Provence I P.

"Shocking, Relentless, Compulsively Gripping!"
Publishers' Weekly

" . . . in this fascinating and perceptive book Anthony Lukas makes it plain that it is, indeed, from our loins that the present generation has sprung . . . you'll understand what it is that makes a young man burn his draft card—a young white woman devote her life to the cause of black equality—and why their parents didn't do these things. Your prejudice will be gone—replaced by insight."

Minneapolis Tribune

"The personal stories of 10 individuals who have taken strong, even extreme, positions . . . One reads it with growing admiration."

The New York Times

" . . . Lukas' book makes for compelling and important reading . . . provides much illumination on the direction of this country." *Indianapolis Star*

"THE BOOK IS GREAT JOURNALISM." KURT VONNEGUT

"A VERY DIST'

Cleveland Public Library

Don't Shoot— We Are Your Children!

J. ANTHONY LUKAS

A DELL BOOK

Published by
DELL PUBLISHING CO., INC.
750 Third Avenue
New York, New York 10017
Copyright © 1968, 1969, 1971 by J. Anthony Lukas
All rights reserved under International and
Pan-American Copyright Conventions.
For information, contact Random House, Inc.
Portions of this book first appeared in *Esquire* and *Audience*.
"Two Worlds of Linda Fitzpatrick," by J. Anthony Lukas,
first appeared in *The New York Times*.
Copyright © 1967 by The New York Times Company
Dell ® TM 681510, Dell Publishing Co., Inc.
Reprinted by arrangement with
Random House, Inc.
New York, New York 10022
Printed in Canada.
First Dell printing—February 1972

To my father,
I am his son

"We're the Daughters of the American Revolution,
but we'll never be the mothers of another."

—*The Little Group*
1939

CONTENTS

Before

One evening in October 1967, shortly after I returned from five years as the *New York Times* correspondent in the Congo and India, I had dinner with a lovely young woman who lived in Greenwich Village. Over enchiladas in a noisy Mexican restaurant, she told me excitedly about her current project: a massive peace march in Washington which would culminate not with the usual rally at the Washington Monument but with a "confrontation of the warmakers" at the Pentagon itself. It was going to be the biggest, most significant protest against the war yet mounted in this country. Why didn't I come along?

So I told her. I told her that kind of protest was naïve and futile. I told her that foreign policy grew from a delicate calculus of the national interest, not from popular notions of right or wrong. I told her that policy-makers listened to men with real political power, not demonstrators in the street. And I told her they certainly wouldn't listen to the scruffy lot of hippies and radicals who seemed to be leading such demonstrations. I told her that one of my last stories from the Indian subcontinent had been about hippies in Nepal and those young people clearly didn't have an idea beneath all that hair. I told her I hadn't met any of the new radicals, but the ones I'd read about while abroad seemed shrill and uninformed.

The next morning, the loudspeaker in the *Times* city room summoned me to an editor's desk. Two "hippies" had been killed in a Greenwich Village basement; now the girl's parents had agreed to see a *Times* reporter and tell the "true story" of her life. So that afternoon, I drove to the parents' home in Greenwich, Connecticut, and for several hours listened to their earnest explanations that their daughter had been a "good girl" who couldn't possibly have been involved with hippies. With great conviction they gave me details of her life in New York they were sure would prove what they said. Armed with these details, I began checking around the Village, talking with the girl's friends and acquaintances there. It soon became clear that her parents knew little about the life their daughter had been leading—and perhaps very little else about her.

When the story of Linda Fitzpatrick was published on October 16, 1967, it brought an extraordinary deluge of letters and telephone calls from parents. Several mothers told me they had wept when they read the story because they felt they knew equally little about their daughters. Others urged me to tell them how to "reach" their children. I told them I didn't know; I was just a reporter.

But somehow Linda's story nagged at me. It made me realize that after five years abroad I was just as out of touch with American young people as most of the parents I'd been talking to. The assumptions I had voiced only a week before seemed shallow and insensitive. Yet, in the weeks that followed, I came to distrust most of the other generalizations about "youth" or "hippies" or "radicals" which journalism and sociology were then producing.

In the end I concluded that I might learn something if I could avoid such broad inquiries and take a close, concentrated look at other particular young people.

I began with Linda, digging further into her background for other clues to the sources of her disaffection (which produced a chapter three times the length of the original article). Next, I decided to look at Groovy, the young man from such a different background, who was killed with Linda. And then I began a search for others who would represent a broad spectrum of youthful disaffection.

But a truly representative spectrum proved elusive. For, even as I wrote, the movement was changing. Many hippies turned political; Women's Lib and the Panthers waxed while the Mobe and the Yippies waned; SDS splintered, its factions drifting off into ideological polemics or windshield-busting street violence. I couldn't go on juggling my chapters with each new and perhaps transitory realignment.

So, ultimately, I chose the ten people in this book not so much because they represented anything but because they intrigued me, because I wanted to know more about them and, in most cases, because I liked them.

Needless to say, I owe them my gratitude. In a real sense, this is their book. Except for Linda and Groovy—who were dead before I began writing—they gave me their full cooperation. Except for Don, who was already in prison and could only write me through his mother, they submitted to lengthy taped interviews running up to fifteen hours each. With two exceptions, Jim and Dave, they have let me use their real names (in those two chapters nothing but the names were changed). Most shared other parts of their lives with me—their friends, meetings, parties, a favorite restaurant, a new record, a well-loved book.

I have been particularly interested in examining the relations between parents and children, and the heritage which one generation leaves to another. So I am especially grateful to the parents and other family members who have received me graciously, granted me hours of interviews and shown me around their homes and communities.

In writing these portraits I have not sought a consistent tone, but have tried to let my language mirror the style of each person I wrote about. I have tried for the moment to set aside my own assumptions and to write instead within each person's assumptions as they grew and changed.

Chicago, June 1970

J.A.L.

DAVE

On the morning of April 9, 1969, David Goldring woke with a miserable cold. His back ached, his limbs throbbed, he could hardly breathe. After stumbling to the refrigerator for orange juice to wash down a mound of pills, he burrowed under the covers and resolved to spend the day in cozy retreat.

But an hour later, his doze was broken by a clatter of feet in the hallway and shouts of "Everybody up" and "Come on, this may be it." Propped against his pillows, he heard colleagues from Harvard SDS explain that, despite a vote against seizing a building that day, the Progressive Labor faction was going to take University Hall anyway. "Damn!" Dave thought. "Wouldn't you know I'd have a cold on the day of the revolution!"

Popping some more pills, he managed to pull on his "battle dress": a pair of faded Levis, work shoes with steel toes, a thick brown leather Air Force jacket and his flat red cap with its button marking his membership in a Boston Teamsters local. With the cap pulled down over his shaggy hair, his blue eyes glaring out through steel-rimmed spectacles and a wiry blond mustache bristling under his runny nose, he looked like a figure from the October Revolution. One of his roommates suggested they take their "battle flag," so Dave clambered up on a chair to haul down the huge red silk banner with SDS emblazoned in white letters on a black circle. Then everybody piled into a couple of cars, feeling "as though we were getting into a troop train."

But if they were troops, they arrived after the battle

was over. By the time they threaded their way through the narrow streets of the working-class district and then pushed through the throng in Harvard Yard, they found that the Progressive Labor people had already gone into the big gray administration building.

Dave was "a teeny bit miffed." After months of preparing for the Harvard confrontation, he'd wanted to be there for the action. He resented the intense, humorless Progressive Labor types for jumping the gun. But he had to admit they'd pulled it off well, presenting the rest of SDS with a *fait accompli*. There they were already, hanging out the windows of the second-floor faculty room, shouting for others to join them. Many of Dave's New Left Caucus friends were now inside too. But Dave knew he couldn't join them. Still waiting out his appeal from a three-month sentence for a State House sit-in, he couldn't afford another arrest. Moreover, having graduated the year before and now working full time for SDS, he no longer enjoyed the immunities of a Harvard student.

But Dave determined to do all he could behind the scenes to support the hall's liberators. He handed over his battle flag, which soon unfurled from an upstairs window. For a while he and some friends amused themselves rearranging the little white letters on the building directory to read: "Che Guevara Hall . . . Liberated Area . . . Smash Imperialism." Then he drifted outside to watch with satisfaction as the deans were expelled, one of them slung over a student's shoulder. For a while, he stood on the steps as impassioned students, most of them from the PL faction, harangued a largely hostile crowd. Things started getting nasty. While one intense speaker shouted through a bullhorn, "Everyone who wants to end Harvard's imperialism come inside now," a group of counter-demonstrators bunched on the steps below chanted, "Out! Out! Out!" Someone tried to grab the bullhorn and there was a brief scuffle.

Dismayed at the way PL was handling the crowd, Dave decided to try his own brand of public education. Through the rest of the afternoon and into the chilly evening, as more than three hundred students milled through the hall, rifled files, strummed guitars in the deans' offices or stocked food for the siege, Dave strolled under the spreading elms talking to students, trying to explain "why we have to do this." One husky football player in a gray sweatshirt called him a "fucking idiot," but most students listened and showed at least some sympathy with the SDS demand for abolition of R.O.T.C.

Late that afternoon, the administration began rallying for a counter-attack. The gates to the Yard were locked, keeping others from swelling the crowd outside University Hall. Cambridge policemen assembled at the firehouse, setting off rumors of an imminent "bust," and Dave promptly started planning to meet the police action. At a meeting in Memorial Church, he and others resolved to form a human wall around the building. All night they knocked on the doors of dormitories in the Yard, urging freshmen to come out and stay on the hall's steps until dawn. Many did. At one door, Dave encountered the football player who had berated him that afternoon. To Dave's delight, the bleary-eyed jock slung on a jacket and joined the blockade.

About 4:30 A.M. word came that the police were about to move. As planned, Dave and others sprinted around the Yard pulling the fire alarms in each dormitory. "It was kind of a surreal thing. Standing there, watching the lighted University Hall silhouetted against the eastern sky, where dawn was just beginning to break. All over the Yard you could hear the alarms jangling and the freshmen suddenly poured out of the dorms and churned around the hall. People shouted, 'They're coming!' Suddenly, I could see the big buses rolling up and the state troopers with their clubs and those plastic face guards, and all those Cambridge and Boston cops, scrambling out, running across the Yard and breaking through our people around the building. They were swinging their clubs at every head they saw. There was nothing I could do. I just stood there and watched my friends hauled away. I was angry as hell and yet kind of exhilarated too."

When the sun was up, Dave ran down to Adams House, climbed up on a chair in the dining room and urged the breakfasting upperclassmen to go on strike in protest against the police action. For the rest of the day, Dave huddled with his SDS colleagues, many of them just released from jail, planning to "close the university down."

Only late that afternoon, with his head throbbing and his voice gone, did he straggle home, take another mound of pills and crawl into bed for the first time in twenty-nine hours. While Walter Cronkite and Huntley-Brinkley showed films of the "uprising at Harvard," David Goldring fell into a feverish sleep.

Just off the Maine coast near Bristol, tiny Muscongus Island crops out of the icy bay. Once the home of the Wawenock Indians, Muscongus was settled by Englishmen in 1650, and shortly thereafter the first Goldring arrived. The waters of Muscongus Bay swarmed with fish and the new islanders hauled them in, marketing their catch in Bristol, where they also voted. But they were a roistering, independent breed who often brawled with the stolid townsmen in Bristol's taverns. This ill feeling peaked during the election of 1860. The islanders were solidly Democratic, the town largely Republican. When the island's votes threatened to swing the town into the Democratic column, the aldermen suddenly discovered that Muscongus wasn't on the Maine map and promptly invalidated its votes. Enraged, the islanders seceded from the Union, chasing tax assessors and Army recruiters from their shores. It remained the Republic of Muscongus until 1934, when, tired of rowing ashore each day to collect their mail, the islanders swore allegiance to Washington in exchange for a post office.

Most of the Goldrings left Muscongus before the secession, settling down the coast at Weymouth, Massachusetts. But they retained their stubborn Yankee independence—merely moving to the other side of the political divide. David's great-great-grandfather was one of the few Whigs in the predominantly Democratic town and, outraged by the slave issue, helped found the Republican Party. In Boston, a Goldring woman became a prominent abolitionist and ally of William Lloyd Garrison.

Until the turn of the century, the Goldrings were one of Weymouth's most prominent families—two of them cashiers of the Union National Bank, pillars of the Union Congregational Church, members of the Church choir, and, in several cases, Harvard men.

David's grandfather broke the mold somewhat. A Congregationalist minister, he worked as a "home missionary" among the Oklahoma Indians and the Mormons before moving back to Massachusetts in 1914 so his children could get an Eastern education. All three children were precocious. Most advanced of all was David's father, Oliver, who entered Harvard at the age of fourteen.

Oliver recalls that his youth and piping voice brought him some ribbing. He was asked to substitute for a girl in a Radcliffe play, but the same slightness also made him coxswain of the crew. The family was by no means wealthy, and for two years Oliver waited on tables and lived at a Business School dormitory. His academic record continued to be outstanding. In 1929 he graduated summa cum laude in chemistry.

Intending to go on eventually either to medical school or graduate work in chemistry, he took three years off to teach science at the Nichols School in Buffalo. Then he moved to the laboratory high school associated with the Ohio State College of Education. "That was the turning point in my life," Oliver says. "When I arrived I still wasn't committed to teaching. But suddenly I found myself on a faculty of extraordinary educators, all of them strongly influenced by John Dewey's progressive theories. I became professionalized."

About the same time he also became "radicalized." At Harvard he had "disdained" politics and was hardly aware of the Sacco-Vanzetti case thundering around his ears. A month after he arrived in Buffalo, the economy collapsed and he recalls "queues of frozen people lining up for soup." But he couldn't be bothered to vote in the 1932 election ("I was still above it all"). Gradually, however, the plight of the unemployed got to him. One year, while at Ohio State, he taught at a "free school" for poor children in Columbus. He became involved in the Unemployed League, teaching dramatics in trade union halls and settlement houses. In 1934 he taught for the first of five summers at the Bryn Mawr Summer School for Women in Industry. He recalls sitting under a tree there reading alternately from *Das Kapital* and the Bible.

He was influenced too by a young drama student he met at Ohio State. Frances Dworken, the daughter of first-generation East European Jews, had grown up in Cleveland wanting to be a ballerina. Rheumatic fever ended her dancing but not her dreaming. "I wanted to say something. I found that the great writers had said it all better than I could. So I decided to be an actress and speak their words." An emotional, idealistic girl ("I didn't even know who Sacco and Vanzetti were but I sat down and cried with them"), Frances threw herself into the theater at Ohio State and also into a Quaker campaign to end compulsory R.O.T.C. there.

Oliver saw her in a play at Hillel House. Having acted and directed himself in Boston, he agreed to direct a play at Hillel just to meet her. "But she didn't even try out for that one; she was too busy with the Quakers on R.O.T.C." Eventually he did meet her and they were married in 1935.

A year later, Oliver accepted a post at Sarah Lawrence while Frances plunged into the New York theater. That same year the civil war broke out in Spain. "It was the last link in a chain," Oliver recalls. "One radicalizing experience after another. A student we knew from Ohio State joined the Lincoln Brigade and was killed in Spain. Many people we knew lie buried there."

In 1937 the Goldrings joined the Communist Party.

For the next seven years their lives were bound up in New York's radical-intellectual community—or communities, for they lived in several separate but overlapping circles.

One was the strictly political community: the cell where they read and discussed Marxist literature, heard Communist speakers, tried to follow the rapidly shifting party line.

The second was Oliver's academic work, first at Sarah Lawrence and then, from 1940 on, at Columbia, where he got his Ph.D. in education. He was active in the College Teachers Union (which was eventually expelled from the American Federation of Teachers because of Communist infiltration), and spent so much time teaching trade union men that he briefly considered making workers' education his career.

Then there was the Morningside Heights community, where they moved when Oliver started at Columbia. Frances and her friends spent some time going from door to door in neighboring Harlem collecting information to present to the city on rats, clogged sewers and rickety stairs.

Finally, there was Frances' involvement in the socially conscious New York theater. She played several proletarian parts, among them an Italian girl in *Sun Up and Sun Down,* about child labor in the tobacco industry. She worked with the Group Theater and Norman Corwin's Columbia Workshop. For one season she played in a left-wing political cabaret, in which she and three other girls burlesqued the D.A.R. with a song that went: "We're the Daughters of the American Revolution, but we'll never be the mothers of another." Frances worked, on and off the stage, with many of the theater's Communists and prominent left-wingers, most of whom were later blacklisted. "I suppose if we'd stayed in New York I would have been blacklisted too," she says. "I would have ended up like a lot of my friends, driven off the stage, dead of broken hearts."

But they didn't stay in New York. When he got his Ph.D. in 1943, Oliver took a job teaching science at Antioch College in Ohio which was expanding its science program to help train engineers in the Army's Specialized Training Program. But then in April 1944 he was recruited for the Manhattan Project, the effort to build an atomic bomb, at Oak Ridge, Tennessee.

The Army apparently knew little of his political background, but by that time he and his wife had left the party anyway. "By 1943," Oliver recalls, "I found I just couldn't take the party's discipline. Its attitude toward Trotskyites was just as sharp and vindictive as any religious battle. They called them 'mad dogs' and 'fascists.' But I knew Trotskyites and I thought it was ridiculous to be told I couldn't associate with them or read their press. I just found that kind of thing unacceptable. So when we moved from New York to Antioch, I, in effect, dropped out of the party. I didn't leave it like so many did, only to strike back later. I just let it go."

In his first weeks at Oak Ridge, Oliver didn't know what he was working on. But when he was upgraded from a training to a research section he was told. "I wasn't surprised," he recalls, "but it did create a dilemma. A friend and I had continuous philosophic debate about whether we should work on a weapon of this sort."

It was there, in the shadow of the cyclotrons and the incredible weapon they were about to produce, that David was born on April 27, 1945 (the Goldrings' second child; a daughter, Julie, had been born in 1941). A few months after David's birth, Oliver went back as assistant professor of physics at Antioch, where he has remained, off and on, ever since.

In choosing the little experimental college in Yellow

Springs, Ohio, Oliver noted years later in his Harvard 25th-reunion report, "We were at the same time choosing a way of life for our children to grow into—not a Utopia, but a small community (enriched by a liberal arts college) where neighbors could unpretentiously take counsel together for their common welfare."

Dave's first memories of Yellow Springs are nearly utopian—of endless space to move around in, to play in, to grow in. The Goldrings lived in a little frame house they rented from the college, but it had a big backyard, which opened onto one of the college's large playing fields, where Dave first tested his lungs and legs. As he got older, there was even more room to roam—the whole spacious college campus, and then Glen Helen, a huge natural park filled with woods, ravines, streams and pastures which Dave recalls as "this immense playing field, not sculptured or cultivated or overrun by cars or streets or parents or anything else but just a place where everything we cared to dream about was true."

And Dave had this same feeling of unlimited space about school. His nursery school and kindergarten were both connected with the college and run on the same free and easy lines. They were right around the corner on a street with little traffic and he was allowed to ride his tricycle to them.

First grade at the Antioch Experimental School was a little further away, but it maintained Dave's sense of freedom. "We didn't have texts or homework or marks," he says. "The only academic things we worked on were reading and arithmetic. There were long hours for just sitting at your desk doing whatever you wanted to do, drawing, reading, art, shop, or playing around outdoors, walking in the glen, picking up a little natural history and stuff like that."

He drew even greater liberation from summer camp, an experience which many boys find stultifying but which Dave found "one of the most important in my life." Part of Dave's zest for camp came from his father. Oliver had gone to Camp Medomak in Maine as a boy and had come to value highly what he later described as "the very special consequences of community living in the out of doors." So in 1952 he decided to spend the summer as a counselor there, taking his seven-year-old son with him.

Thus began Dave's ten summers at the camp he came to love as much, or more, than his father. He loved the emphasis on "self-reliance," through acquisition of skills in athletics, woodsmanship, arts and crafts. He felt challenged by the idea of "self-competition"—against a standard for each age group rather than against each other. Enough points in each skill earned you the medal for your age group. Dave didn't win the "cub" medal because of an intense fear of the water, but he overcame that and won both the "junior" and "senior" medals. Most of all, he loved the forays into Maine's wilderness. From the start, there were sleepouts in the cool pine forests, and as a boy grew older there were longer treks up Mount Katahdin or along the winding reaches of the Allagash River.

Dave feels Medomak formed some of his best traits: his love of the outdoors ("To this day, I feel most alive when I'm out where things are absolutely open and quiet"); an emphasis on community ("A community where one ate, slept, worked, played and shared responsibilities together is very different from the kind where you might go to school with people but everyone ate, did homework and got their allowances separately. I've continued to believe in the completeness of association and responsibility for common problems"); a "workmanlike" approach to life ("The camp put great stress on keeping your gear in order, and carrying through a process from beginning to end. When you're camping, these are practical necessities—and I've found they are outside camp too"); and a sense of discipline ("We used to have inspection every morning, standing at attention by your bed. It was kind of military in some ways, but I think the Spartan virtues come in handy for all sorts of progress. The Cubans and Viet Cong need discipline, and I think the American movement is now at a point where we ought to have a better sense of where we are going and how we're going to get there").

The fall after Dave's first year at summer camp, his father got a grant for research at Harvard. The family rented a house in Auburndale, a Boston suburb, and Dave went to public school there. It was a rude awakening to the realities of urban life. "The school was a nightmare compared to the Antioch school," Dave recalls. "It wasn't fun any more. One of my biggest memories was staying after school one day because I had done something stupid and writing on a piece of paper 'two, four, six, eight, ten' up to one hundred, like ten or twenty times."

And, for the first time, Dave also encountered anti-Semitism—Auburndale kids chattering about "kikes" and "yids." They didn't know Dave was Jewish, but it was humiliating all the same. "I knew who I was. I knew they were talking about me. But I kept my mouth shut."

Dave may have picked up some sensitivity to anti-Semitism from his mother who, at the age of eighteen, had suffered a traumatic blow. She had won a scholarship to Barnard, but a week later received a letter saying their "quota" was full. "I didn't understand," she recalls, "but my mother explained it to me. The principal was so outraged he called an assembly and told the whole school. It was the worst moment in my life. I went blind for twenty minutes, psychosomatically. I think this may have had something to do with my later radicalism. Growing up a Jew, I knew all wasn't light and justice in this world."

And Dave was Jewish on both sides because, shortly before their marriage, Oliver had converted to his wife's faith. As he explained in his Harvard 25th-reunion report, written that very year in Cambridge, "I experienced, not during my undergraduate years but soon thereafter, a serious interest in religious and philosophical issues. This led me quite soon and painlessly to an essentially humanist position—with a deep respect for the beautiful core of every living faith and a deep regret that religious differences should divide rather than enrich the peoples of the earth. My own preference in religious affiliation is, of course, limited by my being 'of the West' and it is powerfully influenced by my deep respect for the lifework of my father, a liberal Congregational minister. It would be first of all unorthodox and then it would find as equivalently attractive: liberal Unitarianism, Reform Judaism and—if I could reach a pacifist position—the Quaker faith." When they had to decide how to bring up their children, Oliver said, his wife and he had affiliated with "the nearest, most liberal Jewish temple."

Their objective, Oliver says, was "that the children should be free—intellectually and ethically. We wanted to do this not by giving them no religion at all, but by transmitting a heritage and letting them make of it what they would as they matured."

Dave recalls little ritual in the home. They celebrated Sabbath and holy days and went to Hebrew School but they didn't keep kosher or do much praying. "I guess you'd call it a humanistic, libertarian, democratic, universalist interpretation of Judaism, stressing the themes of justice, peace and equality within the Jewish tradition." The Goldrings repeatedly reminded their children that not all Jews were middle-class, that there were more poor Jews in the world than rich ones.

This approach implanted Judaic values in Dave perhaps far more deeply than a more Orthodox upbringing would have. Unlike many young Jewish radicals who have turned against the faith of their fathers, Dave continues to find Judaism relevant to his current concerns.

"I've always felt the need for a philosophy, a culture, which integrates the human drama from the beginning of time into the unforeseeable future," he says. "I think Judaism does that better than a lot of other cultures. And I think there's much to be said for rituals which symbolize this integrated view of the significance of human life. A lot of my Jewish friends in the movement don't see that at all—even in an obvious case like the exodus from Egypt. Several times at Passover I'd be with some movement people and I'd say, 'Why don't we have a Seder?' and they'd all say, 'Nah,' so I'd say, 'O.K., let's just read the Haggadah,' and they'd say, 'Christ, we don't want to read that whole thing,' so we'd start reading just part of it and you'd hear snickers. I'd get really annoyed and say, 'Wait a minute, is it true there were a people in Egypt that were enslaved? And is it true that they were freed? And isn't that an essential part of what we're about today, not just the abstract idea of liberation, but the living question of those people? Why are they less important to us than the Bolsheviks or the Vietnamese peasants?' I don't think they are. Of course, in practice we deal with more immediate questions, but I think we have to keep in mind the completeness of the struggle, the whole drama of just trying to be human beings. And I think that philosophical frame of reference comes straight out of my parents' early approach toward religion."

And the Goldrings' religious approach was strikingly

similar to their political approach—in fact, it was often difficult to distinguish between them. Like many of those who joined the Communist Party in the thirties, they were less political dogmatists than concerned humanists searching for a scheme which would make sense of their suddenly disrupted world. In his 25th-reunion report, Oliver noted that he has long been "without orthodoxy" in philosophy. "Attracted about equivalently to pragmatism, logical positivism and Marxism, my preference for over fifteen years now has been for the latter."

In the years just after the war, a man so inclined naturally turned to the Progressive Party. "At Antioch, I kept running into ex-Communists who were now Progressives," Oliver recalls. "I joined almost right away." By the spring of 1948 he was Ohio state chairman and waged a successful fight to get the ticket on the ballot. At the convention in Philadelphia he was asked to give one of the seconding speeches for Henry Wallace. During the campaign he crisscrossed the state, campaigning in the urban-industrial centers where Wallace's strength was supposed to lie.

Oliver stayed with the party even in defeat, but growingly it was rent by ideological disputes. As in the Communist Party, he was put off by sectarian dogmatists who insisted they alone had the truth and tried at all costs to suppress controversy. In a 1950 article in the Marxist *Monthly Review,* he argued for open airing of "both our agreements and our disagreements." If the party could thereby demonstrate the true meaning of a political coalition, he said, "perhaps millions of Americans would the sooner recognize that they belong in the still larger coalition that is needed." Although he resigned as Progressive state chairman in 1952 to go to Harvard, he still dreamed of a broad new party. In his 25th-reunion report written that year, he said he hoped to "participate (as my great-grandfather did a century ago) in the successful building of a vast new coalition . . . that will give courageous and appropriate expression, in domestic and foreign policies alike, to the particular democratic-revolutionary experiences of the American people."

Most Americans, however, were increasingly frightened of such talk. In 1948 Oliver could teach nuclear physics at Wright-Patterson Air Base while serving as Progressive Party chairman, but in the fifties he suffered persecution for his views. The Yellow Springs newspaper and others attacked him, demanding his removal from the Antioch faculty. He received threatening phone calls; glass was scattered on the Goldrings' driveway and dead rats thrown at their door.

The Goldrings did their best to insulate the children from all this. "We tried not to burden them when they were too young with all the grief of the world," Oliver recalls. Dave wasn't allowed to answer the phone and was only vaguely aware that all was not well. He wasn't even sure what the Progressive Party was, somehow associating it with a birthday party; for a long time, whenever he heard it mentioned, the image that came to mind was of a "big slice of yellow birthday cake with chocolate frosting."

But the time came when the burden could no longer be kept off the childrens' young shoulders. In 1954 the House Un-American Activities Committee held hearings in Dayton. Several Antioch professors were called. There were reports that Oliver too would be subpoenaed. "I decided I couldn't hold off any longer. I took David, then nine, and Julie out for a drive in the car and told them the whole story." There is some question as to how much they understood. Dave does not remember the conversation today.

For some reason, Oliver was not called before the committee and the whole thing blew over. As Dave reached his early teens, he was still only faintly aware of his parents' political positions. "In the 1956 election," he says, "I remember all the kids at school going around saying 'I'm a Democrat' and 'I'm a Republican' because their folks were. I was quite confused. I didn't know what I was because I didn't know what my folks were. I knew pretty much by that time they weren't either Democrats or Republicans and then I think I heard someone say 'independent' and I figured out, oh, that must be what it is." That was a fair enough description. Through most of the fifties, Oliver considered himself "disenfranchised" and usually invalidated his ballot by voting for the Socialist Labor Party.

But there was a more important reason for Dave's uncertainty. "From way back," Oliver says, "my wife and I made an explicit decision that we would not indoctrinate either of our children. What I wanted was for David to have the same relation with me that I had with my father—that is, we worried about each other in this rough-and-tumble world, but we didn't worry about each other's solutions or motivations."

In his pre-high-school days, Dave recalls virtually no political advice or even conversation with his parents. "My friends and I were great little warriors always waging epic battles. At first we seemed most attracted to the Nazis, maybe because their planes fascinated us. But when the Korean war started, the Communists were definitely our bad guys. In the dogfights I used to draw, the MIGs were always getting hit. But my parents never criticized the drawings."

"Of course," Oliver concedes, "it was a radical home, it was a dissenting home, and the children must have sensed that." Dave agrees that he undoubtedly absorbed a great deal of political thinking at home. "But it came from the way my parents lived and dealt with problems more than from any explicit political direction. Really, the only explicit thematic statement we ever got was in the religious context. Above all, there was a pretty strong, firmly established atmosphere of love in the home. People were on the whole dealt with as human beings.

"And I think this has real implications for radical work today. It's one of my main differences with the Progressive Labor people who seem to think political education takes place through the forceful encounter with a string of political words. I'm sure words do play a very important role at times. But I'm also pretty sure they make a difference only when they mean something in terms of a great fund of underlying experience a person has accumulated. For example, any effort to translate the words used in China to America isn't likely to work. The average Chinese's experience was one of great misery and oppression, so the political words the Chinese Communists employed connected much more with people's experiences than the anti-imperialist, anti-racist words of SDS do with white Americans, working-class or middle-class."

Dave may also have absorbed radicalism through the narrowing of his family's friendship circle. At times, the Goldrings were socially ostracized for their political views. The people who stuck by them tended to be other radi-

cals or liberal intellectuals from the college. And Dave's
best friends were often these people's children.

Two of his closest friends for years were sons of men
subpoenaed by the House Un-American Activities Committee: Russ, who was Dave's age, and John, three years
older. When Dave was twelve, all three became friendly
with Alan, then a freshman at Antioch. It was a peculiar
friendship, linking boys who were twelve, fifteen and
eighteen, but it remained intact for five years. The quartet
talked, listened to music, partied, went for walks, read
and drank together. Dave has no doubt that all the other
three influenced him immensely—particularly Alan, who
was intensely Jewish, intellectually aggressive, and without
being openly radical, militantly on the side of the oppressed everywhere.

Correspondingly, the family had few friends among
the area's businessmen and Dave developed a marked
distaste for the whole business world. "Even to this day
I have a bad feeling when I go into the stores in Yellow
Springs, because there was always something stifling about
those shops. I didn't like the atmosphere and I didn't
like the people." His maternal grandfather was a business-
man, a wholesale fruit-and-vegetable man in Cleveland.
But Dave always exempted him from the indictment because "he was an old-fashioned pioneer kind of business-
man, who worked down in the real jungle of the terminal
warehouse and had to use his fists a lot."

The only businessmen Dave saw much of were those
who went to the temple the Goldrings attended in
Springfield, ten miles north of Yellow Springs. "A lot of
the men in the congregation were sort of classical petit
bourgeois. They ran small stores, pawnshops, jewelry
shops, small department stores. I was friendly with
some of their sons, but there was always a certain distance between us because I just never felt that relaxed
with their families."

After the fifth grade, however, Dave's little world—
focused on his family and the Antioch Experimental
School—suddenly broadened. Over the summer, one of
the school's most popular teachers was stricken with
polio. Dave and about a dozen of his cronies, with no objection from their parents, transferred to the town's public school.

With the transfer came an abrupt change in style. Mills

Lawn Elementary School drew on a much wider spectrum of Yellow Springs' residents and ran on standard public-school lines. For the first time since second grade in Massachusetts, Dave had homework, regular textbooks, little drawing or music, and had to sit "in the same goddamned seat all day long." But there was the compensation of an infinitely more elaborate social life. And this exercised a strange fascination on the thirteen-year-old boy, just becoming aware of the young girls around him in class.

The year before, defying his gang's masculine contempt for the frail sex, he had already had his first date. But Mills Lawn was something else. "All of a sudden we were thrown into the incredibly complicated social thing—dances, parties, clothes, note passing, rivalries and all that. Through the sixth, seventh and eighth grades we just poured our hearts and souls into that—perhaps in compensation for the lack of any academic stimulation."

And there was rock 'n' roll. Perhaps more than anyone else at school, Dave was swept up by the new driving beat. He bought all the new records—Bill Haley and the Comets, Little Richard, the Platters, Ray Charles and, above all, the symbol of the new music, Elvis Presley. "For a while in the sixth grade I thought I was Elvis. I let my hair grow long and combed it wavy like he did. I rolled my collar up like his. I drew pictures of him. I had all his records. I sang his songs—knew them all by heart. People at school even started calling me Elvis."

Dave thinks this infatuation came partly from "Elvis' real vibrancy which touched something inside me at that age" and partly "rebelliousness toward school," which he had grown to hate. "When I look back at all the energy we poured into our social lives, but particularly into rock 'n' roll and everything associated with it, I think this was the only available way for us to prove that there was something more interesting and exciting about being alive than all the things we were permitted to do. Now, of course, that's just commonplace. But we were terribly unsophisticated then, compared to kids today. We had to work a lot harder at being rebellious than they do—it's so easy nowadays. In a way, that may have been our earliest political education—finding out that most of the things we really liked to do were the things we weren't supposed to do."

But Dave rarely found himself in direct conflict with his parents and never regarded himself as a rebel against their values. As early as he can remember, he wanted his parents' approval, wanted them to consider him a "good boy." He remembers putting up with "incredible terror" over a tonsillectomy so that people would say "What a good boy he is!" And there was an almost institutionalized outlet for anger in the family: brief, theatrical disputes in which his mother, with her Slavic temperament and dramatic flair, usually played the central role. In these fights, the children were permitted (almost encouraged) to give full vent to their dramatic powers—raising their voices, waving their arms, calling all sorts of names. But the fights ended almost as suddenly as they began, and like violent summer rainstorms, left the atmosphere cooler and clearer. His father never took part in these family squalls.

Dave sees his father, in sharp contrast to his emotional mother, as "one of the most rational people I know. Not that he doesn't have a full range of feelings like anybody else. But he disciplines himself to deal with things in a rational manner. He has a temper, but rarely shows it." The only physical punishment Dave recalls was an occasional slap on his hands. When he said "shit" at the age of six, his father washed his mouth out with kitchen soap. The only other outburst he remembers came seven years later. They were driving to Springfield and Dave was being particularly obstinate about something. His father suddenly snapped, "God damn you!" Dave lived in such awe of his father, and this was so out of character for the mild-mannered professor, that it hit the boy "like a lightning bolt; it really shivered my timbers."

In some respects, his parents were permissive. Throughout elementary and high school he was free to come and go pretty much as he liked, play where and with whom he liked. But they had some definite rules and stuck by them. "Although I was free all day, I was expected to report back for dinner, and in the entire time I was growing up I can remember only two times I was allowed to sleep away from home, although most of my friends could stay overnight anytime they liked. Sometimes I would be in mortal agony over my parents' rules, but I very rarely disobeyed them on anything they explicitly said they wanted me to do or not to do."

The hitch was that they didn't forbid very much—and they could hardly forbid what they scarcely knew existed. "They were real innocent about what people my age were doing," Dave concedes. "So it was a question of me maintaining a sort of diplomatic silence with respect to a lot of the things I was interested in and I felt they wouldn't approve of. I successfully avoided the issue most of the time by just being a little surreptitious about these things." These things were pretty innocent by most standards: smoking behind the garage from the fifth grade on, some heavy drinking with the gang in high school, a little petting. But they gave Dave at least the pinch of rebellion which every boy needs at some point.

Yet even during his Elvis period, Dave never failed to perform in the area where his father had distinct expectations: the academic world. He was always an intense, conscientious student, ranking at or near the top of his class and winning prizes. There was no rebellion in the classroom. Unless you count the time in the eighth grade when his teacher made a slighting remark about socialism and Dave objected. "Well, David," the teacher said, "will you explain what socialism is?" Dave mumbled something about "for the good of the people." He still had no feel for politics. That same year, Castro was marching to victory and one of Dave's classmates used to bring a radio to class so he could root for the revolution. Dave could never understand why the kid was so interested in Cuba.

By the time he was fourteen, he was thinking in more political terms. Partly this was a result of hanging around the Antioch campus, talking with students or listening to the speakers who came through. He went to several Pete Seeger concerts and loved "the freedom-type songs." And he began listening to discussions at home. He remembers meeting Carl and Ann Braden, the Kentucky radicals, who came up to visit his parents.

About this time, his father offered the first explicit "political" advice Dave remembers. It involved his barbershop. For years, Oliver had taken him to a shop with Negro barbers, the first one in town to cut Negroes' hair. But when Dave was old enough to get his hair cut on his own, he started going to another shop which had better comics, gave lollipops and didn't cut kinky hair. For a while his father said nothing. Then one day he took Dave aside and said, "Look, you can go anywhere you like. But I just want you to know what's involved here." When he understood the issue, Dave not only went back to the Negro shop but helped picket the shops that still discriminated. It was his first demonstration.

About the same time, peace groups in Dayton were sponsoring ban-the-bomb marches and Dave took part in several. The peace question was clearly on his mind when he was confirmed at the Springfield temple on May 29, 1960. His speech that day was devoted to the Sixth Commandment. "Life is sacred and its sanctity supersedes all else," he told the congregation. "Life is a gift from God alone who alone has the right to take it away. This Jewish attitude is basic to civilized living; an attitude held by the Jews long before the rest of the world understood." The next day he and his parents went on a peace march together to Wright-Patterson Air Base.

And during that fall's presidential campaign, Dave remembers feeling only "contempt" for both Kennedy and Nixon, convinced that neither candidate was addressing himself to the country's critical problems. (This closely paralleled his father's position. That summer, Oliver rummaged around in a trunk and found an old "I Like Fiorello" pin, which he wore for the rest of the campaign.)

Dave never had any use for Kennedy. The "Prince Charming act" left him cold. He grew particularly angry after the Bay of Pigs and joined a "Fair Play for Cuba" march to the state capitol. He didn't think Kennedy was doing enough to speed Southern school desegregation, a subject which growingly fascinated him. During the sit-in movement he watched TV news seriously for the first time, outraged when he saw SNCC demonstrators beaten or prodded.

Increasingly Dave found himself taking more radical positions than most of his classmates. And although his radicalism did not yet have any coherent form, he recalls that when the family left for France in June 1961 so Oliver could take a sabbatical leave at the Sorbonne, he was delighted to be getting out of America. "Standing on the deck as we passed the Statue of Liberty, I said to myself, a bit self-consciously, 'Well, O.K., you bitch, I'm glad to get out of your clutches for a while.' I suppose I was thinking about the conditions of the immigrant families I'd seen on the Lower East Side. I knew by then that their living conditions weren't anything like that statue's promise—'Give me your tired, your poor, your huddled masses' and all that. I was also thinking about Cuba and black people, about America as a place where large numbers of people weren't particularly free and as a country that pushed people around quite ruthlessly for its own benefit." Dave concedes he rather savored the image of himself standing there in the ship's prow bitterly defying the lady with the torch. But there was genuine bitterness beneath the pose as he set sail for his first glimpse of foreign lands.

Not surprisingly, Paris proved a liberating experience for a sixteen-year-old boy who had spent most of his life within a few miles of a small Ohio town.

But his liberation maintained a continuity with all that had come before, most of all with the close family circle. The Goldrings moved into a shabby lower-middle-class neighborhood not far from the Place Pigalle. To support his family, Oliver took a part-time job teaching biology at the American School, where Dave was enrolled in the eleventh grade. This gave father and son more time to spend with each other than ever before. Each morning, they set out together, walking fifteen minutes to a spot where the school's bus would pick them up. Oliver also tutored his son in American history so Dave wouldn't have to spend too much time in the school's all-American atmosphere. In the evenings, the whole family frequently went to the theater or visited the wide circle of French intellectuals they came to know. During vacations, Dave and his parents took several trips to Denmark, Holland, England, Italy and southern France, where Julie was studying at Besançon University. Thus the year drew an already close family even closer together.

During this year, Dave's brisk brightness was developing into a searching intelligence. "The academic year was a real turning point for me. Partly it was the teachers at school, most of whom were real expatriates and much more stimulating than teachers at home. But I had a light load at school—just English literature, French and chemistry—and a lot came outside school, in the tutorial I had with my father." Mostly Dave just read, chiefly books with a radical tinge, such as Leo Huberman's *We the People*, an anthology called *Ameri-*

can Radicals, and the Beards' *Rise of American Civilization.*

"For the first time I was actively interested in the stuff I was learning for its own sake. About midway through the year, with a great bolt of lightning, I realized that with each additional thing I learned, ten more things I didn't know opened up before me. I felt that the knowledge I was working on was pushing hard from inside and expanding a little teeny corner of understanding in a huge universe that was virtually unknown to me. That was very exciting."

But more than purely intellectual excitement, it was "a feeling of discovery on all fronts." Dave usually left school after lunch and spent the afternoon with classmates, poking around Paris. In the bookstores of the Left Bank, the workingmen's bars, the produce markets and factories, he developed what he calls now "an existential feeling for one's surroundings—the art of looking at things around you with a fresh eye, taking nothing for granted."

And he feels that this experience led him to certain discoveries about America he might never have made, or made much more slowly, at home. Perhaps most important was the concept of class. "When you go to a foreign country you find yourself marvelously undefined. Like, you can say certain four-letter words in French and they don't have the same weight as they do in English. Well, similarly, you don't have all the built-in channeling with respect to people of other classes that you do in the place where you grew up. So I could go into a Paris bar and it felt no more or less strange sitting down next to a ditchdigger than it did sitting down next to a banker in a theater. They were all slightly exotic; they all had something in common that set them apart from what you were used to, so you could associate with them all about equally. But then it came to me with kind of a shock that if I walked into the Glen Cafe in Yellow Springs where the guys from the road gangs ate, I wouldn't have felt nearly as open to them because there would have been a real class barrier between us. So I realized that I'd been deprived of whole segments of social realities at home."

The other reality impossible to escape in Paris was the Algerian war, then lurching through its last, bloody year. It was the year the Secret Army Organization carried the violence back to France, setting off *plastique* bombs even along the Champs Elysées. On the bus to school, Dave and his father would uneasily try to figure out which building was going up next. One night a bomb exploded right around the corner from the Goldrings' apartment, damaging the house of a lawyer who had been friendly with the National Liberation Front. You couldn't escape from the war anywhere. One day, walking along the street with his sister, Dave started singing a song he'd heard, called "The Deserted." His sister turned white and told him to shut up. The song—about a young man who refused to fight in Algeria—had been banned by the government and singing it in the streets was enough to get one arrested. Dave was horrified by this; by seeing blood on the paving stones of the Place de la Concorde where police had shot down Algerian demonstrators; by finding submachine guns on the hips of gendarmes all over the city; and by hearing the eerie *eee-aw, eee-aw* of the European police sirens snaking through the Paris night, a sound Dave had heard only once before—in the movie of *The Diary of Anne Frank,* when the sirens belonged to the Nazis.

So, by the end of his Paris year, Dave began making connections—between the freedom struggle in Algeria and the freedom struggle in Mississippi; between the gendarmes' clubs and the sheriffs' cattle-prods. The need for such connections was one of his father's deepest-held beliefs. Dave remembers hearing him argue it that year in Copenhagen, where they ran into another Antioch professor on sabbatical. "This guy was a liberal. He kept saying that you couldn't make any sense out of all the things happening in the world—a coup there, a civil war there, an invasion here. How can you take sides on all these different things? My father argued that if you really did your homework you should come up with something like a unified theory of what's going on. Not a theory that lumps everything under one single explanation, but an interpretive framework that would make sense out of all the conflicts between the capitalist world and Laos, Vietnam, Algeria and the Congo—a theory of imperialism. This is something my father has always emphasized—the necessity of applying scientific methods to political problems. As a scientist, he has always as-

sumed that rational problem-solving could be brought to
bear on politics. This made sense to me."

That summer, the family went to Israel, where Oliver
did some work at Hebrew University. In Sunday School,
Dave had been heavily indoctrinated with the wonders
of the promised land, and so before he arrived his vision
of Israel was one of "shining cities and happy, prosperous
people." He was disappointed with the cities—"God-awful
messes, badly planned, filled with exhaust." And he didn't
like the racial discrimination he saw. "The dark-skinned
Jews from North Africa and the Middle East were
looked down on by European Jews. They were second-
class citizens."

But Dave and his sister spent most of the summer on a
kibbutz and he found that "a very fine experience." He
was impressed by how much better the people there lived
than most of the workers he'd seen in Europe. "It was
clean, quiet, relatively peaceful, and it was collective.
The people more or less democratically decided what
to produce and how to allocate the surplus. And it was a
great place for young people." He remembers one day,
after chopping cotton in the fields, standing with a young
Hungarian refugee watching the sun go down over the
lush green valley, and listening to the refugee talk about
how wonderful it was to work the land. And he remembers the glory of a full Sabbath—the first he'd ever known.
"The people worked hard for six days and then, by God,
Friday night they'd get all dressed up, have a nice dinner and dance. Saturday they didn't work at all. Everybody would go down to this little swimming hole formed
by three streams which was the absolute beginning of
the Jordan. So there we'd be on the Sabbath, bathing in
the headwaters of the Jordan. That was nice."

What wasn't so nice was the occasional machine-gun
fire from across the Syrian border, a mile away. Today,
Dave reluctantly sees some truth in the New Left's view
of Israel as an imperialist outpost among the exploited
Arabs. But at that time he identified strongly with Israel,
considering it his "paternal country." He even had difficulty answering friends on the kibbutz who suggested he
come live in Israel. "Finally, I explained—something I
came to feel strongly that year—that I had a duty to go
home. I argued that American influence was everywhere
in the world, commercially, politically, militarily. So if

an American could help make his country a sane place which would treat the rest of the world sanely he had a responsibility to go home and do that."

In September 1962, at age seventeen, Dave began assuming that responsibility. But something about it scared him. He was so afraid of what he might find in Yellow Springs after his year of liberation, or how Yellow Springs might react to him, that he begged his parents to sneak back into town under cover of darkness. But when they pulled up late one night in front of their house, there was a whole pack of Dave's buddies on the lawn waiting for him.

He managed to get through the homecoming; but for the next four months he was strangely withdrawn from his old crowd. His two closest friends were gone: Alan in Chicago and John in New York. So Dave spent most of the fall at home reading history and working on a long paper: "The Concentration, Centralization and Monopolization of Capital in Great Britain Prior to World War I." With spring, he started coming out of his shell, finding the courage to declare his affections for Sue, a girl he had long admired. They stayed deeply involved for the next five years.

And that spring, also, Dave had to make up his mind about college. He'd always assumed he would go to a small liberal arts college like Antioch. But as "one of the promising young bookworms in the area," he was invited to a recruiting dinner at the Harvard Club of Dayton. Dave was surprised. Oliver had never been the kind of old-tie Harvard man who wanted his son to follow him to the Yard. But Dave was flattered that Harvard would go after him, so he decided to apply there as well as to Oberlin and Antioch. In June he was accepted by all three, and decided on Harvard.

But not for a year. By that spring, Dave had resolved to take a year off before college. After years of conscientious schoolwork, he was played out and wanted to be "footloose" for a while. Specifically, he wanted to see New York, which had always exercised a strange fascination for him. So he asked his father to help get him a job on the *Monthly Review*, the New York-based Marxist journal. Its editors, Leo Huberman and Paul Sweezy, were friends of Oliver's and gladly agreed to take Dave on.

The summer between graduation and his New York

venture, Dave spent as a maintenance man at Antioch.
By then he had developed a somewhat romantic attachment to manual labor. (On the way to France he told his
father he wanted to "clasp hands" with the French working class. His father had chuckled: "What do you expect
—a delegation of blue-coated workers when you get off
the train?") In his senior year he became fascinated with
the miners' strike in Hazard, Kentucky; he delivered an
impassioned school report on it, and that summer regularly sent 10 percent of his paycheck to the strike fund.
He realized many of the men he worked with emptying
trash and cutting grass at Antioch didn't share his views,
but he believed he could win them over. One day he
was picketing the last segregated barbershop in town
when one of the guys from work—a Southerner he knew
to be bigoted—walked out of the shop. He just smiled
and said, "Hello, David." Dave glowed for minutes afterward, feeling that, whatever their differences, they had a
mutual respect to build on.

Dave arrived in New York that September and soon
found a room at Judson House, a rooming house owned
by the Judson Memorial Church, a block from Washington Square. But more than just a rooming house, it
was a vague effort at communal living. Twenty young
people—most of them artists, actors, painters and writers
—lived there, each with his own room but sharing bath-
rooms, kitchen and living room. Dave remembers it as
"a nice community," reminiscent in some ways of both
Medomak and the kibbutz.

His real community that year focused on the *Review*,
only two blocks away at Sixth Avenue and 4th Street. In
the cramped office filled with stacks of pamphlets and
books which the Monthly Review Press also published,
Dave served as a general factotum—filing, typing, selling literature, packing books. He got plenty of chance to
talk politics with Huberman and Sweezy, and, through
them, met other veterans of the New York Left.

But, curiously, for someone who was seeking a breath-
er from formal academia, Dave spent much of his time
that year reading. The *Review*'s office staff got free copies
of everything it published and Dave took advantage of
this to build up a substantial library of radical literature.
He supplemented it with dusty volumes plucked from the
shelves of the Jefferson Book Shop: Marx, Engels, Lenin,

Debs, De Leon, John Reed. He pored through the books, propped up in bed at Judson House or rattling beneath the city's streets on the IRT. He learned how to underline books on the swaying subway, a feat of muscular discipline which involved bracing your legs against the floor, pushing hard against the seatback and tucking your elbows in close to your body. The underlining was a little wobbly, but it traced the wavering path of Dave's radical education.

In New York, for the first time, he became aware of Marxism as distinct from socialism. In France he had already considered himself a socialist. But not until one day on the IRT, reading Plekhanov's *The Materialist Conception of History,* did he understand that "there was a theory being expounded that made sense out of things. I was excited not only about the conclusions it reached, but about the methodology itself."

Some of the activities Dave got involved in that year would be regarded now as strictly Old Left—public meetings in Union Square or in musty old union halls celebrating W.E.B. Du Bois' birthday, or marking German executions, Spanish battles, Soviet proclamations and other great moments in the revolutionary struggle. These meetings were all the same: long speeches by veterans of the Left, resolutions, a few old union songs, a table full of red-bound pamphlets. Dave, often assigned to set up *Monthly Review* bookstands at these affairs, grew deadly tired of them. Today, he doesn't hesitate to call them "bullshit."

But meanwhile, he was drawn into other actions which would now be seen as forerunners of the New Left. Through an Antioch graduate working in the *Review* office, he became involved with the Lower East Side chapter of CORE, and with its two major projects that year: the school boycott and a rent strike. He never did much more than picket during the boycott, but he threw his full energies into the rent strike. For months he spent every free moment tramping through crumbling tenements and overcrowded apartment houses in the Houston Street area, talking with tenants, explaining their rights, helping them fill out forms listing the building's housing-code violations. CORE's strategy called for the tenants to withhold rent from the landlord and deposit it in a strike-fund bank account until the violations were corrected.

Dave worked chiefly in a six-story brick tenement at 232-240 Eldridge Street. More than a hundred and twenty persons lived in its thirty-seven apartments, which rented for twenty-five to forty dollars per room. The Italian families who had lived there for years paid the least and their windows faced the street. Two old Jewish couples, remnants of the earliest wave of immigration to the Lower East Side, lived in back and paid moderate rents too. But two thirds of the tenants were Puerto Ricans, recent immigrants from the island. And every time a new family moved in, the landlord raised the rent the legal limit of 15 percent. Dave noticed that the landlord, an Italian from Brooklyn, appeared the first weekend of every month, knocking on each door, cigar clamped in his teeth, hand out for the rent. Sometimes he came back two or three times before the family could assemble enough money; sometimes he threatened eviction. But he got his rent.

The tenants, however, rarely got much in return. In a paper on the building, Dave recorded his observations: "A long, dark hall . . . underneath the staircase at the back, uncollected garbage spills out from the cans . . . walking up flight by flight you enter regions of dim, eye-straining light, and then climb back into darkness, according to which hall lights are working . . . If it has rained recently there will be traces of the water that has come through the yawning, broken door to the roof . . . the hot water is uncertain . . . there is a central heating system but it, too, operates erratically . . . in some apartments tenants have installed small electric heaters at their own expense . . . here a cracked window, there a broken one . . . fissures appear in the wall; some of them have widened into holes . . . Plaster falls from places on the ceiling . . . Not all of the front doors are sound, in this part of the city where the crime rate is fairly high. But even if they were, this would not keep out the legions of roaches and the furtive rats that wage an underground war against the tenants' food, health and sanity."

Noting that few of the tenants knew their rights, or dared to claim them, or got them if they went through "normal channels," Dave wrote, "As workers, as tenants, and as taxpayers, the inhabitants of 232-240 Eldridge Street could exchange similar experiences with most of the people on the East Side. And Harlem, and El Bario, and the Upper West Side, and Bedford-Stuyvesant. And Newark, and Wheeling, and Canton, and Duluth, and Portland, and Meridian, and Fayette County. They could exchange many things, but they all have one thing in common: they are voiceless. Voiceless, they are powerless, and have no control over the crucial decisions that govern the world around them. They are manipulated, exploited and isolated, all at once. As long as Eldridge Street is ruled by absentee power—the landlord's, the employers' and the political machine's—an anarchic poverty will pervade the life of the people."

Dave's outrage was mixed with a certain morbid fascination with the city's seamy side. Some of this, he thinks, came from stories his parents told him of life there in the thirties; some from plays like *Street Scene* and *A View from the Bridge* (in which his mother acted) that portrayed New York as "a big, dirty, tough, but lively and varied place"; some from Charles Dickens, one of his father's favorite authors, whose books gave Dave a feel for life in London's slums; and some from his early Elvis fixation, which carried over to an interest in gangs, leather jackets, tenements, the whole *West Side Story* world.

From the start, this was the New York which attracted him. He rarely went anywhere near the midtown "sights": Rockefeller Center, Central Park, Times Square, the Broadway theaters. He preferred wandering through the Lower East Side, tracing the successive waves of immigrants, almost as an archeologist would, by the layers of *bodegas* overlaying Katz's Delicatessen and Salvatore's Pizzas. John, his old Yellow Springs friend who was working for a medical-instruments company, knew the New York underworld and introduced Dave to junkies, pushers, prostitutes and pimps. Through an artist at Judson House, he met another circle of flamboyant Village nonconformists, forerunners of the hippies who later flocked to the East Village.

Ultimately Dave came to feel that what fascinated and excited him so much about New York was that it was "an ugly and dangerous place; a place of human misery, where about every tenth person you see should be institutionalized." He wouldn't have expressed it quite that way then, but the seeds of his distaste for the city were planted that year.

Dave managed to spend that summer in the mountains of New Hampshire with a girl friend. This was Mississippi Summer, when hundreds of other young Northern whites were going south to work on voter registration and freedom schools. Dave knew many of these activists from his CORE work in New York (among them, Mike Schwerner, who was killed in Mississippi early that summer), but he felt no urge to join them. "I was a fairly orthodox Marxist by then; so I didn't see the South as something special but part of the overall problem of the country. That had more to do with class than race. I just felt less urgency about what was happening in the South because I saw it as part of a thousand-year struggle."

But Dave's historical perspective was soon shaken by a crisis nearer home. In September, as he was about to leave for Harvard, his girl missed her period and they were sure she was pregnant. Dave went through the motions of those first weeks in Cambridge with his mind far away on her condition. Finally, she phoned to say it had been a false alarm and he turned his attention to college.

But long before he arrived, Dave knew how he was going to handle Harvard. "I saw it as an institution of the ruling class, operated to socialize people in a certain way. But I was determined to use Harvard for my own purposes, do research on questions that were important to me, train myself to be a more competent radical." By this he meant largely academic training. He had no idea of radical student action, for there was no precedent yet for such action. The Berkeley Free Speech Movement was still three months away.

So David turned loose his vigorous mind and prodigious capacity for work on Harvard's vast resources. The result was a two-year bout of academic endeavor the likes of which the college had rarely seen. Excluding classtime, he spent between thirty and forty hours a week studying. He read everything assigned for every course, plus all the books on the suggested-reading lists and books he'd brought up from New York. When he wasn't reading he was writing; long, thoroughly researched papers for which he read still more books. "It was excessive," he says today, but it produced a straight A average. Harvard students with straight A's get the

Deturn Award, and with it a ten-dollar book of their own choosing. In a second-hand shop, Dave picked out a leather-bound volume of *Das Kâpital*.

At times Dave found the work incredibly stimulating. He remembers studying for one humanities exam: "I started looking through my notes and got so excited I couldn't stay in my seat. I kept running around the room because all of a sudden I saw clearly the unity and significance of the people we'd been reading."

But many of his courses also threw him into "a state of intellectual anxiety." For they presented a sophisticated, rigorous challenge to his Marxist analysis. "I'd been a little naïve and insulated, I guess, because my perspective was chipped away and broken for a while by the very intelligent criticism I was subjected to."

The book which shook him most was Albert Camus' *The Rebel,* a tough-minded attack on Marxism from an ethical, existentialist viewpoint. "I didn't quite know how to deal with that book," Dave recalls. "Particularly the way he talked about the Soviet Union as the greatest catastrophe that ever happened. I read it and reread it and underlined it and studied it, but it kept nagging at me all year long." Finally, in an attempt to exorcise the demon, Dave wrote a twelve-page paper that May in which he noted Camus' stand against "the deification of history, the legalization of historically 'justified' murder and repression culminating in Stalinism," but in which he seemed to share with Jean-Paul Sartre a view of Camus as "avoiding the real and pressing problems of the time, hiding behind a moral wall to heal a soul in torment."

Curiously, Dave displayed a similar purism that year in his stance toward SDS at Harvard. His roommate, a New York radical, joined the organization early in the fall and urged him to join. Dave went along to a few meetings, but he didn't regard SDS as radical enough. "I thought it was just another bullshit student group."

He did work on some projects where he ran into SDS people. That fall, he spent a few days canvassing for Noel Day, a social worker seeking a Democratic congressional nomination in Boston. Day was no radical, but armed with a strong liberal platform and being black, he attracted support from radical students. One of these was Mike Ansara, a Harvard freshman from an Old Left family, who had already cast his lot with SDS. During

the Day campaign, Dave ran into Mike several times, and
perhaps because they came from such similar backgrounds, they got along well.

"Dave really intrigued me," Mike says. "He knew more
Marx than any of us. He'd just come from the *Monthly
Review,* which to me then was the very pinnacle of Socialist theory. And, in fact, with his mustache and the
little beard he was growing he looked like a nineteenth-
century Marxist scholar. That's the way I always thought
of him."

During the next few months, Dave and Mike saw each
other almost every day—eating together in the Freshman
Union or spending long hours in radical bull sessions.
Mike recalls: "I kept trying to get him into SDS. But
Dave was still absorbed in his heavy intellectualizing. He
said he was going to hold off on joining anything until he
found the truly Marxist, revolutionary party. I argued
that this was an imperfect world, that we had to work
with what there was, and that SDS was the best available."

More than Mike's arguments, it was the Berkeley Free
Speech Movement that winter which made Dave suddenly aware of the potential for radical action within a
university. Following the mass bust at Sproul Hall that
December, Dave joined a hastily organized Berkeley support rally. He remembers tearing up sheets in his room,
scrawling slogans on them in red paint and marching
through the snow to the rally. Only when the banners
were pinned to the blackboard, with TV cameras panning
over them, did he notice they'd misspelled Berkeley.

Then, in late March, Mike came to ask his help. There
was to be an SDS march on Washington that April—one
of the first major Vietnam war protests. Mike said nobody in Harvard SDS was organizing a Cambridge delegation and suggested they take on the project together. This
time Dave accepted. For weeks they worked on it night
and day, putting out literature, coordinating with local
peace groups, renting buses. It paid off. The night of
April 17, eleven buses loaded on Mount Auburn Street,
just opposite the Fly Club and other exclusive societies,
remnants of an earlier, aloof and aristocratic Harvard.
As students clambered aboard, they were taunted by
counter-demonstrators—some of them jokesters from the
Harvard *Lampoon* who put Easter eggs marked "LBJ"

under the buses' tires. Several fistfights broke out in the eerie glare of the headlights. But finally the caravan wheeled off on its all-night journey.

They arrived just as dawn was breaking on a day Dave remembers as the "high point" of his political life to then. His parents and girl friend had come in too from Yellow Springs, as had Leo Huberman and most of the *Monthly Review* crowd. Dave recalls: "We got off at the Washington Monument, and all around, parked under the blossoming cherry trees, were buses lined up for miles. It looked like a railroad yard. Then we marched from the monument up to the Capitol. I was up front with my arm around my girl on one side and around Huberman on the other, with my mother and father next to him in the same line. And when we got up on the Capitol steps I looked back, and all the way to where the road dipped before the monument was solid with people. Oh, man, was that exciting! I was just delirious! More than ever before, I got the direct physical knowledge of a movement we were all part of. It was just a grand day!"

There was another grand day that spring—one which suggests that, for all his intensity, Dave was by no means a purely political creature. He'd devoted himself largely to study and political action that year, with few of the frivolities which can make life in Cambridge so delightful. He'd been to a football game that fall, sung with the Glee Club, and gone to a few "mixers," the crowded affairs where Harvard men meet Radcliffe girls. Partly because he hated this artificial, desperate kind of socializing, partly because he remained intensely loyal to his girl at home, Dave didn't go out with girls that year.

But one fragrant spring evening during exam period, his roommate persuaded him to have dinner at Radcliffe with some girls he knew. "We walked into that dining room," Dave recalls, "and I felt like I was walking into another world. The sunlight was still streaming through the windows at a long angle, giving everything an extra depth. There was all this dark wood, this delicate tinkling of china and silverware from all over the room, and then all those girls, so well groomed and lovely. I was in a daze with all that feminine elegance swimming around my head. After dinner, we went out and lounged around on the grass in the Radcliffe quad and then my roommate and I got on our bicycles and went riding through Cambridge, down along the Charles and through some of those beautiful tree-lined streets with the sun still filtering through the leaves. It was one of the most powerful experiences I'd had all year. I felt like I was being reborn. I realized I'd been studying and working so hard I'd forgotten to take time off for the joys of life."

But his enchantment with the lighter side of life did not last long. Back for his sophomore year—after a summer working as a maintenance man at Antioch again—Dave went to his annual football game at Harvard Stadium. He noticed an attractive blonde in the row behind him with a "Bomb Hanoi" button pinned to her smartly tailored coat. "I looked at her, a well-bred girl sitting there with not a goddamned care in the world except about herself, wearing a button urging the American government to obliterate a city of human beings. I remember that when they played "The Star-Spangled Banner" I stood up and almost cried; I had to choke it back because I was so upset at the things Americans did."

So instead of broadening his life at Harvard to include some of the things he'd missed his freshman year, Dave gradually began to narrow it. After singing in Beethoven's Ninth with the Boston Symphony that fall, he quit the Glee Club, his main tie to traditional Harvard social life. He began spending most of his time with radicals. Even the year before, he had found it difficult to talk with many Harvard students. He would sit down at the long tables in the Freshman Union with anybody who happened to be there and start talking about politics or religion. Suddenly somebody would say, "Yeah, in my daddy's factory . . ." and Dave would turn off.

He discovered that almost everybody at Harvard, even sons of factory owners, were reasonably "liberal," but he found he now had little in common with liberals. In a seminar on Asian revolution, most of the participants were standard middle-of-the-roaders, but Sandy Thompson was the right-wing son of a wealthy Texas family. Dave started by reacting negatively even to Sandy's drawl, but gradually they were drawn together. "We came to realize that we were passionate on opposite ends of the spectrum, but at least passionate. In between were a bunch of marshmallows—liberals, but intellectually timid people—spouting ten-page academic rationalizations for never taking a firm stand on anything. Sandy was conservative politically, but he was radical philosophically. He was a right-winger because that was the only political coloring in the landscape around him when he grew up. And I saw there were deep currents of very fine stuff in his beliefs—introspective, libertarian, individualistic."

They started walking home from the seminar together, stopping off for a beer, and soon developed a deep friendship. By spring, they and Mike Ansara decided to room together the following year with four other sophomores in two adjoining suites in Adams House. By fall, Sandy had begun his swing toward political radicalism; by November, he went on an anti-Vietnam march; within a year he joined SDS.

Of Harvard's residential houses, Adams was already known as the most culturally and politically avantgarde. Suites B46 and B47 helped maintain that reputation. Since all seven inhabitants except Sandy were already committed political activists, the two suites gradually became something of a primitive SDS cooperative. The participants merged their books into one huge library which covered the walls of one living room, and they often tended to merge their political, academic and social lives too.

Although Dave still wouldn't join SDS and refused to go to most of their meetings, he worked actively with the Harvard chapter. Only a year old and feeling its way carefully, the chapter was concentrating on educational projects and some community organizing. Because Dave had taken a seminar on Asian revolution and done prodigious reading on Vietnam, he was designated head of the Vietnam education project. This meant setting up Vietnam study groups at Harvard and other Boston area colleges, drawing up study guides, writing and distributing pamphlets, and dispatching speakers to high schools, churches and community groups. Dave did some speaking himself. He also moderated a major Vietnam teach-in that fall. It was heady stuff for a sophomore to be sitting up on the stage of Lowell Lecture Hall in a borrowed black suit, introducing men like H. Stuart Hughes and Hans Morgenthau to an audience of over seven hundred.

With all his political activity, Dave remained incredibly conscientious about his academic work. Sandy Thompson remembers that he had a little niche ("almost a sacred place") in one corner of the suite where he kept his books and papers in impeccable order and would spend hours hunched in steely concentration over his work. "Dave could compartmentalize his life better than anybody I'd ever seen," Sandy recalls. "Study until five-thirty P.M. Dinner. Study until eight-thirty. Then have fun. If somebody was playing rock in one room, he'd just get up and move to the next one. Incredibly disciplined and a perfectionist about everything—just like his father."

But Dave found less intellectual excitement in academic work that year, partly because it was the second time around, partly because he was beginning to find drawbacks to the Harvard system. He'd decided to major in history and was getting several of the duller required courses, such as Economics I, out of the way. Some of it was sheer "drudgery." But like the "good boy" he'd been since elementary school, he kept plugging away getting good grades (not straight A's this year, but a mixture of A's and B's).

So summer came as a great release. Joining his girl, who was studying in France that year, they traveled through Europe. Among other places, they went to Yugoslavia and Czechoslovakia, the first Communist countries Dave had visited. He carefully limited his expectations so he wouldn't be crushed if he didn't find the perfect society, but even then the visits were depressing. "In neither country did one get the sense people were politically more involved or concerned than anywhere else. They weren't revolutionary or even democratic countries."

In Yugoslavia they met a working-class family who told them that, even with factory councils, party officials controlled everything. "The workers didn't have any real part in running the show. That was clear." He liked some things in Yugoslavia—peasants strolling through the city's streets, the enthusiasm of the audience at a folk festival—but they didn't have much to do with socialism.

If anything, Czechoslovakia was worse. Dave had some names of American radicals to look up in Prague. He only reached one on the phone—a young man who was cold and hostile even after Dave gave him the name of their common friend. To make conversation, Dave asked him what he was doing there. The man exploded: "That's none of your business!" Dave hung up feeling terribly hurt because he had expected to be welcomed "as part of the international radical family." He concluded that living in Czechoslovakia had made the man anxious about talking to people he didn't know, and that made Dave wonder just what kind of country it was.

A few days later, he and Sue went to Prague's Lenin Museum, vast halls filled with memorabilia of the revolution: banners, manifestoes, weapons and oil portraits of Lenin, Plekhanov and other revolutionary heroes. But Dave noticed that there wasn't a single picture, or mention, of Trotsky. And just as Oliver had been disgusted years before by the party's vendetta against the Trotskyites, so this enraged Dave. "Who in the Russian revolution had been more important than Trotsky? Even if they'd pictured him as a left-wing deviationist, he should have been there. But, no, he'd just been written out of the revolution. To me, revolutionaries must be absolutely realistic. Those who falsify their past for advantage or power or factional strength or whatever reason are hurting the revolution."

But one thing in the museum impressed Dave particularly: a statue of a young worker lifting a cobblestone onto a barricade. It stirred him. "Sure, he was idealized in the fashion of Socialist Realism, a little too angularly muscular. But it was moving because one of the things easiest to forget when you're thinking about historical events is that the heart of the drama isn't ultimately systems, institutions or ideas, but individual people. Sometimes we get so abstracted we think of history as big blocks of concrete, glass or ice—cold, silent, impersonal clusters of things moving through space and crashing into each other—when really it's made by people like that worker with the cobblestone."

And this same feeling came even more intensely when they visited Prague's Jewish memorial on the grounds of a cemetery in the old city. Walking between the moss-covered tombstones jutting from the ground at crazy angles, they entered a former synagogue which served as a memorial to Czech Jews killed by the Nazis. Searching through the seventy thousand names embossed in tiny letters on plaster panels, Dave found the family of Jerry Soyka, a friend from the kibbutz. In a letter to his parents, Dave described his feelings: "It's like looking into human faces, one after another in interminable rows . . .

looking from one panel to another, from one camp to another, I have a sensation of swelling pain and horror, as individuals add up to many, and to a people; but they are never a mass, for a mass can be perceived emotionally as a small unit; they remain a swollen collection of individuals . . . Always the feeling of individual faces, each with two eyes that can look into my eyes . . . And this too is Vietnam. How many human beings? How many names written small on blank walls is this? How many more? . . . If only pain taught men their humanity."

Leaving Eastern Europe that summer, Dave as usual took the long view. "I was disappointed, but I knew what kind of socialism was historically represented in Eastern Europe. So it wasn't a test of socialism for me."

Back at Harvard that fall, Dave had a chance to put his own kind of socialism to a test. The seven suitemates had been granted permission to move off campus. They found a big, three-story house at Dana Street and Broadway, only four blocks from the Yard but in a lower-middle-class neighborhood just being penetrated by graduate students and young faculty.

If they had been groping hesitatingly toward a communal life style the year before, now they set out consciously to establish a "socialist cooperative." They put up a bulletin board with charts assigning work—sweeping, cleaning the bathroom, cooking, washing dishes, carrying out the garbage. Around exam time the system broke down, but usually it worked surprisingly well.

Since everyone in the house was by then actively working with SDS, it became the main physical and cultural asset, if not quite the headquarters, of the Harvard-Radcliffe chapter. During the year they took in four other guys. But you could never really tell how many people were staying there. All week, people streamed into the house to visit, for bull sessions or more formal meetings, for meals, or to sack out on couch or floor. On weekends, literally hundreds of people flooded through. "It was tiring to live like that," Dave recalls, "but it was nice too because we ate when we wanted to, lived how we wanted to. We had some personal liberty."

And perhaps because he was living off campus, perhaps because he was more involved with movement people, perhaps just because he was getting older, Dave began taking a more jaundiced view of academia.

Often before, he had been assailed by doubts. There was Thanksgiving his freshman year when he'd gone over for dinner with a philosophy professor who was a friend of his father's. Another professor was there and, at first, the dinner struck Dave as "the good life of the university, with intellectuals relaxing over the turkey bones." Then he happened to mention how dissatisfied his roommate was because his philosophy course wasn't dealing with the "big problems of life." Both professors guffawed and explained to the freshman that philosophy didn't deal with broad metaphysical problems any more but with technical analysis of discrete questions. Dave left hurt and angry.

Later he recalls getting into "personal polemics with professors which they didn't even know about," for the polemics appeared in Dave's papers, which were read only by graduate-student section men while the professors lectured on in Olympian grandeur from the podiums of vast halls.

But his dissatisfaction with the Harvard course structure came to a head that fall in a course on American foreign policy. By then, Dave had read enough to know that the reading list was "absurdly slanted" toward the official view and left off even the most academically respectable critical works. After two years of poring through everything on his reading lists, Dave suddenly realized there was nothing sacred about the lists, that they reflected particular, often very narrow, points of view.

But what bothered him most was a guest lecturer in the course, a Dr. Williams from West Point, who was lecturing on American military action in the Dominican Republic and Vietnam. Dave remembers starting to take notes as he always did: carefully inscribing the date, the name of the lecturer, the title of the lecture, and then a summary of what the lecturer was saying. What he was saying! "After two lines, I stopped and didn't write anything for the rest of the class. I just sat there looking at the man, listening in disbelief as he spun out an academic web of rationalization for two blatant acts of intervention. And then I noticed that the whole room was filled with downturned heads, gently bobbing with the motion of scribbling down every word the guy was saying. And I remember thinking to myself, 'My God, this is what the university is all about. You cloak an ordinary idiot in academic robes and he becomes some kind of a priest. You put him on that podium and he speaks with tremendous authority, authority he misuses to justify American policy!' "

Gradually Dave rejected ever more the Harvard academic life he had once devoured so voraciously. "When I came to Harvard I knew it was an institution of the ruling class, but I thought there could be a good deal of genuine free inquiry here. Now I saw that a university cannot be an autonomous institution in this society. It exists and prospers only because it performs certain functions the society demands and pays for—namely the training and socialization of students for specific roles they will play."

This rejection of traditional academia coincided with a rapid acceleration of Dave's involvement in the movement. That fall, he finally not only joined the SDS chapter but was elected one of its three co-chairmen, although he still declined to become a national member.

Even before SDS could formulate its program, it was presented with an unusual opportunity for action: Robert McNamara's visit to Harvard under the auspices of the Kennedy Institute. Dave recalls their attitude: "We didn't want one of the main architects of Vietnam policy to come to Harvard without having to confront the antiwar movement. If he didn't, then the administration could say, 'People always claim we don't listen to criticism. Well, recently our Secretary of Defense went up to Harvard, certainly one of the most vital centers of criticism. Well, we have differences—blah-blah-blah—but there is a basic understanding—blah-blah-blah—so we are going to proceed with our policy.' We couldn't let that happen."

So SDS asked that after he met several select institute groups McNamara also publicly debate a critic of the war. They selected Robert Scheer, the *Ramparts* editor then fortuitously also a guest of the institute. But, even when supported by 1,550 students and 50 faculty, this request was rejected. So SDS resolved to force a confrontation.

On the afternoon of November 7, while McNamara met a small group of students in Quincy House, SDS held a rally outside before almost eight hundred persons. Under banners proclaiming "Kill for Peace" and "Vietnam: the Edsel of Foreign Policy," while a loudspeaker blared out "Mac the Knife," Dave and others addressed the crowd. When McNamara emerged, the university police car in which he was riding was blocked by SDS demonstrators sitting on the street. McNamara got out, climbed on top of the car amidst jeers of "Murderer!" and "Fascist!" and agreed to answer a few questions. Someone shouted, "How many South Vietnamese civilians have we killed and why doesn't the State Department disclose the figures?"

"We don't know," McNamara said.

"Why don't you know? Don't you care?" students shouted back.

After more angry exchanges, ten policemen forced their way through the jostling crowd wedged into narrow Mill Street. Forming a protective cordon around the secretary, they whisked him into nearby Leverett House, thus ending the most aggressive political confrontation Harvard had yet seen.

The demonstration stirred outrage at the university and around the country. John Monro, dean of the college, wrote McNamara asking him to accept "our deeply felt apology for the discourteous and unruly confrontation forced upon you." A petition signed by twenty-seven hundred Harvard students also expressed regret for the incident.

Dave's reaction to these apologies was blazing anger. "It was a lot of pompous bullshit. You know, 'Here at Harvard we don't do things like that.' Well, Christ Almighty, Harvard people go down to Washington and help make policy which destroys a lot of lives and here we were trying to get a lousy, stinking debate, not even harming the bastard. I almost wish we had. Standing in the crowd looking up at him, I saw he wasn't eighty feet tall; he was only maybe five foot eight, very fleshy, with a tan I guess he got from mountain climbing in Colorado. And I realized as never before that it was guys like this who were sending Americans to their death and wiping out Vietnam. It was infuriating. It made you want to poke him."

Dave got a chance to take a symbolic poke at another government spokesman a few months later when Arthur Goldberg showed up for his Kennedy Institute visit. This time, the institute agreed to let him be questioned by a five-man panel of students and faculty. Dave, representing

SDS, took the initiative. As soon as Goldberg told the capacity crowd in Sanders Theater how happy he was to be there to participate in the democratic process, Dave stood up and said, "Look, what does this so-called democratic process have to do with the war? We can sit here and debate all we want, but the war goes on and this has nothing to do with it."

That January, Dave had a chance to confront the university administration directly. A committee of the Board of Overseers scheduled a hearing on "How undergraduate opinion gets heard and registered in college decisions and policies." It invited the three SDS co-chairmen along with several other student leaders to a meeting in the faculty room of University Hall. It was Dave's first time in the room and he felt as though he was "walking into another century" when he saw the oak paneling, big mahogany tables, maroon draperies, tapestries, chandeliers and oil portraits of Harvard men since the seventeenth century. Then there was the committee itself—presidents and vice-presidents of banks and corporations and universities. But this time Dave was unimpressed. He hadn't even bothered to borrow a black suit. Wearing his "zoot suit," a light gray sharkskin with big lapels, he told the committee bluntly that the Harvard man's conception of himself was "phony," that Harvard men had no more impact on how their university was run than students at educational factories like Ohio State.

Finally, that spring, Dave helped frame the famous "We Won't Go" statement in which he and eighty-five other Harvard and M.I.T. students declared their "determination to refuse military service while the United States is fighting in Vietnam." Such statements have become routine now, but this was one of the first and attracted wide attention in the nation's press. Yet, Dave and others soon concluded that it had been a mistake because it emphasized the moral rejection of the war by university students. "The reaction we got was, sure, these privileged university kids are trying to find a way out, while our kids have to go anyway. There was a lot of truth to that, and from then on we emphasized that nobody should go, and we directed our appeal to the whole community, particularly working-class guys." (Dave has since applied for and received conscientious objector status.)

As Dave's respect for academic life waned, his old romantic attachment to the workers reasserted itself. Back in Yellow Springs that summer where he worked as a coordinator for Vietnam Summer, Dave stressed the importance of reaching workers. In a report late that summer, he said his canvassers had found "considerable interest among social groups, especially black people and factory workers, which have generally been excluded from peace work."

And he had a heartwarming reunion with some of the maintenance men he'd worked with at Antioch. Two of them—a World War II veteran and a guy who served with the Marines in Korea—had been among the most anti-Communist and anti-Negro in the group when Dave worked there, always talking about "niggers" and "Commies" and how they would drop the atom bomb (which they called the "hootenanny") on Moscow if they had their way. But since then, because they wanted to bargain for better wages and working conditions, they'd formed a union which included many black workers at Antioch and got active help from Antioch's radicals. And in the process their views had changed so much that toward the end of that summer these two men even came to hear Dave speak at a Vietnam Summer meeting and then went out drinking with him and some college radicals at a Negro bar.

Dave feels there is a profound lesson in this: "that the only way to reach the working class is through their own interests. I could have preached to those two guys day and night about civil rights and imperialism without making any headway. But when they found out in the union battle who their real allies were, their attitudes changed naturally. And I began to see just how frustrated and alienated most American workers are. Their lives are built around a job which gives them neither much pay nor much satisfaction. They're in debt. They take orders all goddamned day. They accumulate incredible hostility which is dangerous to direct at the real source of their grievances. So, built into our culture are two safety valves for that hostility: racism and anti-Communism. But if you give men a lever which allows them to deal with the real causes of their unhappiness they don't need safety valves. They begin to see who their real friends are. This analysis gives me some optimism about a revolution which will one day involve the working class."

Back in Cambridge the next year, Dave's feeling of solidarity with the workers was further strengthened by several months of working for a trucking company, loading freight at their terminal on the early shift (3 A.M. to noon). At first the men eyed him with suspicion, but gradually the barriers dissolved in the sweat of the loading platform and the men started asking Dave to fix them up with "hippie chicks." What sealed their friendship was a common contempt for the "office people," the formal, proper, coat-and-tie types who worked in a little cage at the end of the platform. Out on the platform, Dave and the others bulled, roared, swore and sweated together and Dave developed a "tremendous affection" for these men. After he quit, he'd drive by the terminal at night with a friend and say, "That's the concentration camp where I worked. The guys are still there and they're going to be there for years."

During his senior year, Dave lived with three other SDS members in another off-campus house. The old co-operative had disbanded because everyone was "a bit tired out." Dave still believes in the need for "movement centers" where activists can come together in all sorts of informal ways, but he doesn't think they should be where people are trying to live.

That fall, Dave also decided to ease up somewhat on his political activity to concentrate on his senior honors thesis. His growing disdain for the traditional trappings of Harvard academic life did not yet include the thesis, which he saw as a chance to demonstrate the possibilities of real radical scholarship. Ken Waltzer, Dave's tutor and thesis supervisor that year, recalls him as "heads and tails above any student I ever had at Harvard; a very knowledgeable intellectual socialist." But he feels Dave went into his thesis with unrealistic expectations. "He wanted to analyze the entire sweep of American foreign policy and I kept telling him it couldn't be done."

Dave's outline for a thesis to be called "Imperialism and the State" was truly formidable. "My goal," he wrote, "is to explain the rise of the State as a semi-autonomous political force regulating, balancing and stimulating the domestic economy, on the one hand, and protecting and promoting American economic expansion abroad, on the other—especially with reference to the historical expansion abroad of the maturing industrial corporate economy." His approach was heavily influenced by William Appleman Williams, the radical historian at the University of Wisconsin; Charles Beard's books (particularly *The Idea of National Interest*) and other theoretical works. Waltzer kept urging him to narrow the scope and seek out primary sources.

Eventually Dave agreed to focus on 1919-1939 and to dig into trade, productivity and market statistics. "But the more I got into it the less exciting it seemed. All the requirements about how it had to be written, how long it should be, when it had to be in, began to get to me. They just seemed irrelevant."

Something else happened that fall which eroded Dave's devotion to even radical scholarship. On October 25 Dave helped block a Dow recruiter in a chemistry lab. Until then, he and other Harvard radicals had avoided such direct violations of college rules for fear of being thrown out. "I'd always believed it was crucial for me to get my Harvard degree—with high honors if possible—so I could go on to a good graduate school and fulfill my ambition to become a college professor." But when he and seventy-three other students were placed on probation for the Dow sit-in and he realized he could now be expelled for any further violation, Dave's viewpoint began to change. "I began to see that I didn't really have that big a stake in staying at Harvard, that there were other colleges, other ways of living. I realized I hadn't faced up to the implications of my radical views."

Dave recognizes that his changing outlook that fall also stemmed in part from growing tension with his girl. She was working in New York that fall and although he saw her frequently, their relationship was deteriorating. "Part of it was that she'd always had this image of me as a professor, leading the life she'd seen in my father's house and other faculty homes in Antioch. I disappointed her when I made clear I wasn't going to offer her that kind of life. She was never that much attracted to my radicalism." By Christmas vacation, they seemed on the verge of breaking up.

In January, Dave found it increasingly difficult to concentrate on his thesis. One day his roommate asked, "Why don't you drop it?" With the academic reflex of sixteen

years, Dave snapped, "Don't be silly. I couldn't do that."
But his roommate, who had recently dropped his, reminded Dave that many radicals were doing the same,
partly to protest against traditional Harvard scholarship,
partly to spend more time on political work. After an
agonizing week, Dave abandoned his thesis too. "All of
a sudden I felt a couple of chains fall off me, almost physically."

A few weeks later, Dave was scuffing through the
snowdrifts along Massachusetts Avenue when he noticed
ahead of him a man who seemed to be a Harvard professor: tall, about forty-five, well groomed, well dressed
in a black coat and hat. "He looked just like my image
of a professor. Suddenly I had this gut reaction: there's a
guy going to work. His work is different from most people's because he deals mainly with ideas and books. But
still he's going to work. And for the first time I saw
the academic profession without any special dignity or
sanctity or excitement, but as just another kind of work in
a complicated society."

Dave was reacting against his lifelong adulation of his
father the professor; but it was a complex form of liberation, nothing so simple as rebellion. For Dave retains
great admiration for his father, who has never been a
typical professor (he has steadfastly resisted the pressure to publish and has concentrated on teaching, thereby giving up many opportunities to move on to more
prestigious universities). Moreover, he had long been a
radical professor. After the trauma of the McCarthy era,
Oliver pulled in his horns somewhat during the rest of
the fifties. "It was a difficult period," he concedes. "People thought twice about saying anything. A great silence
set in—the period of disjuncture which had given the New
Left such a vivid sense of independent discovery." But
when the Southern sit-ins broke through the country's
crust of complacency, Oliver—and his wife—enthusiastically enlisted in the civil rights movement, and later in
the antiwar movement.

Yet, whatever movement he joined, it was always as
the professor committed to the rational processes of a
liberal arts institution. For example, as an elected member of the Antioch Assembly on Vietnam, he urged ending all secret research and other ties with the Defense
Department, but strenuously opposed efforts to put the

college itself on record against the war. In a draft he wrote for the Assembly, Oliver argued that "the only proper institutional stands for the college are on issues scrupulously identified as educational." The public, he said, would give greater weight to counsel from "an academic community with an earned reputation for free inquiry, for responsible controversy."

Oliver proposed a new field at Antioch called Theory and Practice of Social Change for students who wished to stay "continuously in 'the movement,' seeking solutions to the problems of poverty, racism and violence." Arguing that teaching and studying at Antioch could be honorable occupations "even for radicals," he suggested that such a new field would keep academicians in constant encounter with "activist scholars." This prompted a snippy retort from Carl Oglesby, a founder of SDS who was then radical-in-residence at Antioch. Oglesby said this was like "chasing a butterfly during a lion hunt; radicals may need the school as a sanctuary in the future, but now we have to get out of it and organize for action." To which Oliver replied by accusing Oglesby of "an astonishing disregard of the theoretical struggle."

And this was the nub of the issue between Oliver and Dave. The father still valued the academic community both as a protected arena for the theoretical struggle and, to some extent, as a base for a political struggle outside. Dave increasingly regarded the academic community as corrupt and moved toward radical action—even against that community.

Dave's rejection of the Harvard brand of academic life was appropriately expressed at his own graduation (cum laude) that June. SDS had decided to focus its protest on the granting of an honorary degree to the Shah of Iran. So when the Shah was introduced at the ceremony in front of Memorial Church's dazzling white spire, Dave and a dozen other seniors jumped from their seats, red arm bands tied around their black robes, and ran forward unfurling a banner which read "No Degree for a Dictator." They also distributed a leaflet explaining their view of the university: "The official and widely accepted image of Harvard is that of a center for the free exchange and generation of ideas . . . [But] Harvard's most significant educational function is, we believe, to train individuals to take their places in the elites which benefit from, and to some extent, control, the present workings of our society . . . We believe Harvard must be changed . . . Since the greatest crisis of our time is the struggle of the disadvantaged and the oppressed for fulfillment and freedom, Harvard must be made to take their side in the struggle. Of course, the limits of Harvard's transformation are determined by the society of which it is part. Our fight to change Harvard can only succeed as part of the larger movement for freedom and equality in our society and in the world. We who are graduating will do our part to fight the war and the draft, and to build this larger movement . . ."

As he plunged deeper into the movement, Dave felt increasingly embattled. He saw his friends as colleagues-in-arms—"I realized suddenly that here was a group to whom I would trust my life"—and he found enemies, "not just in some ideological sense, but real physical enemies."

These enemies emerged in a series of movement "confrontations." First, a policeman threw him off a five-foot platform at a Chelsea market as he and others tried to stop the loading of California grapes. Then, he was tossed off an Army base by MPs after he tried to get antidraft information to draftees about to take their pre-induction physicals. Finally, he and eight other SDS members were arrested and sentenced to three months in prison (later reduced to a twenty-dollar fine) for joining welfare mothers sitting in at the Massachusetts State House to demand larger winter-clothing allowances for their children.

Oliver does not feel entirely comfortable with the New Left's confrontation politics. He detects both "nihilistic" and "anti-intellectual trends," and he is particularly concerned by those who have rejected nonviolence. At Antioch he has counseled students to "consider all likely eventualities and not to be provoked into actions they would later regret."

Nevertheless, Dave continues to see his radicalism as growing naturally out of his parents' radicalism: the Old Left giving birth to and nurturing the New Left. He feels strongly that his values and goals are very close to theirs.

Asked what he wants for the world, Dave still says "Communism," and when asked what that means he says, "An end to men's afflictions, an end to exploitation and oppression, an end to competitive and abusive social relationships, an end to the alienation between man and man, between man and woman, between men and nature, between intellectual and physical and artistic labor; between men's activity and their human selves; the beginning of men's collective mastery over their fate, of brotherhood as the functional principle of social relations, of material and cultural abundance for all, of the full development of each as the condition for the full development of all."

Dave believes the Old Left and the New Left differ chiefly in their methods:

"My father is an educator. In the Communist Party, he worked chiefly in worker education and the teachers union. In the Progressive Party, he spent most of his time going around speaking to various groups. I guess that's one of my criticisms of the Old Left. Most Communist Party members never really had to change their lives that much. There were a lot of professionals, even some wealthy people, who wanted to think of themselves as revolutionary without making any significant changes in the lives they led. Not so much my folks, because they thought very deeply about what they were doing. But to be in SDS today usually means committing yourself to a great deal of activism."

He also sees a difference in style:

"Often the Old Left tended to accept middle-class culture while fighting middle-class politics. We need a whole new culture too. This doesn't mean just music, drugs, long hair, pretty clothes, communal apartments and free love. A lot of that can be just another form of the consumer culture, too, unless young people understand clearly what it is they find unbearable about the world around them—namely a social order which makes it impossible for people to live as full, creative, independent, happy human beings."

"Dave has a lot of what black folks call soul," says one of his friends. "He's much more free and spontaneous than a lot of SDS people." Dave smokes pot, but he doesn't need to be high to enjoy the world around him. He loves people and seems to have literally hundreds of friends. He enjoys parties, likes to dance, and often pulls out his harmonica to play along with the music. Although he usually wears a faded blue workshirt, he surprised his friends by showing up at one Cambridge party wearing a purple satin shirt, blue bell-bottom trousers and pointed black shoes. "He gets tremendous excitement and enjoyment out of life," says another friend. "I remember him walking along the shore at Rockport a whole afternoon, picking up sea urchins and shouting, 'Wow, look at this, look at that.' "

"If we're going to appeal to the whole person in our work," Dave says, "then we're going to have to be whole people ourselves."

From August 1968 on, Dave threw his whole person into the movement. Giving up a lucrative fellowship at Wisconsin, he took a job with the SDS New England regional staff. In his spare moments, he also worked hard trying to form an SDS rock band. They had a few sessions, with Dave as lead singer, but often the drummer or the sax would simply fail to show. "SDS people are undisciplined enough and musicians are doubly so," Dave says with a mock sigh. "The combination is impossible."

But he spent most of his time working with college chapters in the area, trying to tighten their organization and develop new techniques for reaching uncommitted students. As the year wore on he was often back at Harvard helping his old colleagues in their campaign against R.O.T.C. By early April the campaign seemed to be building toward the long-sought open confrontation with the administration. Exhilarated, Dave worked so long and hard through the cold, damp days that on the evening of April 8 he felt a bad cold coming on and went to bed early.

ROY

Every April the Garden Club of Holly Springs, Mississippi, sponsors a "pilgrimage" through the town's finest ante-bellum houses. There are few architectural masterpieces on the tour—nothing to match the splendor of Natchez or New Orleans—but Holly Springs offers not so much buildings as a way of life. "Her dreamy, restful Southern spell is cast on all who come within reach of her enchantment," promises a Garden Club brochure.

For those with the four-dollar fee and a day to spend tramping up honeysuckle walks and across parquet floors, the pilgrimage provides a redolent sniff of the Old South at nearly every stop. At Grey Gables, a spiral stairway and Bohemian glass window once looked down on some of the grandest balls of Holly Springs' "grand period." The Mimosas boasts an underground tunnel where Confederate fugitives and valuables were concealed during raids. Montrose, a mansion of slave-baked bricks, was built by Alfred Brooks as a wedding present for his daughter. General Grant once stayed briefly at the Walter Place and left behind some private papers which were returned by a chivalrous Confederate general. Cedarhurst still has its original cypress floors, hand-hooked rugs and French walnut furniture. At the Magnolias, the handsome Gothic door bears the mark of a Union bayonet and, around back, the old Slave Quarters have been restored as a guest house.

In 1851 an eighteen-year-old slave named Ionie was purchased off the auction block in Charleston, South

Carolina, by a Memphis dealer who sold her to the master of the Magnolias. There she married a slave named Louis Hearn and they served together for a decade until the war broke out. When the slaves were freed, Louis and his wife got themselves some land a few miles from Holly Springs, began sharecropping and raised a family which soon spread through surrounding Marshall County.

In 1917 one of their granddaughters—Ardean—met a young man named Harrison De Berry just before he went off to fight in France. The next year, she gave birth to a boy she named Roy De Berry after the absent father, whom she never saw again.

Later, Ardean did marry and went off to live with her husband across the county, leaving Roy to grow up on his grandparents' farm. When he was still very young, Ionie came there to live her last days—she died at ninety-four—and Roy can remember sitting around the sputtering wood stove listening to her tell stories of slavery days.

Roy began school at six, but in those days rural Negro schools ran only four months a year, so he didn't finish eighth grade until he was eighteen. Two years later, he married Willie Mae McEwan, an eighteen-year-old seventh grader, and they both left school. Roy helped his grandfather on the farm for a while and then did "day work" on other farms or on the highway, earning twenty-two and a half cents an hour. In 1937 he began sharecropping his own little farm—a ten-acre patch of cotton and peas next to his grandfather's. The landlord supplied the land, equipment and fertilizer; in return, Roy split the profit with him fifty-fifty.

But his share was hardly worth the trouble. So in 1940 he moved to a larger farm owned by Harris Gholson, president of the Bank of Holly Springs. Set on a grassy plateau about five miles from town, it had about fifteen acres of cotton patch and ample pasture for cows and hogs. He made do there for a couple of years.

Meanwhile his family was beginning to grow. A son, James, was born in 1936, and a daughter, Elnora, in 1938. When his wife became pregnant again in 1941, Mr. De Berry decided he had to find more money and began working part time in Memphis. For the next dozen years he stayed on the farm during the spring planting season and the fall harvest, but worked in Memphis during the winter and summer.

It was a strenuous life, particularly in the off-seasons. He would rise then at 4 A.M., do the essential farm chores and leave around five for the fifty-mile trip to the city. Changing jobs often, he worked on a construction site, in a Firestone rubber plant, in a furniture company's planing mill and a wholesale grocery warehouse. They were all hard manual jobs, by no means easy for the small-boned man who looks almost delicate behind his glasses and spidery mustache. Often when he got home at night, his wife recalls, he was so tired he could barely spoon down his beans and grits before tumbling off to sleep.

But the De Berrys needed the money to keep pace with the children who kept appearing at regular two-year intervals: Lee Etta in 1941, Doris in 1943, Melvin in 1945 and then, on June 13, 1947, a boy they named Roy, Jr.

"Junior," as they called him, remembers sleeping in a little crib stuck sideways in the narrow hallway between his parents' room and the front room, where the other children slept at night. That's all there was to the tin-roofed, tar-paper shack—two square rooms set one behind the other with a long porch running down the side —until they tacked a little cookhouse on the other side with a stovepipe tilting out of the roof.

The best part of the house to Roy, Jr., was the huge gnarled cedar tree in the front yard, more than a hundred years old, with thick branches which coiled around each other like a nest of pythons. From the top you could see for miles, but for years Roy was scared to climb that high.

His other favorite plaything in those years was a cow named Ole Beulah, a swollen, lumbering, gentle creature with a white streak down her black nose. For some reason Roy thought she was funny and he'd stand in the yard laughing while his mother milked her. The De Berrys also had a horse named Lou and a mule named Bob. Roy remembers how his father would hoist him up on Bob's spiky spine and hold him tight while they jounced together across the bumpy pastures. He treasured those moments with his father, who didn't have much time to spend with the children.

Roy saw more of his mother. Unlike other farm women, Willie Mae rarely worked in the fields because of a chronic back problem. Roy remembers her then as "always around the house, cooking or mending or taking care of us—very attentive, very warm."

Roy's most frequent companion was his brother Melvin, two years older and a seasoned guide to the world around them. Beyond the grassy plateau where the De Berrys' house stood, the farm dropped off into acres of brambly woodland, rocky hillsides and winding gullies. Roy and Melvin explored every foot of it, devising a sport appropriate to each locale. They slid on cardboard boxes down one long, sandy slope, rolled car tires along a boulder-strewn obstacle course and nudged Lou and Bob into a shambling race through the underbrush.

The farm was isolated, with only five other houses scattered in a mile radius, and the De Berrys rarely went into Holly Springs during the week. Like most rural black families, they were largely self-sufficient, growing most of the food they needed in a "truck patch" behind the house. On Saturdays they'd go into Holly Springs to buy salt, pepper, sorghum and bolts of cotton from which Willie Mae would make the family's clothes.

On Sundays they went to the Baptist church in Cedar Grove, a tiny settlement three miles down the dirt road. Roy liked Sunday School there with a fat, jolly teacher named Ethel who let them giggle and whisper while she recited Scripture. And he liked the hymn singing which his father often led in his soaring baritone. But he didn't care much for the sermons by the itinerant preacher who came once a month on "Preaching Sunday." It was a fundamentalist service with lots of "Hallelujah" and "Preach on, brother," and in the rhythmic lull of call and response Roy often fell asleep.

Just across the road was the Cedar Grove School, a tiny shack of weather-beaten planks, where Roy started when he was six. The school ran six months a year in a split session—two months in the summer (July and August) and four months in the winter (November, December, January and February)—so the students would be free to help their parents plant in the spring and harvest in the fall.

All eight grades—up to eighty-five pupils—crouched on

low benches in the single room, so close that the toes of one row often scraped the heels of the next. In the center of the room was a great iron stove which glowed orange through its layer of soot. The children took turns cutting logs for it in the forest which crept right up to the school's back door. They also fetched buckets of drinking water to put on a shelf in the corner next to the big tin ladle and a row of glasses. The nearest well was a mile down the road at the County Poor House, and Roy remembers how the bucket's handle dug into his palm as he tottered back along the sandy track.

But Roy was used to walking. Every day he hiked the three miles to school and three miles back, often with his shoes slung over his shoulder to save the leather. (Many kids came to school barefoot, but Willie Mae had "a thing about shoes." She insisted her children wear them in school although they never did around the house.)

The walk to school took an hour and a half each way. So Roy had to be up at six to feed the hogs and eat his breakfast of rice, molasses, biscuits and milk before setting off. Usually there were five of them—Elnora, Lee Etta, Doris, Melvin and Roy—as they tramped down the hill and through the underbrush. When they reached the blacktop highway they were often joined by neighbors' children for the last stage of the walk through a dense pine forest.

With eighty-five students and eight grades in a single room, the school might have been pandemonium. But Roy remembers it ran quite well by dint of an intricate staggering system. While the first, second and third grades had their spelling lesson, the fourth, fifth and sixth grades were out playing and the seventh and eighth were studying their geography books. The school never had enough books. Those they got came down secondhand from the county's white schools and were usually tattered, with pages missing or scribbled on.

But all the school's weaknesses were balanced by one major strength—its lone teacher, Henry S. Boyd. Roy remembers Mr. Boyd with warmth. "He was beautiful—a very good teacher and a very good man, too." A graduate of Mississippi Industrial College in Holly Springs, with a year of teacher training at Tuskegee Institute, Henry Boyd was the second black college graduate to teach school in Marshall County. Although he'd specialized in social science at Tuskegee, he quickly learned to teach everything at Cedar Grove. And he embellished the thin curriculum with some of the talents he'd picked up along the way. A powerful baritone in his college chorus, he led his students every morning in spirituals like "Swing Low, Sweet Chariot" and "I Ain't Going to Study War No More," carefully explaining their origin and what they meant. Every Easter he wrote a play the students gave at the church across the road. And he helped write speeches for the seniors to give at graduation.

But most important to Roy—in retrospect, at least—was the emphasis Mr. Boyd put on Negro history. From his Tuskegee days he brought a deep respect for the institute's founder, Booker T. Washington. Roy recalls his speaking of Washington as "a black man who had achieved something, who was born a slave but went on to educate himself and then founded his own school and became a very powerful figure, a black figure we could relate to."

Mr. Boyd remembers speaking not only of Washington but of George Washington Carver, W.E.B. Du Bois, Carter G. Woodson, Joe Louis, Jack Johnson, Marian Anderson, and black men closer to home—Hiram R. Revels and B.K. Bruce, both United States senators from Mississippi during Reconstruction days. Revels, who lived in Holly Springs, is buried in the town's Hillcrest Cemetery, and Mr. Boyd often took his students there to see the grave.

"I just thought our children ought to know something about these people," he says. "We'd been taught that Negroes were always servants, never anything worthwhile. Even when we studied Mississippi history we didn't learn about Negroes. Lots of Negroes had that kind of image of their own history. I wanted them to know we had done something. I wanted to give them some pride in themselves."

But Mr. Boyd never openly blamed white men—his job depended on them—and neither did the De Berrys. Roy never developed conscious animosity toward the white man in his childhood years, but he picked up subtle cues. One of the De Berrys' few neighbors was a white man, a farmer named Jack Lemmon whom most of the Negroes regarded as "poor white trash." Roy remembers hearing his parents call Lemmon "a cracker." But they managed to maintain cordial enough relations with him and occasionally he would drop by for a chat.

Once, when Roy was five, Lemmon wandered down to the truck patch where Willie Mae was picking beans. As he approached, Roy asked, "What's the cracker doing here?" Lemmon heard him, but took it surprisingly well, laughing with Willie Mae about what the boy had said. Willie Mae laughed, too. What else could she do? But that evening Roy Sr. warned his young son that that wasn't the way you addressed a white man.

The next white man Roy became conscious of was the Marshall County school superintendent, who occasionally dropped by Cedar Grove to talk with Mr. Boyd and check attendance records. "He'd drive up in this big late-model car," Roy recalls, "and that was pretty impressive because we didn't see many cars out there. For that reason alone, the cat's visit was always pretty exciting. He'd come through the door without even knocking. He might say something to Mr. Boyd but he never spoke to us at all and we never spoke to him. I think I vaguely felt the cat was intruding, but not very strongly, because he was just too remote at that time."

Roy stayed at the Cedar Grove School through the third grade in 1956, when Marshall County abolished the school and consolidated it with Holly Springs' Negro school (the Supreme Court had ordered the integration of segregated school systems two years before, but Mississippi was still refusing to comply).

Partly because of the school consolidation, the De Berrys decided to leave the farm. "We wanted to get the children closer to school," Mr. De Berry recalls. "And I'd just got to the point too where I couldn't make a living out of farming at all. The farm wasn't big enough and the land wasn't good enough. So I decided to give it up altogether and start working year round in Memphis." The Precision Tool Co., where he'd worked two years, agreed to take him on full time, and in the spring of 1956 the family moved to Holly Springs.

Holly Springs in those days still bore the strong stamp of its Confederate past. Unlike many Southern towns, it hadn't changed much since the Civil War. Three thousand strong when Fort Sumter was fired on, its population was held in check by the war and then ravaged by the great yellow fever epidemic of 1878. By the turn of the century it was only two thousand and by World War II had grown to barely four thousand.

Spared the urban growth which was bulldozing so much of America, Holly Springs retained about sixty ante-bellum houses which it preened and polished with an antiquarian's zeal.

But the Garden Club pilgrimage covered only a small part of Holly Springs—a manicured strip running northeast and southwest of the Marshall County Courthouse. The tourists were never led toward West Memphis Street where it juts off Court Square and jounces north toward the city that bears its name. For this is "darky town," a stretch of rutted hills, muddy roads and splayed frame houses, where most of the town's Negroes live.

In 1956 the De Berrys moved into the heart of this area. They rented half of a widow's home, a tar-paper bungalow with a porch across the front and a big pecan tree in the yard. The widow stayed on in the other half, but the De Berrys had more room than they'd had on the farm: two bedrooms, a living room, dining room and kitchen. More comfort, too. For the first time they had electricity, a coal stove, running water, a bathtub and indoor toilet. With Mr. De Berry working full time at Precision Tool, they were also able to afford a few other amenities. That first year, he made twenty-seven hundred dollars, more than he'd ever made before. The next year he went over three thousand dollars—a big step for a black man in Mississippi.

But to Roy the best thing about the new house was its location: scarcely a hundred yards from the Julius Rosenwald School. No more rising before dawn. No more three-mile walks. He could stay in bed until the last moment, then jump up and be in the classroom before he finished buttoning his pants.

The Julius Rosenwald School was one of the rural Negro schools the Chicago philanthropist helped finance early in the century. Beginning in 1911, Rosenwald offered to match whatever funds could be raised by local people through public taxes and private donations, and more than five thousand communities throughout the South took him up on it.

For years, Holly Springs' only Negro school was the old Miller's Institute, huddled behind the county jail, so the children had to pass right beneath the barred windows twice each day. This stigma growingly irritated the town's black community, which was inordinately proud of Holly Springs' two Negro colleges, Rust and Mississippi Industrial. If the town could lead the way in Negro higher education, people asked, why couldn't it have a decent Negro grade school? So, in 1926, they raised about fifteen thousand dollars, got a matching Rosenwald grant and built a sturdy wooden schoolhouse on Valley Street. In 1951, with the fight against Southern school segregation beginning, the county built a new brick Rosenwald School across the road; and when the original school burned down in 1954, added a junior high school on that site.

When Roy started there in 1956, the complex was still new and a bit overwhelming to a boy whose only school until then had been a one-room shack. White school officials, determined to show they meant separate but really equal, saw to it that the physical plants at least matched anything at the white schools across town. With their yellow brick façades, glass doors and neat white trim, the buildings looked a bit like the "modern" but starkly utilitarian schools then being built in Northern cities.

But Roy soon learned that "separate" still meant inferior. For the books they got at Rosenwald were still hand-me-downs from the white schools and there were never enough of them to go around. "I was always a book short in some subject," Roy remembers. "I'd have to share or at exam time I'd borrow a book quick and cram up. The brick outside was beautiful but in the things that really counted we were still second-class."

But that still didn't bother Roy much. He was more worried then by a different kind of inferiority. His first day in the fourth grade at Rosenwald, his teacher took one look at him and nicknamed him "Shortie." The name stuck, for Roy was a couple of inches shorter than most of his classmates and he stayed the shortest boy in his class through high school.

He was self-conscious about his size but determined to overcome it, and he soon found he could turn it to his advantage on the athletic field. For if he was smaller than the other boys he was also faster and nimbler. Too small to play the line in football, he spent hours passing to a friend and won the quarterback job on a church team. In baseball, he wasn't much of a hitter but he became a sure-handed, far-ranging second baseman.

Roy was an enthusiastic sports fan, too—a trait he undoubtedly inherited from his father. Through all his years of incessant labor, Roy Sr. relaxed most completely when he was hunched over his crackling radio set listening to some sort of game. His son vividly recalls listening with him to a Joe Louis–Ezzard Charles fight (although the last time they fought was in 1950, when Roy was only three).

"My father was a real Louis fan," he says, "partly, I'm sure, because Louis was able to whup white folks. I remember him talking about the way Joe beat Max Schmeling and there had to be some race pride in that, you know —a black man beating a blond German. For us down in Mississippi that was something."

By 1957, Roy Jr. was avidly following Negro baseball players. That was the year the Milwaukee Braves won the National League pennant and also the year the De Berrys got their first television set. Roy can remember his enthusiasm for Hank Aaron and Bill Bruton, the Braves' two Negro stars, and his joy that fall when the Braves whipped the Yankees four games to three in the World Series.

There was another struggle on TV that fall: the bitter dispute over integrating Central High School in Little Rock. Roy remembers how the World Series games would go off and the news would come right on showing troops patrolling the streets of the Arkansas capital. Although his parents didn't say much, Roy sensed their quiet satisfaction when Eisenhower sent troops in and the soldiers escorted black kids up the sidewalk to the school. "I didn't completely understand what was happening. But I could empathize with those kids, feel both pride and fear, you know— What would I have felt if I'd been making that walk?" For the first time he heard people talk about something called "civil rights." He wasn't sure just what they were, but he was vaguely aware that he should root for them just as he did for Hank Aaron.

Yet nobody applied the lesson of Little Rock to Holly Springs. It was a full three years after the Supreme Court's decision, but integration of Holly Springs' schools

—or other facilities—didn't seem a real possibility to either blacks or whites.

"We just never talked about integration then—at home or at school," Roy recalls. "I was always with black people. I was at a black school and I went to black restaurants. I knew there were white places where I couldn't go but I don't think I questioned why I couldn't. I suppose it was this thing about black people and white people knowing their place. It's your parents' responsibility to get this across to you at an early age. I'm sure mine did."

The black man's "place" in Holly Springs was mainly West Memphis Street, the commercial, amusement and educational center of the Negro community. Straddling the street were the town's two Negro colleges, and trailing after them, the restaurants, snack bars and record shops which spring up around any college: College Inn ("Barbeque Ribs, 65 cents"), Modena's ("Fish Sandwich, 55 cents"), Fox's Inn. Nearby was Olmstead's, a black-owned grocery store, and Brittenum's Funeral Home, which belonged to Holly Springs' wealthiest Negro. Brittenum's was one of the town's social centers. Almost every afternoon, if there wasn't a wake in progress, people would wander down to the funeral-home lounge to relax in the big easy chairs, watch TV, sip ice water from the fountain and trade gossip.

It was a constricted life, tightly defined by the town's rigid racial categories. But Roy had a special outlet. His family's roots, and relatives, were still in the county and this gave him a chance to touch base frequently with the more self-sufficient, self-confident rural Negroes.

For a couple of years after they moved to town the De Berrys kept some hogs penned on the farm. One night a week his father and Roy would take a truck into Memphis, where a friend who worked in a café would let them have a barrel of garbage to dump in the pigs' trough. On weekends his father would often take Roy and Melvin hunting for squirrel, rabbit or 'possum and afterward they'd stop by one of their old neighbors' for some coffee and a chat.

And every Sunday they went back to Cedar Grove for church. There were plenty of churches in Holly Springs, but somehow it never occurred to the De Berrys that "church" was anyplace but Cedar Grove. It wasn't the preaching and praying that drew them; it was the home folks singing the old hymns or chatting afterward beneath the bending shade trees. Cedar Grove, Roy recalls, was "where the spirit was."

Every August the church held a three-day revival meeting, culminating in "the mourner's bench," a ritual designed to save the souls of twelve-year-old children. Twelve was said to be Christ's age when he first impressed the lawyers and doctors in the temple, and Roy was brought up to believe that a person was responsible for his soul when he reached twelve.

Although his parents were regular churchgoers, Roy had never been overly pious and he had a twelve-year-old boy's natural skepticism when it came time for him to take his place on the mourner's bench.

In a paper he wrote years later, he described his feelings as he walked up the aisle that first night. "People were looking from both sides of the church as I walked in. They seemed to be saying, 'Is he serious? Does he know what he's doing? Is he playing with God?' " Seated on the bench with three other twelve-year-olds, he was "tense and afraid of the mysteries ahead." Would he feel Jesus that night? But nothing happened. "As I walked out of the church, I made myself look humble and sad. A voice from the crowd yelled, 'You need prayer, son, you need prayer.' I nodded silently, as if to say, 'Tell me more, I am confused.' "

The next night was much the same. The minister delivered an emotional sermon, which left his shirt drenched with sweat. "We all sat there on the bench, still and supposedly sad. This was a man concerned about us. He was fighting for us, for our souls, but we could not return anything, not even a tear. I felt ashamed." At home that night, his mother told him, "Roy, the Devil and the worldly things got a hold on you, and won't let you go."

The next night one of the mourners didn't show up, and there were just three of them left on the bench. "I wondered who would get up first, gleaming with happiness. The lights were as bright as ever. The singing was beautiful. The church was quiet for a few seconds, then the congregation started to sing, 'Don't you want good religion?' The girl jumped up, praising God to the top of her voice. She was not afraid any more, but alive and glorifying. I looked at the lamenting faces and the mourning ministers; they all seemed holy and good. At that moment, I went blank to all shyness. I was no longer conscious, but brave and cheerful. It seemed as though I had entered a whole new world. I felt light and happy all over. I shook hand after hand. I can recall going home with my sister and one of them asked how I felt. The only answer I could give was, 'Like a different person entirely.' "

However intense this experience, Roy lived most of the time on a more pragmatic plane. Summing up his nights on "the mourner's bench" years later, he chose to put it in ethical rather than spiritual terms: "I learned more than how to live a religious life, I learned a sense of responsibility. It was a chance to direct my own life and struggle with my own problems."

Part of his new responsibility was to bring in some cash. So when school let out at planting and harvest time, Roy went to work in the cotton fields. Before dawn, he would join the other "hire-out people" huddling in clumps on the street corners of darky town. White men, in rattling pickup trucks, would pick them up, haul them out to the fields, then deposit them back on the corners after dusk. It was a long, hard day for a twelve-year-old; but Roy had been chopping cotton since he was six, and he could earn five dollars a day without straining himself.

Roy made even more money selling pecans. It started with the huge pecan tree in their front yard which every year showered mounds of the delectable nuts on the grass. Roy and Melvin gathered them up in a bushel basket and sold them to "the pecan man," who in turn sold them to a factory in Memphis. Soon they went further afield, rattling trees all over town and turning a tidy profit. Once a white man almost caught them stealing pecans from his yard, but they jumped his fence and got away. After that, they didn't take any chances. For Roy had seen enough of the Holly Springs police to know they ought to stay out of their grasp.

"I'd seen them come into the cafés up on West Memphis Street on a Friday night when folks had been drinking and were getting a little warmed up, not drunk, just a little tipsy. The policemen would walk in like they were invading foreign territory. They'd grab some black man, hit him on the head, rough him up and drag him out to their car. People said one policeman had killed three Negroes in his time. I saw them as invaders, with their authority that was white, that was uncaring, that was not sensitive. Right from that time, I don't recall ever digging cops too much."

But Holly Springs wasn't Meridian, Philadelphia or Hattiesburg—the red-necked Klan towns to the south. Proud of its "genteel tradition," it had never been strong Klan territory. Dedicated to "the gracious life," it did not regard lynchings as appropriate. Blessed with a relatively large black "middle class" who had a stake in the system, it could afford to eschew the grosser forms of racial repression. White supremacy in Holly Springs played itself out in subtler ways.

Roy felt it when he ventured out of darky town onto the broad reaches of Court Square, the center of white power and prestige in Holly Springs. On a grassy plot in the middle of the square was the symbol of white political power—the Marshall County Courthouse. And facing it from all sides were the economic foundations of that power: Hale & Tucker and D. Shep Smith, "cotton offices"; the Bank of Holly Springs and the Merchants and Farmers Bank; Cohn's Department Store; the Ben Franklin 5 & 10.

"The Square" made Roy uncomfortable and he went there as little as possible. "It seemed like the salesladies up there had this routine to make you recognize their authority. You'd go in and say 'I'd like some Colgate toothpaste,' and she'd say 'What?' and you'd say 'I want some Colgate toothpaste,' and she'd say 'What kind?' and you'd say 'Colgate,' and she'd take a tube and say 'Is this what you want?' All this was aimed at getting you to say 'Yes, ma'am,' or better 'Yes, 'um.' A lot of black men would go in and hang their heads and shuffle their feet and say 'Yes 'um' this and 'Yes 'um' that. But I'd always get around it somehow. I'd say 'That's right' or 'Nope.' It was sort of a game I played. I didn't want to give them that satisfaction and it just seemed there were certain things you shouldn't do."

But such games were themselves a form of resistance in Mississippi and Roy could play them only after he realized that resistance was possible. That took a long time. As late as 1959, he sat resentfully through the required seventh-grade course in Mississippi history. They used a book with the Confederate flag on the cover and a picture of Governor Ross Barnett inside. They had to memorize the state song, the state flower and the state bird. "And right there in a Negro school, we learned how happy the slaves were and how the slave traders had done the Africans a favor by bringing them here. I didn't believe all that. But it never occurred to me there was anything we could do about it. I just sat there and nodded."

Roy first realized that Negroes might stand up for their rights as he watched, mostly on television, the unfolding of the civil rights struggle during the early 1960s.

"I used to watch the news a lot and I saw all the stuff about the Freedom Rides and Birmingham, Bull Conner and the fire hoses and the four girls who got blown up in the church. A consciousness began building in me that there were black men out there who were doing something about the way we lived and that perhaps I ought to get involved, too."

This consciousness was also spurred by events closer to home. In 1961 Bob Moses and other volunteers from the Student Nonviolent Coordinating Committee began their Mississippi voter-registration efforts at McComb near the Gulf coast. Soon they spread across the state and in the summer of 1962 began a small registration drive in Holly Springs. Operating out of Rust College, a SNCC volunteer named Frank Smith mobilized a small corps of workers and began canvassing door to door in the Negro neighborhoods. Within two months they had reached one thousand persons and persuaded a hundred and fifty of them to go down to the courthouse and take the voter-registration test.

Roy, then just fifteen, took no part in the SNCC efforts that summer, but the presence of civil rights volunteers in his hometown helped develop his sense that resistance was possible. That sense was heightened in October by the drama thirty miles south in Oxford, where James Meredith, backed by federal troops, insisted on his right to enroll at Ole Miss. The troop trucks, on their way from Memphis, rolled right down Highway 78 through Holly Springs.

So when voter-registration efforts continued the next summer, Roy was ready. One night in June he wandered down to a meeting of the Voters' League, a group founded by SNCC and supported chiefly by Negro churches and middle-class blacks. "Somebody was saying that the only way black people were ever going to improve their lives was through the ballot. But first we had to get them down to the courthouse to register. He asked for volunteers. Before I knew it I'd stuck up my hand. I really didn't understand what he was talking about, but I knew I had to get involved."

Several days a week for the rest of the summer, Roy canvassed door to door and then brought potential voters down to the courthouse. Occasionally, he drew angry gibes from whites. Once, a farmer in a pickup truck yelled, "I'm going to get you, nigger," and a man he passed in Court Square just grinned and drew his finger across his throat.

But, unlike McComb, Clarksdale and Laurel where volunteers were beaten, there was no violence. Holly Springs preferred other methods. A Negro farmer who came to register would often get a notice the next week that his cotton acreage had been reduced. Or his taxes would be raised and when he couldn't pay, the Chancery Court would sell his land out from under him. When voter-registration meetings were held, the sheriff would ride by, writing down license numbers, and soon anybody who'd been doing "public work" for the county would be fired.

No wonder so many people turned Roy away at the door. "Some people didn't understand what we wanted," he says. "But those who understood were scared. I couldn't blame them."

His mother was scared, too. "When Roy started that civil rights stuff I was worried out of my mind," she says. "Lots of nights I didn't get any sleep at all. I knew somebody had to be doing all that, but I thought he was too young." She appealed to her husband, who was worried, too. "I didn't like it," Roy Sr. recalls. "Knowing the South as I did, I was afraid of what could happen." But he had been watching television, too, and he realized the South was beginning to change. He had never voted himself, never tried to register, certainly never joined a protest march. That wasn't his style. But he understood why people would want to do these things and he certainly wasn't going to stop his son. "I didn't try to discourage him. If he had to do it, he had to do it. I just told him to be careful."

But 1962 and 1963 were just warmups for the Mississippi Summer Project of 1964, the most concentrated burst of civil rights activity ever mounted in the South. Hundreds of Northern white college students poured into the state to help with voter registration and freedom schools. Holly Springs was selected as a regional headquarters for the project in five counties, and SNCC opened an office in a small frame house just across from the Rust campus.

One of the few young Negroes in town who had served an apprenticeship in the movement, Roy was an asset to the office. He was invited to the orientation session in June for the forty volunteers assigned to Holly Springs and he was flattered when several students took him aside and quizzed him about what they might expect.

As an established canvasser, he was assigned to work on voter registration with a young white student from New York named Michael Clurman. They usually went out two hours in the morning and two hours in the afternoon, and soon they built up a reputation as one of the most effective teams in the project. "Roy was just very good at it," Mike recalls, "I remember schoolteachers were regarded as among the toughest people to register, because they were naturally conservative and they naturally feared they might lose their jobs. But Roy would just stand on the doorstep and banter with them. He was so persuasive, we got two teachers down to the courthouse—some kind of a record, I think."

When he wasn't canvassing, Roy would drop down to the SNCC "Freedom House" to play Ping-Pong and checkers or talk with the volunteers. Some Holly Springs Negroes resented the Northern whites who wore faded blue jeans and workshirts and even went barefoot. "They were trying so hard to be poor and people didn't like that. We knew there was nothing beautiful about being poor."

Some people were also bothered by the sexual activity around the house, particularly the way many of the white girls went after Negro men. But these things didn't bother Roy much. "I thought what we were doing was so important, it outweighed all that."

Roy particularly enjoyed the weekly rallies at the Asbury Methodist Church where SNCC leaders, such as

Ivanhoe Donaldson and Cleveland Sellers, spoke and where everyone joined in singing freedom songs: "We Shall Overcome," "Do What the Spirit Says Do," and "No More Sorrow, No More Bloodshed." He was invariably stirred by black and white voices raised together in those defiant anthems.

But probably his most important experience that summer was the Holly Springs freedom school. Like its counterparts across the state, the school was designed to give young Negroes new skills and new confidence in themselves. Roy was assigned to a class of ten teenage boys taught by Aviva Futorian, a twenty-six-year-old schoolteacher from a Chicago suburb.

"I'll never forget the first time I saw Roy," Aviva recalls. "It was a beautiful day and the class was meeting under a tree on the Rust College lawn. As soon as we started I noticed Roy because he had none of the shyness or reticence the other kids had. He looked very young for his age, like a little kid, but he was a smart little whizzer. While the other boys just sat there, he bristled with questions."

The class, which met three or four times a week for an hour, covered Negro history, civil rights, interracial sex and Holly Springs social structure. "Roy was surprisingly sophisticated," Aviva recalls. "He knew that Crispus Attucks, a Negro, was the first man to die in the Boston Massacre. He also knew who ran Holly Springs, who the big Uncle Toms were and why they were Uncle Toms."

But he was impatient, too. He was depressed that summer about the poor response to the voter-registration drive. "Sometimes I wonder if the things white people say about Negroes aren't right," he told Aviva one day.

Gradually they became close friends. After class they'd go for a coke at Modena's or just sit and talk at Freedom House. "I couldn't believe him," Aviva says. "He was like a plant that had miraculously thrived without water. He had this incredible thirst for knowledge. He told me stories about kids he knew who were brilliant, and about so-and-so who had memorized such-and-such a book. I was a friend, but I was also an available resource to be drained dry."

Roy impressed another freedom school teacher that summer. Mrs. Deborah Flynn, a Brooklyn widow who taught English at Washington Irving High School, came south with a delegation from the United Federation of Teachers and ended up running a creative writing workshop in Holly Springs.

"None of those kids had done any real writing before," she recalls. "There wasn't much I could teach them technically in a couple of months. So I suggested we might all write a play together. Most of the kids just laughed and shook their heads, but Roy's eyes lit up like Roman candles and he said, 'We could write a play about Medgar Evers.'"

Evers, the head of the Mississippi NAACP, had been assassinated the year before. Roy had never met him. But Evers was one of the few Mississippi Negroes prominent in the civil rights movement and he was a natural hero for a boy just starting in the movement. His death hit Roy hard. "I was shocked and dismayed," he recalls. "I saw it as another example of white folks visiting atrocities on black folks." It was still very much on his mind a year later when the freedom school began.

The other members of the writing workshop picked up Roy's idea with enthusiasm. But nobody knew how to write a play, and Debbie Flynn suggested they improvise it. She went to the Rust library, pulled out everything she could find on Evers' life, and bit by bit on the college lawn they acted out the story. Only after two weeks did Debbie sit down and compile the scenes into a script.

One day, as the class was talking about Evers' life, a girl said, "I don't think of him as really dead. I feel that from his grave is growing a huge tree which is sending seeds of freedom all over." They decided to call their play *Seeds of Freedom*.

The fifty-minute production began with Evers' murder outside his Jackson home and then recounted the two trials of his alleged assassin, Byron de la Beckwith, which both ended in hung juries.

Roy played Darrell Kenyatta Evers, Medgar's son. On the way back from the funeral he turns to his mother:

DARRELL (*bitterly*): Momma, I hate white people. I hate them all.

MRS. EVERS: Oh, Darrell, don't talk that way, son. Your father wouldn't have wanted you to talk that way.

DARRELL: I'm going to get me a white man. If it's

the last thing I do, I'm going to get me a white man!

MRS. EVERS: Darrell, your father taught us that we must love. In the movement we must love even our enemies. Hate what they do, but love them as suffering human beings.

DARRELL: But Daddy's with us no longer. He loved and they killed him.

MRS. EVERS: I know, Darrell. And we must learn to . . . Darrell, if you hate, or if you kill, you will also be killing your father again, killing everything he worked for, everything he stood for. Pray to understand, my son.

In the last scene, the narrator sums up:

Here today we have talked of two men: one alive but forever dead. The other, Medgar Evers, dead. But having died for a cause, a noble cause, he will live forever. Don't you believe me? Then come see, come watch the hundreds, the thousands who are carrying on the work, who are joining the movement.

One by one, the freedom school students troop on stage and tell why they joined the movement:

I believe it is time for the Negro to progress, to assume all the rights and the duties of free men. Attending Freedom School gives us the chance to learn to make that progress.

As Freedom School students, we are helping in Voter Registration because we feel that the fight for freedom in Mississippi must be fought not only by the adults, but by the teenager.

We go to Freedom School because we feel this is the era of changing conditions, and we want to participate meaningfully in that change.

And the play ends with the entire cast on stage singing:

"We're voting now
We're voting now

We're voting now for liberty.
Our years of slavery now are ending.
We'll walk and talk till we are free."

At the start of August, they gave the play for the first time at Rust College. Two hundred and fifty people —freedom school children, their parents, black and white volunteers, Rust College students and a few black townspeople—packed the tiny hall. The response, Roy recalls, was "fantastic"—more like a revival meeting than a play. The spectators, who had lived through the same terror and hope themselves, wept, cheered and sang along with the cast.

"I cried, too," the usually phlegmatic Roy concedes. "In fact, I'd say that was the first time I really became personally, deeply, emotionally involved in the movement. Up to then, it was sort of a job, something that had to be done and so we did it. But this was different."

They gave the play several more times that month at churches in Marshall and Benton counties. Then, at the end of the summer, they were invited to give it again at the first freedom school convention in Meridian. The Mississippi Free Theater, a semiprofessional group, was presenting *In White America* on the same program, and the kids from Holly Springs were terribly nervous. But the young volunteers packing the school auditorium gave them a standing ovation.

A few days later, Roy left to join the Mississippi Freedom Democratic Party's protest at the Democratic National Convention in Atlantic City. To dramatize its demand for disqualification of the regular all-white Mississippi delegation, the MFDP planned a vigil outside the convention hall which would be as broadly representative as the regulars were exclusive. Roy was among those chosen to represent young Negroes.

With three other Negroes and two white volunteers, he drove twenty-four straight hours through Mississippi, Alabama and South Carolina to Atlantic City. They were all a bit edgy. One of the whites was a girl and they were driving one of the cream-colored Plymouths SNCC used that summer in Mississippi. Just a few days before, the bodies of Schwerner, Chaney and Goodman had been found near Laurel, and all volunteers had been cautioned again to be extra careful.

But nothing happened. They pulled into the packed convention city relieved and exhausted, only to find that somebody had forgotten to reserve rooms for them. So they slept out on the boardwalk that night, curled up in Army blankets, lulled to sleep by the roar of the unfamiliar surf.

That didn't bother Roy, who was exhilarated just to be there. It was far and away the longest trip he'd ever taken (he'd been to St. Louis earlier that summer for a ball game, the only other time he'd been north of Memphis). He spent much of the next few days strolling along the boardwalk, munching candied apples and saltwater taffy, playing pinball machines in the shooting galleries and buying postcards to send home.

But when time came for the vigil he took his role seriously. Outside Convention Hall, about three hundred MFDP, CORE and SNCC members sat cross-legged and silent on the wooden planking for more than twenty-four hours. Nobody stayed all the way through, but Roy came close. He put in three or four stints of about four hours apiece, squatting there until his thighs and back ached so much he had to get up and run along the beach to shake out the kinks.

His effort was in vain. The credentials committee rejected the MFDP challenge, seated the regular Mississippi delegation and offered the dissidents only two new at-large seats—which were promptly spurned. Yet the setback did not depress Roy, partly because he had expected it, partly because those were still the heady, optimistic days of the movement in which every demonstration was seen as a step forward, a necessary stage in a process moving inevitably in their direction. Roy recalls: "We knew we didn't have much chance of winning then because of the power cats like Eastland had in Washington. When I thought about Eastland and all his plantations I could get pretty mad at just the thought of him being in the same party with Kennedy. But we were very patient then. We didn't expect to knock him off in one try."

Roy got into Convention Hall one afternoon on a guest ticket and was overwhelmed. "It was fantastic. I'd never seen so many people in one place in all my life before. I didn't really feel part of all that, but I didn't hate it either because I was pretty strong for Lyndon Johnson. A whole lot of black folks were that year, because against Goldwater he was pretty obviously the lesser of two evils." With the nomination of the lesser evil, Roy's Mississippi Summer was over. He drove right back to Holly Springs.

But no sooner was he back than he plunged into a new round of demonstrations—this time over discrimination at the Holly Theater. The Holly, on Court Square, was the town's only movie house. Whites sat downstairs in padded seats, Negroes upstairs in straight-backed wooden chairs. The theater even had two box offices back to back, served by the same cashier. For years Roy and his friends had lined up patiently at the right-hand window, bought their fifty-cent tickets and trooped up to the sagging balcony which the whites downstairs called "the monkey gallery." But somehow that didn't seem possible any more.

The Voters' League, some remaining SNCC workers and a few local activists like Roy first tried to organize a Negro boycott of the theater. They urged people who wanted to see a movie to drive forty-five minutes to one of the Negro theaters in Memphis, but that didn't work too well and gradually they turned to more direct action. First, an integrated group of ministers tried to buy tickets downstairs, but they were turned away and the manager put up a "Closed" sign for a couple of days. Then rumor had it he was letting whites sneak in the back door, and Mary Ethel Crockett set out to prove it. Mary played a white woman in *Seeds of Freedom* and some of her friends insisted she didn't "talk white" at all. So she called the theater and, in her best honeysuckle voice, said, "I think it's so terrible you're closed. The ladies and I are sitting here playing bridge and it's so hot we can hardly breathe. What we really feel like is a nice air-conditioned movie." The manager whispered, "That's O.K., ma'am, just come right on down and rap three times on the back door." Nobody ever said anything about Mary's voice again.

That fall, Roy and four other Negroes who had been active in Mississippi Summer decided to try again. One Saturday night they walked up to the white booth and asked for seats. "To our surprise," Roy recalls, "they let us right in. By then I think they were expecting it and they didn't want any trouble. So they just sold us tickets—for a dollar and fifty cents, which we found later was an overcharge. It was one of those Elvis Presley movies and the theater was filled because it was Saturday night. All around us were these real cracker types and we expected trouble. It was a pretty scary moment.

"But nothing happened for about half an hour until the sheriff showed up. The manager must have called him. Sheriff Ash—they called him Flick for short—was pretty much a liberal by Mississippi standards. He came down the aisle and asked us politely to move out of the center seats over to the side. By then we'd appointed a spokesman to do the talking for us and he said we weren't going to move. He and the sheriff had some words and went out to talk in the lobby. Later we learned he'd been arrested—for something like disturbing the peace. But they let the rest of us stay. And the next weekend, another group went down and there was no incident at all. It was as easy as that."

That fall, Roy also took part in a campaign of "selective buying," a gentle term for boycott, against several stores which discriminated in their hiring practice. Picket lines were thrown up around some of the stores, and Roy spent many an afternoon trudging around the Big Star Market, their main target. Whites made no effort to break up the line. Most of the time they brushed by the demonstrators without a word. But once, Roy was standing on the street and a white farmer drove his car right toward him. Someone yelled, "Watch out!" and Roy jumped back on the curb just in time.

Along with the demonstrations, there was another carry-over from the summer, too. Aviva Futorian had been so exhilarated by her months in Mississippi she decided to stay on as the SNCC project director in Benton County, just north of Holly Springs. Sometime in early October, she and another SNCC worker, Frank Cieciorka, decided to start a freedom school class for eight or nine particularly bright students they thought might be college material. Not surprisingly, Roy was one of the first they asked.

Twice a week that fall, Aviva, Frank and Roy drove out from Holly Springs in Aviva's blue Corvair to the home of Howard Evans, a Benton County farmer whose two daughters, Earnestine and Janevial, were members of the class. For two or three hours, they sat around the table in the Evans' pine-paneled kitchen discussing ancient civilizations or contemporary Negro literature. "That's where Roy's brightness really showed," Aviva recalls. "He got terribly interested in abstractions like 'What is the meaning of civilization?' and 'Why did Egypt decline?' "

And Aviva noticed something else, too—a new edge of toughness when Roy talked about the race issue. He responded enthusiastically when they read James Baldwin's *The Fire Next Time*. When they discussed that summer's riots in Harlem, most of the class said they'd been "ashamed" or "embarrassed," but Roy said "I was proud." And he took a bold stance at home, too. That November, a Negro schoolgirl wrote a letter to a local civil rights newsletter reporting how a white girl had laughed at her on the street. She just nodded back, reminding herself, I am a girl scout and am friendly, but in her letter she asked, "How can you be friendly to someone like that? All you can do is act like they do. Am I right?" Aviva asked everyone in the class to write back, and most of the letters took issue with Edith, advising her to "walk on by and don't pay them any attention" or "return good for evil." But Roy took a different tack. He wrote: "If I saw a group of whites laughing at me as I passed their way, I would say to them, 'Go to hell.' My reason for saying this is that they would be astonished to hear a Negro boy alone react to them that way. To be honest, I would be hurt, but to hide my feelings I would say this in order to make them know I am not humble and afraid, as they probably think I would be. So my inner pride would be lifted for me."

This sort of response delighted the freedom school teachers. "Roy was the very model of the proud young black man we were trying to build down there," Aviva says. But it dismayed the teachers at Roy's other school, the all-black W.T. Sims High School (formerly the Rosenwald School). High school and college teachers were almost a privileged caste in Holly Springs—the closest thing to a genuine black middle class—and the civil rights movement was at best a mixed blessing to them. Many recognized they might gain advantages from it in the long run, but in the short run it made them very nervous. At St. Mary's High School, the Negro parochial school, two students were expelled for taking part in *Seeds of Freedom*. Nothing like that happened at Sims,

but the teachers watched the few student activists closely and reported their activities to the principal.

The Negro principal was most nervous of all. Directly responsible to the county's white school superintendent and fully aware of what the town's whites expected of him, he was desperately afraid of his students'
getting involved in "the civil rights thing." Understandably, Roy was one of his major concerns. By then, Roy
had emerged as one of the school's best students: first
in his junior class of eighty, president of both his junior
and senior classes, rated "outstanding" in independence,
leadership and self-confidence. But the principal clearly
distrusted him and gave him several stern lectures about
his work with SNCC. Others flatly labeled the principal
an "Uncle Tom," but Roy says simply, "I'd say the man
was trying to survive. I can't blame him for that."

But the freedom school and Sims agreed on one thing
—Roy was a prime prospect for college. Barely 20 percent of Sims' graduates went on to any form of higher
education, but Roy's record clearly put him in that category. The only question was: Where? His two older sisters
had gone to college in Holly Springs—Elnora to Rust and
Lee Etta to Mississippi Industrial. Roy assumed he would
probably go to Rust, if only because the tuition was low
and he could save money by living at home. The teachers
at Sims agreed that would be the wisest choice, although
one suggested he might consider Tougaloo College in
Jackson.

But Aviva was thinking bolder thoughts. She felt Roy's
talents—and, more important, his initiative—would be
stifled in a Southern Negro school. A 1959 graduate of
Brandeis, she knew that the predominantly Jewish college in Waltham, Massachusetts, was looking for Southern Negroes. One day that fall, she asked Roy whether
he might be interested, and almost casually he said he
would. So Aviva fired off a letter to Phil Driscoll, Brandeis' director of admissions, in which she extolled Roy's
"incredible awareness of conditions around him," and his
"pride and self-respect, which is all the more unusual
when one considers that he comes out of a system whose
chief aim is to destroy the self-respect of its Negro citizens." Driscoll wrote back immediately, suggesting that
Roy come up for an interview.

But Roy might never have made the long, expensive

trip had he not been offered a free ride to New York. All fall, Debbie Flynn had been seeking to arrange a New York engagement for *Seeds of Freedom*. By early December she had booked several performances during Christmas vacation and raised two thousand dollars among Brooklyn CORE, the Metropolitan Synagogue and reform Democrats.

When word reached Holly Springs, the reaction was mixed. Most of the cast were delighted. But four families, under heavy pressure from white employers, refused to let their children make the trip. Finally, four replacements were found, and on Christmas morning, eighteen students clambered aboard a chartered Greyhound bus for the drive north. For thirty-two hours, as their surly white driver huddled over his wheel, they rehearsed the play, sang freedom songs and held a nonstop bull session. "The morale was fantastic," Roy recalls. "For some reason, it seemed much more significant than the trip to Atlantic City. I remember climbing off at the Port Authority Terminal and thinking, So this is the North."

During the next week they gave the play three times— at the Macedonia Baptist Church in Mount Vernon, the James Methodist Church in Brooklyn and the Community Church on Park Avenue. The audiences responded warmly. At the Macedonia Church, eleven hundred people sang along and clapped rhythmically during the freedom songs. At the Community Church, the audience (which included Pete Seeger and Norman Thomas) rose together at the end and sang "We Shall Overcome." Claude Lewis, a *Herald Tribune* critic, said he would "long remember [the play] for its wit, its pathos, its naturalness," and word of the unusual performers spread rapidly. They were interviewed widely by the press; they taped the play for WBAI and sang at the Village Gate.

Roy enjoyed his brief stint as a celebrity, but just as satisfying was the surprisingly warm relationship he developed with his hosts for the week. Helen and Louis Silverstein were among the fifteen families who answered Debbie Flynn's appeal for places to lodge the Mississippians. Louis, then a thirty-five-year-old designer in the *New York Times'* art department, and Helen, just starting a career as a film-maker, had recently suffered a personal tragedy. Their young son, hit by a car, suffered severe brain damage and had to be sent to an institution.

So when Debbie called to see if they would put up two boys, the Silversteins had an empty room and something of an emotional void, too. They promptly agreed.

When the two boys, Roy and sixteen-year-old James Stevenson, showed up on their doorstep, the Silversteins were immediately drawn to Roy. "He had lots of drive and aggressiveness," Lou recalls, "but there was something else, too, a kind of poise and natural grace that made him particularly appealing."

Roy was a bit uncomfortable at first. He had never been a guest in a white home before, and the Silversteins were very different from most whites he had known in the South. He didn't know what to say when they began questioning him about life in Mississippi. "But then I saw they were decent questions, not like so many whites ask. Lou was an artist and wasn't all new to the scene. He knew that injustices existed in the country. He realized that there were certain issues people didn't want to talk about all the time. It was a very relaxed kind of atmosphere, an atmosphere of respect."

Helen set out to show the boys New York. They saw the standard "sights": the Empire State Building, Rockefeller Center, Central Park, Radio City Music Hall, the Brooklyn Bridge, Greenwich Village. And, at Roy's request, she also took them to Harlem. "Roy said he wanted to see how Negroes lived up North." Afterward, over a fried-chicken lunch at a place on 125th Street, they discussed what they'd seen. "Roy was appalled by the closeness and the congestion of Harlem," Helen recalls. "He thought living conditions for black people were better down South. But I remember he said, 'People up here still got it better, because they have freedom.'"

One night over dinner, Helen recalls, "Roy began talking about despair, which he said was the lot of most black people in the South. He said one reason he could talk to us was that we had experienced the kind of despair very few white people had." But what struck Lou and Helen most was how little overt bitterness that despair had left in Roy. Once, after he had described the way Mississippi whites tried to intimidate blacks who joined the movement, Helen asked angrily, "Why don't you get guns and shoot back?"

"We don't believe in that," Roy replied evenly. "That's just not the way we do it in the movement."

On January 5, as prearranged by Aviva and Phil Driscoll, Roy flew to Boston and then took a bus to Waltham for his Brandeis admissions interview. His first impression of the university was of the way the buildings fitted into the rocky hillside as though they belonged there. "It was impressive, the way everything seemed to fit together—the buildings, the rocks, the terrain. It was all part of one campus. And the architecture itself was beautiful. All that glass. It was sort of like a castle. Like an ivory tower on the hill. I was quite overcome."

The forty-five-minute interview with Driscoll went smoothly. They talked about the play, about Mississippi, about his trip north. Driscoll, the first white man who had ever interviewed him, struck Roy as "a detached type, very cool." But beneath his professional calm, Driscoll was overwhelmed. A teacher of Irish literature on the side, he found Roy "gentle as a chrysanthemum, smiling as a sunflower. I remember when he left my office I rushed out and told my secretary, 'Just take a look at that guy. There's a beauty there, if we can ever unlayer it he'll be great.'" Then he went back and wrote on Roy's admissions form: "an absolutely enjoyable boy —much more sophisticated than I had expected. I was very taken with him and I'm sure that he has good ability. A delightful kid."

Back in Holly Springs the next week, Roy labored over a Brandeis application. Listing social science as his intended major, he said he was aiming at a career in college teaching. Then, with ample help from Aviva, he drafted a long essay explaining these aims.

"Since the day my father had a talk with me about my future," he wrote, "it made me think seriously about school and a career. He told me that he dropped out of school to work for a living . . . [but] I can remember him telling me at this time—study hard, do good work, attend college and be a success in life. He was always saying, 'Be independent, stand on your own.' But education has come to mean more to me than simply a road to success. Since I entered High School I have been increasingly concerned about the 'Negro problem' or, I would say, our problem.

"I feel I can best help my people by broadening my knowledge of life inside and outside the South through a good liberal arts education . . . When I finish college I plan to return to Mississippi to help change the system in the South . . . I would like to see the two races get together and iron out their differences as man to man and not as Negro to white. I would like to see them build together in harmony, with everyone having a part in the making and enforcing the laws of the state. That will give me a chance to feel secure as a man—knowing that I have done something of value for my people and for mankind."

But Roy took weeks to complete his application—so long that Phil Driscoll called Aviva to find out if he was still applying. Aviva feels Roy's delay stemmed from a "certain ambivalence" about Brandeis. "I think he was terribly impressed by what he'd seen up there and part of him really wanted to get in. But I think he was also a bit frightened of it all and never sure he wanted to risk it."

Under Aviva's prodding he finished the application. In April, Brandeis admitted him and awarded him the Reeb-Jackson Scholarship, a new grant for Negro students established in honor of James J. Reeb, a Boston Unitarian minister beaten to deaths by whites in Selma, and Jimmie Lee Jackson, a young Negro shot during a night march in Marion, Alabama.

Roy's parents were thrilled, his classmates pummeled him on the back and his teachers buzzed over their coffee. For Roy was the first Sims student ever accepted by a Northern college. Roy took all the fuss with laconic grace, but inside, he concedes, he was elated. "I felt I was on my way," he recalls. When he got another letter inviting him to take part in a summer pre-college program at Brandeis, he eagerly accepted.

Meanwhile Roy stayed active in the movement. Early that spring he became embroiled in a new conflict with his old antagonist, the principal. For years the school had bought its class rings from a company in Jackson that openly discriminated in hiring. As senior-class president, Roy asked the principal to switch to another firm. When he refused, Roy and several friends contracted separately with another company and went into open competition in the ring business, outselling the principal nearly two to one. Not surprisingly, although Roy graduated third in his class of seventy-seven, the principal recommended him to Brandeis only "fairly strongly."

This kind of activism bothered some Negro parents who feared white retaliation. That spring, a number of older people sought Roy out and warned him about the consequences of what he was doing. "They said we shouldn't rock the boat too much, that things weren't really that bad, that we should just let them be," Roy recalls. "My parents never said anything like that. They were worried all right, but I think they knew there were things they should have done and hadn't." Ultimately Roy's persistence won his parents over, and late that spring they even joined two protest marches in town. "It was great to see them in there with us," Roy says. "They were my favorite recruits."

The spring's biggest demonstration took place in mid-June, when hundreds of demonstrators poured into Jackson to protest a special session of the Mississippi legislature called to evade provisions of the Federal Voting Rights Bill. Roy and several other SNCC workers drove down from Holly Springs and took their places in the picket line outside the capitol. Within ten minutes they were arrested, piled onto a truck and taken to the State Fair Grounds on the outskirts of the city. There they were put into one of the exhibition halls, usually used for displaying preserves or livestock, which had been turned into giant stockades for the nine hundred persons arrested during the demonstrations.

One hall was for women, the other for men; and within each hall, Negroes and whites were ordered to stay on opposite sides of an imaginary line. But the halls were often so packed that rigid segregation was impossible. For two nights the prisoners slept on the concrete floor. On the third night the police guards tossed in some mattresses and blankets, but there weren't enough to go around. Each hall had only one toilet, which became stopped up within hours, and a single cold-water shower. The food was always the same: molasses, dry bread and powdered milk for breakfast; beans and rice for lunch; beans and rice for supper.

Roy stayed in the hall for fourteen days.

"After a week, it got pretty foul in there," he recalls. "With the sun beating down on the tin roof all day, people would start sweating up a storm. Since everybody was wearing the same clothes they came in and nobody could really wash much, it began to smell terrible. Then there was the constant harassment by the guards. They never beat us really. But they kept after you. When one was searching me, he kept sticking me with his pen and shouting 'Straighten up.' But the worst thing was the boredom. They didn't let you have any books or newspapers or even writing paper. So we slept most of the time, or talked or played football with two socks rolled together.

"It was a concentration camp, that's what it was. But I was willing to go through it because I was with all those people and I thought what we were doing was right. You might say I felt a sense of destiny. I felt ultimately we were stronger than the cops."

Finally, toward the end of the month, civil rights lawyers got a judge to throw out the charges (picketing without a permit). Roy's parents drove down to pick him up, but he had only three days in Holly Springs before he flew to Boston to begin his pre-college program.

The program grew out of Brandeis' concern that it was becoming a Jewish ghetto, drawing primarily middle-class Jews from Great Neck or Brookline. The administration had already decided to begin recruiting Negroes and "underprivileged" whites; but the records showed that of the fifteen Negroes then at Brandeis, fourteen were in serious academic trouble. The deans recognized that if they were going to increase minority enrollment they would have to find some means of easing the transition from mediocre high schools to the more demanding university. They persuaded the Carnegie Foundation to finance an eight-week pre-college program that summer for thirty-three high school seniors bound for Brandeis or other New England colleges in the fall.

The group that showed up in Waltham over the July 4 weekend was an ethnic jumble: ten Negroes, eight Puerto Ricans, two Italians, two Irish, two Chinese, a Japanese, a French-Canadian, a Polish Jew, among others. Bill Goldsmith, the program's director, recalls the extraordinary air of fellowship among both participants and the all-white staff: "It was a golden era, a terrific, exciting time. The civil rights movement was in full bloom and everybody still believed in integration. We believed blacks —we still called them Negroes then—and whites and browns could work and live and play together. And we did all summer."

There were echoes of Mississippi Summer, but much

of this was a new experience for Roy. He had never gone to school with whites before, and except for the few days with the Silversteins in Brooklyn, he had never lived with them. But he didn't have any trouble with the whites, who went out of their way to be helpful and considerate.

The only friction that summer came in his relationships with nonwhites: a Puerto Rican boy and a Japanese girl. The Puerto Rican, an unusually light-skinned boy from New York, was his roommate. "We didn't get along at all," Roy recalls. "He was constantly trying to put me down. And I thought he was quite naïve about what was going on in this country, particularly about how blacks and Puerto Ricans were exploited. He thought his light complexion was all he needed to make it in this society. I told him he was kidding himself. It got pretty hostile."

The Japanese girl, on the other hand, was warm and beautiful. Roy and she liked each other immediately, and one night he said, "Why don't we go to a movie or something like that?" She said, "Yeah, why don't we do that." But she called her parents in Boston and when they heard Roy was a Negro they said she couldn't go. Roy didn't see her much after that.

But Roy's most difficult adjustments were in the classroom, where he took courses in writing, math, philosophy and social science. The sheer technical demands—particularly in writing and math—were far greater than he'd anticipated. His grammar and punctuation were so bad he was offered special tutoring. Late in July he wrote Aviva that the work was "very hard," but he added, "I'm going to work as hard as I fight those white folks in Mississippi. We shall overcome!"

In a report summing up Roy's progress, written late in August, Bill Goldsmith noted his "will of iron" and "dogged determination" to improve. "His tutor has told me that he has started to do papers over at one o'clock in the morning despite his tutor's admonition that the present work was all right and that he'd best go to bed. He wants to really get it right and he is willing to go the extra mile to guarantee it. Because Roy works so terribly hard, thinks so hard, tries so hard and cares so much, one cannot help caring deeply about him."

But Goldsmith reluctantly concluded that Roy was not ready to enter Brandeis. "It is not only his academic background that is weak," he wrote. "He has seen so little, read so little, and been so few places that his frame of reference is just not big enough to cope with too many new things at once. One feels that he is beginning to become a little strained and nervous . . . He still believes that he can 'make the grade' through hard work, but he is beginning to get the unnerving understanding of the extent to which he is behind the others of his age. What he needs is a year in a quiet place where too many social and intellectual demands will not be made upon him; where he can be given essentially individual instruction so that he can get some sense of accomplishment from his work without being perpetually overcome by his growing sense of all he does not yet understand."

Phil Driscoll called an old friend, Charles Merrill, the headmaster of Boston's Commonwealth School, and Merrill promptly agreed to take Roy for a year. Then Goldsmith had to tell Roy. "It was one of the hardest things I've ever had to do. I remember we sat for hours in the front seat of my car on one of the university parking lots. Roy took it very hard. He felt the whole Brandeis thing was blowing up. But I assured him it wasn't, it was just being postponed so it could be a full success. Finally, he agreed."

The conversation left Roy shaken for weeks. "It was a matter of pride, I guess. I thought I could have made it at Brandeis and I was kind of hurt when people kept saying 'You're not quite ready.' It was never a racial thing, because I saw other blacks in the program go on to Brandeis or even Harvard. It was just a personal feeling. I felt I was falling back just when I should be going ahead."

For this and other reasons, the next year was a dismal one for Roy. He found a tiny room in the South End with an elderly Negro widow who took in boarders. Roy ate breakfast with the widow, had lunch at school, and came home to find dinner left in the oven while the widow watched television. He'd prop a book against the toaster and read while he ate, then retire to his room and work until early in the morning.

"Everything I did that year I did alone," he recalls. "I'd just go to the movies or walk around the streets a lot or sit in my room reading. I became a real loner." This was a startling change for Roy, who was naturally open and gregarious. Part of it may have stemmed from depression over his failure at Brandeis, his first prolonged absence from home, or his drab surroundings, but Roy feels it was a natural reaction to the social situation he found at Commonwealth.

A small day school, Commonwealth attracted many children of professors, doctors or engineers—intelligent, articulate youngsters who grew up in Brookline or Wellesley, attended good suburban elementary schools and regularly went to the Fine Arts Museum or the Boston Symphony. Ninety percent were white. Roy concedes that they were "quite bright technically," but he found them remote and insensitive. "Their knowledge of the outside world was almost nonexistent. And actually most of the ones I talked to were quite superficial. We never talked about anything I considered of value. As a matter of fact, we never really talked. They were a small, elitist group—protected, spoiled brats. I found most of them repulsive."

By winter, Roy was openly at odds with his surroundings. In a letter to Aviva he commented briefly on Mrs. Louise Day Hicks, the virulent critic of busing to achieve school integration. "She's only a representation of what the entire city of Boston is like," Roy wrote, "[but] deep down, I respect her. She isn't hypocritical about how she feels." On December 4 he wrote Aviva again: "As the days go by, I find Boston more and more depressing and the students at the school even more so . . . I miss working down South, but I can see just as much or more needs to be done in this heaven so many of my people have talked about as 'the good North.' "

His only strong ties in the North that year were with the Silversteins, with whom he still maintained an extraordinary rapport. He came down to their house for Thanksgiving dinner and five or six other times during the year. They gave him a key, and he would often call from Boston on Friday and say, "I'll be in tonight; don't wait up." Helen recalls: "We knew Roy was going through a tough period during which he was closing himself off from many whites, but he remained open and warm to us—and we to him."

Roy did have a casual relationship with two white students at Commonwealth—but they were decidedly unorthodox. "That's the only reason we got along," he says, "because they were sort of out of it, too. They were from different backgrounds than the rest of the kids. The girl's mother was from Hungary and the boy's old man had been active with the labor movement in the thirties. They had a different way of looking at the world. They were sort of beginning to rebel against the school and the headmaster, saying this school stinks, it's too homogeneous, it doesn't really teach relevant stuff."

Roy shared their mood but not their grievances. He noted that his reading lists for literature courses didn't include any black authors, but somehow that didn't really seem too important. "At that point, I guess, I didn't spend much time wondering how relevant a book was or how relevant the whole educational process was. Because for me, at that time, it was relevant. It was getting through that place, and getting to Brandeis and getting on."

Roy's determination to "get on" in life was manifested everywhere. That winter, the school distributed a questionnaire asking, among other things, "What do you see yourself doing fifteen years from now?" Some of the white students answered with bemused irony or cynicism: "Being a Jewish mother," "Taking care of my grandmother" or "Leading a meaningless, day-by-day existence, rescued only by my profound hope that I am not destroying my children."

But not Roy, who wrote simply: "Standing on a Mississippi platform running for Governor."

So, despite his mood, Roy kept at his studies with a fervor that often astounded his teachers. In February, Mr. Merrill wrote: "If you criticize what he has done he will sit up to midnight rewriting it. He has bought the idea of education in its most simple and direct meaning. I think he would pay any price if he knew it would mean that he'd eventually arrive."

In the same report an English teacher noted: "In class, surrounded by articulate, even flashy students, Roy pretty well disappears. But when he is writing about something related to his own experience or about something he can relate to it, he can make sense." Once, after reading *Oedipus Rex* and *King Lear*, the class was assigned a paper defining tragedy in relation to some contemporary play or movie. Roy chose *Nothing But a Man,* a film about a Negro laborer torn between frustration and outrage at racial injustice and love and loyalty to his wife. Roy's paper may have told less about the film than about his own state of mind:

"When a man faces limitations, restrictions, and bias in a closed society, he takes on a different form of character, sometimes in order to survive, other times in order to destroy. He might become angry and furious. In other instances, he might give in to the last and most retreating phase of life, a phase of idleness, lack of concern, loss of identity. When he reaches this phase, he has become a vegetable . . . Instead of fighting, he retreats from a society of bias, hate and ignorance. This wouldn't be a tragedy; it would be defeat!

"A tragic hero is one who faces the problems, but can't solve them. One who has pride, and is proud he is a man, though his environment tells him differently. He seems invisible because society fails to see him. The tension grows and grows, but to explode is useless, because the tension is caused and perpetuated by the general force of society.

"The hero in *Nothing But a Man* accepts his fate. He does not retreat, neither is he defeated psychologically. He maintains pride and identity."

Roy managed to maintain his pride at Commonwealth, but several teachers detected a seething frustration and disorientation in him. One wrote of Roy's "wire-taut nervousness" and "high-tension grid." Another summed it up this way: "In a way Roy has lost his identity and I think that this explains a good part of his trouble . . . We have plucked him from a Mississippi environment in which his future was tiny but sure and placed him in a school where he knew nobody and, by our standards, nothing. His pattern of life in Mississippi has been broken for good; his confidence in his abilities to deal with academic work has rusted, and as a result, his future is bouncing around as crazily as a roulette ball . . . It is going to take time for him to take root in New England academia."

When Roy finished the year with a mediocre record— C+'s in philosophy and history, C— in English, D in math—there were those at Commonwealth who felt he shouldn't go any further in New England academia. They suggested that he go instead to Morehouse College in Atlanta. But Merrill argued that Brandeis ought to take "an honest gamble" with Roy. "A Southern Negro college," he wrote, "would be an admission of defeat for Roy at this stage, something we should not subject him to."

On Merrill's recommendation, Brandeis decided to gamble. So, after a summer at home working as a stock boy in Memphis, Roy finally entered Brandeis in September 1966.

He was assigned to Fruchtman Hall, a two-story brick dormitory on a green quadrangle, that always reminded Roy of a motel. His roommate was a Jewish boy from Brookline named Bruce, who played a good tennis game and had a reputation as a jock. Roy had always been interested in sports, so they had something to talk about, but Roy found him "incredibly naïve" on other matters. "He'd grown up in this nice little home and they told him all people were equal and I don't think it ever occurred to him that some people might not be treated equal. He never gave any overt manifestation of racism. I just don't think he ever thought about it."

Although Bruce may have been unusually naïve, Roy found most of the other white students almost equally aloof from his world. "They never said anything insulting. In fact, they were always very kind in this cool, sort of reserved way. But there wasn't any gut feeling there. Not like between blacks."

Brandeis parties seemed to symbolize this difference. Many parties were financed out of the Student Activities Fee and anybody who'd paid his fee was welcome. Roy would often drop by, grab a drink and a sandwich and dance a little. But he never felt at home.

"It was something about the music. Generally, I can't dance to most records by white singers. Maybe I'm biased there, but I just groove to black music, rhythm and blues type or blues singers more than I can to the Rolling Stones or the Beatles. There's just a vast gap between the two. White groups have a different feeling in their songs, a different mood. At those parties, I'd stand and watch the whites dancing to that sort of 'blue-eyed soul' stuff and I'd have to laugh because their sense of timing and coordination was so off. I just never felt at ease, so I'd go back to my own room and put on some real soul stuff."

Roy felt equally ill at ease sitting with whites in the

dining rooms. "I don't recall ever being able to sit with white people and feel the same way I felt with black people," he says. Soon, he began joining other Negroes who sat together almost every meal in one corner of the room. "At that stage, we weren't consciously separating ourselves or anything, we just felt more natural that way."

Roy's growing concern with what was natural for a black man showed up in a paper he wrote that fall for a sociology course. He took off from a sentence in *The Autobiography of Malcolm X*, which he had read the year before at Commonwealth: "I could not get over marveling at how their [Harlem Negroes'] hair was straight and shiny like white men's hair." Roy wrote that processed hair had "intrigued, fascinated and irritated me for quite a few years. I had friends many years ago in grammar school that straightened their hair. Most of the boys were very young, some so young that the hair was really too short to straighten. Nevertheless, the 'in' thing was to have a long, greasy 'conk.'" Malcolm's remark, he said, had set him thinking about just what the conk meant.

Roy went down to Roxbury, Boston's largest black neighborhood, and asked dozens of young men why they processed their hair. Most said they wore it that way because "the movie stars do" or "James Brown has one" or "the girls like it." But Roy concluded that "the change of hair is a subtle way of attempting to assimilate white men's features. Some of these boys assume psychologically that they are 'accepted' if they have straight hair." He quoted Malcolm's denunciation of those who "will even violate and mutilate their God-created bodies to try to look pretty by white men's standards."

But Roy found another group, chiefly college-age young men in the ghetto, who wore a "natural," or "Afro," hairdo. "This group," he wrote, "is extremely proud of their hair, their African heritage, their blackness. . . . The 'natural' hair gives them a sense of pride and identification with their African brothers. They challenge any black American male who straightens his hair out of shame or wish to be white. There is a feeling of articulate anger that the time is over for the 'Sambo' image; it's over for self-denial of one's hair and blackness."

By spring, Roy and other Brandeis Negroes began to feel a need of some rallying point for their new sense of blackness. "To survive psychologically," Roy says, "a black living in a predominantly white society needs something to relate to, to go back to. You need a base and you find that in the black community. And let's not kid ourselves, Brandeis to a black was an alien society."

In March, several Brandeis Negroes attended a conference at Harvard of black student groups from New England campuses. When they got back, they called a meeting from which grew the Brandeis Afro-American Organization. At first the organization had little program. As Roy recalls it: "That spring, we were more concerned with getting ourselves together as a cohesive unit. We felt there were things that had to be done for black people at Brandeis that could only be done if we came together as a unified group. We also decided to make contacts with the greater black community outside, which we saw as our greatest source of strength."

Not surprisingly then, when school ended in June, Roy decided not to go back home for the summer vacation but to get a job somewhere in Boston's black community. He found a position as a recreation assistant with the Jamaica Plain Neighborhood Action Center, a branch of the poverty program operating out of a big housing project on the edge of Roxbury.

His work was simple: producing a newsletter, organizing a softball team, helping with tenants' meetings. The program's efforts to organize the project people had obvious parallels with his Brandeis experience. "I got a kick out of seeing the community people do things for themselves. These were people who didn't have formal education, didn't have the technical equipment, but they were gradually coming together to get some power over their own lives."

But Roy was depressed by the conditions he saw in the projects. When he'd first seen Harlem with Helen Silverstein two years before, he had felt the living conditions were worse than down South but the psychological climate was better. Now he wasn't so sure. "In Jamaica Plain the sheer physical poverty wasn't so bad, but the lives people led were terrible. Men without jobs, women on welfare, kids twelve and thirteen drifting the streets, drinking wine, smoking pot or taking the heavy stuff. If that was the Freedom Land we'd all been singing about, I didn't want any part of it."

And Roy's growing rejection of the North was intensified that summer by events in Newark and Detroit. Three years before, he'd been "proud" of the Harlem rioters; in 1965 he'd welcomed the Watts explosion; now in July of 1967 he was outraged by the methods police and National Guard used to put down the Newark and Detroit riots. "I watched both of those things on TV and I saw cops brutalizing, shooting, killing; the Guard moving into cities and completely occupying the black community with overwhelming force. In Newark, there was this kid who was shot thirty-nine times, his face just blown away, and they showed this cop standing there with a cigar stuffed in his mouth. And that thing in Detroit where they shot those people right in the motel. Things like that changed pretty quickly any feeling I had that life was going to be different up North. I saw there really wasn't any difference between the state trooper in Alabama and the special-forces trooper in Detroit. When it comes to dealing with black people, they're brothers."

Something else may have contributed to Roy's discomfort that summer. In late June he got word that Brandeis had placed him on "warning" for his academic record. This came as something of a surprise, because Roy felt he'd done reasonably well that year: B's in sociology, humanities and English composition; C's in politics and physical science. But he'd gotten a D+ in economics and flunked Spanish—enough to produce the warning. Ever sensitive about his academic performance, Roy brooded about his future. From then on his academic record improved steadily until he reached dean's list his junior year.

Back at Brandeis that fall, Roy and others in Afro found themselves in their first confrontation with the administration. To get their constitution approved, they were told they had to admit white students. Afro balked, pointing out that there were many all-white groups on campus—among them, Hillel House, the Jewish community organization. All fall, the dispute dragged on, with Afro meeting in its members' private rooms so they could invite whomever they wanted. When they started inviting black speakers—Stokely Carmichael, Langston Hughes, Cleveland Sellers, Louis X—they usually co-sponsored the event with the Brandeis Civil Rights Group, an integrated organization, and admitted all comers (primarily to help pay the speaker's fee). But often their guest spoke to a "blacks-only" meeting after his public appearance.

As his sophomore year wore on, Roy's life became increasingly involved with Afro and with other blacks on campus. He was living now with a black, and their room in Fruchtman was a favorite spot for "soul sessions" well into the night. Over Roy's bed was a poster of Stokely and one which read simply, "The Governor of Alabama is a Mother."

But throughout this period, Roy maintained cordial relations with whites. Bill Goldsmith saw him occasionally and they chatted with no strain. Phil Driscoll still found him "the most gentle of souls." And Roy continued to visit the Silversteins regularly. Once, they even came up to visit him, and he showed them around the campus as though they were his parents.

But Roy's dissatisfaction with Brandeis as an institution was clearly growing. He began noticing things he hadn't noticed before. Several nights that winter, returning from dates in Boston, he was stopped by the campus security guards. "Most of those guards knew me, knew all the students pretty well, but they'd stop me anyway and ask me for my ID card just because I was black. I don't think they ever stopped a white student." Or, one night in the dining hall a black student was playing his flute and a white woman came over and told him to stop. "Hell, he wasn't bothering anybody. He played real well and soft, but she said the rules said no music in the dining room. Well, the rules say no dogs in the dining room, too, but these white kids brought in their dogs all the time—strays that hadn't had their shots or been bathed in years—but nobody ever told them to get out. It was small, very tedious, very boring examples of white racism like that which began to bother me, bother all of us."

But Afro did nothing overt until that evening in April when Martin Luther King was killed in Memphis. Roy remembers vividly the moment he heard the news. "I was sitting in my room studying and listening to a Boston rock station when they interrupted to say King had been shot. I jumped up so quickly I hit my nose on the wall. I was shocked. The rest of that night was incredible. The black students just drifted together and we started meeting and we met all night. Everybody felt we had to do something."

On April 8, Afro presented fourteen "demands" to the administration, among them an Afro-American Studies concentration, intensified recruitment of black students, ten Martin Luther King Memorial Scholarships for black students, intensified employment of black people in all university positions, an advisory committee of students, faculty and administrators to implement the demands.

In the extraordinary climate of urgency which followed the assassination, President Abram L. Sachar accepted all the demands "in principle," and the advisory committee was established to work out the details. Roy, who was elected president of Afro in May, became a member of that committee.

To take part in its work and to organize Afro for the year ahead, Roy decided to stay in Boston again over the summer. He signed up once more with the Jamaica Plain Neighborhood Center, but he spent most of his time meeting with Afro members in the Boston area, helping to recruit black students and developing a special orientation program for them.

The advisory committee met three times during the summer, and two of those meetings were attended by Brandeis' new president, Morris L. Abram. When Roy first heard of Abram's appointment, it struck him as "odd" that a Georgian would become president of a Massachusetts university. And when he heard Abram's lilting Southern accent across the table, it reminded him of the voices of the white merchants on Court Square. But assured that Abram was an enlightened Southern liberal, Roy decided to take him at face value.

Before the summer was over, Roy and the new president were at odds. The issue was a debate Abram wanted to sponsor: "Can America Integrate?" between Bayard Rustin, the civil rights activist and advocate of integration, and Robert S. Brown, a black economics professor who espoused separatism. Roy and other Boston members of Afro vehemently opposed the debate, labeling it "another black cockfight for a white audience." Instead, they proposed a symposium on "White Racism and Black Survival" in which black students would also take part. Abram accepted the suggestion, but when the panel took place late in September, he and the black students became embroiled in a heated debate over Brandeis' "racism." The black students walked out. Roy wasn't there at the time, but the incident got relations between Afro and the new president off to a shaky start.

Through the fall, they deteriorated further. Afro had assumed that once the Afro-American concentration was accepted in principle it would be introduced quickly. But the step had to be approved by the faculty, which meant a lengthy process of committee actions. Not until December did the full faculty vote to approve the concentration, but even then its introduction was postponed.

Late that fall, Roy came down for a weekend visit with the Silversteins, and it was clear to them that he was contemplating bolder action. "We sat and talked late into the night," Louis recalls. "He said he was convinced that the key to history was that the guy with the biggest guns won out. We reminded him of that conversation years before when we'd ask him why he didn't use guns in Mississippi and he said, 'We don't believe in that.' Roy said he'd always believed in nonviolence in the South because it seemed the best tactic down there. But he said it was a tactic, not an end. If violence seemed the best tactic, he said he was prepared to use it. He wasn't advocating violence. He just said he was ready to use any tactic necessary to obtain his goals."

Late in December a black student lying in bed at breakfast time was shot by a white student with a pellet gun. The student was not seriously injured and the motivation for the shooting was cloudy, but it heightened the tension on campus. Finally, by early January this atmosphere was further charged by two outside racial confrontations—one over community control at the Timilty–King schools in Boston, the other the black-led strike at San Francisco State College. On January 7 two faculty members from San Francisco State spoke at Brandeis and reportedly urged action there to support "the brothers in California."

Returning from a brief Christmas vacation in Holly Springs, Roy felt the time had come for some kind of action. "I felt very stagnated. We'd been talking with the administration for all those months and we still didn't have the concentration we'd been promised the spring before. I was convinced that we'd talked long enough and the university wasn't going to move until we confronted them in some sort of power relationship. I felt we needed to try something different, something more aesthetic and more dramatic."

At 2 P.M. on January 8, Roy called a meeting of Afro in the organization's new office in Ford Hall to consider what action should be taken on the administration's "breach of promise," the Timilty–King situation and the San Francisco State strike. More than sixty members showed up. After a few minutes of discussion somebody got up and said, "Why don't we just stay here?" It was an audacious proposal, for Ford Hall was the university's communications center, housing the main switchboard and a huge research computer. Roy was apprehensive. He had favored a student strike like the one at San Francisco State, But he put the new proposal to a vote and it was overwhelmingly approved.

Once the decision was made, they moved swiftly. Within fifteen minutes they cleared all whites from the three-story building. A committee quickly drafted a new set of ten demands similar to those of the spring before, except that this time Demand No. 1 called for an Afro-American Studies Department headed by a black professor to be chosen by black students. Late that night President Abram came to the hall for a meeting. After reviewing the demands he told them he was not prepared to negotiate in an atmosphere of "violence and coercion." Roy folded his arms and said, "We have nothing further to say and will not leave until all demands are met."

The next day, Abram agreed to meet with a "discussion committee." They quickly reached agreement on most of the demands, but an impasse developed over Demand No. 1. So the sit-in went on. Sympathizers on the outside passed in mattresses, blankets, food and medicine. They renamed the hall "Malcolm X. University." Then they sat and waited.

After his initial apprehension, Roy found he rather enjoyed the situation. "It was like you had your own car for the first time and you were at the controls and you had to drive no matter how dangerous the situation was. That was what I liked. It was the first time in my whole life I'd ever really been at the controls. Up to then, I'd been a passenger in the white man's car, so to speak. Now I was driving. Sure, there was danger. We knew the police might come at any time, might bust our heads and throw us in jail. But we held the building and a lot of valuable equipment. So they had power, but we had some power, too, for once, and we figured they'd have to deal."

But as day after day went by, Afro realized it did not have enough power to make the university yield on Demand No. 1. So on January 18, eleven days after they'd gone in, sixty-four students marched silently out of the hall. A spokesman held a brief news conference, pledging to "continue the struggle in new forms." Then they walked away.

Roy ducked newsmen, and headed for his room where he slept almost twenty hours. Only the next evening did he sit down to write his reflections on the experience: "It is Sunday night. Blacks at Ford Hall have dispersed. I don't know where most of them have gone . . . It seems kind of clear now that many of us were somewhat politically naïve about the nature of the power apparatus in this country. Many of us now know without a doubt that the power apparatus is strong and sound. It will bend and co-opt. It will be extremely difficult to break . . . Many of us appear to have taken Brandeis out of the context of the American society. I think that we had naïvely assumed that over a period of time of applying pressure Brandeis would grant the ten demands. We were partly correct. She would grant more than two-thirds of them. This was within her power. Demand No. 1 means a policy change. If Brandeis would allow blacks to select a director, that would mean a redistribution of power—student power and power in black people to control the direction of their lives. Brandeis and the U.S. are very much aware of this. They will use any means necessary in order to hold on to this power. It has to be broken. The first phase has given us a clear analysis of the power apparatus. I do not know where the second phase will lead."

SUE

The catfish is a bewhiskered scavenger. Nosing along muddy river bottoms for grubs, worms or refuse, it is hardly a glamorous fish. But on a hot summer's day anywhere in the southern United States there is no pleasanter way to pass the afternoon than sprawling on a grassy river bank dangling for catfish. And nothing makes better eating than a big blue cat deep-fried in a blackened pot set under the trees in the backyard and served up with plenty of French fries and soda pop.

Nowhere in America do catfish grow plumper or tastier than in the turgid waters of the Tennessee River as it slides through sloping farmland near Savannah, Tennessee. Particularly since the TVA people built big Pickwick Dam twelve miles south of town, the fishing has been so good that every July Savannah puts on what it calls the National Catfish Derby. Beginning with a beauty pageant to select a Catfish Queen, the derby goes on all month as thousands of fishermen from miles around assemble to try for the weekly prizes awarded for the biggest fish. Then at the end of the month, at the big wind-up parade along Main Street, a grand prize is given for the biggest cat of all—often weighing over a hundred pounds.

The Catfish Derby—and the abundant supply of bream, pike, bass, sauger, crappie and perch in the river —have spawned a major fishing industry around Savannah: motels (Little Andy's, Sportsmen's Center, Callens Riverside), boat rentals, fishermen's supplies, and half a dozen "worm ranches," which give the town claim to the title Worm Capital of the World. Thousands of worms are bred each year in the long earth beds on Savannah's ranches, then shipped up and down the Mississippi River and all over the world. The ranches also sell almost every other kind of bait: minnows, shrimp, chicken liver, mussel meat and guts—but the big jumbo worms are their real pride. Savannah's pride too. The town is so proud of its squirmy product that the local radio station is called WORM.

The Tennessee and the countless creeks which wander off it also water some of the best bottom land in the state. Herman Thrasher grew up on such land, a few miles south of Savannah. As a boy, between chores for his father, he would sneak down to the river any chance he got and throw out a catfish line. The river beckoned him as it has most boys who grew up there. But the Thrashers had been farmers for generations, and so, when Herman finished seventh grade, he went to work full time hoeing cotton for his father.

And in 1927, when he was twenty, he met and married Cora Agnes Delaney, the seventeen-year-old daughter of a farmer who lived down the river a ways in a tiny cluster of houses they called New Hope Community (after the New Hope Church). Mr. Delaney always preferred lumbering and cabinet-making to farming. Cora can remember her father with a team of eight big oxen snaking huge logs out of the pine forests and down to his sawmill in Crump, on the river. So he was happy to have his new son-in-law move in with him and take over most of the farm work.

Mr. Delaney had 133 acres of cotton, corn and soybeans. But just two years after the Thrashers were married the Depression hit, and farm prices skidded. Unable to afford laborers, the two families did all the field work themselves, but managed to eke only two or three bales of cotton from the land.

When war broke out in Europe, Mr. Thrasher decided he could earn more money at construction work, using the carpenter's skills he'd learned from his father-in-law. For a few months in the summer of 1941 he worked at Milan, Tennessee, helping to build an arsenal. While he was there, Cora went to the nearest clinic, twenty miles south in Jackson, and gave birth to their fifth child, a daughter they named Sue.

Sue was the first of the Thrasher children not born at home. Cora's doctor insisted on a sterile delivery room because the baby was two months premature. It was lucky he did. For when Sue was born she weighed only three pounds, four ounces. "She was so small and delicate," Cora remembers, "they had to carry her on a pillow."

And she was born with gland trouble so severe that the doctors gave her little chance of living. She couldn't control her muscles, falling over so often she ruptured herself. The doctors tried every drug they could think of, but nothing seemed to work, and Sue saw a physician every week until she was eight years old. At first the malfunctioning glands kept her from growing—at eight she weighed only thirty pounds. But when the glands started working, they overworked. From the age of eight, she rapidly put on pounds; since she was twelve, she has been substantially overweight.

Soon after Sue's birth, Herman got a job building housing at Oak Ridge, where scientists were gathering for some special project (the Thrashers never knew just what kind of project until four years later when the Bomb exploded at Hiroshima). Sue remembers living in a trailer on a hillside among the raw construction sites of the atomic city.

When the war was over, the Thrashers moved back to Savannah. They lived briefly on a farm, but Herman decided he didn't want to farm again. So they moved into town, and for two years both parents worked at the Brown Shoe Co.

The company is the oldest factory in town. Recently it has fallen on hard times, partly because of foreign competition. (The Savannah *Courier* has been running tirades by the company warning that "hard-working, self-supporting, tax-paying U.S. shoe workers are gradually losing their jobs to European and Asiatic Nationals all because the government Foreign Trade Policy holds the door wide open to shoe imports.") But in those postwar years it was expanding and offering the best-paying jobs around.

The Thrashers lived only a block from the factory in a white frame house with a big back porch, where the family gathered on soft summer evenings for catfish fries. Sue has especially fond memories of summer evenings in Savannah when she was six or seven—memories reminiscent of James Agee's description of summer evenings in Knoxville. She recalls people sitting out on their front porches after dinner, watering their lawns, walking their dogs, or just visiting with each other. It was a comfortable sort of feeling, surrounded in the peace of the setting sun by friends, neighbors and family. Sue remembers feeling "completely safe."

Every Saturday night, after dinner, the Thrashers would walk down to the movies. In those days, the Savannah Theater showed chiefly serials—spy stories, mysteries, westerns, which went on from week to week. Almost always there was a western starring Gene Autry or Roy Rogers. After the movies the family would walk home together through the quiet, tree-lined streets, with her father usually carrying sleepy, weak-legged Sue in his arms.

But during the day, Sue saw little of her parents, who rose at dawn to get to the shoe factory. The first year in town, Sue was minded either by a family friend or by her sister, Mildred. Eleven years older than Sue, Mildred was the eldest child (one daughter died just after birth). Sue describes her as "kind, sensitive, good; the kind of person other people rely on." For a year or so, Mildred was almost a surrogate mother to Sue, cooking many of her meals, taking her places, buying her things. But in 1948, when Sue was six, Mildred married one of the Blount boys just back from the Navy. Sue remembers crying when Mildred left home. But the Blounts settled in a house a few blocks away and Mildred remained part of the family.

The family's second child, Joe Frank, was nine years older than Sue and already working at the drugstore downtown. So, when Sue started school, she was cared for chiefly by Carl, just two years her senior. This may seem a heavy responsibility for an eight-year-old boy, but it is common enough in Southern families where working parents often depend on the oldest child, no matter what age, to mind the rest of the brood. Carl usually fixed Sue's breakfast, walked her back and forth every day to the big brick schoolhouse about ten blocks away, and then kept track of her until their mother got home around four. But since Carl was an avid baseball player and the games started right after school, Sue often had to traipse along to the ball field, sitting by herself along the third-base line while the boys played. "I would much rather have gone off by myself," she recalls, "but they made me just sit there because they were responsible for me. I got very angry, but I also became a big baseball fan."

This close identification with Carl had its drawbacks. Carl was extraordinarily bright, sailing through school at the top of each class. Sue, following two grades behind with the same teachers, suffered terribly by comparison. In the first grade her marks were poor, and from then on each successive teacher always asked, "Sue, why can't you be like Carl?" The more they harped on this, the more discouraged Sue became, the more convinced that she was not very bright. Her deportment began to match her grades: she talked a lot in class; frequently she was spanked by uncomprehending teachers.

Her parents may have expressed some disappointment too. The Thrashers had both left school early (Herman after the seventh grade; Cora after the eighth), and they were determined that their children get fuller educations. So when they moved back to a farm in the winter of 1948 they made a special arrangement with the Hardin County school superintendent to keep their children in the Savannah school. "We knew what rural schools were like and we wanted something better for Sue and Carl," Cora says.

But Herman had to get out of town. A proud, independent man, he couldn't stand the shoe-factory job, which he regarded as women's work. "Herman was really a carpenter at heart," Cora says. "He'd picked that up from my father and he would have liked to do it full time. But he couldn't get enough work, so he decided to go out to a farm again, raise cotton in the summers and carpenter some in the off season."

The Thrashers moved first into a log cabin about ten miles from town while they waited for their farmhouse to be ready. They only lived there a month, but Sue loved the little cabin. "It was very cold. We had no electricity and had to heat the place with a wood-burning stove. But I guess I kind of relished the newness of it all, the roughness, the adventure. It was the first time I'd really experienced country living and I liked it."

The living was considerably easier at the farm in Morris Chapel, a tiny community named after Charlie Morris, general merchant, who once had a store there. It was a tidy little farm set halfway up a hill from which you could see all the way down into the river bottom and even the church spires of Savannah ten miles away. They had a white frame farmhouse resting on concrete blocks with a long porch along the front; a big gray barn; a henhouse; a smokehouse; a small peach and apple orchard; a pond; sixty-seven acres of land, most in pasture but some in cotton, corn and soybeans; down the hill, a small creek where the cattle were watered; and down in the river bottom, more land they rented for the bulk of their cotton.

The house had four rooms: kitchen, living room, a big bedroom and a small bedroom. Sister Mildred and her husband, Delmas, who came to live with the family then, took the big bedroom. Cora and Herman had the small bedroom, and they put a bed in one corner for Sue. Carl slept on a cot in the living room. Joe Frank left home about that time to serve in the Air Force.

The house never had plumbing. At first it had no electricity either. But Mr. Thrasher was partly responsible for persuading the electric company to string lines into the area; the Thrashers had had electricity in Savannah and they were used to it.

Even after the move, Cora kept right on working at the shoe factory as a "cushion skiver," cutting pads on the bias so they would fit in the shoe bottoms. This was common enough for farm wives in the area, whose husbands never could be sure of making a good living from their farms; and Cora had to drive into town anyway to take the kids to school. But since her factory shift started at 7 A.M., a full hour before school, all three of them had to get up at five. Sue remembers rising on those chilly mornings while a faint mist hung over the cotton patch, washing her face in a tin pan of water heated on the stove, spooning down some eggs and grits and then climbing sleepily into the car, with Carl scrunched up next to her. Along the way, Cora picked up other women who worked at the factory, so the old car was packed with bodies as it creaked down the narrow dirt road toward the river.

Sue was always nervous about that morning drive. They had to cross eight or ten creeks on their way to the main highway. In rainy periods the creeks flooded over the flimsy wooden bridges and they had to thread their

way through tortuous detours. Moreover, when they
reached the river bottom, the road carried them about a
mile and a half along a narrow earth levee with a steep
drop on either side into the muddy water. Mounds of
morning fog hung over the levee, and Cora had to squint
hard through the windshield to see the road.

But they always made it safely, and just before seven,
their mother would drop them at the schoolhouse. Nobody was there at that hour except the janitor, an old
man named Isaiah, who worked in the basement. Carl
and Sue would often go down in the basement and talk
with him until the other children began arriving at seven
forty-five.

Waiting there for the others, Sue was gripped with a
sense of her own specialness. This feeling probably origi-
nated with her illnesses and her continuing gland problems. But certainly the long ride every morning, the lonely wait at the schoolhouse, and the consciousness of being "farm" children confirmed Sue's view that she was a
little different from the other children at school. And she
was different too from the children back at Morris Chapel, who went to the country school. In neither place did
the other children make much out of this specialness.
But Sue felt it intensely.

There was another special routine in the afternoons
too. For while school ended at three, their mother didn't
get off work until four. So again, as the other children
trooped home Sue and Carl had to stay around the
schoolyard until Cora pulled up in her car, honked the
horn and drove them another half-hour home.

By the time she was ten, Sue was strong enough to bear
her share of the chores. In the evenings, after they got
back from school, she was expected to help her mother
in the kitchen. And one morning the next summer, as her
mother started in to the factory she said casually, "Today you fix dinner." Sue decided to make fudge, only it
didn't get hard in time, so when Herman and Delmas and
Carl sat down at the table they were confronted with a
pot of cold chocolate syrup. Her mother gave Sue a quick
course in meat and potatoes, and she cooked regularly
from then on.

Eventually she did much of the family shopping too.
There was a little country store at the crest of the hill
which sold beans and flour out of big wooden barrels. It

was run by two crippled brothers, the Barnes brothers, both of them grotesquely deformed. They couldn't walk, so they put rubber tires around their legs to crawl across the store to get things off the shelves. For longer distances they would get up on little wheeled carts. The brothers revolted and terrified Sue and for a long time she wouldn't go there. But eventually she overcame the fear and even became friendly with them.

During the picking season, Sue often stayed home from school to work in the fields. The Thrashers almost never hired labor; a Negro cost three dollars a day and that was a bit much for the family in those days. Usually Herman worked the farm nearly alone, with help in summer and after school from Carl and, occasionally, from Delmas, who spent most of his time clerking at the drugstore and getting started in the insurance business. Sue worked some in the fields during summer vacation. And during the fall picking season, Herman often had to keep both Carl and Sue out of school to help.

Sue hated it. Certainly it must have been excruciating labor for a ten-year-old girl whose muscles were still not fully formed. Bending over from the waist, both hands down in the sharp branches, yanking the bolls free and stuffing them into the heavy canvas sack she dragged behind her on a strap, she found it "dehumanizing." Weighing time was particularly shameful for Sue because her bag was always the lightest. An average picker should be able to do at least a hundred pounds a day, but Sue never got over eighty. Sometimes her father punished her because he thought she was lazy. Once, she sat down on her bag and started singing to herself. Her father came over and spanked her right there between the rows.

Herman didn't pay Carl and Sue for farm work, but he usually gave them the last picking. That is, they got whatever money was realized on the cotton they picked the last time around in the fall. For Sue it was usually about seven dollars and she used it to buy Christmas presents for the family.

Hoeing was different. Sue liked that, partly because you didn't have to lean over so much and could chop away at the weeds with a long-handled hoe, but mostly because it was a cooperative effort. Various cousins would come over and stay for a week or so to help out and there was much visiting back and forth with aunts and uncles.

Both Cora and Herman came from big families and when they all got together they made a massive clan. Besides exchanging visits at cotton-hoeing time or other occasions, the whole clan would gather every Christmas at one of their houses. When Sue was young, there were always upwards of sixty people at these festivities. There were too many people to give presents to, so everybody's name was put in a box. Each person drew out one name and gave that person something. And, of course, there was a big turkey dinner, which all the women cooked, and which went on all day, with people wandering around the house nibbling on turkey bones or cracking nuts under their Sunday shoes.

Sue loved this kind of warm family affair. She also liked the neighborly feeling in Morris Chapel. Although the farm was far out in the country, with only two other houses in sight, there was a lot of visiting and mutual help.

Sue recalls the first night she spent in that house. It was a stormy evening, with thunder and lightning crashing outside, made even spookier because, a few days before, the bank in nearby Enville had been robbed and state troopers with dogs were still hunting the robbers. All the Thrasher men were down at the log cabin moving the furniture, and Sue, sitting alone in the still-bare living room and listening to the baying of hounds in the distance, was frightened. All of a sudden, a bright flash of lightning lit up the porch, and Sue saw a tall figure standing there. She shrieked. But the man walked in, stuck out his hand and introduced himself as Bob Taylor, who owned the farm down the road.

For the next few years, Bob walked into the Thrasher home like that at least once a day, and they walked into his house the same way. Sue adored Bob and his wife, Nora. They were older people whose children had moved away and they returned the affection. Almost every evening, Sue would go over and talk for at least a few minutes with the Taylors. If Herman needed help on the farm, Bob—and other farmers—would lend a hand, usually bringing their equipment with them. And Herman returned the favor when they needed it. "It was my first real experience with what a community could be like," Sue says, "and it stayed with me."

The main focus of community life was the church, and for the Thrashers this meant the Bethlehem Methodist Church. It's a pretty little country chapel set in a grassy glade with a spring of bubbly water right behind it. Built in 1872 and reconstructed in 1947, it is a solid structure of white cinder blocks topped by a black peaked roof. Inside, there are twenty wooden pews, ten on each side of a broad aisle which leads up to a wood-paneled altar and the choir loft behind the altar. In each pew there is a bamboo fan supplied by Schakelford's Funeral Home in Savannah ("For the Finest in Funeral and Ambulance Service"), adorned with a picture of worshipers strolling to church and above it the admonition: "The Church is the greatest influence in a community. Therefore it needs your support. The Church needs you and you need the Church."

Herman and Cora both came from devout Methodist families. Herman said grace before each meal; for years Sue never understood what he was saying, but she never dared ask. Only when she reached high school could she decipher "Bless this food for the nourishment of our bodies." Herman never worked on Sunday. He broke the rule only once, insisting that the corn would spoil unless he got it in before the approaching rain. Cora didn't want him to do it, convinced that something terrible would happen to them. Herman had grave misgivings too, trembling between damnation and deficit, but ultimately he decided to save the corn at the risk of his soul.

Curiously enough, for people who took their religion so seriously, the elder Thrashers were not regular church-goers. Perhaps they lived their religion every day. Perhaps Sunday was a genuine day of rest for people who worked terribly hard. Perhaps it was because country ministers preached only once every three or four Sundays at each church on their circuit.

But they insisted that the children go every Sunday and the children needed no encouragement. Church was the best place for them to make new friends and see old ones, particularly for Carl and Sue who went to school in town. Moreover, Mildred and Delmas became sponsors of the Methodist Youth Fellowship. So twice each Sunday, once in the morning and once in the evening, Delmas drove his pickup truck the two or three miles over to the church. Mildred, Carl and Sue piled aboard and as the four rode along they sang the old gospels, such as "I'll Fly Away" and "When the Roll is Called Up Yonder."

At church they didn't sing gospel songs. Gospel was considered a bit too emotional, a little too close to the fundamentalist atmosphere of revival meetings, or to Negro music. The Methodists didn't want that much emotion creeping into the service; it wasn't dignified, and at all costs the Methodists craved dignity. The Methodist Church had just issued the Cokesbury Worship Hymnal, a collection of standard hymns sung throughout the country, and Bethlehem had promptly ordered a stack of the new books. So on Sunday morning the farmers in their wrinkled suits and the women in their starched dresses sat primly in the wooden pews singing staid hymns: "Holy, Holy, Holy," "The Old Rugged Cross" and "Come, Thou Almighty King."

But Sue was curious about revivals. When she was eleven, one of the nearby fundamentalist churches staged a tent meeting and she went with her sister. Sitting way in the back, Sue heard a stem-winding country preacher give one of his most fiery sermons, ending with the exhortation: "Come up and be saved, repent of your sins, for otherwise you may die and live in hell." Then, while the preacher prayed, everybody starting singing with his eyes closed, swaying back and forth and moaning, "O why not tonight? If thou wilt be saved, why not tonight?" This wasn't like the singing in church. There was a terrible intensity about the song, as though people's lives really depended on it. Sue was both fascinated and terrified, particularly when the preacher told the story about the man who almost got saved but decided not to and on the way home his car overturned and he was doomed. "I was really clutched," Sue recalls. "All the way home in the car I was afraid we would have an accident and I'd burn in hell forever." After that, she always found fundamentalist religion alien.

Sue loved to sing and longed to play the piano. But she never took piano lessons, as some of her classmates did from a teacher at school. They cost ten dollars a month and that was too much for the Thrashers. Sue never even asked her parents for lessons. She just understood that they didn't have the money.

The Thrashers were never exactly poor. Sue can't recall ever going hungry. They always came up with the one dollar a week for hot lunch at school—perhaps not on Monday when they were supposed to pay, but sometime before the week was over. They always had a car, although always an old model. Sue had enough clothes, though not as many as most girls at school.

Yet, their move to the farm meant insecurity. When both her parents were working at the shoe factory, there was the reassuring feeling that two paychecks would be there every Friday. But the farm income was sporadic and uncertain. One didn't expect income during the winter; much of what they earned had to go back into seeds, equipment and fertilizer, and so much depended on the weather. "All those years on the farm," Sue recalls, "I was very conscious that money was not something you had all the time. I don't remember wanting a lot of things I couldn't have. But I guess I matched my desires to what I knew our resources were."

The Thrashers were far better off than many farmers in the area. They owned their land, which alone set them a slot above the sharecroppers, black and white. And, of course, just being white meant a lot in West Tennessee.

There are at least three Tennessees: the East—from the Great Smokies to the Cumberland foothills—hilly, underdeveloped, Goldwater-Republican in politics; the Middle—from the Cumberland foothills to the Tennessee River—a growingly urban area, looking east and north, somewhat "liberal" on race and politics; and the West —from the Tennessee River to the Mississippi River—still largely rural, decidedly Southern-looking, "conservative" on politics and, particularly, on race. They say that Mississippi really begins in the lobby of the Peabody Hotel in Memphis, and if Mississippi is a state of mind, then certainly its boundaries include most of West Tennessee. Savannah is very much part of this region—only fifteen miles north of the Mississippi state line and a hundred miles east of Memphis. For most of Sue's young life, Savannah and its surrounding countryside were still firmly in the grip of classic Southern racism.

In Savannah itself, there are two black neighborhoods: one known by everyone as Nigger Town and the other called New Town. Sue rarely ventured into either section, although she occasionally drove through Nigger Town to get to her uncle's house. She recalls no reaction to it then "except just that it was Nigger Town." The only Negro she knew at all in those early years was a woman who sometimes took care of her while Cora was at the factory. The only other place she ever talked with Negroes was down on the banks of the river where the family often went to fish for catfish. There would always be Negroes sitting nearby with poles dangling in the same muddy water. They'd get to talking, and Sue recalls that her parents knew many of them by their first names and would chat in a friendly but "Southern paternalistic" fashion.

Yet Sue feels her parents' attitude toward Negroes was very different from that of most whites in West Tennessee or Mississippi. "They were paternalistic, yes, but their paternalism was really a kind of basic human decency toward other people. They approached Negroes as human beings who were less fortunate than they were but nevertheless human beings. That is a very different kind of paternalism than that of the plantation owner who sees Negroes just as people who work for him, his 'boys' or something like that. My father never worked with black people in that kind of relationship and he never had that attitude. Neither did Mother."

Cora today puts it in much the same way. "Herman and I always felt Negroes were human beings the same as we were. And we taught our children to treat them like other people. I remember, once, Herman was working on an out-of-town construction job where there were a lot of Negroes and he overheard some white men talking about how 'the only way to keep a nigger working for you is to pay them just enough so they can get a few groceries. Pay them too much and they just won't work. But let them owe you money and they'll stick around.' Herman was so mad when he heard that, he just went back and stayed in his room. He and I both felt that a Negro should have the same pay, the same privileges, as any white man. Integration didn't bother us a bit."

But in Morris Chapel, Sue had even less to do with Negroes than she did in Savannah. There was a Negro settlement nearby called Satillo. The one time her father hired Negroes to pick cotton he got them from there, but Sue never went to Satillo herself. She knew that the kids who lived there had to take a bus all the way into Savannah to go to the Negro high school because no rural high school would take them. She remembers feeling that was a long trip for going to school, but she didn't carry the thought any further.

And Roy Campanella, the Brooklyn Dodgers' Negro catcher, was one of her first heroes. He really was reflecting the greater glory of brother Carl—Sue's true hero from the start. Carl was a fine natural athlete—co-captain of the high school football team and a hard-hitting outfielder in baseball—and Sue used to go down with the rest of the family almost every week to watch him play one sport or another. Carl was also an avid sports fan. So Sue read all his sports magazines and books too. When Carl announced one day that he was a Dodger fan, she became a Dodger fan. When Carl picked Campanella as his favorite player, so did Sue. They knew he was a Negro, but it didn't make any difference. She remembers something about his being "a credit to his race."

The Thrashers were still very much Southerners, steeped in the traditions of the Confederacy. Morris Chapel is only ten miles from Shiloh, site of one of the Civil War's greatest battles. Herman worked off and on for years helping to construct parts of the elaborate National Military Park there, and Sue visited the park frequently, as often as two Sundays a month during her early summers.

She was fascinated by the cannon which raked the Confederate forces of General Albert Johnston in the peach orchard that April afternoon in 1862; she often stood musing over the Bloody Pond, a sheet of dark water where the wounded of both armies crawled to drink and bathe their wounds; and she stood before the monument constructed by the United Daughters of the Confederacy to honor the Confederate dead: a huge slab of stone topped by three maidens with heads bowed, and engraved: "Let us covenant each with the other and each with those whose sacrifices hallow this field to stand for patriotism, principle and conviction as did they even unto death. As a greeting to the living remnant of that host of gray and in honor of its dead whether sleeping in distant places or graveless here in traceless dust, this monument has been lifted up by the hands of a loving and grateful people."

In 1954 the Thrashers moved again—back across the Tennessee River to another, smaller farm. Herman had found the Morris Chapel farm a strain to run alone and wanted one he could manage easily.

The new farmhouse was a rambling, old building with wide porches front and back. By this time, Delmas and Mildred had moved into their own home and with the family now numbering only four, it was drawn still closer together. "We started doing more as a family," Sue recalls. "We ate together every evening. My father seemed to be around home more and we had these little family projects—one was canning vegetables from our garden. We worked incredibly hard and must have canned close to five hundred quarts of tomatoes, beans, cucumbers— all sorts of stuff."

Then, in August, the house burned down. Nobody was home. Cora had driven Carl in to football practice; Herman was in the fields; Sue was at her sister's home freezing corn. Somebody called to tell them, and Sue remembers watching helplessly as the old house shriveled among the flames. What hurt her most was the sharp popping of cans and bottles as all those vegetables exploded.

But the fire also reinforced Sue's sense of community. All the family's friends and neighbors, and many people they didn't even know, rallied around. WORM broadcast appeals for help. The workers down at the shoe factory collected money to buy a new stove and refrigerator. The family's old neighbors at the New Hope community brought furniture and clothing. Others gave money or just their labor. Someone lent them a house to live in. And with the insurance money and what had been contributed, Herman built a new house.

So this, rather than any sense of disaster, was what Sue carried away from the incident. "It was a decent kind of human response to people in need. Of course, I was a little ashamed that we needed to depend on everybody that way. But I think that early experience of just how supportive a true community could be was important to me. I've never agreed with those people who feel you can go out deliberately and set up a community. But from the fire on, I knew how important it is to have people around you who support you both physically and emotionally."

That fall, Sue entered high school. By this time, she had begun to do well academically, largely because she had shucked off the specter of Carl. That began in the sixth grade, when she had a sensitive teacher who never mentioned Carl and encouraged her to believe in her own ability. Seeing the effects, Cora went down the next fall and warned the seventh-grade teacher not to mention Carl either. Sue, who had always read eagerly, began turning from sports magazines to schoolbooks. In the seventh and eighth grades, she ranked near the top of her class. By the time she entered Central High School she had confidence in herself as a student.

Social confidence came harder. Now substantially overweight, Sue found seventh and eighth grades an "awkward period." She wasn't asked for many dates. But this was not uncommon at a high school where girls far outnumbered the boys (who often stayed home to work on the farm); Mildred recalls that she hardly dated either when she was at the school. Yet, Sue had a particularly difficult time.

Gradually, though, she found her place with a clique of seven girls who stayed together throughout high school. "That was the way the social system worked there," she says. "You were able to survive by gathering your girl friends around you. You would meet them between classes, eat lunch together, go places after school. If you didn't have that, you were left out." There were many such cliques among the seven hundred students at the school. Sue estimates that on the popularity scale hers ranked about in the middle. "We were into a lot of things, but certainly not the most popular."

Sue's closest friend in the group was Edna Ivey, the sister of a boy who played football with Carl. Ivey, as Sue called her, came from a farm way up in the hills. The rest of the clique came from Savannah, largely from comfortable if not wealthy homes. It was a congenial little group with which Sue could sip lemon cokes at the drugstore, go to the movies or just share girlish gossip, and it provided her with a social buffer against less congenial forces.

But, unlike the others in the clique, Sue never restricted her social life to it. Once she had that basic security, she wanted to look outside. "I always refused to be limited by that little group and kept venturing outside to find others—maybe not close friends, but interesting people. I insisted on my right to float. I needed that freedom, which the other girls didn't seem to need."

This streak of independence showed up increasingly as Sue got older. In her early teens, she began to rankle at the provincialism of farm life. Though there were things she liked about the farms—"the sense of space, the freedom to run anywhere"—she hated the hard scrabbling in the cotton patch. And she associated the town not only with shops and money but with books, sophisticated people, and the wider world for which she began to yearn.

So she was delighted when, in the spring of 1957, Herman decided to give up farming and go into carpentry full time. They sold the farm and moved into the heart of Savannah. Herman got a job with a bridge-construction firm which kept him traveling much of the time in the eastern part of the state; often he was home only weekends.

But the move into town merely stimulated Sue's craving for independence and brought her into increasing conflict with her mother. Sue remembers Cora as the family disciplinarian during high school. This was partly because Herman was away so often. But there was more to it than that: by this time, Sue was much closer to her father than her mother. They didn't talk much, but there was an instinctive understanding between father and daughter. He was generally lenient with her as indulgent fathers are with their little girls.

Correspondingly, Sue felt Cora was much closer to Carl. Sue always respected her mother—particularly her resilience and independence, which to some extent Sue imitated. But she resented her mother's demands on her, both for work at home and in her behavior outside. "Very few of my friends did as much cooking and housework as Mother expected of me. And almost all my friends had far more freedom to run around and stay out late."

Cora doesn't feel she was overly hard on Sue. "I wasn't strict, but we didn't just turn her loose. We had rules and regulations and expected all our children to respect them. I'd have to say Sue was the most rebellious of the children. She seemed to resent the rules more than the others. She always wanted her way."

Most of the fights between mother and daughter focused on where Sue could go at night and how late she could stay. Cora didn't approve of the Truck Stop, a café on the highway which became the high school hangout. The truckers pulled up in front, but around back the teenagers would toot their horns for service and then sit in their cars for hours shouting back and forth. Cora said this wasn't the place for a nice girl to spend her time, but Sue insisted on her right to go where she wanted. Cora also set 10:30 P.M. as check-in time at home; Sue thought this was ridiculous and sometimes came home much later.

If Sue was something of a rebel at home, she was a model student at Central High. Her first two years there were still somewhat shadowed by Carl, who was president of his class for four straight years and star halfback on the football team. Sue always insisted she was proud of him, but when he graduated in 1957 and went off to study engineering at Tennessee Tech, she was relieved. "I had two years then without the pressure of being 'Carl's sister.' Already, I'd been deliberately trying to develop a separate personality, and when he left I really began to strike out on my own."

The main testing ground for this new personality was the student newspaper. In her senior year, Sue became editor and did most of the writing, editing, layout and proofing alone. It was a modest monthly covering sports, clubs and school activities. The editor was not allowed to editorialize on either school or public issues and Sue never tried to. But she did such a good job with the rest of the paper that the editor of the Savannah *Courier* offered her a job.

Although her grades remained consistently good, Sue never found anything faintly approaching intellectual excitement in her high school classes. She recalls the school as being "incredibly bad." All incoming freshmen got an aptitude test which determined their course of study: the highest-ranking students were assigned to Latin and languages; the middle group to civics, and the lowest to the sciences (this was before Sputnik). Thus, Sue had plenty of Latin, English and French along with some algebra, home economics, drama, journalism, typing and shorthand. But she had no science course and only one year of American history. She didn't know what sociology meant until she got to college.

Not surprisingly, Sue had little interest then in social issues or politics. Her father was an essentially unpolitical man. He voted for Eisenhower, but supported Democrats in Tennessee. Sue can remember echoing her father's support for Eisenhower. She also recalls becoming quite concerned about "the Communist threat," although she can't remember why. But on the prime social issue of the time in the South—school desegregation—she had no strong feelings either way. "I didn't think the schools should be desegregated, but I didn't think they shouldn't be either. I really didn't think about it."

The issue simply didn't impinge on her life. Though the Supreme Court outlawed school segregation when Sue was in the seventh grade, no effort was made to integrate Savannah's schools until after she had graduated from high school and left town. The battles over desegregation elsewhere in the state and throughout the South were discussed all around her, but the issue seemed remote to Sue. Unlike most whites in the area, though, her parents seemed quite willing to accept the Court's decision. One night in the summer of 1954, Sue sat in the living room and listened while her father and a neighbor heatedly argued over it: "My father said Negroes should be allowed to go to school with whites. The neighbor came back with the old line about intermarriage. And my father said, 'If you educate a Negro he won't want to marry a white person.'"

Sue now traces her later commitment on the race issue to her parents' stance: "I got many of my basic values from them. They were both decent, kind people. I never saw them hurt anyone. I'm sure I wouldn't be what I am today if they hadn't instilled those values in me."

But her parents' simple humanism was rather low-key, and in those days Sue was hardly conscious of it. Her first awareness of values, of a set of standards against which she could judge the world, came from the church.

From her days at Bethlehem Methodist Church, Sue became increasingly active in church life. She succeeded her brother as president of a Methodist youth group and later taught Bible School. When the family moved to Savannah, she started going to East End Methodist

Church, where shortly afterward a young minister named Luke Dunn arrived.

Not long out of seminary and more attuned to the times than the older country preachers she was used to, Mr. Dunn gave Sue her first glimmer of a social conscience. After meetings of the Youth Fellowship, she and the young minister would often sit in his office and talk about the church's teachings. Once she recalls asking him whether he would let a Negro attend East End. This was not yet a live issue in Savannah. No Negro had ever sought to attend, and if one had, the congregation clearly would have objected. But Mr. Dunn said quietly that any Negro could come to services if he wished. Sue remembers being pleased with his answer.

For, while she did not yet have any direct commitment on the race issue, she was beginning to approach it indirectly through a commitment to religious values. "One big difference between the fundamentalists and the Methodists is that Methodists have creeds and doctrines —like the fatherhood of God and the brotherhood of man. I took those doctrines seriously. After all, I said them every Sunday. I took them literally too. I thought you were supposed to. I was very upset when I found out that other people didn't; that, for example, they didn't apply to black people, not even to all white people. Politics and civil rights still didn't mean much to me as such. But religion did. I was working out my own values within the religious realm, and gradually they provided the foundation for action in every other realm."

So, when Sue finished high school, she decided to go to a church college. Although most Central High School students didn't go on to college, Sue had long since determined she would. "From way back I'd thought I was a little bit better than other kids—in the sense of being better educated, more aware of other possibilities. I felt very strongly the limits of the world around me. I was constantly straining against boundaries that tied me in. I didn't know just what I wanted to do professionally. But I knew there were other people, other places, and I wanted freedom to get out and see them."

At first, though, she didn't get very far—only fifty miles northwest to her birthplace in Jackson where Sue received a scholarship at Lambuth College, a small Methodist school.

When she arrived there in the fall of 1959, Lambuth was a dreary place with an underdeveloped campus and an even less developed curriculum. But Sue was lucky enough to find two extraordinary young professors of religion who recognized her ability and encouraged her. They suggested she transfer to Scarritt College, a far more rigorous Methodist institution in Nashville.

But this implied plunging deeper into church work. Run directly by the General Conference of the Methodist Church, Scarritt was designed to prepare students for "careers in Christian service." This put Sue off. "I didn't want to be a full-time church worker because, in my mind, that meant you didn't dance, you didn't do all sorts of things I liked to do." Sue was just beginning to develop a social life at Lambuth. She didn't join a sorority, but she had started going to dances and out on a few dates, and she didn't want to cloister herself.

One weekend, Sue did go over to Scarritt for a mock United Nations session put on by the Tennessee Methodist Youth Fellowship. Sue played a delegate from India. But, more important, this was the first time she had ever participated with Negro students on anything like an equal level.

The Methodist Youth Fellowship had Negro members and, in fact, that year had a Negro president, a bright young man from Lane College, the Negro Methodist college just across town from all-white Lambuth. Sue recalls becoming rather friendly that weekend with one Negro boy from Lane because he too was playing a delegate from a "neutral country." She ate several meals with Negroes and even danced with a Negro at the Wesley Foundation on Saturday evening, feeling she was doing a "very brave thing."

The next year, though, she was not so brave. For a while Lane and Lambuth held joint Intercollegiate Fellowship meetings—one week at Lane, the next week at Lambuth. But when Lane students began sitting in at lunch counters in Jackson, Lambuth's board of trustees ordered the meetings halted. "A few of us felt badly about that," Sue recalls. "We talked about it, but we didn't have any sense of how to fight it. There was no inkling that you could confront the administration over it."

One day, Sue was walking through downtown Jackson and saw a boy from Lane, whom she knew slightly, sit-

ting in at a lunch counter. "I knew the counter discriminated and I was bothered by it, but I never knew what
to do about it. I really didn't have enough guts to picket
at that stage. I felt that if I joined any demonstrations I
would be immediately alienated from my family, from
everyone else at home, and probably kicked out of
school."

So she did nothing, just slogged through three semes-
ters at Lambuth, and probably would have gone all the
way through had her mother not crashed into the side of
a bridge that winter and been severely injured. Near death
for three days, Cora then went through an agonizing
series of operations. The doctors weren't sure she would
ever walk again; clearly, she would need constant care
for a long time. Although Sue dreaded the idea of going
home to Savannah, she finally asked her father if he
wanted her back. Herman said that this certainly would
be the best solution, but that he didn't want to pressure
her and she would have to make up her own mind. Reluctant to leave college but appreciating her father's understanding, Sue went home at midyear.

Partly because of the accident, partly because Herman
was getting tired of traveling, the Thrashers then moved
again, to become managers of a Savannah nursing home.
For the first six months, Cora was a patient in her own
establishment and Sue did much of the managing. For a
girl who had often rankled under her mother's demands,
the job must at times have seemed like a new hobble on
her independent spirit. She hated much of it—particularly the nursing ("I don't like blood"). She often found
the atmosphere oppressive. "They kept putting a pin in
mother's knee and then taking it out again. Mother almost had a nervous breakdown. The pressure on all of
us was fantastic." But somehow the experience drew the
family closer together. "Despite everything, the three of
us got along very well. We found we really had built
something inside that family."

By fall, with her mother on the way to recovery, Sue
again got restless. So, overcoming her misgivings about
its churchly flavor, she went off to Scarritt that September.

Sue was still so terrified of the college's stern reputation that instead of taking the bus to Nashville, she prevailed on Carl to drive her.

Her first glimpse of the college could hardly have been reassuring. It is a center of religious activity. The streets leading off the campus are honeycombed with small wooden frame buildings marked "Tennessee Association of Christian Churches" and "Bahai Faith—Nashville Center." Just across from the main college buildings is the headquarters of *The Upper Room*, a devotional guide published by the Board of Evangelism of the Methodist Church. *The Upper Room* now brings three million people around the world a daily Bible reading, prayer and "devotional thought." Its headquarters boasts a museum containing a Russian icon dated 1350, a Dresden porcelain figurine copied from Raphael's Sistine Madonna and sermons written in shorthand by Phillip Doddridge, an English clergyman (1702-1751).

Scarritt's official name is Scarritt College for Christian Workers. Founded in 1892 by the Women's Missionary Society of the Methodist Episcopal Church, South, it was first known as Scarritt Bible and Training School and was designed to prepare women to become foreign missionaries. In 1902 the program was enlarged to include training of deaconesses and home missionaries, and since then has been further broadened so that its aim is now "the preparation of enthusiastic, creative, capable, devoted and informed Christian lay leadership for the Church and society." The college, which begins with the junior year, has a heavy complement of graduate students studying for specific careers in "Christian service."

Its campus is officially designed as "a laboratory for Christian living." Uniformly neo-Gothic, the brown stone buildings with leaded windows and arched doorways are carefully set on the grassy rectangles to form quiet courtyards and shaded walkways. Over the main archway is the inscription "Attempt Great Things for God."

When Sue walked through that archway on her first day, she felt she was entering a "monastery." But in many respects Scarritt was far from monastic. The girl who took her to her dormitory gave her a key. That evening, Sue wanted to go out for coffee and asked one of the other girls when she had to be back in. "You have your key," the girl replied. "You can come and go as you like." Sue was incredulous. Coming from Lambuth, where one had to be in the dormitory by ten-thirty, Scarritt seemed incredibly free.

Moreover, Sue soon found that the students were by no means as square as she'd feared. They were brighter, older, more sophisticated than those at Lambuth. And while many of them took their religion very seriously, there was a lot of partying and outright gaiety. Partly this was because the school was simply more cosmopolitan than Lambuth. Scarritt was in the heart of an educational complex which included Vanderbilt, Fisk, a branch of the University of Tennessee and the George Peabody College for Teachers. Around it were the wider resources of Nashville, Tennessee's capital and second largest city. At Scarritt, one fifth of the student body was from abroad—reflecting the college's missionary tradition.

And Scarritt was a "liberal" institution, in the tradition of American Protestant liberalism. A few of its faculty had been mildly implicated in the McCarthy era. The college itself proclaims that its "interracial and international situation makes possible a unique atmosphere of world-wide concern in which future Christian workers can stretch their minds and enlarge their horizon." Scarritt had been integrated since World War II. The year Sue came, there were five to ten American Negroes and several Africans there. In fact, when Sue entered her room, her brother whispered, "I think your roommate is a Negro." She turned out to be a very dark-skinned Mexican girl named Emma Ibarra, who was sometimes mistaken for a Negro. But there were three Negroes in Sue's class, and Sue and Emma quickly became friendly with them.

That Christmas, Sue took Emma home to Savannah, where she was warmly received by the Thrashers. But one day, while Cora, Sue and Emma were shopping downtown, a clerk openly snubbed Emma. Cora was furious. "They shouldn't treat her that way," she said as they marched out of the store. Another time, while Emma and Sue sat in a drugstore booth, the manager and his staff caucused at the other end of the store deciding whether Emma should be asked to leave.

These incidents had a cumulative effect on Sue, making her suddenly more conscious of what a Negro had to go through in the South. Increasingly she felt an emotional sympathy with Negroes she met and spent more time talking with them. But she still was by no means ready to enlist in the civil rights movement. Her attitudes had less to do with anything the Justice Department or SNCC were doing than with the values she carried from home and the stance of the liberal Christian church.

That spring, Sue came to enjoy Scarritt more. As always she enjoyed the sense of community—a community in which people of varied backgrounds could come together, in which nobody ever locked his door because everyone trusted each other, in which one frequently switched dining-room tables so as to have a "family eating experience" with everyone in the college at least once during the year. As she began to feel more at home, Sue's leadership and organizing abilities became apparent. She was asked to serve on the Student Council. And she started working for the college's public relations office. Since Scarritt had no newspaper, this was the closest Sue could get to her old love, journalism. She was already beginning to think of combining her two chief interests and seeking a career in religious journalism.

Sue was still not entirely at ease socially. Her weight put her at a disadvantage in the dating game. At times, she felt lonely. But she didn't brood over her problems. Her energy, her independence, her warm, outgoing personality allowed her to transcend them. By the end of her first year at Scarritt, she was a recognized campus leader.

After a summer in Nashville working for the college public relations office, she plunged even more enthusiastically into student activities that fall. Named chairman of the Student Council's Social Life Committee, she became the campus' main organizer of dances, parties and other gatherings.

Then, abruptly and in rapid succession, came two events which pushed Sue from social life into social activism.

First, Abel Musorewa, a black Methodist minister from Rhodesia, was refused membership in the Belmont Methodist Church. There was a particular irony in this because Belmont sponsored the white missionary couple who had sent Mr. Musorewa to Scarritt. Sue knew the minister from a course they were both taking in religious journalism, and was outraged by the church's action. "I'd talked about this very issue with Luke back in Savannah. To me the teachings of the church were so clear on this point that they just couldn't refuse Abel. But they did."

Before Sue had time to catch her breath, the Campus Grill refused to serve Lorine Chan. Lorine, a Scarritt student from the Fiji Islands, was a Melanesian with coffee-colored skin but a naturally flaring hairdo which made her look a bit like an American Negro. The Campus Grill, a small frame shack with a corrugated tin roof, was a popular hamburger-and-coke hangout for Vanderbilt and Scarritt students. It didn't serve Negroes, but none of Scarritt's Negro students tried to test it, preferring to eat in the cafeteria or go downtown to the Negro section. But Lorine thought she was entitled to eat there, and when the manager came over and told her to get out, it created quite a stir.

Sue was still reluctant to become an activist. She concedes that she was pushed into what followed by others who were already drifting into the civil rights movement. One of these was Archie Allen, a white minister's son from Virginia, who'd started going to SNCC meetings. Archie came up to her shortly after the Campus Grill incident and asked what the Student Council was going to do about it. Sue was taken aback. "Do?" she asked. "There's nothing we can do." Archie said sure there was —they could pass a resolution condemning such discrimination and calling for a boycott of the Grill.

Sue had never even considered such a step. But the more she thought about it, the righter it seemed. She talked to Peggy, a former missionary, who was also serving on the council, and they agreed it was a good idea. So at the next council meeting the two girls urged that some such resolution be passed. "The response absolutely floored me," Sue recalls. "Immediately, almost everybody was against it. They kept saying, 'What can we do?' 'That isn't our responsibility,' 'We can't go out and wave flags.' I was surprised, because we never thought of the resolution as a radical action. But by the end of the meeting I was being seen as a radical by almost everybody else in the room."

Sue was still anything but radical. For, confronted with such surprisingly strong opposition, she and Peggy decided to take what seemed the path of least resistance. They drafted a resolution which did little more than express the Methodist belief in the fatherhood of God and the brotherhood of man. "We didn't say anything about the Campus Grill incident, about a boycott, even about discrimination. But in the context of the incident and Abel's case it was clear what we were talking about. It seemed like a completely wishy-washy statement, which would have been an easy way for the campus to get off the hook without really offending anybody."

She was all the more surprised when this innocuous draft stirred a furious debate in which she, Peggy, Archie and a few others found themselves cast as radical trouble-makers. Several Southern students vigorously condemned the resolution, arguing that the college had no business getting involved in a private matter. Most students seemed to agree, if only out of apathy. Finally a campus-wide meeting was called in a hall underneath one of the classroom buildings. Sue got up before a hundred or so students, read the statement and explained why she and the others felt it should be passed.

"I was terrified," she recalls. "It was the first time I'd gone against a major part of whatever group I belonged to. It was clear to me then that we were in the minority and our position was looked on as radical. Even the black students didn't support us completely. Some of them were very conservative and others didn't dare take a stand. So, as I stood up there I felt very isolated, very exposed."

Some of the opponents shouted antagonistic questions at her which she remembers fielding ineptly. Then she sat down and the debate surged around her for hours. Ultimately the meeting decided to take no action at all on the resolution, but to simply post it on a bulletin board and let anyone who wished sign it.

"It was incredible," Sue says. "Somehow it was considered a big radical thing to sign a statement which did little more than reaffirm the Methodist creed. Suddenly, I realized that Scarritt *was* really an isolated little monastery. I'd been enjoying the good things about it so much that I thought I'd found a whole new world. But now I saw the old world was still there and that people at Scarritt just weren't willing to extend our community beyond its boundaries into that world. If you tried to confront the issues out there they'd just say 'That's all right, it's not like that here.' I was starting to say 'It's not all right.' "

Of the thirty signers, Sue and about fifteen others decided to form a group to work on social issues. For the rest of the year, they met irregularly and sponsored a few forums to discuss issues. Even then, Sue hadn't made the decisive turn into the civil rights movement. "I knew it would be a big emotional break and I didn't want to go through it," she says. "I think at that point I would still have been quite content to stay within the group and go through the motions of being concerned with things outside."

One day that winter, Sue went to the administration building to pick up her mail. In the lobby, she ran into Alice Cobb, one of two faculty members who had signed the statement. Miss Cobb was one of the few genuine radicals on campus. She had taught at the Highlander Folk School, which had been accused of being a Communist training center, and now she was active in the freedom marches. She had always liked Sue and on that day she cornered her by the mailboxes and invited her to come along to a civil rights meeting in Nashville that evening.

Sue remembers: "My immediate reaction was—Why doesn't she leave me alone? Why doesn't she stop pushing me? I don't want to go to that meeting. I don't want to get involved. But there was no real way I could say no to her."

So Sue went along to the meeting with Miss Cobb and Archie Allen. Sponsored by the Nashville Christian Leadership Conference (an affiliate of Martin Luther King's Southern Christian Leadership Conference), the meeting was held in the First Baptist Church, one of Nashville's major Negro churches.

It was the first Negro meeting Sue had ever gone to; in fact, it was the first time she'd even heard Negroes talking openly about repression, because the ones she knew just didn't talk that way. But almost immediately she liked it. She liked the way the Reverend Kelly Miller Smith, who headed the Nashville conference, spoke simply but powerfully of freedom. She liked the singing—gospels she remembered from her days in Morris Chapel and the "freedom songs" which had become part of the movement. She liked the broad, rumbling streak of humor which ran through even the most intense moments. She even liked it when they poked fun at white people.

Perhaps Sue had been reluctant to go because she knew how attracted she would be once she got there. As she wrote later to a friend: "I was drawn in—and I'm not sure that I could have resisted even had I tried, for it is life. I mean by that I felt like I was living life—joy, pain, love, tragedy."

From then on she went to the meetings faithfully each week. Soon she started going down to the church on afternoons to help Mr. Smith get out newsletters and leaflets. "Before I knew it, I was spending more time there than at school. I'd rush down there right after classes, and soon I began cutting classes altogether. The day I took my oral exam I was at the church instead of back studying like I should have been."

Around the church that spring, Sue met many of the SNCC leaders: Lester McKinnie, John Lewis and Bernard Lafayette. This was before the break between SCLC and SNCC, and the two were almost indistinguishable in Nashville. Sue was excited by the fire and determination the young SNCC people showed in sit-ins, marches, and picketing at Nashville's places of public accommodation.

For months, Sue could not bring herself to join the picket lines. "I was scared of getting my picture in the paper. A white person would have been singled out immediately by the press and I knew everybody at home in Savannah would see the picture. I wasn't so much afraid of my parents' seeing it; I was pretty sure I could work it out with them. But I knew it would create a stir in town and what trouble that would cause Mother and Daddy."

So, for the time being, Sue worked as a support troop, doing all the things which the activist on the front lines needed to keep them going: grinding out press releases on the front lines needed to keep them going: grinding out the old mimeograph machine in the church, making coffee, raising bail money, carrying messages.

Sue remembers one day in particular that spring when SNCC had mobilized several hundred high school students for a demonstration. "I was driving uptown to see what was going on and I passed this little girl named Helen whom I remembered from meetings. She was sitting on the curb with her head bleeding all over from a policeman's night stick. I put her in the car and took her back to the church. Then some of the other kids started straggling in all bloody too. It was awful, and I felt kind of guilty not being out there with them."

Later that afternoon angry young whites carried the

battle to the church itself. Metz Rollins, a black Presbyterian minister working with SNCC, was hit in the eye by a rock—another shock to Sue, who had grown close to Metz and admired his quiet courage.

A few hours later, Metz, John Lewis and Sue were talking in the church when several young whites came through the door. Metz, with a big white bandage over his eye, walked back and in a quiet voice asked them please to leave. They left. Sue said she didn't understand "how those hoodlums had the nerve to come in here." John Lewis looked at her in a funny way and said, "Don't call them hoodlums. They're human beings just like you and me."

Sue recalls: "I was really taken aback. I couldn't believe that someone who had gone through what John had could sit there and say that. It was my first real lesson in what nonviolence means. I've never forgotten it. I admired John even more after that and we became very close friends."

That June, John Lewis and Lester McKinnie came to see Sue graduate. Standing with her parents in the swirl of other gowned graduates and beaming relatives, she saw them across the lawn, ran over and hugged them, not thinking how others might react. Later, in the dining hall, her father said, "Sue, I didn't think much about that, but I saw other people looking at you."

"I'm sure he did think a lot about it," Sue says now. "For a Southern man to see his daughter hugging the necks of two black guys must have been quite an experience. But he didn't reprimand me. He just said I should be careful."

That new relationship with her parents crystallized a few weeks later when Sue had her first brush with danger in the movement. When she graduated, her parents had given her the family's old 1957 Pontiac, and in July, Sue, John Lewis, Lester McKinnie and a white friend took off in the car for a civil rights conference in Atlanta. Lester was driving when they ran into a heavy rainstorm about sixty miles from Nashville. Coming around a curve the car skidded on the slick roadway and turned over in a ditch. Incredibly, nobody was hurt. A policeman took them to a nearby town, but they were soon drawing hostile stares. Clearly, whites and Negroes traveling together shouldn't linger there, so Lester walked over to the Negro section and found somebody to give them a lift back to Nashville.

Sue was terribly nervous about what her parents would say: about the demolished car, about letting Lester drive it and about traveling with two SNCC leaders (John Lewis had just been elected SNCC's national chairman). But when she called home, her mother was only concerned about her, whether she was injured, whether she shouldn't see a doctor just in case. She didn't say a word about the car or about Lester and John.

Sue was so touched by her mother's attitude that she sat down and wrote her parents a long letter, saying how much she appreciated their understanding of her involvement in the movement. For the first time, she told them how much she had changed, how different her life would be from theirs, but how much she hoped they would still love her.

That next weekend, Sue went home. She and her parents talked about the accident, but still there was no suggestion that she had done anything wrong. Back in Nashville, she found a letter from her mother saying that they were sometimes frightened that something might happen to her, but they understood what she was doing and why she was doing it and, above all, they still loved her.

"That exchange of letters was terribly important to me," Sue says. "I realized that they respected me for what I had to do. That was very important. If I'd been cut off by my family it would have been a great trauma. But they made it very clear to me that the family relationship would continue. They did warn me from time to time to be careful, but that was because they loved me."

The Thrashers may also have had some concern about their own position in Savannah. Sue remembers she once took home a movement songbook called *We Shall Overcome* and left it on the piano downstairs in the nursing home. Her father brought it up to her and said simply, "Don't leave this downstairs."

But Cora today says most of their concern was about Sue. "We worried ourselves sick. We feared for her. Of course, we felt there were a lot of things that weren't right in the South and something ought to be done. But we felt children weren't the ones to do it and Sue was still a child to us. Gradually, I guess, we just accepted that she had to do what she had to do."

Sue was sure she had to remain active in the civil rights movement. But she thought she still might combine that with a career in some sort of church work.

By that time, Sue's feelings toward the church were at best ambivalent. Shortly after Abel Musorewa was turned away from the Belmont Methodist Church, Sue stopped going to services. "I was upset by the church's hypocrisy, and I also began to find it just plain boring and irrelevant. Maybe if it had been a country church like we had at home I might have kept going. But the Nashville churches were huge monstrosities full of wealthy people. They just turned me off."

Then, that spring, there was an incident which soured her even further on the institutional church. For years she had thought about becoming a missionary and that winter decided she wanted to go to Indonesia. But up at the Methodist Board of Missions in New York she had a "terrible encounter" with a bureaucrat who told her that she had to go somewhere else because it was "the only slot open." Sue deeply resented that, as she always resented being forced into any slot.

The board sent her to a psychologist at Vanderbilt for a routine examination. Afterward the psychologist told her she had scored very high on ambition and would make "a very good insurance salesman." That infuriated Sue, who conceded she was ambitious—but to excel in things she thought were important, "which doesn't include insurance." Finally the psychologist said she was extremely independent. "If you were told to do something you thought was wrong you wouldn't do it. In the mission field it's very important to take orders. You're too independent to work in a structure like that." Sue complained to Scarritt's dean about the psychologist, but the dean told her, "He's probably right, you know. You wouldn't take orders and you might not be comfortable as a missionary."

So Sue told the Board of Missions to "forget it." Yet, soon after graduation, she went to work at the Methodist Publishing House in Nashville. "I had rejected the institutional church, the framework people wanted to push on you. That was totally meaningless. But religious values were still terribly important to me. And I could still be attracted by the church militant—the church that wasn't satisfied with preaching good values but went out to change society."

Sue took the job at the Methodist Publishing House partly because of her continuing interest in religious journalism and partly, as she wrote to a friend, because "I was hoping against hope that there I would at least find the church striving to be what I think it can be." But she quickly became disillusioned both with the publishing house's brand of journalism and its level of churchly aspiration.

She worked chiefly on two Methodist publications. *Mature Years*, designed for elderly church members, carried health hints ("Problems of Constipation"), daily meditations, and articles entitled "Mending China," "Have You Tried Playing Chess by Mail?" and "You Can Grow Roses Indoors Too!" The *International Lesson Annual* was a guide for adult Sunday School classes and included a lesson for each day ("Personalities Around Jesus," "Israel in the Wilderness") and inspirational poetry ("A door is closed behind me/Another opens wide/Before it lies a welcome mat/With faith I step inside").

Sue felt most of the material was "just plain garbage" and she found the atmosphere at the house stultifying. Most of the women with whom she worked didn't interest her at all. "They were either all wrapped up in their nine-to-five work, or worrying about getting married. I'd have coffee with them, but I just didn't fit in." At times she encountered open hostility. One woman obviously resented her civil rights activity. When Sue got a phone call from SNCC, the woman would shout across the room, "There's a colored boy for you on the phone."

Sue had similar problems outside. After living that summer with Joe Frank and his wife, she found an apartment in East Nashville. One day she had a visit from Lorine Chan, the Fiji Islands girl who had been refused service at the Campus Grill. After chatting in Sue's apartment, they came downstairs, where the owner met them in a blind fury. Spitting at Lorine's feet, he shouted, "Don't ever bring a nigger into this house again." Sue stayed calm long enough to drive a shaken Lorine across town, but then she went to Joe Frank's house and wept for an hour before she could tell him what was wrong.

Sue finally found another place in a changing neighborhood. The family next door were Negroes and there were other Negroes down the block, so Sue's visitors were no longer an issue. For the next year, the apartment was a virtual open house, with activists, white and black, coming through at all hours.

For by then, Sue was leading two lives: from 8:30 A.M. to 4:30 P.M. at the publishing house reading manuscripts by eccentric ladies and impassioned Bible students, and from four-thirty to two or three in the morning working with Nashville civil rights groups.

That fall, Sue helped organize a serious effort to integrate the Campus Grill, spearheaded by students at the Vanderbilt Divinity School. This led to the formation of a group called the Joint University Council on Human Relations, with students from Scarritt, Vanderbilt and Peabody who met each other on the picket line.

But Sue wouldn't join the picket lines at the Grill, still fearing repercussions on her parents at home. Not until that winter did she overcome her fear. One day she drove down to one of Morrison's cafeterias where SNCC was picketing. She was standing on the sidewalk talking to friends as pickets patrolled in front of the entrance. "Suddenly it seemed silly for me to stand on the sidewalk while everyone was picketing. So I just got in and walked. It was that spontaneous."

As she plunged deeper into the movement Sue developed a thirst to meet other Southerners who felt as she did. She wrote later to a friend about the "isolation" which a white liberal felt in the South in those days. Most of the civil rights activists then were either Negroes or Northern whites. Sue found common cause with both, but she knew she was neither. The greater her own commitment, the greater became her need to prove that she was not a freak, that there were other Southerners who shared her anguish and her vision.

At Scarritt she met a few, such as Archie Allen and a Texas girl named Gerry Bode. Through Alice Cobb she also met Carl and Anne Braden, who ran the Southern Conference Education Fund and edited a radical paper called the *Southern Patriot*. Anne was particularly important because she was a radical woman from Gadsden, Alabama, interested in journalism and committed to civil rights. Sue looked up to her and identified with her. That winter, she also met Sam Shirah and Bob Zellner,

SNCC staff members working with white Southern students; Robb Burlage, an SDS member from Texas; and most important of all, Ed Hamlett.

Ed meant a lot, partly because he was from West Tennessee too, only fifty miles from Savannah. "I hadn't known there was anyone else from that area who thought the way I did. Ed shared both my rural background and my feeling for the church. I felt close to him and learned a lot from him and I didn't feel stupid around Ed the way I did around a lot of the SDS Northerners; like most Southerners, his and my involvement with the movement was more emotional than intellectual."

Ed, who had dropped out of Southern Illinois University that winter to work with the white Southern student project of SNCC, remembers that he liked Sue immediately when he met her on a trip through Nashville in February. "Sue is rooted in time and place in a way that, say, Tom Hayden isn't. And I'm like that too. Down here in the South, our radicalism is less ideological than it is soul, heart and gut stuff. And I understood Sue's religious impetus. I'd been very active in the Baptist Church, particularly on the musical side. Sue and I used to sing gospel and hymns together."

The small group of Nashville activists quickly developed an intense camaraderie. Almost every night there was a meeting or party at somebody's house. One night that January they got together at the home of a Fisk psychologist. Sue soon fell into discussion with Archie Allen, Carl Braden and Dave Kotelchuck, a physics professor at Vanderbilt. "We were talking about the problem of white Southern students, how isolated they were. We didn't feel they could be reached through the Northern white students who were beginning to come South then. I felt that particularly because I resented the moral judgments Northerners made about the South. We agreed that the best way to reach Southern students would be through other Southern students. We got terribly excited about the idea and decided to have a meeting about it the next day."

A somewhat larger group was there that next morning and again nearly everyone was enthusiastic. With the help of Sam Shirah, who in his travels for SNCC had ferreted out most of the Southern white-student activists, they put together a list of some twenty groups at colleges like Clemson, Tulane and North Carolina where some white civil rights activity had already begun. Invitations were sent out for a conference in Nashville on April 3 to discuss ways of coordinating and expanding their efforts.

About forty-five students from fifteen predominantly white Southern campuses showed up that weekend. A carload of students drove up from New Orleans; one boy took a bus all the way from Florida. After three days the meeting decided to set up the Southern Student Organizing Committee. Robb Burlage, who had helped draft the SDS founding statement, now wrote one for SSOC. He called it "We'll Take Our Stand," echoing the book by Nashville's Fugitive Group of writers. It read, in part: "We as young Southerners hereby pledge to take our stand now together here to work for a new order, a new South, a place which embodies our ideals for all the world to emulate, not ridicule. We find our destiny as individuals in the South in our hopes and our work together as brothers."

Another smaller meeting was held the next month in Atlanta to coincide with a SNCC executive committee meeting. The white students of SSOC wanted to clear their idea with the predominantly Negro leadership of SNCC. Somewhat surprisingly, Stokely Carmichael, Bob Moses and most others went for it and even donated three hundred dollars to get it started. So SSOC elected its own leadership: Gene Guerrero, an Emory University student, chairman; Ron Parker, the Vanderbilt student who led the Campus Grill protests, treasurer; and Sue, executive secretary.

Within a few weeks, Sue and four other SSOC leaders left for the Mississippi Summer Project. But before they could get there, word came that three civil rights activists, Schwerner, Chaney and Goodman, had disappeared. Sue recalls going through her training in the wild glory of the Great Smoky Mountains struck by the contrast between "all that natural beauty and that ugly thing down there."

She arrived in Mississippi fearing she might be dead in a few weeks, but her work turned out to be relatively safe. While most Northern students worked in the countryside registering Negroes to vote and running freedom schools, SSOC people went into a white organizing project

Shirah had set up in the bigger towns and cities. For several weeks, Sue worked in the office of the Mississippi Council on Human Relations in Jackson, the state capital. Later she went to Biloxi, on the Gulf of Mexico, to do public relations for the project there. The most hostile Mississippian she met during these weeks was a Methodist minister in Biloxi who refused to speak to her when she tried to explain their goals.

On her way back to Nashville, Sue stopped off in Savannah. She told her parents she was giving up her job with the publishing house and going to work full time for SSOC. "They weren't terribly pleased," she recalls. "But they made no effort to stop me."

By then, Sue probably couldn't have been stopped. "My decision to go ahead with SSOC was my final break with the life I was expected to lead," Sue says. "It meant a total commitment, a change in my whole life style. That wouldn't have been necessary if I'd gone to work, say, for the Tennessee Human Relations Council. There you could say you were working for 'civil rights,' but your style would still be bureaucratic. I might have gone that way. I was accepted as an intergroup relations intern, but I decided not to accept. Instead, I put everything I had into SSOC."

Everything she had didn't seem much. Only twenty-three, Sue had no organizational experience. "I felt very much that I wasn't competent to do the job. All of us felt that. But we didn't see anyone else around. So we went ahead and did it."

Sue rented an office in one of those frame houses near Scarritt and hired Archie Allen as a full-time staffer. They split responsibilities, with Archie out traveling the campuses and Sue running the office. It was hard work—fourteen to eighteen hours a day, setting up conferences, finding speakers, compiling mailing lists, getting out newsletters. For the next eighteen months Sue lived only for SSOC. Making twenty dollars a week, she cut her life down to Spartan necessities, staying rent free in a friend's apartment, partying rarely and then only with SSOC people.

Sue soon showed a natural talent for organizing. Warm, genuinely interested in other people, she easily gained and held loyalties. Meticulous and intensely pragmatic, she was the perfect office manager. And she loved the work

—hours on the telephone talking to her contacts, encouraging them, finding out what they needed. By the end of the year, SSOC was growing fast. Its mailing list was up from sixty to two thousand. It had individual or group contacts on about a hundred campuses throughout the South, as well as "fraternal" ties with SNCC and SDS.

That winter, SSOC brought thirty-seven students back to Mississippi to help remodel community centers in Palmer's Crossing and Meridian. The project was held in two sessions, before and after Christmas. Sue went home for Christmas, stopping in Corinth, Mississippi, to buy presents for her family. Coming straight from the poverty of Palmer's Crossing, she was a bit repulsed by all the tinseled merchandise and clanging cash registers in the stores. At home, the Thrashers had a typical Southern Christmas—only the immediate family, but a table loaded with three kinds of meat and six vegetables. "I sat there eating and knowing that the people in Palmer's Crossing didn't have much of anything to eat that day. Suddenly I felt more alienated from my family than ever before—not because of any break between us, but because of the difference between their life and what I was going back to." When she went back, Sue stuffed a paper bag full of fruit, nuts and candy, but when she got to Palmer's Crossing she was so embarrassed she didn't know what to do with it. She finally gave it to a Negro staff member and asked him to do whatever he thought best.

Sue drove in and out of Mississippi frequently that next year—often down the road through Meridian and Laurel, the area where Schwerner, Chaney and Goodman had been killed. She always put on more than her usual Southern accent when she stopped for gas; that and the Tennessee license plate on her car may have kept her out of trouble. But somewhat later she learned the Klan knew the dates and times "the girl in the red-and-white Falcon" had traveled the highway. Unnerved, she changed cars frequently from then on.

It was impossible to escape fear in Mississippi. Sue often stayed with Ed King, the white Methodist chaplain of Tougaloo College, a national committeeman of the Freedom Democratic Party, and a member of SSOC's advisory board. Once when she arrived, the Kings had just received a bomb threat; another time, the Klan threatened to kill Ed. Over in Batesville, on the edge of the Delta, she stayed with Robert Miles, a Negro farmer active in the movement. "Once, we were sitting there watching the news when we heard all sorts of commotion outside. Mr. Miles got up, went to the window and said calmly, 'Well, those people done left us a cross.' I got up and rushed to the window and there was a cross burning, a fairly big one, about five feet high. It was the first time I'd ever seen one and I was terrified. But Mr. Miles stayed completely calm. He just exuded this feeling that he wouldn't bow to anyone without a struggle. That night, when I went to bed, I looked up at the wall and there were bullet holes—about ten of them—right across the top."

Even in Nashville, the breath of danger was always on the back of their necks. They got threatening phone calls; once, a man followed them into a gas station and told everybody they were a bunch of "Communist agitators." Appeals to the police were fruitless. One day, several policemen came barging into the office and said, "We understand you have a picture of Khrushchev in here."

But the danger helped weld people together. After staying with the Kings for a weekend, Sue wrote to a friend, "I suppose the thing I love the most about my work is finding people like them. Together we form a community . . . and the unity and strength found there in that community is, in the end, the only reward and that is enough."

Within its first year, SSOC's community changed somewhat to include a few Negroes on Southern campuses where SNCC was not organizing. But soon SNCC's own shift from a multiracial group which welcomed whites to an all-black one seeking to develop race pride created problems for SSOC, caught moving the other way. There was some agonizing within SSOC about how they should react to the shift, but it bothered them much less than it did many Northerners in the movement who identified strongly with Negroes and hated Southern whites. "After all," Sue says, "we'd been working primarily with whites all along. We were really the first people to decide to work with our own people, and when SNCC began to shift in that direction it made me feel we'd been proven right. I suppose if my relation with John Lewis had been cut off—as it was with some others—I might have felt differently. But John and I continued to like and respect each other, although we worked with different constituencies."

And just as SNCC sought to give Negroes pride in their black heritage, so SSOC began seeking out what was good in the Southern white's heritage. This merely reinforced a theme that had been there in the group all along: a search for roots. Just as each of them had to prove that there were others in the South then who felt as they did, so as a group they had to discover some precedent for what they were doing. "We had to find ourselves rooted in history," Sue says. "We had to show that we weren't that different, that the ideas we represented had some kind of tradition in the South and that there had been other people who had gone through the same things we were going through."

This began with a search into white Southern culture. Like many others in SSOC, Sue had heard country music all her life but had early come to equate it with the provincialism she rejected. "By the time I graduated from high school I thought of it as 'hillbilly music,' not the kind of thing I wanted to identify with." Although Nashville was the home of country music, the site of the Grand Ole Opry, Sue never went to the Opry all the time she was in college.

But at SSOC conferences she joined the others in singing gospel songs, then started listening to country music again, and finally went with some others to the Opry. And she sang a song Sam Shirah had taught them about "Big Jim" Folsom, the former governor of Alabama who had several paternity suits brought against him. The song —something about a poor girl who met Folsom, got pregnant and went on the streets as a prostitute while Big Jim was in the State House—became the unofficial SSOC song. Sue believes it was because the song "made us come to terms with our own backgrounds, which were largely poor and rural, and admit that was where we came in, that was where we had to begin." Eventually, SSOC sponsored an annual Southern Folk Culture Revival Festival with black and white performers like Bernice Reagon, one of the original Freedom Singers; Johnny Cash; Eleanor Walden, an Appalachian balladeer; and Bill Monroe, the father of "blue grass music."

And this led them to a search for the roots of Southern white radicalism. Sue and Gene Guerrero spent one whole afternoon with Lillian Smith on her Georgia mountaintop talking about the work of the Southern Conference for Human Welfare in the forties and about Miss Smith's other radical activities. They invited Don West, one of the first CIO organizers in the South, to talk about the history of the Southern labor movement. Sue became interested in the radicalism of Harlan County, Kentucky, scene of some of the CIO's most bitter battles with mine owners, and once she visited the home of Sam and Florence Reece. Sam had been one of the key CIO men in the county and his wife wrote the famous union song "Which Side Are You On?" Standing there in her log cabin, Florence Reece sang them her song—"They say in Harlan County/No neutrals are there/Either be a Union man or a thug for J. H. Blair" (one of the major coal operators). The song had been adapted for the civil rights movement ("They say in Mississippi/No neutrals are there"), and Mrs. Reece talked about the parallels between the union fight and the new movement. "She was a great woman," Sue says, "who had gone through her own struggle and understood instinctively the trouble of black people."

People like the Reeces were terribly important to Sue because she had never rejected the rural Southerner. "I rejected the out-and-out racists, the Klansmen, the women who shouted dirty names at Negro children going to school. They were my enemies. But I could never reject the average white Southerner, because that would have meant turning against my family. I always believed that there were deep reservoirs of very decent, good, even radical feelings in many rural Southerners which could be tapped if only we worked hard enough."

And this view led Sue and the others from a racial to a class analysis of the country's problems. "We came to see that the Southern white man was—as Bob Dylan sang about the man who killed Medgar Evers—'only a pawn in the game.' His racism often wasn't his fault; he was exploited and used in much the same way as the black man. We saw that we had to fight for all poor and oppressed people and, in the South particularly, that meant many whites."

As they began thinking in terms of class, they extended their activities beyond civil rights to the whole spectrum of concerns adopted by the New Left. They worked with textile workers and migrant labor, campaigned for university reforms, urged a boycott of Dow Chemical Co. products, and finally organized the Southern Coordinating Committee to End the War in Vietnam.

This shift in emphasis forced Sue to rethink her position. She had started with a narrow focus on civil rights and, in fact, a distrust of the sweeping radicalism of the Northern SDS people. "In those early days I felt very insecure politically. I hadn't thought seriously about politics on a national scale because nothing I'd been involved in demanded it. Hell, I was still voting for Nixon in 1960 because my father was an Eisenhower man. So when I met SDS people like Tom Hayden, I didn't understand what they were talking about. There was a lot of sectarianism—lots of talk about the 'Trots.' I didn't even know who the 'Trots' were. Things that meant a lot to SDS people didn't mean anything at all to me. I thought they were a bit arrogant. And I thought they were awfully romantic in the way they approached poor whites."

And the war issue brought Sue into more conflict with her family than civil rights ever had. Although the Thrashers all support racial integration, they are instinctive patriots who believe an American's simple duty in time of war is to support his country. Joe Frank, who served in the Army for four years, says, "Our family doesn't think much of those antiwar demonstrators and draft-card burners." Carl, whom Sue idolized for so long, became a career Army officer and served with the engineers in Vietnam.

But the injustice of the war came home to her when Gene Guerrero and several other young SSOC men refused induction and faced jail sentences. Talking to them and to more SDS people, she gradually became convinced that Vietnam was an atrocity, and that it involved basically the same issue as the civil rights movement—the right of people to control their own lives. In April 1965, Sue went to Washington for an antiwar march sponsored by SDS—her first peace demonstration. And that summer, she went North for her first extended stay, to work on the staff of the Encampment for Citizenship in New York. The encampment, a six-week seminar on world affairs and government, was run that year by Allard Lowenstein, whom Sue had met in Mississippi. Lowenstein asked her to come up and be the "staff radical," which surprised her a bit. "At that time I didn't really consider myself a radical. But when I got up there I found I was to the left of almost everybody. Strangely enough, I got along best with a girl who had been a founding member of Young Americans for Freedom, a far-right-wing group, because both of us distrusted the stock liberal position which predominated there."

That trip to New York reinforced a restlessness which had begun to gnaw at her. It continued all that fall as she plunged back into her sixteen-hour-a-day schedule in Nashville. She was beginning to feel, as she wrote a friend, that she was "imprisoned" in her own "ghetto." This was an old theme with Sue, stretching back to the days when she felt trapped on the farm or in her high school clique. This time, after nearly three years of total immersion in the civil rights movement, she wanted to move on.

Robb Burlage, her SDS friend from Nashville, was working at the Institute for Policy Studies, a radical research center in Washington. He had launched a seminar on Southern politics and wanted Sue to come work with him on it. SSOC insisted it couldn't get along without her, and Sue stayed on month after month. But finally, in April 1966, she broke loose and went to Washington.

From then on, Sue moved rapidly and easily into the New Left. At the institute, she worked closely with Dick Barnett and Marcus Raskin, the co-directors, and with Arthur Waskow, one of its leading intellectual lights. Moreover, Washington was swarming with old SNCC and SDS hands whom she saw frequently. In the spring of 1967 a friend in SDS told her about plans for Vietnam Summer, a concentrated bout of radical organizing around the war issue. So, in June, Sue moved to the Vietnam Summer headquarters in Cambridge, Massachusetts, where she worked as Southern coordinator, operating through scores of old contacts and friends spread across the South. It was an important period for her, she feels, because it marked a shift from strictly regional organizing to national activity. "Even though I was responsible for the South, I was part of a national staff, and I saw more than ever before the need to make the South part of the national movement."

The pouring of Southern energies into a great national movement was symbolized for Sue that October, when SSOC people marched as a contingent in the March on the Pentagon. "We had a big SSOC banner, and several of the states had banners of their own. I was walking with Ed Hamlett, and as we approached the Pentagon I could see about fifty soldiers with gas masks on advancing toward us. It was the first time I'd ever seen that and known it was directed at me. For the first time I realized what I had become: an enemy of the state. I realized that I was now totally alienated from my government. A very disconcerting feeling. The soldiers marched by us, but I started crying. Ed asked me what the trouble was and I just said, 'It's going to be so awful.' I knew instinctively that it was going to be bloody. My gut reaction was to go with the rest of the people. It was kind of stirring to watch the great waves of people moving up toward the Pentagon. I identified a lot with them. But I had no intention of getting arrested. I'd always felt that arrests just took a lot of money for bail, and didn't prove anything. I never wanted to do it."

For, despite her increasing radicalism, Sue remained the pragmatic organizer. While she felt there was a need for continuing confrontations with authority, she didn't think everybody ought to take part in them. "There is a need for somebody to give a backdrop to the confrontation politics, with the nitty gritty of organizing, and educating people. This didn't mean conventional politics. I've long since abandoned hope in the ballot as a means of change. But I still think in terms of changing people by getting them the information they need on which to make the right decisions."

Her pragmatism set her off from many of the younger radicals, even many of the Southern kids who stayed at her apartment when they came to Washington for demonstrations. "They weren't the people I'd worked with down there. They were into the hippie thing, the drug culture. I wanted to say, 'Look, man, you can't do any serious organizing on dope. Cut it out. You've got to be serious!' I wanted to say that, but I didn't."

Sue was also turned off by the radical tendency to romanticize the working class. "I've always felt that the people who talked the most about the 'workers' were the comfortable middle class who were alienated from middle-class existence and were therefore projecting values onto the working class. That isn't realistic at all in terms of organizing. We have to pay as much attention to middle-class people and students as we do to the workers, because the working class just isn't a great revolutionary vanguard."

Perhaps even more than most New Left people, Sue did not act out of a theoretical framework. She acted because she had lived through certain experiences which had changed her. "I sense that society has to change because I've seen oppressed black people in the South; I work for university reform because I've experienced alienation as a student; I want political change because I've felt powerlessness as a citizen of this country; I want to change our stance toward the world because I pay taxes which go to a war I don't support. These are just very specific things you can't ignore. They are there. I don't have a very clear picture about what ought to replace them. I know I want a society in which people have control over their own lives. I don't know whether that means a socialist society or a restructuring of the democratic system we have. But I don't know that there is a great deal to be gained from trying to sketch out a scenario for the future."

Above all, Sue brought to her work a more sober, less apocalyptic air than many of the young radicals. She avoided both the extremes of deep alienation and wild expectations. Perhaps because of her days in the civil rights movement, she had more faith in human nature, in the essential decency of many Americans. But she also had a profound awareness of how small the New Left was in the nation as a whole. "I saw how powerless we were. Despite all our protests, the war still goes on. If it continues much longer, my brother may have to go back for a second tour. I don't really look at the future with a great deal of optimism. There's something in one of Camus' notebooks about 'You understand that what you are doing isn't really going to change things.' Well, I understand that. I do things because I can't do anything else, because I have to do it."

In December 1967 Sue went home for Christmas as she always did. It was the usual warm family affair: the table heaped with food, relatives passing through at all hours, singing the old songs around the piano. On December 30 she was preparing to drive to Washington in time for a New Year's Eve party when somebody noticed a big black rat rooting around the greenhouse. Her father loaded the shotgun and went out back to shoot it. But he slipped on the ice, the gun went off and blew shot into him. He was in the operating room for eight hours, lived for the next forty-eight, and then died.

"It was a three-day nightmare for me," Sue recalls. "I was very upset that my father should have died by gunfire. He was such a gentle man, kind and good and sensitive, that it seemed terribly wrong for him to be taken violently that way. I was very angry about the gun being in the house, angry at my family because they didn't understand how I felt about guns, angry that Carl should have been in Vietnam at a time like that, even angry at the Rose Bowl which created so much air traffic into Los Angeles that the Army couldn't get Carl home before Daddy died."

For a while, Sue was annoyed too by the townspeople who streamed through the house. The day Herman died, more than thirty people stopped by to leave food. It was a Southern tradition to bring food for a bereaved family because you assumed they wouldn't want to cook. By evening the Thrashers' kitchen table was covered with fried chicken, catfish, hams, potato salad, cakes and pies.

"At first I deeply resented those people being there at all," Sue recalls. "On my trips home, I'd always come just to see my immediate family. I felt pretty alienated from the rest of Savannah. I didn't identify with anyone else in that whole town, even my aunts and uncles. So, particularly at a time like that, I wanted them to go away and leave us alone.

"But then I realized that they were coming there out of respect and feeling for my father, and for my mother too and all the rest of us. And I found that very touching. All of a sudden, I was thrown back against my roots in a way I hadn't been for years. I'd been standing outside because I could no longer feel comfortable living in that town, or sharing in that culture for any length of time. But that week I had to live in it, to experience all the rituals of death in a small Southern community, and to understand that that was my father's life, a part of it, and a part of mine."

LINDA

The windows of Dr. Irving Sklar's reception room at 2 Fifth Avenue look out across Washington Square. A patient waiting uneasily for the dentist's drill can watch the pigeons circling Stanford White's dignified Washington Arch, the children playing hopscotch on the square's wide walkways, and the students walking hand in hand beneath the elms.

"Certainly we knew the Village; our family dentist is at 2 Fifth Avenue," said Irving Fitzpatrick, the wealthy Greenwich, Connecticut, spice importer whose daughter, Linda, was found murdered with a hippie friend in an East Village boiler room on October 8, 1967.

For the Fitzpatricks—who lived in a thirty-room house a mile from the Greenwich Country Club—"the Village" was the Henry James scene they saw from Dr. Sklar's windows and "those dear little shops" Mrs. Fitzpatrick and her daughters occasionally visited. ("I didn't even know there was an East Village," Mr. Fitzpatrick said. "I've heard of the Lower East Side, but the East Village?")

But for eighteen-year-old Linda, the Village was a different scene: crash pads and acid trips, freaking out and psychedelic art, witches and warlocks.

If the Fitzpatricks' knowledge of the Village stopped at Washington Square, their knowledge of Linda (whom they called Fitzpoo) stopped at the unsettling but familiar image of a young, talented girl overly impatient to taste the joys of life. Reality in both cases went far beyond the Fitzpatricks' wildest fears.

It is perhaps futile to ask which was "the real Linda"— the Linda of Greenwich, Connecticut, or the Linda of Greenwich Village. She was a strange mixture of these two worlds, so tangled that Linda herself probably did not know in which she belonged.

Her first world presents the burnished image of wealth, elegance and comfort to which most Americans aspire. The Fitzpatricks have been wealthy for generations. Austin Fitzpatrick emigrated from Scotland in the mid-nineteenth century, settled in Brooklyn and entered the coffee and tea business. Impelled by a Calvinist dedication to work, he accumulated enough capital by 1898 to purchase the Knickerbocker Mills, a Brooklyn spice company, which he handed down to his son.

Irving Fitzpatrick, Sr., was an even harder worker than his father; some recall him as nearly compulsive. Working six days a week, he was supposed to take Wednesday afternoons off. But he spent most Wednesdays driving upstate, stopping at grocery and bakery shops to see whether they used his products. In later years, when his health failed, doctors prevailed on him to winter in Arizona. He would go with reservations for three or four months, but would be back at work after a few weeks. Before he died, he had built a fortune of several million dollars.

Irving, Jr., the eldest of his two sons, was born in Hollis, Long Island, but the family moved to Montclair, New Jersey, when he was five. There, he went to Mount Hebron School, Montclair High School and, finally, Mercersburg Academy, before entering Princeton in 1927. Although he stayed four years, Princeton's records show he never graduated.

The summer after his senior year he married Elizabeth Stockton Trenbath, a Montclair girl with distinguished lineage: direct descent from Jedidiah Preble, first Brigadier General under George Washington, and Richard Stockton, a signer of the Declaration of Independence. They had known each other for years, gone to school together, worshiped in adjoining pews at St. James Episcopal Church, where her father was rector. And they were married in that same church, joining wealth and social standing in a partnership which seemed to augur well for the family.

Shortly afterward, Irving Jr. moved to Harrisburg,

Pennsylvania, where he became a salesman for Proctor and Gamble. His younger brother, Craig, joined Knickerbocker Mills directly out of Princeton; but their grandfather felt that Irving, as the eldest son, should get experience elsewhere first.

He stayed with the soap company only two years before coming to the mills in 1934. The young couple moved into a home Grandfather Fitzpatrick bought them in Montclair—a handsome white frame house with black shutters and big shade trees, just right for the life of quiet elegance the Fitzpatricks now cultivated.

And it made a comfortable home for the family they began building. Their first child, Perry, was born in August 1935, followed by Robert in July 1937, Carol in June 1940 and David in June 1942.

But by the time David was born, the marriage had fallen apart. As sales manager, Mr. Fitzpatrick traveled all over the country, building Knickerbocker from a regional into a national company; and he saw less and less of his wife, a strong-willed woman who resented his lack of attention. Sometime in 1942 they decided to recognize the situation; Mr. Fitzpatrick left home and moved into a Manhattan hotel.

They were separated for three years. During that time, Mr. Fitzpatrick met Patricia Binger, the daughter of Roy Binger, a well-known Hollywood cameraman who worked with John Ford on *Stagecoach*. An attractive brunette, Patricia had come to New York to study painting and was living with another girl on the East Side when she met the older but still ruggedly good-looking executive. They fell in love.

Finally, on October 8, 1945, the Fitzpatricks were divorced in Reno, Nevada. The next day, Irving married Patricia at the Reno Unity Center.

The couple lived in New York for a while, then moved to Larchmont, where they bought a ten-room house at 19 Dogwood Lane. The house, which backed up on the Rockefeller estate, was more of a showplace than the Montclair home. By then, Mr. Fitzpatrick was making a lot of money and he spent it freely to please his pretty, young bride. They hired a Negro couple as live-in maid and butler, the butler doubling as chauffeur for their two cars. They bought a sailboat and joined the fashionable Larchmont Yacht Club.

On July 8, 1949, at New Rochelle Hospital, Patricia gave birth to a daughter, whom they named Rae Binger Fitzpatrick.

Some of the Fitzpatricks' friends suspected Patricia wanted a child partly because she resented the attention Mr. Fitzpatrick still paid his first four children. But if she thought the baby would bring them closer together, it didn't work. On the contrary, soon after Rae's birth, serious strains developed in the marriage.

"Patricia was a gay person who liked parties, liked to have a good time," says a friend who knows her well. "Remember she was from Hollywood, where people live life fast. She had an artistic temperament, very temperamental. And she took pride in saying she was 'part Latin' —a de Silva on her mother's side, I think. She loved to dance, particularly Mexican dances. Fitzpatrick just couldn't keep up with her. She felt he was too straightlaced."

Mr. Fitzpatrick had his artistic side too. In his youth, he had been a better-than-average painter. Although he had given it up, he enjoyed having good paintings around him and bought several valued at over ten thousand dollars apiece. He also enjoyed music and built a sizable record collection.

But, for Mr. Fitzpatrick, art and music were domestic graces to be built into a fine home along with a swimming pool. For, as friends describe him, he was essentially a homebody. "He's never really known what to do with all that money," says one. "He doesn't enjoy running around to parties, the races or other jet-set affairs. If he had his way, he'd putter around home. And that just wasn't Patricia's bag."

Gradually, this clash of temperaments intensified. Patricia started making frequent trips to New York, seeking gaiety at the theater, restaurants and night clubs.

One of her favorite restaurants was L'Aiglon at 13 East 55th Street, which advertised its "Continental cuisine of distinction." She often ate lunch there before a matinée, and one day in 1950, the restaurant's owner introduced her to another of his regular customers—a tall, suave Cuban-born journalist named Jorge Losada.

"We had lunch together," Mr. Losada recalls, "and I began seeing her regularly. She told me her marriage was going very badly and she wanted to leave her husband."

On September 12, 1951, she did just that. While Mr. Fitzpatrick was away on a business trip, Patricia packed her things into one of their cars and drove to the city, where she checked into a hotel.

Alerted by his maid and butler, Mr. Fitzpatrick flew home. Friends recall that he was deeply hurt and angry. Although he let his wife file for divorce, he took a hard line on its terms. Eventually, Patricia accepted an unusual agreement. She not only waived all alimony and any claim on his property, but gave him custody of their daughter (she could visit Rae only at times specified by her husband).

Mr. Losada recalls how surprised he was that Patricia gave up custody of her child. "She loved Rae. It was a real sacrifice. But she said Mr. Fitzpatrick was better able to care for the child and assure her a secure life and an education."

In December 1951, Patricia moved to Florida to establish residence for the divorce, which became final on April 10, 1952. Eight months later, she married Jorge Losada in Havana.

For about a year after the divorce, Patricia visited her daughter—first every two weeks, then once a month. Then the visits stopped altogether.

On June 5, 1953, Mr. Fitzpatrick symbolically cut his daughter's last ties with her mother when he officially changed her name from Rae Binger Fitzpatrick to Linda Rae Fitzpatrick. Linda had always been one of his favorite names; he had almost given it to his daughter by his first marriage.

And about this same time, Mr. Fitzpatrick remarried—to Ann Rush, a striking blonde who had been a Powers model and a leading cover girl in the thirties. Ann had been divorced several years earlier from Douglas Leigh, the electric-sign magnate, and had an eight-year-old daughter—Lucinda, called Cindy—from that marriage.

Sometime in 1954 the Fitzpatricks and their two daughters moved to a large white frame house on Zaccheus Mead Lane in Greenwich, Connecticut. It was Mr. Fitzpatrick's biggest house yet—about fifteen rooms—and he embellished it further by building a swimming pool and stone fireplace out back.

In contrast to the ebullient Patricia, Ann was reserved. ("Patricia would throw her arms around your neck and kiss you; Ann would peck you on the cheek," says one member of the family.) Trained as a model, she was always impeccably groomed and she kept her house the same way. "She was always rushing around emptying ashtrays," a friend says, "but the house never looked lived-in."

Ann recognized Linda's need for a mother and, by most accounts, gave her all the affection she could. But in 1959, she gave birth to another child of her own, Melissa, who took much of her time, energy and motherly love.

For a while Linda got some of the warmth she needed from her stepsister Cindy. Although three years older, Cindy spent a lot of time with Linda and the two girls grew very close.

But Cindy had inherited her mother's blond good looks which Linda, a bit pudgy and ill-proportioned, couldn't match. As she grew older, Linda learned to sit patiently with her hands crossed in her lap while boys asked her stepsister and other pretty girls to dance.

She wasn't very popular with girls either. "I don't recall that she had any close friends at school," says one classmate at the Greenwich Country Day School.

But if this bothered Linda, she didn't show it. Much of her energy at Country Day went into athletics. She excelled at field hockey, winning a place on the Stuyvesant Team, Fairfield County's all-stars. She also won swimming and riding awards. In her early teens, Linda became fascinated with horses and rode regularly at the nearby Round Hill Stables, where Theodore Wahl, the owner, recalls her as "a nice, quiet little girl—always outfitted proper, in jodhpurs."

John R. Webster, headmaster at the Country Day School and a friend of Mr. Fitzpatrick's, says Linda had "quite a decent I.Q. and really a very acceptable academic record." But her classmates recall that her grades were poor and, in fact, that Mr. Webster suggested she might do better at another school. So when she left Country Day in 1965, Linda had fewer options than she might have had. The Oldfields School in Glencoe, Maryland, was the solution.

Oldfields is old (founded in 1867), expensive (thirty-six hundred dollars a year), small (one hundred girls), exclusive (the roster is studded with names like Rockefeller, Vanderbilt and Stettinius), and not overly intellectual (it emphasizes "development of Christian character"). It has two courses of study—an "A track" for girls seeking entrance to four-year colleges, and a "B track" for those aiming at junior colleges or artistic or technical training. Yet even A-track girls rarely get into Radcliffe, Smith or Vassar. In some quarters, Oldfields has a reputation as "a rich-dumb-girls school."

But many girls from Greenwich and other manicured Connecticut suburbs end up there. In Linda's class of twenty-nine, four girls were from Greenwich, two from Darien, and one each from Cheshire and Old Saybrook.

In fact, as she set off for Oldfields that fall of 1965, Linda seemed not unlike many other daughters of affluent American suburbia. Mrs. Fitzpatrick recalled her then as a "well-rounded, fine, healthy girl."

"My first impression of Linda was of a soggy, lumpy, lackluster girl," says Robert McGuire, who taught English at Oldfields. "She didn't seem to have any confidence in herself—academically, socially, in any way.

"Of course, a lot of Oldfields girls felt a bit that way. Most of them had brothers or sisters who went to much better schools. They felt their parents had shipped them off to a kind of dumping ground for 'non-producers' and this made them feel stupid. But Linda was worse off than most. She felt ugly, worthless, unloved."

Linda was on Track B, heading nowhere. "In most classes she seemed like an absolute clod," Mr. McGuire says. "Her name kept coming up at faculty meetings. 'What's the matter with Linda? Has she done anything for any of you?'

"This was deceptive, I think. She could have been one of the best students in the class. She had sensitivity and intelligence. I think she could have made it even on Track A if you could have kept up her confidence. That was her key problem. She felt she was a real loser."

The only subject in which she showed any real interest was art. But her art teacher that first year didn't like Linda and openly ridiculed her efforts. This blocked her one creative outlet and intensified her crisis of confidence.

Some of those who knew her at Oldfields feel that Linda's lack of confidence stemmed partly from sensitivity about her looks. "She kept telling us about how good-

*looking her mother was, how she'd been a model and all,"
one classmate says. "But I think Linda resented her too,
because she didn't look that way."*

*The girls often remarked that Linda could have been
"quite presentable" if she'd cared for herself. But she
didn't seem to try. She rarely washed her hair, didn't
take care of her complexion and continued to put on
weight. "She kept saying she was going to diet," one girl
recalls, "but she ate all the time—in the dining room or
in her room."*

*Nevertheless, Linda had more friends at Oldfields than
she'd ever had before—if only because of sheer proxim-
ity to others in the dormitory. She started off living in
Lower North, but didn't get along with her roommate
and moved to Centennial Center. There she found several friends and soon became part of a clique of six or
eight girls.*

*But those friendships proved costly. "Linda was very
easily led," one girl recalls. "If her friends wanted her
to do something she'd go along." That winter, about eight
girls went on a shoplifting expedition at Hutzler's Department Store in nearby Towson—taking some nail polish,
underwear and lounging outfits. One girl turned herself in
and the others were eventually caught. No criminal
charges were brought, but several of the "ringleaders"
were expelled from school and others, including Linda,
were put on probation. This meant restriction to campus
for the rest of the year. So when summer vacation came,
it was a particular release for Linda.*

By then, the Fitzpatricks had moved to yet another
house. In 1962 Mr. Fitzpatrick paid $125,000 for the
thirty-room fieldstone mansion on Doubling Road near
the Greenwich Country Club. Called Graystone, it is an
impressive house set back from the road across a circular
graveled driveway, surrounded by spreading shade trees
and four lushly landscaped acres. In back is a big rectan-
gular swimming pool.

Linda spent the first few weeks of her vacation lounging around that pool. Then, in July, she joined the family
for a month's vacation in Bermuda.

"The family always takes its summer vacations together," Mr. Fitzpatrick said. "Sometimes we went to
Florida, sometimes to Antibes, but for the past few

summers we've rented a house in Bermuda. We're very close."

"Her parents didn't pay much attention to what she was doing," recalls Herbie, a boy she met in Bermuda that summer.

The Fitzpatricks' house was off Riddell's Bay Road near the Riddell's Bay Golf and Country Club, but Linda, who turned seventeen that month, managed to spend many of her evenings alone in downtown Hamilton. Herbie met her there one night at the Hog Penny Discotheque.

"She was supposed to be with this guy who played in the Clockwork Orange, the rock group at the Hog Penny. But we got to talking and I said I was going to a beach party down at Elbow Beach. I asked her, Would she like to come? She said sure. So we went."

That night, on the white sands of Elbow Beach—her friends believe—Linda smoked her first pot. She smoked it several more times before the month was over.

Back in Greenwich that August, Linda picked up her first world with apparent ease. Her friends recall shopping with her for dresses at Ann Taylor's, listening to records, helping her take care of Melissa.

By then, Cindy was married and living in Oyster Bay, Long Island. Linda and Melissa ("Missy") soon formed a relationship very much like the one Linda and Cindy had some years before. "Linda needed to be really close to somebody," one of her friends remarks. "Since she couldn't get that from her parents she got it first from Cindy, then from Missy."

One of her best Greenwich friends was Linda Vanderbilt, who also went to Oldfields. The spring before, the two Lindas had agreed to room together the coming year. The Vanderbilts were driving their daughter down to Maryland in their big Oldsmobile station wagon and agreed to take her new roommate with them.

"I remember we picked Linda up at her house," Linda Vanderbilt recalls. "Her parents were there helping her get ready. When we left, their goodbyes were warm enough, I guess, and they kissed at the door. But I could see Linda was very happy to get away.

"She obviously had something to tell me. As soon as

we got in the car—Mother and Dad were in front, Linda and I in back—she started whispering to me about the summer. But that bothered Mother. She was mad because I'd gotten poison ivy and had a doctor's appointment which made us late getting on the road. So I told Linda to stop whispering and tell me later."

Within a week at school, Linda had told her roommate everything. "She just couldn't stop talking about Bermuda, about the boys she met there, the beach parties they had, but especially about the pot she'd smoked. I'm sure she hadn't smoked before she went down there, but that fall she'd obviously turned on. She thought it was the big thing in her life and she wanted to do it a lot more.

"Linda didn't have any pot at school," her roommate insists. "It was too dangerous. We had this housemother, Miss Godfrey, who made room checks all the time. After the shoplifting thing the year before, Linda knew she had to be careful."

Robert McGuire, the English teacher, noticed the change in Linda as soon as she got back that fall.

"She looked puffy and gray, perfectly awful," he says. "If you'd jabbed a needle in her I don't think you would have gotten any reaction.

"I had her in English lit. that semester. She'd sit by the window with this expressionless, glazed look on her face. I brought this up at a faculty meeting; I wanted somebody to do something about it, but nobody would. So I said I'd wait until her parents came down for Parents Weekend in October and talk to them."

Parents Weekends, as Mr. McGuire recalls them, were "great big fantastic, drunken houseparties." He recalls intercepting Mrs. Fitzpatrick at one occasion over the weekend. "I told her I was seriously worried about Linda because she looked so gray and sick. Her mother said, 'Oh yes, doesn't she look awful; she looks older that I do.' She said it was probably her teeth and we ought to have the dentist look at them. Later in the weekend I talked to her father and he said 'Yes, I'm worried about her, too. I'm very unhappy about her grades. You're her English teacher, aren't you? Can't we get them up?'"

The Fitzpatricks went back to Greenwich that Sunday convinced Linda needed to do something about her appearance and her schoolwork, but confident that she was essentially sound. "She was such a nice, outgoing, happy girl," Mrs. Fitzpatrick said. "If anything changed, it happened awfully quickly."

During Parents Weekend, Linda Vanderbilt recalls, both Lindas told their families they were coming home the last weekend in October, and got them to sign the required permission. "We'd devised this system for getting away on our own. See, at the last moment, we called up and told our parents we had too much schoolwork and couldn't come. They didn't expect us, but the school thought we were going home. So we were free."

They caught a taxi to Baltimore and a train to New York, ducking into the ladies room to change from their prim Villager dresses into garb more appropriate for Greenwich Village. "That was the whole point of the weekend. Linda had been to the Village a couple of times in August after she got back from Bermuda and she really liked it. She'd met some people down there and she couldn't wait to get back."

After a night on the women's floor of the YMCA, they went down to the Village looking for Linda's friends. "We found them at The Cock and Bull, right next to the Cafe Wha! There was this twenty-three-year-old guy, David, from Brooklyn who used to come into the Village on weekends. And there was a colored guy from Jamaica who everybody just called Jamaica. They all played instruments. Dave played the harmonica, Jamaica played the bongo drums and there was another guy who played guitar.

"They were going to this party and they asked us to go with them. We walked down the street playing the instruments and then went up to this crummy apartment with no furniture. Nobody was smoking pot. Just drinking, a lot of drinking, but we didn't. Linda never drank. It got pretty rough. Two guys got into a fight in the hall. One of them had a knife. But the police came and broke it up.

"Linda met this guy at the party and went off with him. When I woke up the next morning, she wasn't there. I looked all over but couldn't find her. Finally, I just went down to the train and the first car I came to—there she was."

On the train, Linda told her roommate she wanted to leave school after the Thanksgiving weekend. "She said *she just didn't like school any more. She hated it. She had her friends, or what she thought were friends, in New York and she wanted to be on her own. She wanted me to come with her. But I didn't want to."*

Linda went home to Greenwich for Thanksgiving. Later her family insisted they never sensed anything was wrong. And they found it hard to believe that Linda would purposely deceive them. "Linda didn't have the guile to make things up," said Mrs. Fitzpatrick. "She wasn't tricky."

"Linda was two different people—one at home and one at school," Linda Vanderbilt says. *"That Thanksgiving she had her parents buy her a coach ticket to Baltimore. She was going to get off in New York, cash in the rest of the ticket and use the money to find a place in the Village. But when she got on the train Monday she was really sick. Maybe the idea frightened her a little. Anyway, in New York she went to a girl friend's house and the girl called Linda's parents, who told her to come home. The next morning she was feeling better and went right back to school. Her parents never guessed what she almost did."*

But soon Linda was off to the Village again. At least twice, her roommate recalls, she told her parents she was going to stay with another girl from school in New York. She went with the girl as far as Penn Station, then disappeared into the Village. After one of these weekends, she reported that she had met a boy she liked and slept with him.

But even with these deceptions, Linda couldn't get away many weekends. Oldfields doled out pleasure and pain on a complicated scale. Every two weeks, each girl was placed in one of four groups—A, B, C or D—on the basis of cards which faculty and staff members deposited in a padlocked "card box." Girls assigned to the upper groups were given certain privileges, those in the lower groups certain restrictions. Since Linda was usually in C or D group, she wasn't permitted to leave school often.

But she found a form of escape at the McGuires' house. Linda had always felt close to Bob McGuire, a lively, erudite man who seemed out of place at Oldfields. That fall she also got to know Bob's wife, Nancy, who *taught art. Unlike her art teacher the year before, Nancy praised and encouraged Linda and was repaid with gratitude and devotion. Linda also became friendly with the McGuires' daughter, Sue, a senior at Oldfields. So, increasingly that year, she spent her free time at the McGuires' house.*

"We had quite a group of girls who came over regularly—Saturdays, Sundays or for a couple of hours in the evenings," Bob McGuire says. "They liked to come and we liked having them. Oldfields was extremely uptight on rules and we weren't. We felt the girls ought to be kind, pleasant and polite, but we didn't go in for all the crappy discipline and formality."

The McGuires lived in a handsome old farmhouse with a two-story living room, a wallful of books and a big stone fireplace. They had decorated it with zest, covering the walls with Japanese puppets and masks, African sculpture, Chinese tapestries and Indian miniatures.

"Linda took a special fancy to the grotesque, exotic things around the house," Bob recalls. "We used to burn incense in the fireplace, and on Easter we'd have some of the girls over to fly Indian kites. Linda loved that sort of thing. She liked to talk about Oriental religion, Yoga, the supernatural."

Linda told people she was a witch. "She did what she called her 'witch trick,'" Bob says. "Her face would go expressionless; her eyes would get narrow, reptilian, with only the whites showing. Sort of an evil eye. The other girls would go hysterical when she turned it on them."

Linda went home for Christmas. By her family's account, it was a perfectly normal Greenwich holiday: the lawns covered with snow, a holly wreath tied with a red ribbon on the door, eggnog, heaps of presents under the tree and all the family around the table. "We always do things as a family," Mr. Fitzpatrick said.

"I don't think we realized then how much we meant to Linda," Bob McGuire says. "I think she regarded us a bit as surrogate parents. She didn't feel her parents loved her." That spring, Linda wrote a goodbye note in Sue McGuire's yearbook in which she described the elder McGuires as "the most wonderful parents in the world."

"She would have liked to be close to her parents,"

Linda Vanderbilt says, "but she didn't feel loved. She felt she couldn't tell her parents anything. She told me she'd been close to her father until he remarried, but then he was more aloof."

The McGuires say Linda occasionally talked about her "real mother," but they don't know how much she knew about Patricia. Once she told them her mother had "run off." And the McGuires say Linda remembered her father once told her, "Your mother was wild and you're just like her."

That spring, Linda began trying new drugs. Sue McGuire recalls the day she came over to their house to roast some banana peels she'd gotten from the school kitchen. "She smoked them, but she didn't get much out of it." Sue also remembers Linda saving tranquilizers and sleeping pills from the infirmary and then taking them all at once.

One day in art class, Nancy McGuire heard Linda and another girl whispering about LSD. "Linda was saying that everybody down in Greenwich Village was using it and how much she wanted to try it. I told them, 'Kids, that's extremely dangerous.'"

The only aspect of school which engaged Linda's interest that spring was her art work. "She had a real feeling for it," Nancy McGuire says. "She needed to express herself and painting seemed to do that for her."

Nancy was art adviser to Tidbit, the Oldfields literary magazine, and she persuaded Linda to contribute some drawings. Three were accepted, but they were very different from the flowers, carousels, and millponds elsewhere in the magazine. One showed a girl slumped on a barren landscape staring apathetically at a dollhouse, toys and dresses around her. Another was a full-page psychedelic abstract, an intricate maze suggesting waves, jellyfish and eyes. But the third was the most striking: five figures in various attitudes of despair—one with what appeared to be blood on its hands.

Her work for Tidbit helped win Linda the post of art editor for the following year's yearbook. It was Linda's first genuine distinction at Oldfields and she was pleased. But late that spring, Linda heard that the McGuires weren't coming back the next year. Suddenly, the yearbook job and her whole senior year seemed profoundly uninteresting.

"She started talking about going to California, particularly Haight-Ashbury," Linda Vanderbilt says. "Her half-brother worked out in Los Angeles and she said she wanted to go out and see him, then go up to Haight-Ashbury and never come back to school. She talked about that a lot that spring."

Oldfields let out on June 7. Linda told her parents she was going to stay with a friend for a few days, but instead she went to the Village again. This time, her parents sensed something was wrong. They called the friend's house, found Linda wasn't even expected and notified the police.

When Linda didn't show up for a few more days, they hired a private detective to find her. He had no luck, but on June 15 she called to say she was all right. Her father told her to come right home. Linda said she had no money, but Mr. Fitzpatrick told her to get a cab and they'd pay the driver when he got there. The driver was very nice and even bought her something to eat on the way out.

Linda got a lecture from her father and she promised never to go off like that again. Later, Mr. Fitzpatrick told someone he had had "a good talk" with his daughter and thought he had straightened things out.

"It's difficult to talk to Irv," says a friend. "When he has his mind made up he just won't listen. He's a rock-ribbed Republican—Goldwater and Nixon rather than Rockefeller—and when his son David turned out to be an ardent civil libertarian, went on the Selma march and all, Irv just wouldn't listen. I don't know how much he ever listened to Linda."

"Irv has a tendency to ignore disagreeable things," says another friend. "Unconsciously, I think, he felt Linda was a blight on the family honor—a throwback to her mother. And for a man so intent on being socially acceptable, that was too disagreeable. I think he just closed his eyes."

A few days after Linda got home, she went to her half-brother David's wedding. Mr. and Mrs. Fitzpatrick, Linda and Missy all drove down from Greenwich together. Linda didn't look well, but an outsider might not have sensed anything radically amiss. Even Holly, David's bride, found Linda only mildly upset. A designer and artist herself, Holly had a long chat with Linda at the reception. "She said all she wanted to do was paint. The other courses at school were all a bore and she didn't want to be distracted from art. I told her I'd felt just the same way when I was in school, that it was entirely natural."

Linda spent the rest of June in Greenwich. Then, on July 1, she joined the family for another vacation in Bermuda.

This time they rented a place on South Shore Road just up from Elbow Beach in Paget. It was a pretty pink stucco house surrounded by a low stone wall, terraced gardens and leafy bay grape trees. About twenty yards down a paved brick walk was a tiny pink-and-green cottage. Irving, Ann and Missy stayed in the house, with a maid the Fitzpatricks brought along to look after Missy. Linda lived alone in the cottage.

As the Fitzpatricks remembered it, Linda passed "a typical Bermuda vacation"—swimming in the crystal ocean, beach parties on the white sands, hours of painting, occasional shopping expeditions to Hamilton.

During the day the family spent much of its time at the Coral Beach and Tennis Club, one of the colony's most elegant and exclusive private clubs. Set on a high cliff, the club has a series of verandas and terraces where one may sunbathe, drink or dine while watching the waves splash on the broad coral beach hundreds of feet below. For the more active, there is swimming, boating, spearfishing, tennis on six finely groomed courts, and putting on the club's eighteen-hole green. Coral Beach is also the playspot for the island's most sophisticated young set—sons and daughters of well-to-do residents who go away to college in the States during the winters but flock back to the colony in the summers. It was here that Linda spent most of her sunlit hours that month.

Once night fell, Linda was free to go where she pleased.

A few evenings after she got to Bermuda, she was walking down Burnaby Street in Hamilton when she ran into Herbie, the boy she'd known the summer before. He took her to Elbow Beach again, where she met his friends: Peter, an eighteen-year-old dropout from a Connecticut boarding school; "Red," a seventeen-year-old wanderer; Curt and Charlie, English-born brothers; and Weed, so named because he once worked in a flower shop.

These five and several others formed a loose gang which hung out together on the beaches and lichen-covered rocks or in the island's jazz spots and bohemian bars. They were very different from the sophisticated, cool young men at the bar of the Coral Beach Club. Although most were from "good" Bermuda families, they hadn't followed the expected path to college in the States. They were not yet "hippies," for the hippie phenomenon was just coming to public attention in America. But they were dropouts from the well-groomed, British-styled "Bermudian way." Getting by on odd jobs or handouts from tourists, they grew their hair long, wore colorful clothes and cultivated a "hip" language. Most important, perhaps, they had ready access to good pot—from Jamaica, other Caribbean islands, or Mexico.

Linda had nibbled at the edges of this group the summer before, chiefly with Herbie. But in the summer of 1967 she became a regular member, at least after dark.

"We never saw her until after six P.M.—often not until nine or ten," Weed says. "She'd spend her day up at the Coral Beach Club, although she called the people up there 'a bunch of squares.' She had to have supper with her parents. They were nice and good to her, she said, although she liked her father more than her mother."

"She never wanted us to see her parents," says Peter. "That was a big thing with her. Once I went up to her house. I just went to the door and asked whether Linda was there. When she heard about it she got very upset and made me promise never to do it again. See, her relations with her parents were good as long as she played up to what they wanted her to be. And she wanted her parents to think the best of her. I don't think they ever knew what she was doing."

Most of the time, Linda would ride her motorbike down to Elbow Beach early in the evening and the group would congregate there. But sometimes they would come up and slip into the little cottage.

"There were these French doors in back, away from the main house," Red recalls. "You'd go through a gap

in the hedge there and tap lightly on the glass. She'd let you in. You could go up there any time during the night as long as you were quiet."

Most evenings, the group would walk along the beach, clamber on the rocks or climb trees. "Linda would do anything," Weed recalls. "Most girls, if you say 'Do something,' they'll think about it. She'd do it right away." Herbie is more blunt: "That girl didn't have any mind of her own; she'd do anything you asked."

Sometimes they hung out at the Hog Penny or the Paraquet, another bar. "But we didn't go down to Hamilton very often," Peter says. "The police gave us a tough time, particularly if we were on dope." And they were on dope most of the time. Peter says they smoked pot almost every evening.

"By then Linda was a real pothead," says Herbie. "When I'd seen her the summer before she mostly just talked about it. She was something of a phony then. But in the year between she'd obviously smoked a lot. She really liked it."

"Yeah, it really did things to her," Weed recalls. "I mean she was always kinda funny. She talked kinda funny, about unreal things. But when she was on pot it was more so. She had her mind on a faraway planet and her body here on earth."

It was usually Linda's money that bought pot for the whole group. "I never saw her with less than ten dollars," says Red. "She always had money and she was very generous with it. A twist cost six dollars. She'd buy one and give all the guys some. It was great."

But Linda brought them something besides money—a glimpse of the American hip world most of them had only read about. They all found Bermuda unbearably straight. "Nothing ever happens here," Peter says. But Linda had been to the Village perhaps a dozen times by then. She talked volubly about what she had done there —and perhaps some things she hadn't done.

"She said she'd met these two big hippies named Galahad and Groovy," Red recalls. "She seemed to know them pretty well. She told me 'When you go up there, just ask for Galahad and tell him I sent you.' And once she told me she and Galahad were married."

Peter recalls that Linda did some drawings of people she knew in the Village—among them both Groovy and

Galahad. "She gave me a few. She also gave me this picture of a weird face—more like a skeleton."

Peter was the most sensitive boy in the group. Pale and pensive, with a shock of long blond hair and horn-rimmed glasses, he called himself a nonconformist. After dropping out of school, he tried his hand at pottery, welded-metal sculpture and oil painting. He yearned to be an artist and, not surprisingly, he and Linda were drawn to each other immediately.

"I guess I must have seen her almost every day she was here. We talked a lot about life and art. She said I could send her the pottery I was doing and she'd sell it for me and take a percentage.

"Linda was the most beautiful person I've ever met. She had a personality too beautiful to be true. She talked about beautiful things."

Peter insists he never made love to Linda. Herbie admits sleeping with her several times in the little cottage. Others may have, too. The whole group often stayed in Linda's cottage smoking pot and listening to music until 2 or 3 A.M. and, several times, all night.

"We could do just about anything we wanted down there," Red says.

On July 31 the Fitzpatricks returned to Greenwich, where Linda spent most of August. Again, the family insisted, she was "the girl we knew and loved."

They said she spent most of her time painting in her studio at the back of the house, but found plenty of time for swimming with friends in the large robin's-egg-blue pool, playing the piano and sitting with Missy.

If Linda went to New York during August, the family said, it was "just a quick trip in and out—just for the day."

"Linda came down here every weekend in August, every moment she could get away from home," recalls Mark, a hippie from a small Michigan town who had an apartment at 620 East 11th Street that month.

Next door, at 622 East 11th Street, was the famed "crash pad" run by Ronald Johnson ("Galahad") and Jimmy Hutchinson ("Groovy"). Since late April hundreds of homeless hippies had stayed there and apparently Linda had been one. Although Galahad barely re-

members her, the stories she told friends in Bermuda suggest that she at least met Galahad and Groovy sometime that spring. Evidently they made a deep impression on her.

The first weekend after she got home from Bermuda found Linda down on 11th Street again—this time next door at Mark's place. Arlene, a sixteen-year-old girl from New Jersey, recalls: "She came in and started mumbling about how she wanted some grass or some acid. She looked sort of snobby to me. I didn't feel like talking to her because I thought she was some rich kid getting all involved in drugs. She just sat there talking in the air 'cause nobody was listening to her. She started getting really desperate, saying she'd gone some place to get acid but the guy wouldn't give her any. She was very upset, very depressed. After about forty-five minutes she got up and left."

Mark felt much the same way when he met her later that night. "You could tell she was raised rich just by looking at her face and hair. I know that face. I kind of stayed away from her 'cause she looked like one of those types, ahhh, with their noses in the air."

Linda made a better impression the next night. Mark, Arlene and some others were over at the Robinsons' place at 537 East 13th Street. Sue Robinson is a small shy girl who ran away from her home on Cape Cod that spring and married Dave, a gentle young man with a D. H. Lawrence beard who worked in a brassiere factory over on Sixth Avenue. They were among the "stable hippies" who served as anchors to the floating, fluctuating population in the East Village that summer. The two-room apartment where they lived with their two cats and posters of Bob Dylan, Timothy Leary and D. H. Lawrence served as another crash pad for hippies who stayed a night, a week or a month. Sometimes the coming and going kept Dave and Sue awake. Scrawled in pencil on the tin door was a sign that read NO VISITORS AFTER MIDNIGHT UNLESS BY APPOINTMENT PLEASE. *It was signed with a flower.*

"Linda just walked in that night with a guy named Pigeon," Sue Robinson recalls. "We called him Pigeon because he was kinda angelic-looking with soft blond hair and a face like sculpture. He was the first guy Linda went out with down here. She was tripping on acid that

night and she was very giggly and funny and nice. We liked her.

"*She and Pigeon went over to hear the Mothers of Invention at the Garrick Theater. She paid for it and she turned him on with some acid. And as they were coming back, it was raining and Pigeon fell down. When they got here, Linda said a great big forty-pound raindrop had fallen on Pigeon's back and knocked him over. She hallucinated this. We all laughed and then we smoked some grass and she started talking about witches and warlocks and things.*

"*Linda said she was a witch. She said she'd discovered it one day on a beach in Bermuda. She was just sitting there wishing she had some money and three dollar bills floated down from heaven. Then she thought how empty the beach was and how she wished someone was there. Suddenly a man appeared. She was sure she had supernatural powers.*"

Later that night, Linda and Pigeon and a girl named Judy all went out tripping. They were walking down the street when Linda stumbled over a broom. "Oh," she told Judy, "this is my lucky day. Now I can fly away."

Early that morning, Linda went home to Greenwich. But she was back the next weekend. This time she stayed with the Robinsons.

"*She was really nice to everybody," Susan recalls. "She'd come into town with thirty or forty dollars and she'd buy acid for people who needed some. She was always turning people on. Once, I guess it was that weekend, we all went out to a grocery store. When we got inside she went her way and we went ours. When we met in the checkout line, she had this great big bag of groceries and she said, 'This is for the house.' It was full of incredible things like expensive spaghetti and vegetables. She was a nut about health foods—fruit, orange juice, milk, tomatoes, things that give you vitamins.*"

Even Mark was impressed. "She turned out to be O.K. She wasn't snobby at all. She bought us all kinds of things."

Linda was less thoughtful about absent friends. Early in August, Peter wrote her from Bermuda enclosing fifty dollars and asking her to send him some acid. She and Dave went out and bought three tabs for ten dollars apiece. She took one, gave one to Dave and told every-

body she was putting the other aside for Peter. But she never sent it or any other. Late in August, Peter got a letter from Linda saying she'd been "burned" by a dealer who sold her some fake acid. She said she'd pay him back his fifty dollars after she got to San Francisco.

That tab of acid provided Linda with her most memorable trip. As Dave recalls it: "Linda was always getting burned with bum acid. So that night she kept saying, 'God, I just hope this is good.' We were out in Tompkins Park and we dropped it right there. Forty-five minutes later, around midnight, we were off. The stuff was good.

"We walked over to Mark's pad on 11th Street and picked him up, then we went back to Tompkins Park and swung on the swings awhile, then over to Cooper Union Square, where we had this very good discussion with a drunk. By then we were really flying."

Mark, who didn't have any acid that night, remembers it all clearly. "Linda giggled a lot. Every time she took acid she laughed her ass off. But that night—wow!—she was really gone. She ran around between cars and stuff, pretending she was a spy. She'd run into a store and peer out at me through this little window in the door."

At one of the stores they bought some Tootsie Rolls because Linda wanted to see if she got "chocolate rushes" on acid. "She had this idea that if you ate Tootsie Rolls on acid you'd get these rushes of chocolate taste. It kinda worked. So there we were walking along 12th Street and Avenue B eating Tootsie Rolls and getting rushes."

When they got back to the Robinsons', Mark recalls, Dave sat down and started smoking. "He'd take some smoke into his mouth and let it trickle out while his eyes got real weird, you know, really freaking around. Linda started screaming, 'Oooh! Don't do that. You look like a demon! You look like Satan!' "

They freaked around all night. "At eight A.M. I went to sleep," Dave recalls. "Linda took the subway up to Grand Central and got on the train to Greenwich. She still must have been flying when she got home."

That week in Greenwich, Mrs. Fitzpatrick was getting Linda ready for school. "We bought her almost an entire new wardrobe," she recalled, "and Linda even agreed to get her hair cut."

For months Mr. Fitzpatrick had complained about Linda's hair, which flowed down over her shoulders, but Linda didn't want to change it. Then, at the end of August, she abruptly agreed. "We went to Saks Fifth Avenue and had the hairdresser give her a kind of Sassoon blunt cut, short and full. She looked so cute and smart. Hardly a hippie thing to do."

The first day of school was only ten days off on September 2, when Linda told her stepmother she didn't want to go back to Oldfields. She wanted to live and paint in the Village."

"We couldn't have been more surprised," Mrs. Fitzpatrick said.

"Linda said her favorite teacher and his wife weren't coming back. She just adored them and couldn't face going back to school if they weren't there. She said there wasn't anything more she could learn about art at Oldfields. They'd offered to set up a special course for her there, but she didn't want more courses. She just wanted to paint. She thought she'd be wasting her time at school."

Linda and her stepmother talked for nearly two hours that Saturday morning of Labor Day weekend. Then Mrs. Fitzpatrick told her husband, who at first was determined that Linda should finish school.

"But we talked about it with all the family and friends all through the weekend," Mr. Fitzpatrick recalled. "Finally, on Sunday night, we gave Linda our reluctant permission, though not our approval." Linda left for New York the next morning.

The Fitzpatricks' minds were eased when Linda assured them she had made respectable living arrangements. "She told us she was going to live at the Village Plaza Hotel, a very nice hotel on Washington Place, near the university, you know," her stepmother said.

" 'I'll be perfectly safe,' she kept saying. 'It's a perfectly nice place with a doorman and television.' She said she'd be rooming with a girl named Paula Bush."

The Village Plaza, 79 Washington Place, has no doorman. A flaking sign by the tiny reception desk announces TELEVISION FOR RENTAL *amid a forest of other signs:* NO REFUNDS, ALL RENTS MUST BE PAID IN ADVANCE, NO CHECKS CASHED, NO OUTGOING CALLS FOR TRANSIENTS. *"Sure, I remember Linda," said the stooped desk clerk.*

"But Paula Bush? There wasn't no Paula Bush. It was Paul Bush."

Riffling through a pile of stained and thumb-marked cards, he came up with one that had Linda Fitzpatrick's name inked at the top in neat Greenwich Country Day School penmanship. Below it in pencil was written, "Paul Bush. Bob Brumberger."

"We never met Paula," Mrs. Fitzpatrick said. "But Linda told us she was a twenty-two-year-old receptionist from a good family, a very nice girl."

Paul Bush is the son of a television repairman in Holly, Michigan, a small town between Detroit and Flint. When he got out of high school, Paul worked for a while in a tool-and-die shop but decided "there wasn't that much happening" in Holly and took off for Los Angeles. He "bummed around" southern California for a few months, then came back to Holly, where he met Mark at a dance. Mark told him about all the groovy things happening in Greenwich Village. So, on August 15, 1967, he hitchhiked to New York, where he soon became known as "a way-out hippie" who carried a live lizard named Lyndon on a string around his neck.

Paul joined the crowd sleeping on the floor at the Robinson's place and it was there he met Linda. At first, he recalls, she struck him as "some rich girl who got her kicks by spending money on us."

Then, one day late that month, Linda, Paul and Bob Brumberger, a boy from New Jersey, got to talking. "She told us she was thinking of moving down to the Village and getting a place. Brumberger and I started joking around with her. We said we'd go in on it with her. We were just kidding, but she got real serious. She said, 'No, I mean it, I really want to get away from my parents.' So we said we'd do it."

Sue Robinson had a different version. "Paul and Bob didn't have a place. Linda had all this money. So they talked her into coming down here so they could move in with her. They said, 'Come on, move down, it'll be great.'"

Whoever took the initiative, Linda, Paul and Bob decided that last week in August to get a place together. Since Linda had to go back to Greenwich, Paul and Bob agreed to find an apartment during the week.

They concentrated their search in the West Village.
"We didn't want a place on the East Side," Paul recalls.
"Linda said it was too dirty and there were too many
bugs over there. Also, it had to be a place her mother
wouldn't worry about."

But they couldn't find an apartment. They looked for a
couple of days, but everything was too expensive. Linda
had told Paul she could give them ninety dollars for the
first month's rent and Paul had fifteen dollars. All the
apartments around Washington Square ran much more
than that.

One afternoon, as they were wandering through the
square, they noticed the Village Plaza Hotel on Wash-
ington Place. "We'd never really thought about a hotel
room before," Paul says, "but we went in and they said
they'd let us have a room for a hundred and twenty dol-
lars a month."

Linda had given Paul her telephone number in
Greenwich, and he called her that Saturday morning to
say they'd found a place. She said that was fine, but her
father was in the hospital and she might not be able to
come. Her father wasn't in the hospital. Presumably Linda
was protecting herself in case her parents balked when
she told them her plans a few hours later.

Her fears were unfounded. On Monday, Labor Day,
she went to New York, looked at the room, and gave her
approval. She paid ninety dollars, Paul added his fifteen
and they owed the hotel fifteen dollars. Paul and Bob
moved in that night. Linda went home to pack and came
down the next day with a suitcase, her portable stereo
and a sackful of records.

The desk clerk had promised to set up a folding cot
in the corner, but it never arrived. So that night, Lin-
da, Paul and Bob slept together in the sway-backed dou-
ble bed.

"When Linda told us she was staying at the Village
Plaza, that sounded familiar," Mrs. Fitzpatrick said. "I
thought it was one of those nice hotels near our dentist's
office."

"You want to see the room?" the desk clerk said.
"There're some new people up there now, but I guess it'll
be O.K."

The elevator was out of order. The stairs were dark and narrow, heavy with the reek of marijuana. A knock, and the door to 504 opened.

Against one of the light-green walls was a peeling gray dresser, with the upper-left drawer missing. Scrawled on the mirror above the dresser in what looked like eyebrow pencil was "Tea Heads Forever," and in lighter pencil, "War Is Hell." Red plastic flowers hung from an overhead light fixture. The bathroom, directly across the hall, was shared with four other rooms.

"Would you like to see Linda's room?" Mrs. Fitzpatrick asked, leading the way up the thickly carpeted stairway.

"That used to be her room," she said, pausing for a moment on the second floor to point into an airy bedroom with a white canopied bed. "Then she began playing all those records teenagers play these days and she asked to move upstairs so she could make all the noise she wanted."

On the third floor, Mrs. Fitzpatrick opened the red curtains in a large room. "Red and white were Linda's favorite colors; she thought they were gay," her stepmother said, taking in the red-and-white-striped wallpaper, the twin beds with red bedspreads, the red pillow with white lettering—"Decisions. Decisions. Decisions."

Orange flashed here and there—in the orange-and-black tiger on the bed ("That's for her father's college, Princeton; we're a Princeton family") and in the orange G's framed on the wall, athletic awards from Greenwich Country Day School.

Above her dresser, a NO PARKING ANY TIME sign hung next to a certificate from the Auxiliary of the Greenwich Hospital Association recognizing Linda's service as a candy striper in 1964.

On the shelves, between a ceramic collie and a glass Bambi, were Edith Hamilton's *The Greek Way*, Agatha Christie's *Murder at Hazelmoor* and Ian Fleming's *Casino Royale*. Records were stacked neatly on a bottom shelf, among them Eddie Fisher's "Tonight," Joey Dee's "Peppermint Twist" and Rick Nelson's "A Wonder Like You."

"Linda put her little portable stereo on the floor next to the door," Paul recalls. "She had some really groovy

sides—Country Joe and the Fish, the Grateful Dead, the Stones, Donovan. We used to sit around up there and listen to 'em while we smoked."

They didn't do much else up there. Paul and Bob both insist they never had any sex with Linda, never even wanted to. Bob says she sometimes reminded him of Popeye the Sailor Man because of her funny chin and sometimes of a "pear on legs" because she was so chubby. Paul is more laconic: "She just never appealed to me."

But Linda had her own plans. The Robinsons assume she slept with Pigeon and "the kid from Boston." She once told Pigeon that she wanted to try intercourse on acid because Tim Leary said a woman could have "a thousand orgasms" that way. Then there was Ed, a tall, red-bearded hippie with a leather strap around his forehead whom Linda took up to her Village Plaza room several times during September.

"She had lots of men up there all the time," says the desk clerk, "anybody off the street—the dirtiest bearded hippies she could find."

"Linda was never terribly boy-crazy," Mrs. Fitzpatrick said. "She was very shy. When a boy got interested in her, she'd almost always lose interest in him. She got a proposal in August from a very nice boy in Arizona. She told me, 'He's very nice and I like him, but he's just too anxious.' The boy sent flowers for the funeral. That was very thoughtful."

Toward the end of her first week at the Village Plaza, Linda told Paul and Bob that her mother might be coming down that weekend. She suggested they stay elsewhere. Bob was already spending most of his nights at another pad, but Paul was annoyed. He recalls:

"One night I came back and there was this sign on the door: DO NOT ENTER UNDER ANY CIRCUMSTANCES— EVEN MY MOTHER. *That kinda pissed me off, so I beat on the door, kept beating on it until she came and opened up. There was that tall kid with the red beard in bed naked, and Linda kept shouting, 'Didn't you read the sign on the door? Get out of here.' I said something about it was my room too, but she yelled, 'I pay the rent and I want to spend the night here with this*

kid. So get out of here.' So I left. I don't know what she would have done if her mother had come down there."

Mrs. Fitzpatrick never showed up. "She wanted to go," a friend recalls. "She felt she ought to see where Linda was staying. But Irving wouldn't let her go. He said he didn't want her going into a neighborhood like that."

The Fitzpatricks said they were reassured about Linda's life in the Village because she told them she had a job at eighty dollars a week making posters for a shop called Poster Bazaar. Later she called and said she'd switched to a place called Imports Ltd. for eighty-five dollars a week and was making posters on weekends.

"She sounded so excited and happy when she called," Mrs. Fitzpatrick recalled. "I was happy for her. I thought she was going to be a career girl."

Nobody in the Village has ever heard of Poster Bazaar and Linda's friends there assume she made up the name so her parents wouldn't worry.

At 177 Macdougal Street is a shop called Fred Leighton's Mexican Imports Ltd. where, the records show, Linda worked for two dollars an hour selling dresses for three days—September 11, 12, and 13. On the third day she was fired. "She was always coming in late and they just got fed up with her," a salesgirl recalls.

Before she left, she asked the manager not to tell her parents she'd been fired if they called. "They didn't call," the manager says.

From then on, Linda supported herself largely by panhandling around Washington Square.

"She kinda got a kick out of begging," Susan recalls. "You know, I think she came down here to escape the rich life at home, to experience being poor."

"Yeh, she thought it was cool and funny," Mark says. "She was pretty good at it, too. She'd pick on all the old men that looked rich. They used to give her money because she was so nice and all. She could get two or three dollars in change in a couple of hours. Enough to buy food with."

A few times, she helped one of her Village friends sell pot. "We'd go over to the square and she'd keep the pot in her purse while I went around to find customers. That way, even if they were cops, I couldn't get busted.

After I made sure who they were I'd go back and get it from her."

But even while panhandling or peddling dope, there was still a "rich-girl aura" about Linda.

The desk clerk at the Village Plaza, who disapproved of Linda's behavior, recalls "she didn't pay me any attention, but, you know, she never answered back real snappy like some of the other girls. She had something— I don't know—class."

Susan recalls that Linda always wore "very expensive Greenwich clothes." Her favorite outfit was white wide-wale corduroy slacks and a custom-made tailored blouse. In bed, even with Paul and Bob, she wore pastel pajamas.

She told many different stories about her family, although each one emphasized how rich they were. She told Mark that she lived with her father, "a big advertising man," in upstate New York. She told Susan she lived on a Long Island estate. Adele and several others say Linda told them her family had a town house near Central Park.

And she often talked about making big money herself. "She had a thing about money," David recalls. "Once she told me she wanted to get a job with Hallmark cards drawing those little cartoons. She said she'd make forty thousand dollars doing that and then rent a big apartment on the Upper East Side and invite all her hippie friends up there."

"We're a great card-exchanging family," Cindy said. "Whenever the occasion arose—birthdays, holidays, illnesses—Linda would make up her own cards and illustrate them with cute little pictures of people and animals."

From a pile on the hall table, Cindy picked out a card with a picture of a frizzy-haired girl and an inked inscription: "Please get well 'cause I miss ya, love Linda XOX." In the same pile was a Paris street scene in pastels, two forest scenes made with oils rolled on with a Coke bottle, and several other gentle landscapes. "Linda was experimenting with all sorts of paints and techniques," Cindy said.

"You want to see some of the paintings she did down here?" asked Susan Robinson as she went to a pile of

papers in the corner and returned with five ink draw-ings on big sketching-pad sheets.

The drawings were psychedelic: distorted women's faces, heavily lidded eyes, dragons, devils, all hidden in a thick jungle of flowers, leaves and vines, interspersed with phrases in ornate script: Forever the Mind, Flyin High, Tomorrow Will Come.

Linda rarely discussed her Village world at home. Her family recalls only two occasions.

Early in August, Mr. Fitzpatrick read a newspaper story about Galahad and announced his "disdain" for the flamboyant hippie. Linda defended him.

But her father remembered that a few weeks later he and Linda watched a CBS special about hippies in Haight-Ashbury. "I expressed my abhorrence for the whole thing and her comments were much like mine," he said. "I don't believe Linda really had anything to do with the hippies. I don't believe she was attracted to them."

Her friends say Linda was fascinated by Haight-Ash-bury and talked endlessly about going there. Late in Sep-tember she may have made it.

About mid-September she left the Village Plaza, al-though she'd paid rent for the whole month. Paul be-lieves she was evicted for having too many men in her room. The desk clerk is vague about that. But he re-members standing on the steps as Linda carried her bags out. "I guess I caused you a lot of trouble," she said. "Oh, it wasn't any trouble, really," he replied.

After that, she dropped out of sight for almost two weeks.

In the first week of October, the Fitzpatricks got a card postmarked Knightstown, Indiana, a small town thirty miles east of Indianapolis. Mrs. Fitzpatrick did not want to show the card because "it was the last thing I've got which Linda touched." But, she said, it read roughly, "I'm on my way to see Bob [Linda's half-broth-er who is a Los Angeles attorney and an agent for major rock groups]. Offered a good job painting posters in Berke-ley. I love you. I will send you a poster. Love, Linda."

About the same time, a girl who identified herself as

Linda telephoned Bob's office in Los Angeles, but was told he was in San Francisco. She never called back.

On October 2, Susan Robinson heard a knock on her tin door. When she opened it, there was Linda standing in the dim hallway with a piece of coffeecake in her hand. "Is it O.K. if I eat my breakfast in here and wash up?" Linda asked. Susan said, "Sure."

Between bites of coffeecake, Linda told Susan she'd been in Haight-Ashbury. As Susan recalls the conversation, Linda said she'd stayed only two days because it was a very bad scene. "She said, 'All the good people have gone up into the hills and bought farms. The only people left are speed freaks. The only thing you can get there is speed, cut with baking soda and quinine. It's really cruddy.'"

Linda also told her she'd met two warlocks on the trip. "She said they could snap their fingers and make light bulbs pop. She told me one of the warlocks took her mind apart and scattered it all over the room and then put it back together again. 'Ever since,' she said, 'I feel the warlock owns me.'"

"I never heard Linda talk about Buddhism or Hinduism or any of that supernatural stuff," Cindy said. "I don't think she even knew what it was."

"Pepsi" says he was one of Linda's warlocks. A former sailor, musician, restaurant owner and dope peddler, he is a scrawny fellow in his late twenties with long sandy hair, a scruffy beard, wire-rimmed glasses, Levis and long suede boots with a fringe on top.

He says he picked Linda up in Indianapolis before she reached California. "My buddy and I ran into her in a club called the Glory Hole. She was dead set on going to California and she was working all the truck stops for rides.

"You could see right away she was a real Meth Monster, a real spaced-out speed freak. I told her she didn't need to go to California, that she'd get even more messed up in the meth scene out there. So she came on back to New York with us. We were two days getting back—I got busted in Pennsylvania for driving without a license —and then she put up with me and my buddy in a pad

on Avenue B. She was supposed to keep it clean, but all she ever did was sit around on her fat ass. It sounds like I'm knocking her, but I'm not. She was a good kid if she hadn't been so freaked out on meth. She had a lot of, what do you call it—potential. Sometimes she was a lot of fun to be with. We took her on a couple of spiritual séances, and we went on the Staten Island ferry one day at dawn and surfing down at Jones Beach about eleven at night.

"She had this real weird imagination, but she was like talking in smaller and smaller circles. A couple of times she thought me and my partner were part of the Syndicate, and sometimes she thought we were professional mind-fuckers, and asked us if we had ever taken any courses in how to fuck up people's minds. She'd go on with all these weird fantasy worlds. I guess that's what brought her onto the drug scene, all those fantasies. After a while I got so I didn't even listen to her any more.

"She was supposed to be this great artist, but she really wasn't much good yet. I mean she could have been good if she hadn't been such a Meth Monster. But then it was just teeny-bopper stuff—drawing one curving line, then embellishing it—yeah, kind of paisley."

"Linda's whole life was art," Mrs. Fitzpatrick said. "She had a burning desire to be something in the art world. I knew how she felt. I wanted to be a dancer or an artist when I was young, too."

Linda told Susan she thought she was pregnant. "She didn't know who the father was. It was probably Ed's. But she didn't want to have the baby. She was afraid about what LSD might do to it. Anyway, she said she was too young to have a child."

"She'd ball absolutely anybody," says Pepsi. "She'd gotten the clap a while before and she was raped by some spade, but that didn't faze her at all."

"Yeh, she had a lot of spade friends," Paul Bush recalls. "She liked spades. She used to go down to the Cave on Avenue A all the time—that was a real spade hangout."

About this time her friends began seeing her on the street with Groovy. David saw them together in the Cave on Thursday night, October 5.

Friday night, he saw her again in The Something, a snack bar on Avenue A. "I was in there waiting to get a sandwich. She saw me and came running in. All of a sudden she said, 'Oh. Gosh. I forgot what I was going to tell you.' So she went running out again. I sat down to eat my sandwich and I saw her outside. I sort of smiled at her and she giggled, that childish, ridiculous giggle of hers. That was the last I saw of her."

Linda spent part of Saturday lying in a sleeping bag in front of the Psychedelicatessen with Groovy.

About 10 P.M. on Saturday, Pepsi saw her with Groovy in front of the Cave. "She was stoned. She said she'd shot up a grain and a half and was pretty high. I was really mad because I'd been trying to get her off that stuff. I told her to go home. She said, 'No. You're trying to bum-kick my trip. I'm with Groovy. He's a tin-man.' She'd wind him up and he'd do this stupid number with his arms flapping around. So I left them."

Three hours later, Linda and Groovy were dead— their nude bodies stretched out on the concrete floor of the boiler room of a tenement at 169 Avenue B. Their heads were beaten in with bricks.

On September 2, 1969, Thomas Dennis, a twenty-seven-year-old drifter from Philadelphia, pleaded guilty to killing Groovy. On November 5, 1969, Donald Ramsey, a twenty-eight-year-old ex-convict and black nationalist, pleaded guilty to killing Linda. No motive has been established.

GROOVY

On dusky brown summer mornings, as the big trailer trucks snort toward Woonsocket, the sour-sweet smells of baking dough mix with the diesel fumes over Dexter Street. At the open windows of Gorman's Bakery ("Home of Gorman's Fortified Bread"), men whose beefy forearms are covered with white powder stand sniffing another day in Central Falls, Rhode Island. The steam from the ovens, the choking powder, the heat slowly rising from the macadam roadway, the fumes from the trucks grinding gears and hissing brakes, all work up a powerful thirst in a man. So one figure raises a ghostly white hand in a window, beckons to a boy sitting across the street on the stoop of a three-story frame house and asks him to bring three Seven-Ups from the soda fountain at Barry's News Store down the block.

The boy nods and moves off down the street in his peculiar stride, bouncing up and down on the balls of his feet, bent sharply forward from the waist, his hands jammed deep in the pockets of his brown leather jacket, his head drawn down between his hunched-up shoulders like one of the big brown turtles in Scott's Pond. A few minutes later he comes bouncing back, a paper tray with the three Seven-Ups balanced precariously on his head, his silver harmonica flashing in his mouth, playing "Fingertips" to an audience of grinning, powder-white bakers.

This is how one of Gorman's bakers remembered James "Groovy" Hutchinson a few weeks after his nude body was found beside that of his friend Linda Fitzpatrick in a Greenwich Village basement.

In the East Village Groovy was an all-too-easy luminary, reflecting the gleams in the eyes of a thousand runaways. But to have starred in Central Falls, before an audience of bakers lined up in the windows of a great brick box, among the trucks and the filling stations and the railroad track and the junkyards—that may have been his finest hour.

Central Falls is the very essence of a New England mill town come on evil days. Wedged onto a sandy slab where the Seekonk and Blackstone rivers meet just north of Providence, it lies at the southern end of the Blackstone valley, once a center of New England's textile industry. Towns like Saylesville, Valley Falls, Quinnville and Albion all had their big sooty brick mills which somehow managed to spin out a fine white yarn and cloth, giving no hint of its grimy origin. But after World War II most of the mills moved south, drawn by cheap labor and new power, leaving behind them stagnant pools of unemployment and depression.

With the mills gone, Central Falls has eighty-one manufacturing plants left, employing only 3,812 persons. Corning Glass and the Standard Romper Co. are the only major plants in town; the rest are mostly small companies lodged in converted mills and producing machines, paper, shoes and food products. There are jobs for the young, but men over forty, who spent their best years in the textile mills, find it hard to get work. Central Falls has a welfare caseload of 1,700, the fourth largest in the state, although there are eight communities with bigger populations. The city has steadily lost population since 1930, when it had 25,898 persons; in 1965 it had 18,677. Births continue to decline every year while deaths increase.

One thing Central Falls has plenty of is liquor licenses—sixty-six, or one for every 283 persons—and there is a bar on nearly every corner, most of them rough workingmen's taverns that sell more beer than Scotch and more Scotch than gin. It's a tough city too, sometimes called Little Chicago, known particularly for its numerous bookies, who periodically draw a futile crackdown from the district attorney. Other than drinking, playing the horses or perhaps bingo, there isn't much to do in Central Falls. There's one movie house and one bowling alley. Central Falls calls itself "the friendly city with the forward look," but one teenager says, "You can look right through it."

That's the way Central Falls apparently likes it, though. The city elected the same mayor—Raymond J. Morissette—five straight times; in November 1967, after his latest victory, his son said, "It's a little like the way it was with the New York Yankees."

There are only four business streets of significance in Central Falls, enclosing most of the city's 1.27 square-mile area. "If you want to find a guy," explains one teenager, "you drive down Broad, left on Hunt, left on Dexter and then left on Clay. If they ain't there, they're out of town." In between are row after row of three-story frame houses where the conglomerate people of Central Falls live—about half of French Canadian origin, 27 percent Irish and English, 10 percent Polish, 5 percent Syrian and 2½ percent Portuguese.

Jimmy Hutchinson's family is Portuguese on his mother's side; and his mother, Esther, and her large family were the chief influences in his young life. Esther was one of eleven children born to Mr. and Mrs. Mandel Joseph of Lincoln, Rhode Island, where Mr. Joseph worked in a mill. While she was still young, the family moved to Pawtucket, just across the New Haven Railroad tracks from Central Falls, and it was there at nineteen, in the midst of World War II, that she married Joseph I. Hutchinson, then a sailor stationed at Quonset Point. After the war the Hutchinsons moved to Pawtucket, where Esther helped support the family by making jewelry.

Esther was a dark-haired, well-built girl with Mediterranean good looks and a Mediterranean temperament to match. After her divorce from Mr. Hutchinson, she married a truckdriver named Bob Benoit, but they separated six or seven years ago.

Esther had two children by Mr. Hutchinson: George, born in 1944, was adopted while still an infant by the sister of Mr. Hutchinson's sister-in-law; and Jimmy, born February 14, 1946, in Pawtucket. She also had two children by Mr. Benoit: Brenda, now thirteen years old, and Ronald, now six.

The family lived in Pawtucket until Jimmy was about five and then moved to a comfortable old frame house on Tiffany Street in Central Falls. Jimmy went to kindergarten at the Kendall Street school and then on to first grade in 1952. It was that year that Jimmy's "learning problems," as the school system called them, began showing up. His performance in the first grade was so poor that he had to repeat the grade the next year. The following year, when the family moved back to Pawtucket for a brief stay, Jimmy went on to the second grade and then through the third grade at the High Street school, but school records show that he was a "low achiever, a borderline student, with difficulty in reading, spelling and comprehension." They also show a "below-average I.Q." A school official said Jimmy evidently "tried hard, did what he could with what he had, but he didn't have much."

So when the family moved back to Central Falls in 1956, the school department there assigned Jimmy to an "ungraded class" at the Hedley Avenue school. Miss Sara Kerr, who was the principal and school psychologist at Hedley Avenue, explains that the ungraded class was a remedial program to prepare "underachieving children" to return to the normal grade progression. "As soon as Jimmy's achievement matched his age we would have put him back in a regular grade," Miss Kerr said. But it never did, and he remained in the ungraded class for five long years.

Miss Kerr, a birdlike, sharp-featured woman with blue-tinted white hair which stands up sharply from her head, is now retired from the school system, but she spoke warmly about her former student as she perched on an ornate armchair in her Victorian parlor a few blocks from the Hedley Avenue school.

"Jimmy, poor Jimmy, was emotionally disturbed, a badly upset boy—and that came out in a severe reading problem as well as some behavioral problems. He had no motivation, no desire to learn and he was always disturbing the classes. I never found any meanness in him. We had some kids who killed flies and tortured them, but Jimmy never did anything like that. He was just clowning. But the teachers couldn't put up with his capers so they'd send him to me.

"I can remember him, oh so well, standing there in the doorway of my office. He was always so well dressed —beautiful clothes—no little girl could have been more fastidious. He'd just stand there so neat and clean-looking and I'd say, "Oh, Jimmy, not again!" and he'd start to cry, wiping his eyes on his sleeve. And we'd sit and talk, and I'd ask him why he couldn't pay attention and do his work. He'd just nod and sniffle and say, 'Yes, Miss Kerr.' He was a poor bewildered boy.

"One night I kept him after school. I was determined that he was going to do a single little arithmetic problem, but he couldn't do it, he just couldn't.

"I can assure you for those five years he was never neglected or ignored; he was getting the very best remedial education available. The class was small—fifteen kids —and they had a teacher specially trained for remedial work. We worked with him and worked with him to erase his deficiencies until I guess we finally came to the conclusion that there were just impediments to academic learning."

Jimmy also posed an increasingly difficult discipline problem. Once he called Miss Kerr a "purple-haired monster," referring to her blue-rinsed hair. Another time, one of his teachers was so exasperated she picked up a long wooden pointer and went after him. Jimmy grabbed it, broke it into little pieces over his knee and handed the pieces back to her. By the end of his fifth year Jimmy was fifteen and already bigger than most of the other kids in the ungraded class. As Miss Kerr recalls it, the superintendent came over one day and said, "Miss Kerr, you've had it. We've got to try something else with this boy."

The "something else" was the Butler Psychiatric Hospital Center, where Jimmy was an outpatient off and on for a year. His teachers agree that Jimmy was emotionally disturbed, that all his clowning was his way of saying Notice me, pay attention. But by the second year at the Hedley Avenue school he was already getting most of his attention outside school—in a gang of which he was the informal but undisputed leader.

There was Ernie St. Angelo, a hulking boy with a barrel chest and huge hands which could squeeze a Narragansett beer can flat; there was his brother, Steve St. Angelo, a thin, dark-haired youth with a sensitive face; there were the Zenone brothers, Danny and Jimmy; Russell Wilson, Dave Quebec, Eddie Marco, Gary Larossee and sometimes Jimmy's brother, George, down from North Attleboro.

But of them all, Ernie St. Angelo was closest to Jimmy, more like a brother than George was. "Every day after school," Ernie recalls, "we used to go down to his house on Tiffany Street. Hutchy's Corner, we used to call it, 'cause we called him Hutchy—that's one of the things we called him. And Hippity-hop too, because of the funny way he walked, bouncing up and down like that—oh, yeh, and Bouncy, we called him Bouncy too."

Jimmy collected nicknames the way other kids collected rocks or bottle caps. Groovy, the last one, came much later, the casual gift of a casual friend in New Orleans. But in Central Falls there was Jungle Jim, a name he got after he cut another kid with a machete. There was Gander "because he used to goose guys." There was Steve Ribs, which the gang started calling him one day when he hung on a vine over Scott's Pond making the Tarzan call—"Aaaahhh"—with his puny chest stuck out and ribs showing all over. There was Rock Hutchinson, which he gave himself one night, a night Eddie Marco, another gang member, remembers well: "We useta go drinking on Friday nights. One night we got all dressed up. He had bought some new clothes, a new trench coat and these new square shades. So we come down the street and he says, 'Dig me. I'm Rock Hutchinson. See, girls. You've got a chance to go out with Rock Hutchinson now!' And everything. Ah, he was too much!"

Jimmy, the gang remembers, would do anything and would usually carry the rest of them along. "We wouldn't of ever done this stuff unless Hutchy done it first," Ernie St. Angelo recalls. "You wouldn't see him one day. And next day he'd come and tell ya what he done. And you'd say, 'No, you didn't,' and he'd say, 'C'mon, I'll show ya.' And he'd do it, too. He'd do anything. I'll tell ya he was a nut. A nut! But he was funny. If somebody was on their deathbed and they don't want to see nobody, the one I would advise them to see would of been Hutchinson because I tell you he would of had 'em out of that bed. He was that funny. He was funny not being funny. Even when he got mad the faces he used to make was funny. Serious he was funny.

"I'll tell ya the kind of the things he used to do. When we were real young we useta go down to the dump. There was this bum who useta live down there, Slim the Bum. He was a real dirty old guy living in this shack, a shack made out of doors off old houses they tore down.

We was all scared of him because he was kind of crazy, sort of trapped in the head, you know. We used to throw stones at him and watch him skip. But not Hutchy, not old Hutchy. Hutchy would go up there and shake hands with him, ya know? Pat him on the back and say, 'How ya doing, Slim. How's the wife and kids?' It useta really break us up. One day I says, 'Jimmy, why do you go down there and do that stuff with Slim?' and he says, 'Aw, Slim's my buddy.'

"There just wasn't anything he wouldn't do. I remember when he was 'bout thirteen or fourteen, we started going down to the slaughterhouse to ride the wild pigs. The first time I ever went was with my cousin. So I spread the word around Central Falls. I know a place we can go and ride pigs. So when Hutchy heard this, he never rode any pigs before, but he says, 'Come on, let's go.'

"Well, see, it was a whole day. You'd hop the freight train in Central Falls. And then you'd go up to Pawtucket where it stopped and you'd hop the big freight coming by and that would take you right out to Providence and you'd get off when it slowed down after the lights and go over to the slaughterhouse. Now they got these pigs all in this big pen waiting to be slaughtered and they'd go nuts because they can sense the smell of death coming from the other pigs being killed. See, you ought to watch out. 'Cause they have the male and the female pigs. Now, if you ride the female pigs it's all right, but if you ride a male pig, that's all over. They'll bite you to death.

"Well, Hutchy, he didn't care. He got on this big male, must of been about three hundred pounds. They got some big pigs down there. He rode him all around. And then he got off it, and he started skiing in the mush, you know, the shit. We useta do that. You'd grab their tail and just ride on your feet. And right in the center of the floor was this big hole, a hole about four feet deep where everything drains into it. And Hutchy was skiing by it and he went right into it, right up to his waist. He come home all stinking and everything and his mother says, 'Where were you?' and he says, 'Oh, I was down to the stables, riding the horses.' And she sniffs again and she says, 'They was no horses.' Oh, he was too much!"

Now the gang was really off, one Hutchy exploit tripping on the heels of another.

"I remember one time he bought a case of Ruppert's," Ernie St. Angelo said. "He used to love Ruppert's beer. So he put it down on the ground and he had a stick, one of those voodoo sticks they used to have, you know, with those shrunken heads. He jammed this stick into the case and he gets down on his knees and everything and he goes, 'Oh, Ruppert's Goddess. Oh, Ruppert's Goddess. You're so good to me.' He went to extremes. Anything you did with him, you'd try and keep up with him, you know, so he wouldn't make you look stupid. But mostly you couldn't. He'd start joking and you'd start joking to keep up with him and before you know it you're running out of jokes and this kid's still going, got a book in his head or something.

"One time we was out in Lincoln Woods at this park they have out there. And there were these four guys singing round the snack bar. They was pretty good, you know, maybe semipros, and they had everybody gathered round them listening. So Hutchy, he had these bongo drums, and he went over and sat down across the path on the grass, and he started playing the drums. He wasn't so good, really, but he played real hot, and these people round the singers started coming over one by one. He just took them away. Finally, the singers gave up too and came over. At first they was kinda mad, but then they started laughing and said, 'What are you going to do?'

"Sure, he was a clown. He was half clown, half nut and all hot. Why did he act that way? I don't know. Maybe down deep he might have thought he was really a fool. He probably was hiding something, a bad feeling inside, a feeling that no one really liked him 'cause he was a fool. So he was going to be a bigger fool than even they thought."

Jimmy's problems stemmed, in part, from what could hardly have been a secure, serene home life. Still lively and attractive when she left Mr. Benoit, his mother had many friends, among them a Providence policeman. She stopped working in jewelry factories and collected Aid to Dependent Children.

Friends say she did her best with the cramped five-room apartment on the third floor of the green frame building at 818 Dexter Street where she moved with her three children from Tiffany Street. Jimmy had his own room leading off the kitchen which was decorated with pictures of Elvis Presley and James Brown, his childhood idols, and scattered with records, model cars and airplanes he made and the comic books he scanned but could never quite read.

Jimmy doted on his younger sister, Brenda, and often spent nights baby-sitting with her. His mother says he was "a good son, always doing something for me, for everybody. He never talked the hippie line or nothing like that. I don't understand how my son could ever have lived that life in all that filth and everything. He was always clean, liked clothes and everything. And he liked to work. And he wasn't unhappy or anything. He never said nothin' about worrying or nothin' like that."

In September 1962, after a year of visits to the Butler Center and at the age of sixteen, Jimmy entered the machinists' class at Central Falls Trade School, lodged in a gray Quonset hut beside the high school.

The machine shop, at the rear of the hut, is small and jammed with gray steel lathes, grinders, drill presses, spindles and milling machines. On the walls, hammers, awls and wrenches each hang on a nail over its own black outline. Above them is a neatly lettered sign, WE AIM TO KEEP THIS PLACE CLEAN—PLEASE HELP. Gray lockers bear a seemingly endless roster of French Canadian names: Plamondon, Trottier, Bernier, Rochelle.

The teacher is another French Canadian—Louis Sarault, Jr., a lean, deliberate, thoughtful man who takes sociology and psychology courses so he "can understand these boys and my own job a little better."

"Sure, I had Jimmy in my shop for three years," he recalls. "I remember the day he arrived. Dr. Calcutt, who was superintendent then, marched him over himself. He told me Jimmy came from an ungraded class, that he'd gotten through only the third grade. Normally the trade school accepts only kids who've gone through the eighth grade. But Mr. Calcutt said, 'Let's give him another chance, Louis, see what you can do with him.' Well, that wasn't unusual. Old Sarault usually got all the problem kids. I like the challenge.

"But I got to say Jimmy tried here. He wasn't too shifty with a paper and pencil. If he could write more than his name he didn't show me. If I asked him how much is half of fifteen he'd scratch his head and say that's a tough one. You need more than that in a technical shop like this. I couldn't talk trig to him. I had to do his thinking for him.

"But he made himself some nice tools. I remember this die stock he made, welded it himself. It was so good I kept it around as a model, threw it away only last year.

"And in some respects he had a good head. He could reason. He wouldn't take an unnecessary chance if it jeopardized his safety. He was a real con artist, foxy. In fact, in the con sense of the word you'd have to say he was sharper than most of the other kids. He'd smile at you, but underneath you knew he was saying, 'I'm putting you on, Sarault.' And his friendship—you'd almost have to say alliance—with Ernie St. Angelo was a very shrewd one. Ernie's a big boy and he could take care of Jimmy, but he's not too smart, while Jimmy had it up there, at least in the way you need it on the street.

"He was skinny, real skinny, but if he thought there was an easy mark in the class he'd go after him. I remember, once, he took on Ronald Fannion, a little kid with glasses, and I caught them. I did what I always did. I said, 'If you guys want to fight, then stand up like men, right next to each other, and swap punches in the arm.' "

Ernie St. Angelo, who was in the same shop, remembers that fight. "Ya, it was really funny. Hutchy knew Fannion was cross-eyed, a little goofy and couldn't see for nothin'. So he said, 'I'll fix 'im.' He filled his shirt pocket with nuts and bolts and scraps of metal. Fannion threw a shot at him, took the pocket off and cut his hand bad."

Another time, Sarault remembers, Jimmy went after Ralph Johnson, another kid who looked like a mark. "But Ralphie punched him out real good, made a cream puff of him. Up till then the shop had been a little wary of Jimmy because he talked tough. But once they saw him in action against Johnson they knew he wasn't nothing.

"Under his toughness, Jimmy was pretty timid. Once or twice when I disciplined him he'd cry—a boy of sixteen! A kid needs to be wanted, he needs to be loved, and I don't know how much of that he had at home. Once when he got in trouble I told him to bring his mother in. She was all agitated and said, 'I'm through with him; I've told him he has to conform, but he won't. I've had enough.'

"He'd been tossed around a lot. He said he didn't remember his father. But he carried his father's picture around in his billfold—a sharp-looking sailor in his Navy whites, his hat cocked back on his head, a little mustache. Jimmy said he wanted to be just like his father and go into the Navy. I think I pleased him once when I said he looked a little like his father. He kept wanting to grow a mustache like his father's, but I wouldn't let him. Every once in a while the fuzz would start sprouting under his nose and I'd say 'Shave it off, Jimmy.' And he would. A couple of years later I saw him on the street here, and sure enough he had a little mustache, just the spitting image of his father's.

"Jimmy got through O.K. right up to May of his final year and those last ten days we gave seniors off to get caps and gowns and all that. Then he went and got in some bad trouble."

This was the machete incident. According to members of the gang who were there, Jimmy had persuaded Gerry Bergevine, a twenty-nine-year-old neighbor, to buy him some beer. Some other kids tried to take it away from him and a "real punch-'em-up" developed. A friend managed to throw Jimmy a machete, and in the fight Jimmy cut seventeen-year-old Albie Nickerson on the arms so badly he had to be taken to the hospital. After a hearing before Judge Guillaume Myette, Jimmy was held for the grand jury in $1,500 bail.

"That really blew up a storm," Sarault recalls. "Dr. Calcutt, who had gone out of his way to help Jimmy, said, 'Louis, I don't see how we can give him a diploma now.' But I knew Jimmy wanted that diploma in the worst kind of way. After all those years in the ungraded class, you can't blame him. He was tired of hearing people say all he did was mush. So, although I don't think he attended graduation, we gave him his diploma."

Three weeks after he got his diploma, Jimmy got another break. The grand jury declined to indict him, apparently because Nickerson refused to testify.

Perhaps because of his close call, Jimmy seemed to plunge into work that summer. He worked briefly for Tuppet Screw Co. in Central Falls, and in September switched over to the New England Paper Tube Co. in Pawtucket, where he developed a reputation as a hard worker.

At first, as a floor boy, pushing two-wheeled hand carts of paper tubes around the four-story building, he averaged forty-nine and a half hours a week—nine hours on weekdays and four hours on Saturday. Then in January 1966 he became a baler, raking waste paper from a huge chute into compressing machines, then trotting downstairs seven or eight times a day to wire up the bales of packed paper. As a baler he averaged sixty-one and three-quarter hours a week, working all the day shift and part of the night shift, too, in a room filled with the roar of the nearby splitting machines and the hiss of the relentlessly moving mountain of waste paper.

"He was a real comedian," recalls Frank, his foreman. "He was loud and you could hear him clowning all over, even with all the machines going. But it didn't bother me none. My rule is if it doesn't hurt work it doesn't hurt me and Jimmy worked good. He was absent only seventy hours in twenty months and he was late only three times —hell, that's a better record than mine."

To the gang, most of whom were working only sporadically, Jimmy's spate of industriousness was just another sign he was nutty ("Hutchy was a working fool," Ernie said). He put most of his money (which got up to about eighty-seven dollars a week before taxes) in a Central Falls credit union, first to buy a car and then a motorcycle.

But he had no luck with his purchases. He bought Albie Nickerson's '57 white Ford convertible, but Steve St. Angelo ran it off the road and into a tree. Then Jimmy bought a motorcycle, a Japanese Yamaha, and within a few days cracked that up.

"Yeh, the Yamaha went into a gas station but Hutchy didn't," Ernie recalls. "He and these other kids were out on this rainy night. It was real slick and at the entrance to the station he jammed on the brake. He did a swan dive over the handlebars and the bike just rolled into the station and cracked up. Hutchy was all banged up, but still clowning. He told me the story all Japanese-like, you know, 'Ah, velly honolable bike, So solly, have tell you velly sad tale. Learn number-one lesson—with Japanese bike you do not put front brake on in rain.'"

The motorcycles were part of a new style the gang had adopted even before Jimmy and Ernie left trade school. They began calling themselves the Mondos to differentiate them from the Collegians, another gang across town. The Collegians hung out on Broad Street around Eddie's Ice Cream Parlor and Izzie's Restaurant. They wore white sneakers, chinos or Levis, white shirts and close-cropped hair. The Mondos hung on Dexter Street around Sparky's Restaurant and Duchesneau's Drug Store. They wore black pointed boots with high Cuban heels, black leather jackets, black pants with tapered bottoms, their long hair slicked back with grease.

Jimmy was the sharpest dresser of all the Mondos—everything black except the white buttons on his shirt, a white silk tie, a red vest and maybe a little snap-visor corduroy hat. By now his arms—and chest and legs—were heavily tattooed. He had a girl on his left arm, a little baby with boxing gloves captioned "Baby Jim," some dice and lucky sevens. "The first one he got was a torch with a scroll saying 'Mom,'" recalls Ernie. "I can remember when we got it. We went down to Rocky's Tattoo Parlor in Providence and he says 'Aw, its nothin', we get a tattoo, it's nothin'. You go first.' I says 'Why me?' and he says, 'Look at ya, ya big gorilla'—he used to call me that—'You're a big gorilla, look at the fat on ya. Look at me. I'm like a pole.' So I got this one here and he says, 'How was it?' and I said, 'It's nothin', Hutch, you'll like it!' So he gets up there, trying to show how brave he was, and the guy started the machine and started on his arm and you could hear all kinds of grunts. But he was smiling like it wasn't hurting him. He also had these hinges. Usually they'd put on these big hinges, like they have on sea chests, right at the inside of the elbow, but his arm was too skinny so they put one of these door hinges on. Every time he met somebody new he'd show him the hinges on his arms or legs and he'd bend it and say, 'Eeeekkk, eeeekkk,' like one of those creaky doors."

With his square dark glasses tilted down on his nose, his little corduroy hat cocked back, all his hinges creaking, Jimmy could often be found early in the evenings leaning against the windows of Duchesneau's Drug Store entertaining the rest of the Mondos with his renowned rendition of little Stevie Wonder's "Fingertips." First he would play it on the harmonica, doing a jiggly little dance on the sidewalk as he played. Then he would take

the harmonica out of his mouth, and spreading his arms
wide, would imitate the blind Negro singer's wail:

> Say, yeh, yeh, yeh, yeh, yeh, yeh
> Just a little bit of soul,
> oohhwwaa, oohhwwaa, oohhwwaa . . .

Then he would do his other favorite, James Brown,
or he would do a Jackie Gleason or Red Skelton routine
he had seen on TV, and the Mondos would roar and slap
their knees and shout, "Oh, Hutchy, you're some hot
ticket."

Sometimes the Mondos would spend the whole evening in front of Duchesneau's or Sparky's, watching the
girls, or "snappers," as they called them. "They'd never
really do anything, you know," recalls teenager Karen
Conroy. "They'd just cross their arms in front and
watch you real close and say, 'Dig her.'" There were
some "snappers" who hung out with the Mondos—girls
like Connie Oakley, Cathy Malloy, Madeleine Gilbert.
Jimmy knew them all, dated them, but like most of the
other Mondos he never got serious about girls. On Friday nights the Mondos would often wander up to the
dances at Holy Trinity, but only to watch the girls go in,
and make appropriate remarks.

Almost every spring there was a clash between the
Mondos and the Collegians on Dexter Street, but most
of the time they only growled at each other. They rarely
got into serious trouble with the police. Occasionally they
would steal empty bottles from construction sites and
cash them in, or pull false alarms and watch the fire
trucks race up, or drop lighted cigarettes in mailboxes
and watch the smoke seep out; and one Halloween a
Mondo was arrested for possession of eggs ("Yeh, believe
it or not, possession of eggs! 'Course he'd been throwing
them at police cars").

The police didn't like the Mondos and they took a
particular dislike to Jimmy. "They thought he was a wise
guy," Ernie said. "They really used to get on him. 'Course
they used to ride all of us. You're out on a corner with
another guy, see, and they'd come along, tell you to
move. And you ain't doing nothing. There's old men
across the street, about ten of them, and they don't kick
them off. Hutchy really hated that and I guess he told

some of the cops off 'cause they'd really go after him. I seen cops hit him in the legs with clubs hard enough to knock him on the ground and double him up with pain —just for standing on the corner!"

Most of the time, though, Jimmy was shrewd enough to stay out of serious trouble. If he wanted to raise a little hell he'd let others take the risks. "One guy who would do anything for Jimmy was Shorty," says Ernie. "Shorty was always following us Mondos around and we couldn't stand him. He was a hot ticket all right but we couldn't stand him because he had such a big mouth. So most of us just used to tell him to buzz off. But old Hutchy was too shrewd; he'd say, 'Hey, Shorty, if you want to hang with us you gotta show us you can do something. Why don't you steal a car and come back and pick us up. But for God's sake, make it a good one. No old buggies.' We all laughed 'cause we didn't think Shorty could steal anything. But a little while later Shorty came around the corner with a red T-bird, for Chrissakes. We all climbed in laughing and all, and Shorty he was so small he couldn't hardly reach the pedals, but Jimmy, he held him up by the seat of the pants and told him, 'On, James,' like he was a chauffeur or something."

Jimmy made Shorty the butt of a thousand little jokes, but with the rest of the gang, and particularly with his buddy, Ernie, he could be more than generous. Ernie remembers once he needed a hundred dollars more to get a car he wanted. "Hutchy said, 'I'll give it to ya.' This is while he was working at the Paper Tube place and he had plenty of dough. I said, 'Naw, I don't want your money.' But he went to the bank on Friday and drawed out a hundred and he come to my house and says, 'Here, Ernie, here's the money. Go buy the car. And then when you get the car we'll all go along.' That's the kind of guy he was. Listen. He was a well-loved kid, not well-liked, well-loved." The other Mondos agreed. Eddie Marco said emotionally, "There always was and always will be a Hutchinson."

Others found him less appealing. Seventeen-year-old Wayne Robichaud said, "Well, I guess he was O.K. to the kids who were his friends, but he used to pick on some of us smaller kids. I was a little scared of him." Nineteen-year-old Ken Moore said, "He could be rough. I remember once I walked by a car where he and a girl were in the back seat. I knocked on the window and he came out after me with this knife."

The Collegians remember that Jimmy always carried a knife his last few years in Central Falls—"All kinds of knives, big ones, small ones, curved ones, switchblades." The Mondos concede this but insist it was largely for self-defense. "He was only ninety pounds, for crying out loud. The guy couldn't fight with his hands. He didn't have no defense with his hands."

But it was a knife which ultimately got Jimmy into big trouble. On October 22, 1965, he and Steve St. Angelo went out to celebrate Steve's seventeenth birthday. "We decided to go over to North Attleboro, Mass., and do the town," Steve recalls. "We hit a few of the spots in town and then we drove over to the VFW hall where they was having this teenage dance."

Officers Robert Bray and Antonio J. Casale stationed outside the hall later reported that they observed the two boys "staggering" up to the door and "demanding" admission about nine o'clock. "They smelled strongly of alcohol, were unsteady on their feet and their speech was incoherent," the report said. "They became loud and boisterous and began to hit the paneled wall of the lobby when they were refused admission." They were placed under arrest, but Officer Bray noticed Hutchinson had his left hand in the pocket of his leather jacket and ordered him to remove it. Hutchinson did not respond. According to Bray, he then put one hand on Hutchinson's left wrist and began patting the outside of the pocket with his other hand to see if it contained a gun or a knife. "In the process," Bray's report reads, "Hutchinson's left hand came up and forward, still in his left pocket, and a sharp pointed weapon in his left-hand coat pocket penetrated the pocket and came in contact with Bray's right hand, puncturing the palm of his hand, drawing blood."

The sharp pointed weapon, still kept in an envelope in the North Attleboro police station, is a piece of steel about four inches long with two sharp blades protruding at right angles at each end. When the bar, wrapped in cotton and Scotch tape, is held in a man's clenched fist the two blades jut out just beyond the knuckles.

The boys were taken to the police station, where Jimmy was charged with assault and battery with a dangerous weapon, possession of a dangerous weapon, drunkenness and disturbance of the peace. Steve was charged with drunkenness and disturbing the peace.

Ernie St. Angelo, who went up to North Attleboro that night, recalls that even then Jimmy was still clowning. "He had his hands handcuffed behind his back and every time the cops turned their backs he kept stepping through them so his hands would be in front. The cops didn't know how he did it. Then back in the cell he and Stevie unrolled this toilet paper, draped it all over the cell and through the bars and started singing 'Happy Birthday.' When the cops came back to tell them to shut up Jimmy said, 'Jeez, it's my buddy's birthday, aren't you going to even wish him happy birthday?' "

At his arraignment the next morning, Jimmy pleaded not guilty to all four charges and was held in $1,075 bail. When he could not put up the bail he was taken to the New Bedford House of Correction, where he was held until the hearing on October 29, when he was bound over for the grand jury. On February 11, the Bristol County grand jury indicted him.

Within a week after the indictment, Jimmy was talking seriously about leaving Central Falls.

The Mondos say he had always wanted to travel. Eddie Marco remembers: "When we were twelve a bunch of us took our bikes and went all the way to the Red Bridge in Providence. Hutchy wanted to keep going, but I had a little Mickey Mouse watch and I said I had to be home for five o'clock supper. So I turned around and came back. Gee, I didn't see the rest of them until after eight. They said Hutchy just wouldn't stop, he wanted to go all the way to New York. 'Course, he had an English bike. He could go faster than we could."

Later, he took to riding the freights in and around Providence and he would give his friends a tour of the city from the top of a freight car. Once, Ernie recalls, "He went right up to the front of a freight and he asked the engineer, 'Buddy, can I drive your train?' And the guy started screaming at him, and Hutchy says, 'No offense, no offense.' "

Still later, he and the other Mondos would drive to New York for weekends, fill up the car with liquor they could buy legally there at eighteen and sell it to minors in Central Falls.

In New York, the Mondos usually went to Greenwich

Village, which fascinated Jimmy. "He always wanted to go down there," Ernie says. "We never wanted to, but he kept saying, 'Oh, I want to see them guys with the long hair.' One time we was in this bar down there and the American Beatles were playing. We were sitting at a table plastered, so Hutchy calls this guy over, when they had a break, and he grabbed the kid's hair. 'Excuse me,' he says real nice. 'Is that your real hair?' and then he started pulling. We was all laughing. Finally the kid says, 'All right, already.' "

Early in April 1966 Jimmy told his brother, George, that he was going to leave home. "He didn't know where he was going to go," George recalls. "He said he just wanted to change the scenery. He wanted me to come with him, but I said I couldn't go. Then, before I knew it —boom, he was gone."

Jimmy withdrew all his savings from the credit union and he and Dave Quebec, one of the Mondos, bought a car together. He packed a small suitcase with a couple of sports jackets, two pairs of pants, some underwear and socks, telling his mother that he might send for the rest of his clothes as soon as he was settled. He gave his record player and his large record collection to his sister, Brenda.

Jimmy worked his last day at the Paper Tube Co. on April 22 and the next day he and Quebec drove to New York. A few days later his mother received a postcard date-marked the 23rd from New York with a picture of the New York skyline under the painted legend "Just Arrived in New York." It read: "Having fun. Can't complain as yet. Say hi to Ronnie, Brenda and everyone for me. Okay. Love, Jim H." His friends presume that Quebec wrote this and subsequent postcards for the still largely illiterate Jimmy.

Shortly after they arrived in New York, Jimmy and Quebec apparently joined an itinerant carnival known as Amusements of America, a New Jersey outfit which toured the Eastern seaboard with a string of ferris wheels, merry-go-rounds, "thrill rides" and "children's rides." It is not clear just what Jimmy did for the carnival. Once he told his brother that he and Quebec helped put up and tear down the tents. Another time he said he sold tickets for a freak show.

The record of his travels for the next eight months is

told largely in a series of laconic postcards he sent his mother. The next was from Philadelphia on May 3 in which he said he was "doing all right and don't need anything." In the next weeks the carnival played a series of one-week stands in New Jersey and Pennsylvania but the next card from Jimmy came in early August from Hagerstown, Maryland: "Hi ma. Heading for Canada. How's the family? Fine I hope. See you soon, Jim." And on August 28 came a card from Ottawa, Canada: "Hi, Mom. Had a wonderful time here. Going back to the U.S. now. Will hear from me soon. Doing fine. Being good. Your best son, love, Jimmy."

Soon after he came back to this country, Jimmy left Amusements of America and joined a smaller carnival run by David B. Endy of Mount Dora, Florida, as it headed south toward Florida. In September he sent his mother a card from Enfield, North Carolina, saying, "Took in the sights here—moving on to a new town."

Early in January 1967 a barber known as Frenchy, who ran Frenchy's Barbershop a few doors down from Jimmy's old house in Central Falls, was on vacation in Hollywood, Florida, and wandered into a carnival at a shopping center there. He spotted Jimmy standing by a sideshow. "I remembered him very well 'cause he was one of the first 'round here to wear his hair long. He never wanted any off the top. I said, 'How ya doing, Jimmy.' He said, 'Oh, O.K., I guess.' "

Jimmy apparently stayed on in Hollywood after the carnival left, because on February 7 he sent his mother another postcard saying, "Having a good time and going up to New Orleans today."

In New Orleans, Jimmy worked at odd laborer's jobs, waiting to pick up with another carnival on its northern swing in April. Then in late February he was staying at a small hotel in the French Quarter when he met another young ex-carnival worker from Kansas City named Ronald Johnson. Johnson, known as Galahad, remembers the meeting this way:

"There was this Spanish kid I knew down there—he and I'd been going out with the same chick—and one night I didn't have a place to stay, so the Spanish kid said, 'Come on up to my place.' I went up there and Groovy was up there with this other kid named Chris. At first Groovy came on a little uptight, sort of teed off, you know, because those two guys were goofing off all the time while he was working and paying the rent. But the next day Groovy and I got to rapping and found out the things we had in common. That wasn't only carnivals. There were lots of things. But the main thing was we both liked to goof on people, you know, blow people's minds, doing weird, fantastic things.

"After that, Groovy stopped working mostly and we just goofed off together, just horsing around with the longhairs in Jackson Park and all over the French Quarter." In these weeks Jimmy acquired at least four things —a tattoo of "Bourbon Street" in fancy lettering; a piece of parchment printed like a diploma with the inscription "Nobody of the Year Award" above the name "James L. Hutchinson" which Jimmy later hung in his New York pad; the nickname Groovy, which, as Galahad recalls it, came from a guy they met in a bar one night; and the drug habit. Galahad is a little vague about when Groovy first began taking drugs. The Mondos say he was "a wino" in Central Falls and never did more with drugs than sniff glue. But soon after he met Galahad he was apparently taking LSD regularly.

"One day," Galahad recalls, "we was sitting in his hotel room, just rappin', rappin' about carnivals, and we just decided to take off, like the carnivals weren't due yet and we could catch them in Philly. So we hitchhiked up to New York, took us about a week. We spent this one wild night just wandering around Memphis but mostly we kept on the road."

Galahad and Groovy arrived in New York on April 1 —which later seemed to some an appropriate date—and, as Galahad remembers it, they went first to Times Square. "We ran into some kids up there who were tripping on LSD and were on their way to the movies. We asked where we could stay and they suggested the Peace Eye Bookstore down in the Village. So we went down there and ended up staying a couple of weeks."

The Peace Eye, at 383 East 10th Street in the heart of the East Village, was a hippie bookstore featuring psychedelic literature and the underground press. It was owned by Ed Sanders, the leader of the Fugs. Frank Wise, who ran it for him, let Galahad and Groovy camp in the back room for about three weeks and fed them

in exchange for a little work around the place, most of it
done by Groovy.

"One day," Galahad recalls, "Groovy told me he
wanted to open a crash pad where homeless kids could
stay. I don't know where he got the idea. There weren't
any crash pads down in New Orleans. I think he got the
idea from some girl he met. Finally we met this other
chick who said she'd let us use her pad, really her boy-
friend's pad, over on 11th Street as long as we paid the
rent—thirty-six dollars a week."

The pad was Apartment 11 on the third floor of a
dingy tenement at 622 East 11th Street. On the door was
a hand-lettered sign: GALAHAD'S PAD, PROTECTOR OF ALL
THAT IS RIGHTEOUS AND HOLY. For the next three months
it served as the most renowned of the East Village's
crash pads, where the homeless and the friendless
could stay as long as they lived. Sometimes Groovy and
Galahad would return a runaway child to his frantic parents and be rewarded with a television set or money.
("We're in the people business," Groovy once said.) But
most times there were twenty to thirty assorted hippies
staying there and, later, a whole host of visitors—newsmen, television cameramen, other curiosity seekers and
policemen, always policemen.

The police concentration on the pad was later explained
in an affidavit filed by Police Commissioner Howard Leary
before the United States District Court. The commissioner said there had been "a number of entries" to the
apartment "occasioned by constant requests from other
police departments, but most frequently from parents
themselves to find minors, runaway teenagers in the East
Village area of New York City. Usually the parents themselves have heard that their children are living at Apartment 11 at 622 East 11th Street."

The commissioner's affidavit was filed in response to a
suit on behalf of Galahad, Groovy and several other defendants by John Mage, their lawyer, and Paul Chevigny
of the New York Civil Liberties Union. The suit charged
that the police were conducting a campaign of "harassment, including dragnet arrests, invasions of privacy and
searches" against the defendants. The suit, filed in June
1967, cited eight specific instances prior to May 6 on
which the police entered the apartment "without consent,

warrant or other lawful cause" and intrusions after that "on an almost daily basis."

Among the instances were:

One on April 27, when, according to Mage, a member of the Narcotics Squad banged on the door and demanded entrance. He arrested Groovy for impairing the morals of a minor—a girl found in the apartment. Groovy spent the night in jail, but the next morning the case was dismissed on arraignment when the girl was found to be over sixteen.

One on May 6, when the police again demanded entrance. Under instructions from Mage, who became their lawyer after Groovy's arrest, Groovy and Galahad demanded a warrant. But according to the suit the police said they did not need a warrant and "forced their way in." About fifteen persons were arrested and taken to the Ninth Precinct but were released the next morning without being charged.

One on May 19, when police again banged on the door, Groovy again demanded a warrant and, according to the suit, the police again said they did not need one. After searching the apartment the police arrested Groovy and several others on narcotics charges, which were dismissed the next morning in court.

John Mage, a boyish-looking but deeply committed young lawyer, recalls: "After one of the mass arrests I called the Ninth Precinct and complained that this was something out of 1938 Berlin. I guess because I was a lawyer they assumed that I was a married old man with children because the detective said, 'What if your daughter was running around with these hippies?' I said if I had a daughter I'd expect the police to treat her justly as all people ought to be treated, and the detective shouted, 'These aren't people, they're bedbugs and they should be exterminated.' "

In answering the suit, Commissioner Leary said, "I believe the police officers have acted in good faith to enforce the laws of the state in these situations." But shortly after the suit was filed—and a parallel action against the detectives involved was brought before the Police Review Board—the police entries of the apartment stopped.

Even after the police were gone, the pad was threatened by an ever-increasing horde of newsmen seeking the bizarre and the way-out. "Neither Galahad nor

Groovy knew how to cope with this kind of publicity," recalls Don MacNeill of the *Village Voice*, one of the few newsmen who handled the story with sensitivity. "It just blew Galahad's mind, almost destroyed him. It was just incredible to see how the media's attention contorted the guy."

Groovy was less affected by it because he was more naïve. Eve Cary, who works for the Civil Liberties Union, recalls Groovy coming up to her wide-eyed at one of the court hearings and saying that *"Time* magazine, the Society Magazine," wanted to interview him.

"Groovy was just gleefully enjoying everything that happened to him," John Mage said. "Even during the worst of the arrests he just ate up the attention. Newsmen were baffled and amazed to find somebody down there who would talk to them at any time, tell them absolutely anything that came into his head."

Groovy struck others as somehow different, more truly innocent, than the rest of the hippies. June Tauber, a "straight" girl who met him several times last summer, recalls that he made a particular impression on her the night of the Tompkins Square riot. "Most of the hippies, the whole thing, was so dark, dirty, almost Hogarthian. Except for Groovy. He was ebullient, hopping and leaping around, buzzing around Galahad like a butterfly, his little, dark dancing eyes, his teeny, teeny features, small, delicate, light and bouncy, almost childlike in the midst of that dreary affair."

Another friend remembers Groovy one night as he and other hippies waited for hours amid the forbidding marble columns of the Criminal Court for Galahad to be released on bail: "Groovy would go careening around the hall like a kid on the last day of school, in and out of pillars, leaping, prancing, then skidding sideways to a grinning halt. He would play softly on his harmonica, breaking into a jig every few bars."

Steve Golden, who frequently wrote about the East Village for the *New York Times,* says: "Galahad was the brains of the organization, quick, sharp, though no genius. Groovy wasn't so smart, but he could feel, which Galahad couldn't. Groovy had the vitality, the energy. He was the only one who could put down Galahad without getting him mad. I think of them as Don Quixote and Sancho Panza or maybe Paul Douglas and Judy Holliday in *Born Yesterday*."

One day Galahad and Groovy were sighted on St. Mark's Place in the heart of Hippieland. Galahad had a fireman's hat on and was wheeling a wire shopping cart containing a big fire extinguisher. Groovy would scurry ahead and light a piece of paper in the gutter and then Galahad would race up and put it out. They would panhandle from the bystanders and then Groovy would race ahead and light another piece of paper. Galahad liked the act, which Groovy had invented, and told him to hold on to the extinguisher. But when they got together that night he saw Groovy didn't have the extinguisher. "What you do with it?" Galahad demanded. "I don't know," Groovy said. "I think I gave it to somebody."

Groovy seemed to enjoy giving things away in the Village—part of his newfound "digger" ethos. Sometimes he would stand on the street corner and when he saw someone whose face he liked he would go up and plant a bottle cap in their open palm. "I just want you to have it," he'd tell the bewildered pedestrian.

He also gave away drugs—LSD, speed, pot—or sold them at cut-rate prices far below those charged by the more professional dealers.

Suddenly in midsummer Groovy took off for Woodstock, New York, about ninety miles up the Hudson, where a hippie scene was developing. He drove up with some friends and they stayed about a month. Galahad recalls that Groovy talked vaguely about starting some sort of rural commune there, patterned after those that were sprouting in the California hills, but his Woodstock friends say he never did anything about it.

"Mostly we just clowned around the Cafe Espresso in the middle of town and Groovy was the chief clown," one friend recalls. "One night he pulled some grass out of the ground, you know, real green cow-type grass, and he rolled it up in a cigarette paper and went up to these old proper villagers and said, 'Hey, you want a joint of grass, man?' You had to laugh. Oh, another night, you know, the tables of the café were in this little sunken courtyard with their tops just about level with the sidewalk and one night Groovy just stepped off the sidewalk onto one of the tables and asked these tourists for a light. It broke everybody up—except the tourists. They just sat there and looked amazed."

Groovy and his friends had no place to stay in Woodstock. They moved around, sleeping in fields and barns. One week they stayed at a camp in the woods near Bob Dylan's house and visited several times with the folk singer-poet. Later, somebody said they'd found a vacant barn, and on July 23, Groovy, two other boys and two girls went out there to sleep. It was raining, and they curled up in the hay and went to sleep. About 1 A.M., acting on a complaint by the owner, two Woodstock constables arrested the five for trespassing. The two girls were later released in custody of their parents. But the boys appeared the next day before Justice of the Peace Milton Houst and were sentenced to fifty days in jail or a fifty-dollar fine.

One of the boys arrested with him recalls that Groovy seemed happy in jail. "In the cell he met this old Negro he'd known on the carnival circuit and rapped with him for hours about the old days. When I got out he asked me not to tell anybody he was there because he wanted to stay in, get some rest and three square meals a day for a while. He was already pretty strung out on drugs by then, and I think he just liked the idea of fifty days of peace and quiet. But somebody called Galahad in New York and he came up and paid the fine."

A few weeks after Groovy got out of jail he and Galahad hit the road again. "We were just tired of the scene," Galahad recalls. They rode with some friends from Woodstock up to Montreal (Groovy wanted to see Expo) and then out to Denver. One night they were stopped in a small South Dakota town by a policeman who wanted to see their identification. "Groovy said he didn't have any eye-dentification," Galahad remembers. "But he said he had some tattoos. The cop said he just wanted to see an ID card. But Groovy kept showing him his tattoos. It really blew that cop's mind."

In Denver they were picked up by a girl named Diane in her Volkswagen bus and drove with her and six others to Haight-Ashbury in San Francisco, where Galahad and Groovy put up in the Digger Free Store.

One day Steve Golden ran into Groovy at the Haight-Ashbury Free Clinic, which was giving hippies free medi-

cal care. "He was wearing the only clothes I ever saw
him wear anywhere—a dark shirt under a navy-blue pea
jacket, scruffy blue jeans and a blue wool cap with a button on the top. But he looked a lot worse than he had in
New York. He was sitting on an overstuffed couch, his
hands folded in his lap, and when I said hello he looked
up and said 'Hi.' His eyes were much duller, his skin had
turned sallow and he had a four days' growth of beard. I
tried to talk with him but I didn't get much response. He
said he needed some vitamins but the clinic didn't have
them and he didn't have money to buy them. I offered
him five dollars but he wouldn't take it. He said he didn't
feel well enough to peddle the *Berkeley Barb* like the
others were doing, but he'd panhandled some."

Late in August, Groovy and Galahad left for New
York because Galahad had a date in court. Passing
through Chicago, Groovy pulled a freak-out which is still
Galahad's favorite. "We were busted for loitering and
this cop started frisking Groovy. Groovy had this electric
razor in one pocket, and when the cop touched the razor
case Groovy suddenly yelled, 'Careful, it'll explode and
blow us all up.' Boy, the cop yanked his hands away like
it was a hot stove."

Back in New York the two friends saw less of each
other than they had before. They stayed in different pads,
although they would usually get together at least once a
day. "We still looked after each other, like brothers,"
Galahad says. "But he was really strung out on speed by
then. Seemed like every time I seed him he was on that
stuff, always speedin' all over the place, moving around,
circulating, grooving with all the people. I couldn't keep
up with him at the end. I didn't have all the energy he
did. I wasn't on speed then."

Steve Golden recalls seeing Groovy one day at a be-in.
"His little face, which always looked a bit like John Car-
radine's, was getting down to bones. His chin was sharpened, his cheeks hollowed. His body, which was always
thin, still seemed O.K., but his face looked like it was
starting to die."

Jim Fouratt, a leader of the Jade Companions of the
Flowered Dance and other East Village community
groups, also saw Groovy several times after he got back
from California. "He was getting more and more frantic,
still playing the court jester to Galahad's king, a minstrel

in the midst of all that ruin. He was frightening to look at, all wasted away from the drugs; he looked like a skeleton dancing and singing."

Sometime around this time Groovy met Linda Fitzpatrick, the girl from Greenwich, Connecticut. Nobody paid much attention to her because Groovy was always with girls in the Village—girls named Fran, Shelly, Vina.

He spent part of his last day lying in a sleeping bag in front of the Psychedelicatessen next to Linda. At dawn the next morning their bodies were discovered in the boiler room on Avenue B.

Groovy's head was badly mutilated by the brick, but the family insisted on an open casket at the funeral, so the undertaker worked a day and a half to fix it up. On October 13, he was buried in Highland Memorial Park in Johnston, Rhode Island. Ernie St. Angelo, Danny Zenone and most of the other Mondos were there. So were Galahad and about thirty other flower children from the Village. Galahad played Groovy's harmonica briefly over the grave. "I know how Groovy would have wanted it," he said, "like this."

In the reams of press coverage which followed the murder, Groovy was beatified. One feature writer saw him as "his generation's young rebel, a fugitive from the meanness and materialism he saw around him. An urban Huck Finn. The modern runaway from mendacity and phony respectability. A hot-gospelling psychedelic seeker of lost souls."

After reading most of the stories, Ernie St. Angelo said, "Hutchy would have been in his glory if he was alive and could read all this. He would have loved the crazy things they're saying. He always wanted to be the leader of the laughers."

JIM

He speaks softly, oh, so softly, the words fluttering down like the milky-gray pigeons settling on the ledges along Haight Street. Now and again he skitters into a giggle or snuffles his runny nose, but he murmurs on, calm and deliberate and gentle as the San Francisco mist on the window panes.

All the while he fixes you with those wide, earnest eyes set exactly where they should be in that symmetrical, boyishly open face framed by long jet-black hair. A heavy silver cross ("a life-death symbol," he explains) hangs around his neck over a black T-shirt tucked into brown chinos. Nothing flamboyant, nothing designed to rattle the "straights," except perhaps his half-smiling answer when asked, "What do you think life is all about?"

"Death."

Silence. Outside, the fog wafts around the towers, turrets, parapets and Corinthian columns on the three-story Victorian houses and softly enfolds the old ramrod statue of President McKinley in Panhandle Park. Then Jim Murphy murmurs on.

"I won't learn any more about life than I know now, which is kind of a strange statement to make at the age of nineteen. But I'm sure of it. Because now I know that life is just preparing for something that happens afterwards. I can't go any further now because to go further I'd have to die.

"I've done all the mind-expanding I can. There's nothing more I can take to figure out anything more. I've dropped acid maybe two hundred times, and I stayed up on speed for two straight months, and I've tried heroin, cocaine, opium, hashish, LSD, STP and just about anything else you can name. Then I came down with hepatitis, pyorrhea and malnutrition and I've pretty much stopped. Only not because of being sick. I would have stopped anyway.

"LSD can only take you so far. What it really does is boost you up so you can get your fingers over the edge and then you have to pull yourself up the rest of the way. It turns you on to life. Then it's up to you. Mostly I meditate by myself now—just sit in nature and think. But I'm not trying to plunge into new states of consciousness any more. I think I've expanded my brain about as far as I should. If I expanded it any more I'm liable to regress . . ."

He giggles.

"From now on it's just a kind of waiting thing . . . to see what happens next. Life now is very uncomplicated because I'm, you know, very happy and I understand why I'm here—as much as I can. And I realize that I don't have to hassle any more because I'm not going to find out any more."

No more hassle. No more bumping and breaking your shins on the hard angularities of middle-class America. But no need to rebel, to struggle with all that any more. "I'm a lot more tolerant now. Acid gives you a lot more tolerance for just about everything. You know. Everybody's doing their thing and it doesn't make any difference what it is as long as it doesn't interfere with yours or somebody else's."

No hassle. No rebellion. Just doing your thing high up on the steep hillside called Haight-Ashbury—watching the grayish-white fog rolling in off the bay like one of those fuzzy warm wool blankets you used to pull up over your head on crisp winter mornings long ago in San Leandro.

There is no fog in San Leandro. The sun shines there three hundred and fifteen or more days a year. The air is bright and crisp. And there is a brisk, no-nonsense mood which has given San Leandro the nickname "City of Action."

The Chamber of Commerce proudly boasts of the community's independent pioneer spirit. "The city that would rather do-it-yourself" rejected federal financing for downtown renewal projects because the government attached strings requiring residential renewal too. So San Leandro went ahead on a million-dollar downtown modernization program financed by its own pay-as-you-go funds. The city abhors bond issues—only two have even been brought to a vote since 1947—and it has watched spending so closely that its tax rate has decreased every year "for twenty (count 'em) consecutive years."

"Get the picture?" the Chamber of Commerce says. "San Leandro is a personality city with a prosperity-plus 'purse-onality' economy."

In the last twenty years, more than four hundred and fifty manufacturing firms have gotten the picture. Jostling each other in the corridor between the rushing new Mac-Arthur and Nimitz freeways are dozens of bright new brick and aluminum plants manufacturing everything from trucks and fuel-injection systems to waxed paper and chocolate bars.

But San Leandro consumes even more than it produces. It has seventy-five thousand residents who live in California split-levels, bungalows and garden apartments blanketing the softly rolling land which slides from the San Leandro Hills toward the bay. And San Leandrans keep their houses well stocked. In 1969 the city's retail sales rose to a record $201,500,000.

"For the modern American family," the Chamber of Commerce says, "San Leandro is literally a shopper's paradise." In the recently refurbished downtown shopping area nationally known chain stores are linked with pedestrian malls, covered walkways, fountains, park strips and multicolored sidewalks. The city also has fifteen shopping centers, led by the mammoth Bay Fair. Covering forty-seven acres with nearly six dozen shops and three thousand parking spaces, Bay Fair is one of the biggest regional centers in the state. "The Center with Everything in the Center of Everything," it calls itself.

Since nearly everybody in San Leandro seems to have enough groceries and hard goods, San Leandrans compete chiefly in the size and lushness of their gardens. In the perfect climate, almost anything will grow. So housewives spend hours on their hands and knees in the front lawns planting: spiky stalks of lavender delphinium, domed clusters of salmon phlox, airy white clouds of baby's-breath, pink billows of sea lavender, dainty strings of red coral bells, carpets of fiery begonias, bushy balls of golden marigolds, spears of yellow snapdragons, mounds of white candytuft, drooping arches of pink and white bleeding heart, splashes of yellow daylilies, cascades of pink rhododendron, showers of ruffled white camellias.

And when the bright sunshine fades into night, San Leandro keeps on consuming. Although it boasts little night life, its home bars are some of the best stocked anywhere. According to a recent government estimate, 7 percent of the population in the six East Bay counties suffer from alcoholism. And so it was no surprise when, in 1957, James P. Gilmore chose San Leandro as the site of the Gilmore Hospital for the care and treatment of chronic alcoholics. The hospital was established in one of San Leandro's showplaces, the Casa Peralta, and when visitors come to the "City of Action" they often stop to stare curiously over the high white walls of the gracious old stucco mansion.

On his crumbling hillside in the gray fog, Jim smiles crookedly when he talks of San Leandro. "What began to get me over there was how it was all a farce, a bunch of lies. Well, most of it was lies and half-truths.

"It would be all right if they didn't say 'Liberty and justice for all' and 'Every man is created equal.' If they didn't say it, then they could be as bigoted and prejudiced as they wanted. But the American Dream type of thing says all that and then they don't practice it and they can't understand why people riot. What America says it stands for and what it really stands for are two different things.

"You know, I was so lucky. I was white and I was kind of middle-class and that's *the* thing to be in America. And I had all this laid before me saying, you know, 'You can make it, baby, if you want to.' And I looked around and saw all the people that couldn't make it even if they tried really, really hard—they couldn't make it because they were the wrong color or the wrong religion or . . . they said one thing that just wasn't right and didn't fit. And I decided that I didn't want the whole thing handed to me on a platter because it wasn't worth anything if it was handed to me on a platter.

"And, I don't know, I just didn't fit. I didn't think the way that everyone else thought and I didn't believe the propaganda that everyone else believed, and therefore what the hell was I doing in the middle of something that I didn't believe in? You know, by living in this society and yet saying 'I don't believe it,' I was being just as hypocritical as this society.

"I began asking a lot of Why's and What If's, just to find out what people would say. I'd ask my parents, 'What would you do if a Negro moved in next door?' And they'd say, 'Nothing! We don't mind.' And I'd say, 'What would you do if I wanted to marry a Negro?' and that was completely different. 'No. You can't marry a Negro. No, no. You can't do that.' And I couldn't understand why, because I'd been raised to believe Negroes were just like anyone else. Two and two just never made four.

"And the materialism, the things! I always thought there was more than just possessions, that there were people and that it would be a lot better for me to know one person in my entire life really well than to have all the stereos and the cars and the houses and the money that was ever made. I never wanted any of that stuff. And it was kind of shoved down my throat all my life. You know, it was 'Here, buy this. Here, buy that. Do you want this? Do you want that? You can have whatever you want.' All I ever really wanted was love and understanding, which was kind of spread thin between three children and one parent.

"I don't know. I just look at the divorce rate and I wonder what happened to love. It's pretty stupid for people to get married one year, divorced the next year and then married again the next year. It's all, I don't know, it kinda looks like it's all the sex angle. You know. They want to make love to people but they have to be married to do it, and when they get tired of that person, well . . . Over here, sex and love are two separate things—sex happens all the time and love comes now and then. They're two distinct things. But over there, in a straight-type society, it's all messed up. Love, what they think is love, is just sex.

"In my family, well, I don't think there was ever any love."

Mrs. Murphy is an uneasy mixture of soft and hard. She is a handsome woman with a sensuous mouth and still surprisingly good figure. But she has a strong face dominated by heavy eyebrows and speaks with the crisp authority of a woman used to fending for herself.

She does not gloss over the rough spots in her life, particularly her years with Jim's father.

"It was a mismatch from the start. I came from Protestant, Anglo-Saxon, middle-class stock in Terre Haute, Indiana—you know, bland, typical Midwesterners with never a divorce or any serious psychological problems I know of. My husband was an Irish Catholic from San Mateo, with a typical Irish temperament—smiling, happy, a good-time Charlie who could charm the birds off the trees when he was sober, but loud and profane when he was drunk—which, as time went on, was most of the time."

When they married in 1940, she was eighteen, he a twenty-one-year-old, $75-a-week bank clerk. Their first child, Sharon, was born in 1941. During the war, Mr. Murphy went to work for a shipyard and inched his way up to supervisor before he was drafted in 1944 and went off to serve in the occupation army in Japan. While he was away, Mrs. Murphy worked in a department-store credit office, sending her daughter off to live with her parents.

When Mr. Murphy came home in August 1946, he moved the family back to Oakland. But with only a high school education and no special skill, he found the going tough. He worked for the Veterans Administration, and then as a salesman for a steel company. After his two sons, Frank and Jim, were born in the late forties he gave up white-collar work altogether for a job as a machine operator in a paper-box factory.

"He found he could earn more money there than he could in an office. But it meant working shifts—day, swing, graveyard, two weeks on each. That was the difference between us and other people who had nice regular eight-to-five lives," Mrs. Murphy recalls.

But by 1951, when Jim was three, they had saved enough money to make a down payment on a new $14,500, five-room house in San Leandro. It was distinctly a step up in the world, away from the crowded urban neighborhood in Oakland to which Negroes were already moving, and into Halcyon, a new all-white "suburban" neighborhood.

Halcyon—the name itself conjured up all the magic "suburbia" had for those ex-GIs. One-story bungalows painted in pastel shades of pink, green and blue. Basketball hoops nailed up over the one- and two-car garages.

Palm trees in the lawns, and of course by the white pick-et fences, San Leandro's famous flowers.

"But it wasn't the kind of suburbia you read about in the magazines," Mrs. Murphy says. "You know, with doctors and lawyers and country clubs and all that.

"It was just these veterans, mostly guys who'd finished high school before the war but never got to college, may-be making ten thousand to fifteen thousand. When they came back from the war they each wanted a little house with a plot of grass, a nice place to raise children, to make a new world. So they came to Halcyon; they all lived a little beyond their means, buying a car or a boat on credit, making the best of rotten marriages, getting by, making do."

And it was here that Jim grew up. His first few years were bad ones. "He was a very sick little boy," his mother recalls. "He was born with a congenital duodenal ulcer. And he was a 'bleeder,' not a hemophiliac, but he had a real slow clotting time and needed lots of transfusions. Once he almost bled to death. His veins collapsed. In those first few years he spent so much time in the hospital they almost named a wing after him."

But by the age of eight or ten he could do almost any-thing the other neighborhood boys did. And his parents, who were exceptionally active in community affairs, en-couraged both Jim and his brother, Frank, to do every-thing. They both played Little League baseball on a team their father coached. They were cub scouts in a den for which Mrs. Murphy was den mother and Mr. Murphy was cub master. Later they were boy scouts while Mrs. Murphy served as treasurer of the scouts' mothers club and Mr. Murphy was a committeeman of the scout pack.

But gradually Jim lost interest and began shying away from most of these activities, particularly sports. His fa-ther, an enthusiastic athlete, was furious.

"He beat him, made him feel inadequate because he wasn't a man, wasn't physical. But the more he raved, the more Jim dug in his heels and refused. One time he in-sisted Jim come out onto the baseball field. He threw a hardball at him and beaned him right between the eyes. Wham! After that I don't think Jim ever played again.

"I know now that my husband must have been an alco-holic when I married him. He had it under some control before he left the war, but when he got back he was really belting the stuff. He was a blackout drinker—one of those people who could drink to a certain point and then wouldn't remember anything for twelve to twenty-four hours. When he got like that he'd do anything.

"My doctor told me as early as 1950 to leave him before something tragic happened. But I came from a home where there'd never been a divorce. You made your bed and you'd lie in it. So I made a terrible mistake—I said I'd stay for the children's sake. Then, when I began thinking about it I was too afraid of him to leave him. So we just lived our little nightmare."

Finally in October 1962, after twenty-two years of marriage, Mrs. Murphy told her husband to get out. He did (although she didn't file for divorce until 1963 and the divorce didn't become final until 1964). "The children were so terrified of their father they were overjoyed when I told him to get out. They kept saying, 'Don't change your mind, Mom, don't change your mind.'

"But Jim's real problem wasn't his father. It was his brother, Frankie. Frankie was a year older, but when they were young they were almost like twins. They walked alike, talked alike, got sick at the same time.

"Gradually, though, Jim became Frankie's shadow. Frankie was one of those fabulous creatures everybody swarmed around. He was very gregarious, very outgoing. Jim was becoming an introvert and he let Frankie do the talking for him. They were both bright—Frankie had an I.Q. of a hundred and sixty and Jim a hundred and thirty-five. But while Frankie was getting straight A's in school Jim never applied himself. He wouldn't read when he was young. 'Why should I?' he'd say. 'Let Frankie read to me.' Jim really had better natural coordination, but Frankie made himself an athlete through sheer force of personality. There was nothing he wouldn't try—baseball, football, diving, water skiing. Jim let Frankie excel, never challenged him.

"Frankie knew Jim was too dependent on him. Once he came to me and said, 'Mom, I'm going to make Jim mad. But I've got to make him go out and find his own friends. He can't rely on me all the time.'"

Then a few months later, in February of 1964, Frankie drowned while surfing in a strong undertow. Jim was devastated.

Jim recalls: "It was really strange. My mother and I'd

been out shopping and when we got home there was this policeman there. My mother told me to go into the kitchen, but I heard it and I just kind of crumbled and fell apart. The cop told me I shouldn't cry because I had to be a man now, but the cop was crying, too, which kind of blew my mind because he was like twenty-seven or twenty-eight and I was only fifteen.

"And then started the long brigade of neighbors and terrible things. And the doctor came and gave my mother a whole bunch of tranquilizers, which she kept feeding into me. They were like Miltowns which you're supposed to take half of one every six hours and she was feeding me a whole one every four hours for about two weeks. It was a long time, you know, because they couldn't find the body. We waited and waited but it didn't come up, so we had the memorial service and then two weeks later the body washed up on the beach in San Mateo.

"I was on tranquilizers most of this time and I was so tranquil I didn't know what was happening. Finally I got a little more coherent. Then I didn't want to go back to school, I didn't want to go out of the house. I wanted to die because I felt like I should have died instead of him. Like I was nothing. He got good grades and he had a girl friend and he was going to be a lawyer. I wasn't any of those things and yet I was alive.

"Then I gradually came to accept it. And I think that's when I really became a person. It's kind of like I never existed until he died, because as long as he was alive I was a carbon of him. Then I couldn't be a carbon of him any more because there was nobody to copy. So I had to become me—which is kinda scary. And I guess that's when it all started. I didn't have a father to pattern myself after. I didn't have a brother any more. So I started learning and wondering and questioning and, you know, growing into me."

And drinking. Just a few months after his brother's death, Jim started going regularly to "booze parties" with his brother's friends. "I sort of took his place in this circle and they had these parties all the time. We moved around, wherever anybody's parents were going to be out for an evening. We drank anything—whisky, vodka, gin. I'd go out and get completely shellacked and when I got drunk I'd really get obnoxious."

But nothing showed yet. Jim still played the role.

Healthy California boy. Dates. Basketball games. School dances. Maybe a little quiet, a little withdrawn. But nothing to worry about.

Marina High School was spanking-new, the very model of a suburban California school: one-story white and gray with beige wooden siding, a crenelated roof, broad green lawns and a landscaped patio where students could chat and study while soaking up the San Leandro sunshine.

And all the trimmings too. An alma mater:

> Marina High, Marina High
> All hail your blue and white
> Marina High, Marina High
> Show all your strength and might
> Holding high your banner
> Marina High, Our Alma Mater
> Hail, hail, hail.

A football cheer:

> Somewhere [clap-clap]
> Over the goal post
> There's a [clap-clap]
> Touchdown we want
> Go for it!!!!

A student code:

A. Each student shall uphold high personal standards of honesty, courtesy and cleanliness.
B. Each student shall respect, support and obey student rules and civil law concerning the conduct of minors.
C. Each student shall care for personal property and the property of others in a responsible way.
D. Each student shall try, to the best of his ability, to benefit from the opportunities education offers.

And other rules:

Boys should be clean-shaven. Hair must be reasonably trimmed and clean, with no extreme style or length. Slacks, suits, shirts, sweaters and jackets which are appropriate for teenage boys may be worn. All clothing must be clean.

Shirts must be buttoned.

Radios and tape recorders are forbidden on school grounds.

Tobacco and narcotics are forbidden on school grounds.

Deans are responsible for students from the time they leave home until they return home.

Then, in his senior year at Marina, Jim discovered Haight-Ashbury. It was the fall of 1965, still a full year before the hippie phenomenon broke onto the national scene. But it was already stirring faintly among some San Franciscans, and Jim found his way to them.

"I met this girl who lived with foster parents in the Haight. Her foster mother was really groovy, very intelligent and liberal-thinking and understanding. I felt more at home at her house than I did in my own. She helped me to work out a lot of my problems that I was hung up on.

"She had a hippie son, I guess one of the first of the hippies. And, I don't know, I guess I was just ready for it. A year before or maybe a year later I might have felt just like everyone else would react to hippies—kind of with repulsion. But I was ready for it. It was such an easy thing. You know, complete acceptance no matter what you are.

"We'd come over every weekend and sometimes on week nights too, come over and listen to music and just sit and talk to them. It was a kind of free and open thing. You could say whatever you wanted and do whatever you wanted and it was really nice. I never found anything like that before."

The style was spreading quickly. Back at Marina, Jim started hanging with a few others who were catching on. "My friends and I were kind of the weirdos of the school. There was only seven of us. It was kind of like Future Hippies of America or something and it was pretty terrible. People would yell names at us, because you just can't get away with wearing beads and sandals in a straight suburbia type of situation.

"Well, I went as far as I could at school, but I couldn't get too far-out because it was a very uptight thing. Suburban high schools are very strict-type situations. There's only a certain level to which you can go before they really get mad and throw you out. So it was mainly a question of sitting bored through classes and then in the evening getting your kicks somewhere else."

In March 1966 Jim got his first real kicks. "We were over at the house and the son said, 'Why don't you take some acid?' I said, 'What's acid?' and he told me all about it. He told me what was good and what was bad and I decided 'What the heck.'

"So about nine or ten of us went down to Golden Gate Park one afternoon. It was just barely becoming spring and the wild flowers were growing. It was by this small clear lake up by the ocean. We just sat down on the shore and somebody passed around these little white capsules. I was afraid until I put it in my mouth. And then I wasn't afraid any more because I figured what was going to happen was going to happen. And it turned out it was really nice. Nothing unpleasant at all. It was kind of a childhood-type thing. I just kind of walked in the sun and sniffed flowers and talked and did fun things. It was really nice.

"I took seven or eight more trips that spring. No pot— or only once—because I found out I was allergic to it, sort of a hay-fever-type reaction. I wheeze and my eyes swell shut. But I really liked acid.

"Nobody ever really caught us. But about three weeks before I graduated there was this kind of crisis. There were a lot of accusations about people selling LSD and marijuana at the school. It wasn't my group. It was the hard kids, you know, the kids that always had their hair slicked back, tight rock pants, boots and chains. But my friends were kinda weird, so they naturally assumed we were the ones doing the dealing. They called us in with all these wild accusations.

"I got kind of scared, so I called my sister over in San Jose. She knew what I was doing because I'd confided in her all the time. I told her, 'I can't stand it. I'm going to get arrested. I want to get out of here.' She told me she thought it would be best if she came up and we sat down and told my mother the whole thing so she'd be prepared if anything happened. I didn't want to do it, but she talked me into it. So we went home and broke the whole thing.

"My mother really took it very well. All she wanted me to do was promise that I'd never take LSD again, which I did, knowing that I would take it the first chance I got. But she understood everything else. By this time, you know, I wanted to 'live life' instead of messing myself up by doing things I didn't want to do. I didn't want to go to school. I didn't want to work. I just wanted to look around and see what the world was all about. And so my mother said, 'Well, you can do what you want. There's three more weeks of school and you can either stay in school or go on and live with your sister. If you stay in school and graduate, then you can go look around the country and see what you want.' She was so darned nice about it I decided to stay in school."

Jim graduated in June.

A few weeks later, the police picked him up in San Leandro Park, unconscious from sniffing glue.

His mother was called, and she recalls: "By this time Jim knew he had some problems. He really wanted help and he told the probation officer so. But they said, 'We got lots of kids who need help more than you do.' The police didn't bring charges. The sergeant just told him to go get his hair cut and come back. When Jim returned looking really clean-cut, the sergeant said, 'You're a nice-looking kid, but you look much better this way. Now just keep it that way. You don't want to hurt your mother, do you? Now go home.'

"I remembered Jim came out of the police station with me and he was just disgusted. 'What asses!' he said. 'When I had long hair and dirty clothes they called me a dirty animal. But when I have my hair cut, good clothes on, they pat me on the head and say, 'You're a good boy. Go home.' But, me, I'm the same person inside. All they care is how I look."

The probation officer had given Mrs. Murphy the name of a psychiatrist. "I called him but he could only give me an appointment in three months. By that time, Jim said, 'Forget it; I'll solve it myself.' He never asked for help again."

Jim began spending most of his days and some of his nights in Haight-Ashbury. Soon he was taking acid every couple of days, which kept him spaced out and confused most of the time. Although he came home at night to sleep, his mother seemed to notice nothing. She was busy —working days as an executive secretary for an Oakland engineering company and cooking and cleaning at night.

"Maybe I stuck my head in the sand too," she concedes. "It was so important for me not to lose him. So I never made a scene. Because I knew that if I ever let him go in anger I might never get him back.

"I really didn't realize he was on drugs again. Anyway, I couldn't get all that hot and bothered about the hippie thing. After all, it was the first group he'd ever really been close to. It wasn't the group I would have chosen, but it was someone he could identify with.

"I didn't like the society we live in any better than they do. I just knew I couldn't change it. I always taught my children to conform outwardly, not inwardly. I told them, Questioning, doubting inwardly, was fine. But everybody has to conform outwardly, you can't go out and kill people."

Jim agrees that his mother put few constraints on him. "She was completely liberal about everything. She offered no opinions, let us form our own. All I had to say was, 'I'm going here' and 'I'm going there' and I was allowed to go. I was allowed to question anything I wanted.

"But, you know, kids who have that much freedom get a kind of complex. They think maybe the parents let them do anything because they don't care. What I did, I guess, was rebel and do things that I knew they wouldn't like as often as I could just to see—kind of like: 'I'm drunk. Now punish me so I know that you care.' And it never happened.

"All my mother really cared about was appearances. You know, she really hates the job she has, she hates the people she works with. And I'd ask her why she didn't leave. She'd say, 'Because I have responsibilities.' And I'd say, 'But what about your responsibility to yourself, to be you, do what you want to do?' And she just gets this blank look on her face and she doesn't know what the hell I'm talking about."

For a while, Jim tried to meet some of the responsibilities his mother talked about. In November he got a job at a San Francisco hospital pulling patients' charts.

"It was terrible," he recalls. "I was in with all these really straight, terrible people. There were six guys and six girls, all about eighteen, nineteen or twenty. But it seemed to me the way they acted they were more like fourteen and fifteen, the way they were constantly having rubber-band fights and stupid things. I couldn't talk to any of them because they all thought so differently from me, and I had to sit there all day and listen to them talk about their girl friends that they were going to marry and the houses they were going to buy and all the materialistic things they wanted. If I had said what I was thinking I wouldn't have lasted too long. But I still felt I ought to try to follow what my mother said I should do, which was, you know, to work and earn my way in this society."

But one day in February changed all that. It was the day of the Human Be-in at the Polo Grounds.

"Before I went to the be-in I took some acid. There was this special kind of acid out then—an itty-bitty teeny white tablet which was really powerful and you were supposed to split it up for four people. But I took a whole one and then walked down through the park toward the be-in.

"There were about fifty people all walking along. Everybody knew everybody but nobody really knew anybody. It's kind of like when you're a hippie you know everybody anyhow. But some Hell's Angels came up and they said, 'Is everybody going to the be-in?' and we all said yes, and they gave everyone another tab of acid and so I took that and then I got to the be-in and by the time I got there I was really, really, really bombed.

"And then I saw this friend of mine who was a dealer and I walked up to him and he said, 'are you stoned?' and I opened my mouth to say something. I couldn't say anything, so he dropped another one in my mouth. And I just went 'Ahhh' and I didn't know what to do. So I just got stoned. And I was so stoned I was just walking around in circles, in this little circle, just walking around and around because I didn't know where anybody I knew was and I didn't know what to do. So I was just walking around in circles, thinking. And this girl came up to me and said, 'Wow, you sure are stoned; you better sit down.' And she sat me down and she sat there with me. Then I was really, really stoned.

"By the time we were ready to leave four or five hours later I was just kind of, you know, still pretty far-out. We were walking through the park and I would walk about thirty or forty feet and I'd think of something and I'd sit down and I'd think, you know, about whatever it was that was on my mind. Then I'd get up and walk a few more feet and sit down and do it again. I'd think about myself and where I was in relation to the world. Where do I belong? What is my purpose in being here? About God and stars and things. And I just decided I couldn't go on living in this farce of a society."

So a few days later, Jim left the file room at the hospital for a coffee break and never went back, leaving a hundred and fifty dollars in pay. It was almost a year to the day since he'd first taken acid.

For the next few months, Jim drifted. First he moved in with a girl he knew in Oakland. Then he moved to Berkeley, living off some money he had in the bank. Three friends moved in with him for a while, but Jim was always taking off, flying down to Los Angeles to see friends or going surfing at Big Sur.

Then he and two friends decided to drive to New York. "We were going through Seattle, which people don't understand, but we just decided it was nicer and we wouldn't have to go through the desert. We didn't think the car would make it through the desert and we were probably right because it didn't even make it through Seattle. It nearly blew up there. So we sold it for ten dollars and just moved in with some people there.

"Then my friends decided to go back to San Francisco to get married. They left me all alone. I had nowhere to go and I had no money and there was nothing to do. I didn't want to come back because it would be admitting defeat, admitting I couldn't do it. So finally I moved into this big house with about ten other people in it.

"They were shooting speed all the time. They kept offering it to me and I kept saying no. I'd never shot speed up to then and I didn't want to. But it's an easy kind of thing to fall into if everyone around you is doing it. You just kind of put up a resistance as long as you can. Finally, one day I came home and everybody had done up speed and some people were doing it up again in the kitchen and they said, 'Do you want some?' and I said, 'I guess so.' It didn't make much difference because, oh, I don't know, I didn't even care any more. I'd fought so long to resist that I just couldn't resist any more.

"But I liked the feeling. You stick the needle in and about ten seconds later it's kind of like this warm-feeling hand clasping over your brain. It's just nice—this great surge like an orgasm.

"But every time you start to come down it's so terrible

that you do up again. So since a high lasts four to six hours, you're doing up every four hours or so for about four days, which is about as long as you can take it. After two or three days you get pretty screwed up. Just running around bumping into things and it feels like your head is going to drop off any second. You're just exhausted because you've run so long your body is overworked.

"Well, I just kept this up from the middle of July until the end of August, maybe a little longer, it's kind of a blank-type area. About two months, I guess, during which I was hardly ever off speed. For a while I lived in the big house, in the basement, with this whole group of people who were doing speed all the time twenty-four hours a day. Once when I was off speed, there was this girl I knew there, and realizing I was really screwing myself up, I said, 'I just gotta get out of here' and she said, 'Come and live with me.' So within fifteen minutes I was packed and went with her. I thought I could get off speed there, except after I moved in I found she did speed too. It was cleaner and there was food and it seemed better until I realized that it was no good either because it was pretty hideous.

"Then in September I was really messed up. I'd lost about thirty-five pounds and my teeth were falling out, my gums were rotting, and I decided 'Oh, dear,' so I called my mother and asked for some money to go to the dentist. But he told me I had malnutrition and that's why my teeth were all messed up. So, I called my mother and told her I had to have three teeth pulled and she said, 'Come home,' and finally I decided I'd better go home. I was sick and tired and I wanted to come home. Then when I got home they found out I had hepatitis too."

For several weeks Jim rested at home and then Mrs. Murphy again suggested he go out and get a job. "If I was a sitar player I could have gotten a job easy," Jim recalls. "Otherwise, the agency said I'd have to cut my hair before they could find me a job. But by this time I'd decided, hell, I've been through so damn much I'm not gonna go back where I was six months ago." Then, one day, he wandered into the Haight-Ashbury Medical Clinic, an agency set up to offer hippies free medical care. The clinic needed another staff assistant and Jim found the atmosphere "groovy," and so he just stayed on, first for no pay at all and then for a nominal fifteen dollars a week.

His mother was getting remarried, to an engineer she'd met on the job, and so he was going to have to move out and find a place. But not in Haight-Ashbury, he'd decided. "It's dirty and it's noisy and I don't like dirt and I don't like noise."

Jim doesn't know what he'll do next. "I'll do whatever comes along that seems right at the moment. And when it stops being right, then I'll stop doing it. Most people don't do what they want to do. Not really. If they can do what they want to do and still live in straight society, fine, more power. But I can't."

Jim doesn't think he can do much about straight society. "I don't think a crusade to turn on America is ever going to work. The only way you can do it is by being yourself. The more hippies there are, the more straight people are gonna realize that maybe there is something wrong. If there's that many people who do exactly the opposite of everything our society stands for, then maybe they're going to realize there are a few things wrong."

Jim has gone to several peace demonstrations. He attended four or five San Francisco rallies sponsored by the Vietnam Day Committee "just to see what it was like." And later he picketed for an hour in front of the Oakland induction center. He regards himself as a pacifist. "I just don't believe in war. It's kinda like legalized murder. I don't see how people can go to Vietnam or any other war and shoot people. I could never shoot anyone." He was recently granted a 1-Y deferment on the basis of a psychological report by a doctor at the clinic.

He would like to do something in "the civil rights movement," but he's not sure what he can do. "You know, I won't go out and riot with them, and there's not really anything peaceful being done any more that I can see."

Moreover, he's skeptical about the effect of radical movements. "I think it would be nice to change society, and slowly but surely things are happening, but there's nothing I personally can do to change it. Except be what I am. Be one more body for peace."

Since Jim's troubles began, Mrs. Murphy has been thinking, too, about what's wrong with society. And she thinks she knows.

"There was no love in any of those homes in Halcyon.

Everybody was always doing something for their children instead of just loving them. Parents were too busy for real love, so they bought their children off with things, possessions. The children just wanted Momma and Dad. But Momma and Dad were such unhappy, miserable people themselves, with lousy marriages.

"And, oh, the hypocrisy! They told their children to be honest, but they stole. They told their children not to drink, but, oh, how they drank. They told their children to be faithful, but you've never seen so much hanky-panky as we had in old Halcyon.

"It was all a front and our kids saw through it. I blame the parents—and I suppose that includes me. But don't say we were bad people. Just say—we blew it."

JOHN

Hernando Pizarro rode confidently before his finest cavalry as they pranced through the froth of the Urubamba River that morning in 1536. Above on the rocky hillside towered the parapets of Ollantaytambo, the Incas' great gray fortress; and as his horsemen clattered up the hillside in the first touches of the Andean dawn, the conquistador never doubted he had caught the Indians asleep. "But thousands of eyes were upon him," Prescott says in his history of the Spanish conquest, "and as the Spaniards came within bowshot, a multitude of dark forms suddenly rose above the rampart. At the same moment the air was darkened with innumerable missiles, stones, javelins and arrows, which fell like a hurricane on the troops, and the mountains rang to the wild war-whoop of the enemy. The Spaniards, taken by surprise, and many of them sorely wounded, were staggered; and, though they quickly rallied, and made two attempts to renew the assault, they were at length obliged to fall back, unable to endure the violence of the storm."

"It was the last triumph of the Incas," Prescott concludes. A quick reversal of fortunes destroyed the great native kingdom and subjected Peru's Indians to the rule of the Spaniards and their light-skinned descendants ever since.

When John McAuliff, a slim, intense Peace Corps volunteer from Indiana, came to Ollantaytambo in May 1965, he found the famed citadel on the hill a ruin. Only six huge stones remained from the fort's Sun Temple, and just a short stretch of the once formidable battlements still loomed above the Urubamba.

Yet, the spirit of the Incas was not entirely dead. Among the twenty-five hundred Indians and other dark-hued people who lived in the village which has grown up around the old fortress, McAuliff found a suddenly revived pride and an urge to reassert themselves against the light-skinned landlords and officials from the coastal plain.

A "land-invasion" movement had sprung up in the highlands in which farmers, led by a Trotskyite named Hugo Blanco, seized their landlords' property and grain mills. As the Army put down the movement, President Fernando Belaunde Terry sought to meet some of its grievances. Proclaiming the ideal of *mestizaje* (a blending of Indian and Spanish virtues), he pushed through agrarian reform and technical-assistance programs for the mountain people. Some of these social reforms were watered down by the opposition-controlled Congress, and others were hampered by lack of money. But once aroused, the Indians' aspirations were not easily dampened.

So when John McAuliff reached Ollantaytambo that spring he was reminded of Mississippi, where he had worked in the Student Non-Violent Coordinating Committee's "Mississippi Summer Project" the year before. Here again, he thought, he would be working with a dark-skinned people, long oppressed by whites, a people who had not yet fully realized the power they could have if they jointly demanded their rights. John thought he could help develop this spirit and give them the techniques they needed. It was an exciting prospect.

For nine months he worked as a community-development adviser, showing farmers how to use fertilizers, insecticides and hybrid potato seed and helping with a school-construction program. Then, in early 1966, he found his issue.

The absentee landlord of Tanccac, a small hacienda four miles from Ollantaytambo, had abruptly raised the rent for his thirty-five tenant families by 300 percent. Outraged, John plunged into an effort to block him.

First, he discovered that under the new agrarian-reform law if tenants objected to a rent increase they had a right to an official investigation—a right rarely invoked but one which gave them a position from which to bargain for a more reasonable sum. John and community leaders consulted lawyers who suggested that in the meantime Tanc-cac's farmers deposit their rent with the state attorney general (a stratagem which reminded John of Jesse Gray's Harlem rent strikes). Then the tactic had to be explained to the community.

Finally, in April, Tanccac was ready for its showdown. The landlord was a wealthy man named Delgado de la Flor who lived in Lima and owned several haciendas like Tanccac; so the farmers had to negotiate with his lawyer in Cuzco, twenty-three miles from the Urubamba valley.

One day in early spring, John, Orestes Becerra, Tanc-cac's most vigorous young farmer, and two other tenants set off on the three-and-a-half hour bus ride to Cuzco. The farmers wore their city clothes—faded jackets and trousers and scuffed leather shoes—but they carried home-spun ponchos over their arms. As the bus jolted along dusty roads up the side of the valley, with the snow-covered Andes glistening above them, John and the farm-ers chatted excitedly about their coming confrontation. That night they stayed with Orestes' sister, and the next morning walked over to the lawyer's office.

The office was tiny—barely large enough for a desk, a bookcase and a few straight-backed chairs. So when John and the three farmers crowded in they were sitting much closer than they'd expected to the landlord's representa-tive, a lightish-skinned man in a business suit.

The lawyer began politely but somewhat paternally, ad-dressing the farmers with the familiar *tú*. He hinted at the possibility of a compromise, but when the farmers talked of their rights under the law he began to threaten.

"You'll just have to pay the rent or get off the land," he warned.

"But the agrarian reform law says—" Orestes interjected.

"No, the law doesn't say any such thing," the lawyer shot back. "Whoever's been telling you that is just trying to mislead you. Now you all know Delgado, and he's al-ways been good to you. You should do what he says."

The farmers said Yes, Delgado was a kind gentleman, but the land was very poor, they had had a bad crop, there wasn't much water and, anyway, the agrarian reform law said—

"Well," the lawyer broke in, "we've heard stories about Communist agitators up there trying to disrupt the good relationships which have existed." Then turning to John, he said, "Mr. McAuliff, you are an American and Americans are very much against Communism. What do you know about these agitators?"

A few months before, Peruvian troops, advised by American "counter-insurgency" experts, had put down an abortive guerrilla movement in the highlands, allegedly led by Cuban cadres. But the guerrilla movement had not touched Tanccac and so John told the lawyer, "No, there are no agitators up there, just people who've talked to the Agrarian Reform Office and who know their rights, just people who feel they're being unfairly treated by the landlord, but who are willing to talk and reach a fair settlement."

Obviously irritated now, the lawyer said, Well, if that's the way things were he would have to turn the matter over to the *prefectura* for legal action. "People just can't stay on the land if they won't pay the rent," he said. The interview was over.

Ten paces down the narrow street, in the dark shade of the high Spanish-style houses, John, Orestes and the other farmers burst into laughter, slapping each other on the back and repeating over and over with broad mimicry the lawyer's phrases: how "Communist agitators" must be behind this, how "that isn't what the reform law says," and how "Delgado has always been so generous."

"It was an exciting moment, maybe the most exciting one I had in the Peace Corps," John recalled a few years later. "The conversation in the office had been so much like those I'd heard between white Southerners and humble blacks in Mississippi. But when we all started laughing out there in the street, I realized that the three guys from the community had been very conscious all along of what was going on in there.

"You know, I guess until then I'd thought it was up to me to give these people a consciousness of themselves, of the landlord-peasant relationship, and of the power they could have if they stood up to it. Now I'd discovered they were in fact very conscious of all that. Oh, they'd gone along with the phony bit of honoring the landlord, but they knew what the lawyer was up to. They knew they weren't strong enough to openly challenge him, but they could laugh openly at his attempts to scare them."

And in months to come, as John drew closer to the

younger farmers, they told him other stories gleefully, laughing as they had together outside the lawyer's office. Orestes told about the time the Army came to arrest some men in a village down the valley and everyone went out and stood in the road, the women in front, until the young lieutenant not only let the prisoners go but complimented the villagers on their determination. Or, with even more laughter, of the day the *prefecto* came up from Cuzco to try to arbitrate a dispute with the landlord, and when he said something the villagers didn't like, the women went at him with their whips.

Gradually, John developed ever more admiration for the *campesinos* and ever more doubts about what the Peace Corps—or the United States—was doing to help them.

Sitting in his straw-roofed, whitewashed mud hut in Tanccac, he typed out his random thoughts on a portable set on a rickety fruit box:

"Despite the usual middle and upper class self-justification about the laziness and irresponsibility of the campesino, one great truth of rural Peru is the widespread campesino desire to improve his way of life. The drive for change is clearest in the young men who have not yet been destroyed by the cruel exploitation of the economic and social system. If these men are given an opportunity which is meaningful to their own experience and sophistication and are protected from the traditional power structure they will change their communities and the nation."

Or, in a more bitterly ironic tract he called "Justification by Faith":

"The Peace Corps is a middle class, bourgeois organization. As such it has middle class bourgeois ideas about backward and deprived peoples. Its approach to the poor is their need to be saved. The missionary of the last century used more blatantly spiritual vocabulary to explain his call. *We* benefit from the snow white vestments of sociology and anthropology . . . The influence of Martin Luther is seen in the Peace Corps' belief that spiritual change or faith is the only path to salvation. Without new attitudes and the organized expression of them there is no progress. The prime heresy continues to be Justification by Works [which preaches] that all the poor need for their own salvation are material resources and the freedom to use them. Justification by works turns the Peace Corps volunteer into a mere technician with the mechanical job of material and advisory support to an independent and self-defined community."

But his doubts went beyond the Peace Corps itself. He looked with increasing distrust on United States policy toward Peru, which he felt was largely influenced by Belaunde's election pledge to nationalize the International Petroleum Co. (a 99.9 percent-owned subsidiary of Standard Oil of New Jersey). He suspected that the United States was "blackmailing" Belaunde, refusing to let him have money he badly needed for his agrarian and other reforms unless he agreed not to touch American oil holdings.

And when United States troops moved into the Dominican Republic, John shared much of the outrage expressed by Peruvian students. Back in his mud hut he banged out some rough notes:

"The intervention has put in even greater doubt exactly why the United States government has aid programs in Latin America. Are we here to fight Communism because Communism is Evil and its success would change the world balance of power and so threaten the good thing we've got going for us back home? Or has humane concern for our fellow man truly prompted a program of mutual help without consideration of the political affiliations of the partners? Evidence from American editorial opinion, the general political climate and the recent House resolution suggest Holy Alliance is a more accurate indication of our motivation than Alliance for Progress."

So as John moved toward the end of his tour in Peru that summer of 1966, he was filled with deep misgivings not only about the Peace Corps and its role in developing countries but about the nature of his own country's intentions toward the world around it.

If I were the personnel director of a major American company, I would look hopefully to the pool of returning [Peace Corps] volunteers. They have been selected by a rigorous process from the cream of the nation's youth. They have survived a demanding training program. They have displayed qualities of high motivation, capacity to adjust, and skills which have enabled them to spend two successful years working with the people of a foreign country. All of this is becoming obvious to alert companies . . .

—SARGENT SHRIVER

(Speech to the Los Angeles World Affairs Council October 7, 1963)

Peace Corps Volunteer John Francis McAuliff, Jr., was born August 26, 1942, in Brooklyn, the first child of John Francis McAuliff, Sr., an X-ray salesman, and the former Cecile Castor. His parents were both children of the Depression and have intense memories of hard times.

McAuliff Sr. recalls that although his father, a dentist in Garden City, Long Island, had a good practice, few of his patients paid their bills during the Depression. "After my freshman year at Colgate in 1932 I came home and announced that I wasn't going back to college. It was too expensive. I wanted to go to work. But one of Dad's oldest patients came to dinner and offered to pay a couple of hundred dollars on his overdue bill. So I went back to college." Finally, like most of their neighbors in the heavily mortgaged suburb, the McAuliffs lost their house on a foreclosure and moved back to Brooklyn, installing a dentist's chair in their home. "It was rough, but we scraped by," McAuliff Sr. recalls.

After graduating from Colgate in 1936, he went to work for Household Finance as a collection agent. "It was real nasty work in those days, chasing down poor Negroes and shanty Irish who owed us money." Making only ninety dollars a month himself, he married Cecile, a Brooklyn girl he'd known since childhood. A few years later, after one of the agency's debtors committed suicide and another fainted in the office, Mr. McAuliff couldn't take it any longer. He went to work as a salesman for the Picker X-Ray Corporation, for which he has worked ever since.

When John was born the next year, his mother recalls, he was a "normal, healthy, happy little boy." He was in both the cub and boy scouts and remembers scrapping with kids from the next housing development in Wantagh, Long Island, where the family moved when he was six. But by ten, John had largely lost interest in boyish horseplay and sports, preferring to spend his time indoors reading. This was apparently due to at least two factors: an operation for a ruptured intestine which kept him in the hospital for several weeks around the age of nine and required six months of recuperation; and discouragement at the unusual athletic prowess of his younger brother, Peter, whom John at the age of fourteen described as his "arch-enemy."

Whatever the reason, John recalls spending most of his time sprawled out on a couch reading first comics, then horse books and historical novels, and finally—turned on by something called the Rick Blane Science Adventure Series—becoming a science fiction fanatic. He went through every science-fiction book in the school library and then turned to the library in town—by then Wilton, Connecticut, where his father was transferred in 1953 and where John attended the seventh and eighth grades. He became so enthralled by the "space operas" he read that later he considered going to the Air Force Academy to become a space pilot. But he was most fascinated by stories about the creation of new societies and contact between earth and other civilizations—the kind of tale written by Heinlein and Asimov.

Today, John sees a connection between his science-fiction craze and his later radicalism. "It not only started me thinking about what it would be like to create a new kind of society; it put my own society in context, kind of like reading anthropology."

But its most immediate effect was to help undermine whatever respect he had for the Catholic Church, of which his mother is a devout member (Mr. McAuliff, an Episcopalian, didn't attend church but supported his wife's insistence that the children do so).

"I think the kind of scientism and rationalism implicit in the science fiction I was reading both undercut Catholic dogma and, in a way, provided its own kind of theology which was much more interesting to me. I was simply bored with having to sit in church once a week and have a ritual going on that I didn't understand and didn't care about. I thought it was all silly. I never really memorized the catechism."

But at that time John was not strong enough to defy his mother for long. He went to church and sullenly day-dreamed through the long services.

His agnosticism revived, however, in Indianapolis, where the McAuliffs moved in 1956. At first they lived in a small city house, but after a year rented a sprawling farmhouse on several acres of land in Fishers, sixteen miles from Indianapolis. The farm, an adjoining cattle farm and a nearby golf course provided endless room for the six McAuliff children to roam.

But there was also a new Catholic church in nearby Noblesville, manned by a priest with a conservative bent well suited to his substantial rural parishioners. While a sophomore in high school, John announced that since he could not accept the church's teachings he would no longer attend Mass.

This set off a head-on confrontation with his mother. There were long family wrangles, often followed by discipline, such as cuts in John's allowance. Finally, he returned to church, but he devised ingenious ways of keeping his mind off the Mass. Sometimes he would sneak out just after it started and return five minutes before the end. Or he would bring books to church and read them hunched down in the pew.

When he was a senior, an outraged parishioner reported him to the priest who complained to his mother that John was reading a "paperback novel" in God's house.

Indignantly John fired off a letter to the priest confessing: "I do indeed read other than the propaganda disseminated by your church during the time in question." So that the priest should not form "false impressions of my moral structure," John wanted him to know that his reading during Mass was confined to *The Age of Analysis,* a survey of modern philosophy edited by a Harvard professor, and *Henry Esmond,* by William Makepeace Thackeray.

"You may ask why I have engaged in such pursuits," John concluded. "Frankly I find them much more interesting than listening to your rather bigoted comments, such as those concerning birth control. I believe it is each individual's right and duty to make such decisions unilaterally without having others tell him what to think. I wish that in the future you do not bother my mother with complaints about me, but rather take them up with me. Since you already control her mind, I think it unsporting to take advantage of this fact by threatening her 'eternal damnation' for my 'error.' "

By this time John was already a declared iconoclast. Until high school, although he had preferred reading to sports, he had been a generally gregarious boy who traded baseball cards, was a patrol leader in the scouts and conformed outwardly to most standards of a mid-fifties American boyhood.

But at Indianapolis' Shortridge High School, to which he rode the bus from Fishers every morning, John quickly became a member of a small group of individualists. "All of a sudden I became conscious of isolation and proud of it," he recalls. "The group I was associated with were the very intellectual people, self-consciously political, critical of most of the mores and culture of the rest of the kids."

John recalls that the group developed first around the Shortridge Senate, an organization patterned after the United States Senate and devoted to debating public issues in an intensely realistic political atmosphere. But it spread out from there to include perhaps forty students who were involved either in the Chess Club, the Classical Musical Club (which John joined) or some other consciously "intellectual" pursuit.

The group was openly contemptuous of many of the twenty-five hundred students at the huge urban high school. "There was a real 'we–they' feeling. We were particularly hostile to the popularity people, the social people, the class presidents, the 'Normies,' as we called them. It was a very nonsocial group. Next to none of us dated or were involved in high school social events. I think I went to one basketball game and one football game during the whole time I was there—and remember, basketball is very big stuff in Indianapolis."

John recalls that the group developed around a nucleus of eight or ten classmates who shared these "common values." But Paul Harmon, a member of the nucleus who has remained one of John's closest friends, remembers it a little differently: "I would say the nucleus was made up of shy, socially awkward people. This certainly applied to both John and me. We preferred intellectual rather than social pursuits because they were more convenient, more comfortable for us."

However they thought of themselves, the group was regarded by other students as "kooks." Generally unconcerned with dress and grooming, most carried book bags, an unusual accessory at Shortridge, and some were self-consciously "artsy."

But the group's major focus was the Senate, one of the

school's oldest extracurricular activities but one which had always attracted intense students somewhat out of the school's mainstream. The senators, each of whom took the name of a United States senator, spent more time in parliamentary maneuver and factional infighting than in debate.

But when "Senator Kenneth Keating, Republican of New York," rose to speak he often took positions that ten years later John could hardly recognize as his own. One resolution he introduced, noting that the national debt totaled more than $290 million and that "no organization, public or private, can perenially remain in debt without weakening its foundations," called for a constitutional amendment providing that the debt be reduced by at least one percent per year and never be increased except in wartime.

In the classroom John took similarly conservative stands. One social-science paper inveighed against the New Deal for introducing the dangerous doctrine of "free bread and bureaucracy." Another warned that labor unions were becoming so powerful that the government should invoke the anti-trust laws against them. And in a twelve-page senior paper, which won an *Atlantic Monthly* certificate of merit, he marshaled his full case against creeping "governmentalism." "The function of government," he wrote, "is simply to provide those services which it would be inconvenient for individuals to provide for themselves, such as fire and police protection . . . To liken a government and its citizens to a mother and her child, as does United States Senator Vance Hartke (D. Ind.), is simply a sign of immaturity. To believe in a maternal or paternal government is to declare yourself incapable of independence and liberty . . . unless there is a change in attitude and those forces are resisted which tend to deteriorate our American ideals by extending federal power in the welfare state we have failed to prove democracy is practical."

But already it was foreign relations which fascinated John most. His interest was kindled in his sophomore year at Shortridge by a modern-history course taught by his favorite teacher, Mrs. Elsie Howard. That fall, assigned a paper on what he wanted to do when he grew up, he wrote earnestly, "When I first started this report I was not sure what I wanted to be. So I decided to investigate a career in which I was fairly interested, the foreign service. Now I am fairly sure that is what I want to be. Because there is still some doubt in my mind I intend to do some more research work on my own to resolve this all-important question."

His views on foreign affairs were by no means consistent. At times he took a hard anti-Communist line which matched his conservative domestic policies. For example, in his junior year he wrote a paper, "The Yalta Story or How We Lost the Peace," in which he argued that "because of a hyper desire for peace, a cry to 'bring the boys home' and other manifestations of war weariness, the Russians were given the impression that the United States would yield on any question." The same year he wrote a letter to John Foster Dulles on his retirement, concluding that "without your leadership in the Department of State our foreign policy might have come under the control of those individuals who value life more than liberty" and thanking him for "providing an example which I may profitably follow in pursuing a career in our nation's foreign service."

But within a year he was taking positions which would hardly have cheered Mr. Dulles. One paper, calling for the admission of Communist China to the United Nations, argued that "it is silly to think that the piddling few millions on Formosa can speak for the 600 million mainlanders" and concluded that the U.N. should be "a place where all views may be voiced."

Then, shortly after Fidel Castro seized power in Cuba in 1959, John wrote a column for the school newspaper attacking United States policy in Latin America and praising the Cubans, the Venezuelans and the Argentinians for overthrowing their "despotic governments."

"And which country is it that supports these criminals? Why, it is the freedom-loving, liberty-conscious United States. In seeking support against Communism we have looked the other way when undemocratic governments were concerned, never bothering to consider their oppressed citizens . . . It is neither our right nor our duty to intervene in undemocratic nations; but the least we can do is to refuse aid to these despicable despots who bleed their own citizens white. If we do not do so in the three remaining dictatorships of Latin America (the Dominican Republic, Nicaragua, Paraguay) we will lose the respect of all Latin America."

But the column was rejected by the paper's faculty adviser, who wrote across it in blue pencil: "John— It is not the policy of the *Echo* or any *school* paper to criticize our government. We have not had sufficient background material or training to merit this responsibility."

John was furious. A few weeks later he vented his anger in a paper for Composition I: "Freedom of the press is a proud slogan. It has been fought for and died for. The uninitiated would say that all the press in the United States is free. Someone writing for the daily *Echo* would disagree. I, possibly more than any other, have come up against censorship in the *Echo* because that which I submit is likely to be controversial. Controversy is generally banned from the *Echo*. So is criticism of government policies or suggestions of alternatives to them on the grounds that the high school student is neither wise enough nor mature enough to criticize constituted authority." But already John was developing a shrewd sense for the locus of power. "It is doubtful," he noted, "that the program of censorship originates from the *Echo* office, but rather from the Indianapolis Public Schools (i.e. the board of school commissioners, the downtown office, etc.)."

In response he got only another teacher's comment in the margin: "What about the idea that freedom is not license or that freedom means self-discipline?"

In his last year or so at Shortridge, this concern with individual self-expression and free inquiry became almost an obsession. In one *Echo* article he attacked the ban on "subversive materials" in high school libraries. After attending a "school for anti-Communists" he wrote: "Rather than being educated, I heard lengthy, fiery speeches which appealed more to emotion than to the intellect. I was informed by some speakers of such relevant points as 'I wouldn't allow my children in the same room with that murdering butcher' (referring to Mr. Khrushchev) . . . Such comments are a symptom of that disease—fanaticism. If the fanatic feels his way of life challenged he will strike back like a cobra at the challenger, accusing him of being unpatriotic, un-American, 'pink.'" And in still another paper, entitled "To Protect Our Freedom?" he wrote: "Restricting the rights of a 'dangerous' minority may eventually lead to restrictions of everyone's rights to protect one group's concept of freedom . . . What good does it do to defeat a totalitarian dictatorship in the name of liberty and freedom if you have become one yourself to do so?"

From this welter of sometimes inconsistent attitudes, John had begun to mold a distinctive world view. Conservative on economic and social issues, distrustful of big government, big business or big labor, opposed to much of American foreign policy and fiercely determined to maintain his right of dissent and free expression—it was a position not far from the brand of militant, old-style Calvinist individualism found throughout the Midwest and particularly in a city like Indianapolis.

In some respects it was similar to the position of the *Indianapolis News*, whose young editor, Stan Evans, John met and admired during this period. Evans was a leader of youthful conservatives, and about this time John joined such a group—the Intercollegiate Society of Individualists. Sponsored by the Foundation for Economic Education, the ISI was an effort to develop intelligent young conservatives. It was from this same effort that Young Americans for Freedom later grew, but while YAF often attracted far-right-wingers, ISI drew a more iconoclastic, libertarian breed.

And John was above all a libertarian. His favorite author in those days was John Stuart Mill. He read *On Liberty* first during a Great Books course at Shortridge, but he kept coming back to it time and again. "I really dug it," he says today, "the concept that every man should have unlimited freedom as long as his freedom didn't interfere with anybody else's freedom. Mill was the formative, crucial figure for me—the key to my political philosophy at that time."

And since then, too, libertarianism has remained the leitmotif of his political philosophy. "My radicalism still stems fundamentally from that kind of motivation. In a funny kind of a way, I've remained an individualist or populist. The communal drive has never been as strong in me as the anarchistic 'Every man should be free' thing.

"I don't think I've really changed so much. What change there has been came as a result of learning more about the world rather than shifting my basic values. Even my attitude toward the federal government. Indianapolis was always an anti-establishment town, very paranoid about the Eastern liberal establishment they thought controlled the country. Well, I haven't made such a big switch emotionally. I still don't trust Washington bureaucrats—I just don't trust them for different reasons now."

There was a streak of the same kind of independence in John's father too. He opposed Roosevelt from the start ("I thought he was an out-and-out phony, just out for power"), but in Long Island's Nassau County and Indianapolis, both heavily Republican areas, he voted Democratic almost for the hell of it. "In 1960 I put a Kennedy sticker up on the front door, even though, or maybe just because, I knew it would annoy our friends and neighbors. I was getting sick of all these people voting and thinking the same way just because everybody else was doing it." If anything, on most social and economic issues the McAuliffs were more liberal than Indianapolis and even than their own son during his anti-welfare-state period. "We had some disagreements about that," his mother recalls. "We couldn't understand why he was against social security." But essentially it was a nonpolitical household, with *Reader's Digest* condensed books the main reading matter on the shelves, and John had to go outside the home to feed his increasing appetite for political argument.

He was a decidedly contentious young man. "According to Dale Carnegie one should always avoid an argument," John wrote then. "I am of the opinion that only personal arguments should be avoided. Otherwise argument is fine for it sharpens our minds, challenges our beliefs and theories and increases our knowledge. Consequently I seize every opportunity which may be fortuitous to argument."

One opportunity was the Indianapolis Youth Council on World Affairs, which sponsored programs on foreign relations every couple of weeks. John became program director, and the summer after he graduated from high school he arranged a forum on "the elimination of one of mankind's cherished possessions, the sovereign nation state." In a printed circular, he wrote, "Anachronistic as this concept is, there are still some individuals who believe in it, such as the American Legion, the D.A.R. and Barry Goldwater"—strong stuff for Indianapolis.

Now he was ready to leave Indianapolis, but college admission proved a problem. With all his outside activities, John's academic record at Shortridge had been only mediocre. In courses he enjoyed—social science and advanced English—he worked hard and got A's. But in those which did not interest him—Latin, science, math—he did much less well. Ending with a C+ average, he ranked 114th in a class of 495. Yet he demonstrated his potential when he got almost the highest college board scores in the school. As a result he qualified for a National Merit Scholarship sponsored by his father's company for its employees' children.

Encouraged, John applied to only three colleges, Harvard, Princeton and Yale, and, he recalls, "On the same glorious day in spring I got rejections from all three; it was the first major crisis of my life." A family friend had gone to Carleton, a small but academically excellent liberal arts college in Northfield, Minnesota. Late in May John sent off a letter and he was accepted.

But before he had been at Carleton a week he was engaged in a major personal rebellion. Carleton had an elaborate set of freshman "traditions." During their first term, freshmen were required to wear a green-and-yellow beanie so that its brim was "no more or no less than two fingers' width above the bridge of the nose"; on an upperclassman's demand recite details of Carleton history or give forth with college yells and songs; stay off campus grass and flagstones and remain in the chapel balcony until upperclassmen had left the building. Moreover, during a three-day "hell-week" in October, they had to shine shoes, carry firewood and run other errands for upperclassmen. Violators were subject to discipline, including paddling, by the Men's League Traditions Court.

John flatly refused to perform most of the traditions. In a letter to the college newspaper—which was never printed—he explained why. The traditions, he said, only created "unnecessary tensions" for freshmen. "There are indeed enough hates and prejudices existing in the world today without artificially creating more for the dubious purpose of fostering class unity."

John said he would cease such acts immediately "because I believe that the public disavowal of them by at least one person will help in their eradication. In particular I shall in no way observe the regulations and practices of Hell Week, undeniably one of the most extreme and most childish manifestations of traditions. If and when I receive a summons from the Men's League Court, I shall ignore it for two reasons: first, its jurisdiction is questionable and second, it is a blatant travesty of justice and I would stand as much chance of a fair trial as Sacco and Vanzetti did in the 30's."

And John buttressed his case with no less than three citations from his favorite author, John Stuart Mill, among them: "Where not the person's own character, but the traditions or customs of other people are the rule of conduct, there is wanting one of the principal ingredients of human happiness, and quite the chief ingredient of individual and social progress."

John's adamant stand outraged some upperclassmen. They threatened him with force unless he appeared before the traditions court, and one day in the dining room a sophomore came up and kicked him. But John remained adamant, and the court never summoned him.

Today he still recalls the period with disbelief. "It was just an incredible kind of introduction to academic life. I'd come to Carleton with this really intellectual image of what college was going to be like, and instead I found this! What's more, I got no support from the administration and only a little moral support from faculty and students. Nobody was ready to take a public stand with me. Those first six weeks set the course for my whole college career, partly because the only students who even came down and said they supported me privately were the New York radicals."

John was still far from being a political radical. In a letter to the *Carletonian*, the college paper, during his freshman year, he defined himself as "a non-Communist who occasionally knocks our system (e.g., segregation, attacks on civil liberties, the House Un-American Activities Committee, agricultural aid programs, compulsory social security, gerrymandering, pork-barrel legislation, junketeering congressmen, etc.)."

That was the fall of the Kennedy-Nixon campaign and John arrived at college wearing a Nixon-Lodge button. But after talking politics with one of the New York radicals he put a piece of adhesive tape over Nixon's name and walked around the rest of the fall with only "Lodge" showing.

He was still a member of the Intercollegiate Society of Individualists and read the material they sent him. But soon he found the conservatives at Carleton were not the libertarian breed he had been drawn to in Indianapolis.

"They were traditionalists, the suit-and-tie boys, not at all the kind I was interested in."

And temperamentally, if not yet politically, he was drawn to the radicals. One of these was Jack Barnes, a senior who had been active in the Young Socialist Alliance and had just returned from a summer visit to Castro's Cuba. He and his equally radical roommate were among those who offered John some support in his lonely battle against freshman traditions. Soon John was spending many evenings in their room, talking and listening to Pete Seeger records.

So he was gradually drawn into liberal-radical politics on campus, which meant the Action Party, a group organized by Jack Barnes. This was still several years before the Berkeley revolt, but Action was already advocating something close to student power—attacking *in loco parentis*, urging more responsibility for student government, arguing for freer use of campus facilities.

This was the first aspect of Action's program which appealed to John. Running for a seat in the student Senate he declared, "Treating college students as children is the best way to insure they remain children." In his late freshman and sophomore years, his main target was one which naturally had particular meaning for him—Carleton's religious requirement. Although nondenominational, Carleton required that each student have some kind of "religious experience" at least once each week, either in the school chapel, a downtown church or at a special Sunday evening program. John led a vigorous petition campaign against the requirement, arguing that students were entitled to "freedom of belief and nonbelief."

But Action by no means restricted itself to student-power issues. Contending that "what is done in Washington or in Moscow or Peking can affect the Carleton student in just as real a fashion as what is done in the president's office," it campaigned for repeal of the Smith and McCarran Acts, prohibition of nuclear testing and reestablishment of diplomatic relations with Cuba.

Cuba, another old interest, was the issue which probably turned John definitively to the Left. His interest in Latin America was reawakened the summer after his sophomore year, which he spent at an American Friends Service Committee work camp in Mexico, planting coffee and digging latrines. A few weeks after he returned to Carleton the Cuban missile crisis broke out and John was outraged by Kennedy's tough line.

In an article written for the *Carletonian* he argued that the United States should halt its "illegal blockade" and negotiate a mutual withdrawal of Soviet missiles from Cuba and American missiles from Turkey. "Each country has an equal right to have missiles in the territories of its allies," he wrote, "but is equally crazy to do so." A few days later he took part in his first demonstration, a rally against the Cuban blockade staged by the Student Peace Union at the University of Minnesota. John was one of thirty Carleton students pelted with eggs, oranges and toilet paper by a group of young conservatives.

Years later, John recalled the missile crisis as "the first time I found myself consciously taking a radical position. I might not have called it radical then, but it was the first time I was conscious of taking a stand radically different from what everybody else was saying, what the press was saying, what television was saying. I guess it was then that I started fundamentally questioning the logic, the wisdom, of my government."

That fall he was also active in Challenge, a group which brought controversial speakers to campus. One he invited was George Lincoln Rockwell, the American Nazi leader, whom John explained it was important to hear because "he represents ideas that twenty years ago produced the most terrible war machine in Western history, ideas that students should come up against, from a partisan source, to appreciate their impact upon history."

Challenge also sponsored a panel that fall with a Communist, a Socialist and John (representing the "liberal" position). As treasurer, he sent the Communist a check to cover travel expenses from New York. Within a few weeks, John heard from his friend Paul Harmon, then at Indiana University, reporting that an F.B.I. agent had interviewed him about why John was interested in Communism.

Furious, John fired off a long letter to J. Edgar Hoover which said, "I have a quaint belief that to be a free man means to be able to write to whomever one pleases without having the government investigate you . . . I believe that it is my duty as a citizen of a free country to take no one's word for anything just because he represents Authority. I believe it is my responsibility to find out what Communism is, not only from unreliable sources biased against it (e.g., the American Nazi Party, the John Birch Society), but also from unreliable sources biased for it (e.g., the CP itself). Surely if you have any appreciation of education as distinguished from the indoctrination you would encourage me in this practice . . . Your office bears the very grave responsibility of keeping track of potentially treasonous people without serving as a brake on the free and fearless expression of all ideas. From this experience of mine, I would say you are seriously failing that responsibility."

The letter, printed in the *Carletonian,* was picked up by the Minneapolis *Tribune* and other papers. Mr. Hoover never answered, but John got a rash of other letters, including a brief note from his father which asked, "What is all this F.B.I. nonsense! An adult member of the Carleton Senate would, I assume, conduct himself as an adult, intelligent person. Don't burn your bridges behind you. Build from one to another. Build a sound future. Dad." It was one of the few responses his father has ever made to his political activity.

John's major activity that fall—and for several years to come—was civil rights. All of a sudden, the events in the South had broken with their full impact over him.

Until 1962 John had been only abstractly aware of the developing struggle. He had grown up in exclusively white neighborhoods and the few Negroes he encountered at Shortridge made little impression on him. He attended a few meetings of the Shortridge Human Relations Council, the only group there concerned with civil rights, and later recalled his reaction then as Yeah, they're probably right but they sure get emotional about it. When he arrived at Carleton the college had only one American Negro student, but this did not strike him as peculiar.

Then, on a single steaming hot day that past summer, the issue had come alive. On the bus south toward the Mexican work camp he began to notice the COLORED and WHITE signs on washroom doors and water fountains in the fly-specked terminals (even though the Interstate Commerce Commission had already outlawed such distinctions). When the bus pulled into Huntsville, Texas, John found himself walking into the dingy "colored" lunchroom. But when he sat down at the counter and ordered a cup of coffee, the Negro waitress was terrified and blurted out something in a strangled voice. John couldn't understand her, but a Negro high school student who had been on the same bus said, "She wants you to leave; she's afraid she'll lose her job if she serves you." John said he wouldn't eat in the white restaurant, so the student brought two coffees outside where they drank them together. Later, as the bus rolled through the dun fields of northern Texas, they talked, and the boy told John what it was like to be black and grow up in the South. Once, he turned in his seat and said simply, "I want to walk where I want to walk."

The boy's words were still reverberating in John's mind that fall when Frank Smith, a Negro student from More-house College in Atlanta, came to Carleton to speak about the work of the Student Nonviolent Coordinating Committee. John was exhilarated. Here was a group on the cutting edge of the struggle and he immediately plunged into "support work" for SNCC.

John decided to take advantage of that fall's state elections to dramatize the fight for voting rights in the South. Under his leadership, the Action Party ran off leaflets which read roughly: "While you're calmly exercising your American right to vote there are people in the South struggling, being jailed, beaten and even dying for it. We hope you will consider this and send a donation to SNCC or CORE." They planned to distribute them outside Northfield polling booths, but the city's attorney ruled that the leaflets were "campaign material" and thus could not be passed out on election day. This was John's first direct conflict with the law and he handled it shrewdly. He called the American Civil Liberties Union, which appealed to the state attorney general, who overruled the city attorney.

By November, John was so absorbed in civil rights work that he sent out a form letter to relatives and friends: "In Christmases past you have generously sent me a Christmas present. If it is your intention to do the same this year I would appreciate it if instead you made a donation to the Student Nonviolent Coordinating Committee. This organization of students of my generation is spearheading the courageous struggle of the Southern Negro for equal rights. It deserves and needs your help."

And while others were opening presents and sipping eggnog that Christmas, John and Paul Harmon took off on a two-week hitchhiking trip through the South. They stopped off at Tougaloo College, a black school in Jackson, Mississippi, where they talked with a number of SNCC activists. John was warmed by their enthusiasm but "chilled" by Jackson, where a Negro girl insisted he walk away from her each time a police car approached.

They swung over to Atlanta, where they talked with Howard Zinn and Staughton Lynd, both then teaching at Spelman College. "I didn't have any idea who they were when I got there, but I remember being very impressed by how radical and mature they were."

They talked to the other side too. In Jackson they marched into Governor Ross Barnett's office and talked to him for fifteen minutes about "how things are down here." In Atlanta, at Howard Zinn's suggestion, they went out to Lester Maddox's restaurant, ate a fried-chicken dinner and spent an hour chatting with the future governor. Barnett's and Maddox's views were echoed too in countless conversations with the white Southerners who picked them up on the roads. The one Negro who picked them up couldn't step into the lobby of the white hotel in Thomasville, Georgia, where he dropped them off.

Arriving back at Carleton, John's already considerable commitment to the civil rights movement had been immeasurably strengthened. That spring he wrote a series of articles for the *Carletonian* on what he had seen in the South, raised funds for SNCC and carried on a long correspondence with SNCC headquarters in Atlanta, some of it with a young man named Julian Bond.

And the almost frenzied activity continued that summer in Indianapolis, where, besides making up his language requirement at summer school, he threw himself into the Indianapolis Social Action Council, a newly formed group working to organize the city's one hundred thousand Negroes. One of the few whites in the group, he helped organize rallies and edited several issues of a small newspaper (one of which carried a cartoon showing white faces in the form of a swastika).

John's growing militancy may have stemmed partly from his own guilt feelings about race prejudice. In an essay he wrote that summer called "None of My Best Friends are Negro—The Price of Privilege," he asked, "Why do I find myself nervous as I drive through a Negro neighborhood and much more likely to lock the car when

I park? . . . I have not had a close relationship with a person who was Negro and doubt that I will until I can stop thinking of a person as Negro . . . It is the destruction of this unnecessary bar between people for which I am now fighting . . . I fear a little bit of 'revolutionary' action may be necessary in Indianapolis to accomplish any immediate change."

His senior year, as John recalls it, was "a lot of things coming to fruition."

One of the first fruits to ripen was his running battle with the administration over the dress code. College rules required a coat, tie and other dignified clothes at meals and weekly convocations. John balked. Once when he wore Bermuda shorts and sandals to convocation, the dean of men lost his temper and nearly punched him. From then on, John usually conformed through such stratagems as wearing a shoestring tie threaded through a peace button. But in his senior year when he appeared coatless and tieless at a faculty-student tea, he was asked to leave. John sent a three-page letter to the college's president in which he said, "Dress customs are to me a colossal fraud which say nothing about the person hiding beneath them . . . while I recognize that many people prefer to exist on this shallow level of superficialities I don't feel it is my responsibility to encourage them."

By this time, John had become editor of *About*, a monthly campus magazine designed to express views too unorthodox or pungent for the *Carletonian*. In an opening editorial, John said the paper would be "a gadfly on everyone's neck."

He kept his promise, often in his own column, which he called *The Barefoot Anarchist*. When the administration demanded that lights be kept on in a notorious "passion pit" in the Student Union, John wrote:

> "Lights on" they said in a monologue
>   United, comfortable and prim;
> "Our word is law, our God is gold
>   Our love, the purging of your sin."

In other columns he argued for opening faculty meetings to student reporters, raising the "coolie wages" paid faculty babysitters, improving the quality of films at local movie houses, abolishing freshman hazing, and providing sex education courses.

Somehow he found time for a personal life too. He did not date until he was nineteen, but then he quickly went through what he described shortly afterward as "an emotional revolution." First there was a "stormy" relationship with one girl and then a deeper one which "occupied pretty much my whole emotional and sexual life my junior and senior years." He played soccer, skated and folkdanced (largely to evade the "jock" atmosphere which prevailed in most physical education), and he majored in history (because political science at Carleton was dominated by conservative professors).

That June, almost as a final fling, John ran for permanent class president on an unusual platform. Arguing that past alumni class officers had been devoted to perpetuating the "jolly, jolly alumni bit" and "reminiscing about past experiences," he said he would seek to keep the class "living with each other in terms of the present." Despite strong opposition from more traditional elements in the class, he won.

All that year, John had been juggling three possible careers—law, journalism and teaching. But by spring he wasn't ready to make up his mind; his old fascination, the foreign service, still shone beyond the more immediate domestic concerns, and, besides, he had the draft to worry about. So he opted for the Peace Corps.

John was by no means a Kennedy enthusiast. He had been to Kennedy's right in 1960 and in the meantime had moved to his left. In his senior year, he wrote a paper sharply critical of the country's Vietnam policy. (Even Kennedy's assassination had made him "only sad, not really broken up the way most people were." He was much more affected by the killing of Medgar Evers, whom he met during his trip south. "When I saw a paper on a newsstand in Northfield saying 'Mississippi NAACP Leader Shot,' I had to sit down on a bench and I came close to crying.")

But although only lukewarm about Kennedy, John had been enthusiastic about the Peace Corps from the start. He sponsored a resolution in the Carleton Senate backing the program, and from then on the possibility of volunteering had never been far from his mind.

But there was still the almost equal lure of the civil

rights movement. So when John was accepted for the
Peace Corps' Peru program in May 1964, he had his en-
try postponed until fall so he could join the Mississippi
Summer Project, in which hundreds of Northern students were going south to help in voter registration and
"freedom schools."

John explained what he was doing in a mimeographed
letter he sent from Carleton that June to his friends and
relatives. After asking that any money slated for graduation gifts be sent to Mississippi Summer, he wrote, "I am
too much the advocate to resist the opportunity for the
following short polemic: the reason I am going to Mississippi (and Peru) is that I believe (with the Angels)
that every living person should have political freedom
and enjoy full human dignity. Wonder with me awhile why
our country worries so expensively about defending one
dictatorship against another in Vietnam and all but ignores
the tyranny her own Negro citizens live under in Mississippi."

With the letter he enclosed his final columns from
About and the *Carletonian*. One argued that "a college
of the liberal arts should see its primary purpose in the
recognition by its students of their responsibility for the
world"; the other mused ruefully about his "personal discomfort with the absurdity of the world (Phi Beta Kappa
speakers notwithstanding)."

Some of this discomfort surfaced abruptly during a two-
week group-dynamics laboratory in Maine which John attended just after he graduated. In T-groups with fifteen to
twenty persons, he was made acutely aware of the prickly
parts of him which often put others off. "It was a very
important experience for me. The feeling of being isolated
from people which I'd felt so strongly in high school had
started softening in college. By the time I'd finished Carleton I'd pretty much built up a group of friends and I had
a real image there. But still I guess I tended to alienate
many people who didn't know me closely. At college I
was able to fairly well ignore that. But the T-groups
brought out a lot of these difficulties. They were people
who didn't know me, and they responded simply on the
personality basis. When they felt I was being hostile
they'd really throw it back. The lab accentuated the feeling of being tossed out of the womb, so by the time I went
to Mississippi my psyche was kind of exposed."

In a journal he kept that summer his still-bruised psyche was never far from the surface. On the long train ride to Mississippi he wrote, "Question of motivation: Why are we down here, and they at home—just a question of out-ness there forcing us to seek an in-ness elsewhere—people who are unable to relate directly and openly to real particular individuals insist on the protection of doing it on their 'own terms' through the structure of a grand ideal."

But his first post in Mississippi Summer did not live up to the grand ideal. Vicksburg, a largish city, "liberal" in Mississippi terms, with a steady tourist trade, did not fit John's image of the kind of place where he and other SNCC volunteers were to risk their lives for justice. "The police here *protect* the project workers," he wrote with dismay in his journal. "As long as I am in Mississippi I would learn far more in the tense and more difficult projects. But this naturally suggests some unpleasant and unresolvable questions about my own motivation for being down here. Seeking after adventure isn't exactly the highest idealism. Is there a difference between wanting experience with the sharpness of life and thrill-seeking?"

After days of introspection, John asked for a transfer. He was sent to Shaw, a delta town of twenty-three hundred persons, where he found an even worse situation. The project there was headed by a young Negro who seemed to resent the bright young whites from up North, and this contributed to other strains in the groups. Bursting with ideas for action, John found the stalemate intolerable, but continued to distrust his impulses. "I am still so tied up with my own needs for respect and importance," he wrote in his journal, "that I don't know how to rise to the point of considering the others. The ideal of course is that I get in at the beginning of an operation and be able to run my own show ('run my own show?'—not exactly what I'm preaching—damn it! I want so badly for people to see it my way that I won't let them do it for themselves)."

A few weeks later John moved again to Cleveland, seat of Bolivar County, where he worked in voter registration for the rest of the summer and found fear he'd never seen before. In his journal he recorded the reactions of Negroes he asked to sign voter registration forms: "A lady, afraid to sign because she might not get into the hospital for a needed operation. A retired man (76) afraid his welfare might be cut. A man who wanted to sign but wanted to do it out of sight behind a building. A housewife who said simply 'I'd be scared to—they drag you out the window and break your neck.' "

John, who insisted on wearing his SNCC pin wherever he went, was threatened several times. A post-office clerk leaned across the counter and said, "If I didn't have a wife and family I'd kill you." On the streets, whites shouted "Nigger lover!" or "White nigger!" The Negro family he stayed with kept a shotgun leaning against a wall.

While he was in Cleveland the bodies of Chaney, Goodman and Schwerner—the three civil rights activists killed early that summer—were discovered a hundred and thirty miles across the state. In his journal, John wrote that the murders "probably saved the rest of us quite a few beatings and even deaths." Later he attended a memorial service at the burned church the three men had been off to visit the day they were killed, and heard Bob Moses say, "Through what's going on here, we have to teach the rest of the world to find a way to change people's lives without killing them."

John left Mississippi a few weeks later, changed in several respects. First, he wrote, "Living so closely with Negro people, knowing them in the complexity and diversity which are any group of human beings, has allowed me to get beyond 'the Negro' and to see Roy and James and Nora Lee and Mrs. Barnes. That fear of the Negro which I shared with most whites and is a weird mixture of guilt and ignorance, seems to have completely gone." But he was angrier too. "I'd learned about the federal government. They weren't helping. In fact the F.B.I. were on the side of the local cops. The government made trade-offs. Some of the worst judges we had to deal with were Kennedy appointees, one reason I could never be too enthusiastic about him."

Within days, John was off to join Kennedy's Peace Corps, but not surprisingly he soon found himself at odds with officialdom. After his training in Oklahoma, the selection board called John in and told him they had seriously considered dropping him from the program. His activist record in college, they said, suggested he would be too "impatient" with the slowness of change in Peru. They had decided to take a chance, but wanted to warn him.

A few hours later, John refused to swear "So help me God" at the end of his oath of allegiance and asked to affirm instead. This set off an Oklahoma sandstorm. "They reformulated the selection committee and read me the riot act about this is what they had been afraid of. The training director said that if one wanted to work for the government one should do what was necessary, and they were only words anyway. It was all the worst things I had secretly feared about the Peace Corps. It was like the argument I'd had with the dean at Carleton: principled acts versus 'That's-the-way-the-system-works-so-go-along-with-it.' "

Finally, after the Oklahoma officials sent John home in a state of limbo, word came from Washington that of course he could affirm. After spending Christmas with his parents, he was off to Peru.

Probably because of his mountain isolation, John came into less conflict with American officialdom there than anytime in the past decade. There was one confrontation with the country director who ordered him to shave off his beard (inspiring John to write a bitter little essay concluding with "A beard to the bland is a bush"). But ultimately he shaved it off, and relations became cordial enough, so that when John's tour ended the director offered him a staff job.

By this time John was already severely disillusioned with the Peace Corps. He had gone in expecting the same kind of commitment and emotional involvement he found in Mississippi Summer; he was "shocked" to find little among either volunteers or officials.

But he had not completely given up on the Corps. So he responded with guarded enthusiasm when Frank Mankiewicz, then the Corps' director for Latin America (and later Robert Kennedy's press secretary), sent out a memo calling for just such committed volunteers, whom he nicknamed "gunners."

"Bang—I'm a gunner," John shot back. He warned that most volunteers had only "vague sympathies for the downtrodden [which] are often unconsciously diluted by identification with the better educated and wealthier, but especially in a society like Peru, 'exploiting classes.' The necessity and urgency of finding a revolutionary alternative to totalitarianism is seldom felt or expressed." He urged greater efforts to recruit "volunteers who have the sort of moral idealism and enthusiasm, the commitment to equality and real freedom etc. that most of the people [he had] known in student activism have.

"Gunner recruitment must emphasize the possibility of deep involvement in the lives of people and communities long the victims or forgotten ones of their society," he wrote. But he went on to warn that even after recruitment there were many obstacles along the way for such volunteers. "Gunners are gunned down by cautious selection boards with few exceptions . . . most important, the Peace Corps should not go after the gunners unless it is willing to back them in the field . . . All the carefully directed recruitment and improved selection policies won't matter if letters to friends have given the Peace Corps an Establishment reputation."

Despite these misgivings, when his Peru tour was up, John applied for a Peace Corps recruiter's job—to help make sure the Corps got the "gunners." When he arrived home he found the post filled, but he soon found another in which he felt he could exercise similar influence.

He was named acting regional director for Latin America in the International Secretariat for Volunteer Service, an organization which coordinates forty-five countries' volunteer agencies abroad. He was to help set up a new volunteer project in the Dominican Republic sponsored by the Pan American Development Foundation, a group tied closely to the Organization of American States. John, who had angrily condemned the Dominican intervention, felt the project was largely designed to refurbish the OAS image there. But it involved the kind of agricultural development he felt was vitally important and it was to use only Latin American volunteers. So for several months he plunged vigorously into the work.

But during these months he was torn by doubts about working within the "system" and found himself drawn increasingly toward the "movement." Back in Washington late that spring of 1967, with the ISVS job drawing to an end, he began seeing appeals seeking volunteers for Vietnam Summer, the radical project designed to organize grass-roots opposition to the war. Some of the ads drew explicit parallels with Mississippi Summer, and to John, who had been seeking ever since to recapture the excitement and commitment of those months in the South, this was irresistible.

He went first to Boston to help in the national office, helped set up the training program in Cleveland and finally was named field secretary in Minnesota. He supervised the three-man office in Minneapolis and spent much of his time traveling the state in a Volkswagen bus, sleeping in the back many nights. Carrying a stack of three-by-five cards with the names of possible "contacts" in each town—members of pacifist, church, women's or youth groups—he set up meetings where he gave a short speech, showed slides of North Vietnam and distributed literature.

The public's response was mixed, but for John the summer's experiences were decisive. "This was what I believed in; this was where I wanted to work." Abandoning all remaining musings about law school or journalism, he threw himself into the movement. Yet even then, he was not clear where it was taking him. About this time he wrote a friend, "Like others who came to the Movement because of 'liberal' commitments, I find myself becoming 'radical' without really understanding the implications. My involvement to date (university reform at Carleton, Mississippi Summer, Peace Corps) has grown primarily from moral outrage, which is a good place to begin but not to stop. Effective action requires more than reaction to individual injustices. Insofar as there are systems and interrelation between events, and public actions are prompted by hidden motives, valid countermeasures (and life styles) must be founded on rigorous and comprehensive understanding."

To get this understanding, John enrolled that fall in the Institute for Policy Studies, a radical research center in Washington. He took seminars on the corporate society and the cold war, and organized his own seminar on political repression. This led naturally to ever-more intensive radical activity. He attended meetings of the SDS and the Resistance. And he joined the Committee of Returned Volunteers, an organization of young Americans who have served in Asia, Africa and Latin America either in the Peace Corps or such private groups as the American Friends Service Committee, International Voluntary Services or Frontier Interns.

Although CRV's members include many liberals as

well as radicals, they are all committed to "fundamental changes" in United States policies, among them:

> The United States must recognize the right of people of local communities—here and overseas—to control the institutions which affect their daily lives, and to participate in political and economic decision making.
>
> The United States must realize that revolution is frequently legitimate and necessary to achieve the self-determination of communities and nations.
>
> The United States must accept that unilateral intervention in the affairs of other nations is not in their best interest nor in ours.

That fall he also worked briefly with the Mobilization Committee to End the War in Vietnam, organizing the March on the Pentagon.

At 12:30 A.M. the night after the march, John was sitting fifteen feet from the line of soldiers before the Pentagon when they began advancing into the crowd. A federal marshal grabbed his arms and dragged him to a truck. Refusing to give his name, he was booked as John Doe 281, charged with unseemly and disorderly conduct and taken to Dormitory No. 4 at Occaquan Work House in Virginia. Unlike most of his fellow prisoners, John refused to plead nolo contendere. "I insisted on pleading not guilty because I thought it was important to get into the public record that we had been attacked by the Army and not vice versa." After three days he posted bond and was released pending trial on November 2. On November 1 the government dropped the charge against him.

But the impact of this, his first arrest, helped push John into his own personal confrontation with the military.

John's personal stance toward the draft had developed only slowly. In 1962, when Paul Harmon applied for conscientious-objector status, he took John along to the hearing as a character witness. John told the board he did not agree with Paul's pacifist position but that Paul was "morally bound" to follow his own conscience.

John received deferments through Carleton and the

Peace Corps, but when he returned to the States he found a letter reclassifying him 1-A. Ten days later he applied as a conscientious objector and in a long letter to his draft board explained why. The letter concluded: "I have just completed two years helping to build the world. I hope to spend my life in the same pursuit. I cannot and will not spend two years helping to destroy it."

The board granted him conscientious-objector status. But as he was drawn deeper into the movement he had increasing misgivings about accepting even the required alternative civilian service. "It was an agonizing decision. This time, it meant not only opposing the draft; it meant I was going to live in opposition to the expected standards, norms, values of my society. I remember putting it all down on paper, trying to add and subtract this on one side and that on the other. It didn't help at all."

Then, one day in January 1968 John was sitting in an institute seminar with Marcus Raskin, the co-director, and William Coffin, Yale's Protestant chaplain, when a reporter called them out and told them they had been indicted for inciting draft resistance. The institute's students organized a demonstration at the Justice Department to support them, and a few days before the demonstration John suddenly knew what he had to do.

Before newsmen on the windy street in front of the Justice Department, he read a statement: "After many months of difficult thought and conversation, I have concluded that I am morally and politically obligated to resist the Selective Service System by turning in my draft card . . . As a white son of the middle class I have enjoyed [deferments] . . . Accepting a CO now would be to further take advantage of my race and class-privileged position . . . But more profoundly, the courageous example of the black men and women with whom I worked in Mississippi in the summer of 1964 taught me how much one must risk to be truly free." He faced federal prosecution for draft resistance.

John's next clash with the law came on October 24, 1968. Elected chairman of the Committee of Returned Volunteers in April, he led demonstrations by committee members during the summer and fall, one of them at the Wallace rally in Madison Square Garden. There they chanted "Peace," "Stop hate" and *"Sieg heil"* from the second balcony and showered confetti on the Wallace

supporters below until ordered by police to leave. The
police say John then pushed and shoved the officers, kick-
ing Patrolman James Mongiello in the groin and leg.
John gives a different version. He was moving down an
aisle toward an exit, he said, when policemen started
beating a CRV girl in front of him with billy clubs.
When he tried to protect her, he recalls, "a couple of
policemen started beating me too. As I fell under the
blows I went into the nonviolent protective position which
I learned during training for the Mississippi Summer
Project, holding my arms curled back over my head and
trying to bring my legs up to cover my genitals. But I received a number of blows and kicks around the head,
arms and chest." He was charged with felonious assault,
resisting arrest and obstructing governmental administration.

Since then John has devoted most of his waking hours
to building the CRV for the long struggle he knows lies
ahead.

What kind of struggle will it be? "I hope it will be
nonviolent," he says. "I'm still a liberal in that sense. I
don't conceive of killing a person to advance my politics. That's one part of me.

"But another part of me knows that ultimately what
I'm doing is building for a revolution. Building an opposition, building an alternative way of life, is building for
a revolution. And I suppose a socialist revolution, because
emotionally I don't believe in some people having a lot
of money and a lot of people not having much. I don't
believe in large concentrations of corporate power or
even labor union power which totally disregards the people they are supposed to be serving. One of the things I
learned in Peru was that a lot of changes that were necessary were liberal changes. It was just that nobody was
going to make them if there weren't any revolutionaries.
So, what kind of revolution will it be? I can't answer
that. I can hope it will be nonviolent and I can work to·
make it so. But what determines it will be the response
that is made. I mean, if people are crushed they will
strike back."

DON

On July 1, 1968, one of the strangest hearings in the history of the United States District Court for the Eastern District of New York took place at the Brooklyn federal courthouse, not in one of the paneled courtrooms but in a tiny detention cell downstairs.

The prisoner, Donald C. Baty, described the scene later in a letter from another prison cell ". . . the door to my cell was opened and a robed man with a kindly smile walked in. At this point I had been fasting 15 days. In jail I had been reading the Bible, and *The Pilgrim's Progress* by John Bunyan. I thought perhaps I was having a vision or something. The man turned out to be not Bunyan's Pilgrim but Judge Mishler. When he was told by the U.S. marshals that I would not walk upstairs he had decided to come to my cell to see me. He brought the assistant D.A., the court recorder and assorted other people with him. We had a good conversation. Judge Mishler patiently listened while I explained my behavior. I was quite impressed by him. He was not concerned about the fact that I insisted on defending myself. When the interview ended Judge Mishler said that he was going to send me to King's County Hospital for mental observation. He said I seemed completely sane but my behavior had been very 'unconventional' and he wanted to make sure I was capable of defending myself."

Donald's behavior had indeed been "unconventional" from the moment on June 13 when he was arrested for refusing induction into the Army. On that day, U.S. marshals dragged him from the altar of the Washington

Square Methodist Church while dozens of his supporters shouted, "I'm Don Baty." Taken by paddy wagon to the same federal courthouse, Don refused to walk into the building because he was handcuffed. As he wrote later, "To handcuff me is absurd. I refused induction because I cannot kill. Nor will I condone the taking of life. I won't hurt anybody. I don't even like to slap mosquitoes. Why was I handcuffed? Were the U.S. marshals afraid I would love somebody while they weren't looking?"

The marshals carried him upstairs to a courtroom where they braced him into a chair before Judge Joseph C. Zavatt. The judge ordered him to stand. Don refused. Judge Zavatt cited him for contempt of court. When Don refused bail and counsel, the judge sent him to the federal House of Detention on West Street. Again Don refused to walk, so the marshals carried him from the courtroom.

In his cell at the West Street jail, Don began a fast which was to last thirty days, during which he took only coffee, tea and water. He refused to work because he did not wish to do "anything that will help support the prison." On June 20 he was taken back to the federal courthouse. Downstairs he told the marshals he would walk into the courtroom if his handcuffs were removed. The marshals informed Judge Zavatt, but the judge sent back word that Don could sit in jail until he was ready to walk into court with handcuffs. So he was returned to West Street.

Finally, on July 1, Don was brought back to the courthouse and the impasse broken when Judge Jacob Mishler saw him in his cell.

On Judge Mishler's orders, Don then spent a week under observation at King's County Hospital. At its end, a psychiatrist reported that Don showed "awareness and comprehension of the charges against him and . . . ability to participate in his defense. It is possible that certain decisions of his, including his decision to be his own attorney, show poor judgment on his part, but there is nothing that indicates incompetency."

On July 12 he appeared before Judge Mishler again. This time he agreed to walk into the courtroom, even with handcuffs on. As he explained later, "Judge Zavatt attempted to force me to show respect. Judge Mishler earned my respect. Judge Zavatt thought of me as a prisoner who would either obey orders or sit in jail. Judge Mishler thought of me as a human being. This is one message I'm trying hard to get across. I am not simply a number to be handcuffed, ordered around, tried and sent off to penitentiary. I am Donald Baty, a young human being, struggling to cope with a bewildering world."

That night, after talking with his parents, Don also decided to break his fast. His weight had dropped from 125 to 110 and he was very weak. With the trial set to start July 19, he needed to build up his strength to defend himself.

During the next week his parents and friends urged Don to drop this plan and accept a lawyer, but he was adamant. In a letter on July 14 he explained, "If my aim was simply to 'beat the rap' I never would have gotten involved in this struggle in the first place. I would have attemped to get a deferment, or flunk my physical, or run to Canada. But I don't want a deferment, I won't take a physical and I refuse to run to Canada. I am appalled by the senseless carnage occurring in Vietnam . . . I do not see this as a legal challenge. This has been a moral confrontation from the beginning and that is how I view this trial . . . I shall stand before the jury, armed only with my moral convictions, and attempt to make them understand my heartfelt message."

And Don kept his word. The one-day trial was as unorthodox as its preliminaries. Don made a dogged and often ingenious effort to get his moral message across, but time and again Judge Mishler ruled against him, spurred on by a vigilant prosecutor determined to hew to the narrow legal issues. And this often led to an unusual dialogue between the white-haired judge, high on the bench beneath the angry spread of the United States eagle, and the twenty-two-year-old defendant before him, as lost in judicial procedures as he was in the sports jacket which drooped on his slight frame further wasted by the hunger strike.

At one point Donald tried to explain why he would not have accepted conscientious-objector status although he thought he might qualify. "There are so many people who deserve it who are denied it by the law," he said.

Judge Mishler: "Well, I am not interested in anyone else at this particular point except Donald Baty. . . ."

Donald: "First, let me say that I am interested in everyone else except Donald Baty, and that is why I am here."

Judge Mishler: "Well, I am interested in nothing else at this point except Donald Baty's claim that he might have been entitled to conscientious-objector status."

Donald: "Then we are going to have a little trouble."

And they did. Once, exasperated by Don's moral pronouncements, the judge leaned down and said sternly, "I must rule on the law of this case as I understand it to be, not as I would like it to be. And you are required to obey the law as it is, not as you would like it to be."

Slightly flustered, and a bit angry, Don snapped back, "You are free to do that in this case because you are not being asked to kill or die in a war you don't believe in. You are being asked to do something rather objectionable, and that is sending someone perhaps to jail. But I would be doing something much more objectionable than that, to violate everything I believe in right down to my core . . ."

This exchange occurred in the pre-trial examination that morning. When the trial before jury began in the afternoon, Judge Mishler enforced courtroom procedures even more strictly and Don's frustrations grew correspondingly.

At one point, explaining his reason for refusing induction, Don said, "I have a moral responsibility that is up and above and must take precedence over my responsibility to man-made laws . . . I found a case where this had been put into international law, and I should like to enter this into the record now, the Nuremburg Principles, and read Principle 4."

At this, Michael Rosen, the young Assistant United States attorney, jumped to his feet. "Your Honor," he said, "I object to any such reference as having no relevance whatsoever to the case on trial."

Judge Mishler: "Objection sustained."

Don: "I cannot read this then?"

Judge Mishler: "No."

Clearly dismayed now, Don concluded his case quickly. Then, turning to the ten men and two women on the jury, he summed up: "This doesn't need to be a long summation. I think you know how I feel. I just submit that this was not a willful failure to do my duty. First of all there is a duty to God and mankind and human feelings that comes above the duty to General Hershey . . . You know the individual has to decide in all cases, and I have made my decision. It was hardly hard for me to make. Everything in my life has channeled me in this direction of just not wanting to hurt anybody. So I—I submit that this was not a willful failure to do my duty. First of all, I was doing my duty. Second of all, I had no other choice. Given my background, this was all I could do."

Where does a man's background begin? In Don's case, perhaps one should start with James Nathan Thomas Franklin Baty, his paternal grandfather, whom Don's father remembers as "a cold-water Baptist fundamentalist, a beautiful example of a rigid old man." Schooled only through the third grade, he got a team of oxen and a wagon from his father and at twenty-two started farming in Oklahoma, but he had no knack for it. When his crops failed, he tried side businesses—fixing farm machinery, doing the neighbors' threshing—but none of these went very well either. With little money to feed their nine children, his Czech-born wife decided the family was big enough. But Nathan refused to use contraceptives, loudly declaring that birth control was "against God's will."

So the family broke up. The mother kept the girls, and Nathan took the six boys north to Canada. Among the brothers were twins—Don's father, Wilton, and Milton ("Don't ever do that to your twins," says Wilton). When Wilton and Milton were fourteen, their father drifted into Montana, where suddenly their mother turned up again. "She had two suitcases," Wilton recalls, "one filled with clothes and the other with condoms. She thought Dad had learned his lesson, but he hadn't. Within two months they broke up again on the same old issue. Dad just wouldn't bow to the necessity of limiting himself in any way. He went to his death convinced he was right."

But his sons couldn't accept their father's old-time religion. They preferred science. One brother, Joe, went off to study chemistry at Cornell, and a few years later the twins followed. Wilton wanted to study at Cornell's School of Agriculture because he "came to realize that farming would succeed only if it was scientific." But soon he decided to become a science teacher instead.

At Cornell he met Helen Case, a girl who came from what she later described as "old-line *Mayflower*" stock. Her parents had both studied music in college but they found little accord in marriage and were divorced when Helen was five. Brought up by her maternal grandparents in upstate New York, she had contracted polio as a child and still limped noticeably when she arrived at Cornell in the fall of 1932. "I felt I couldn't go home any more," she recalls, "and I think it was that which let Wilton take me over completely. I stayed taken over for twenty years."

They were married at the end of their sophomore year, and the next year their first child, Charlotte, was born. But money was short. "My young husband wanted to put full time into practice teaching," Helen recalls. "So halfway through my senior year I quit school to support him and my infant." (Some bitterness over this may have contributed to severely strained relations between Helen and her first daughter which continued until Charlotte was killed in an automobile accident in 1958.)

Wilton got his first full-time job nearly nine months after he graduated—teaching science in the upstate town of Hilton, at the skimpy salary of twelve hundred dollars. They spent the next four summers in New York City while Wilton got his master's at Columbia Teachers College. Then in 1942 a job opened up at Huntington High School in Huntington, Long Island, for twice the salary. Wilton took it and has been there ever since, first as a science teacher and now as head of the department.

When they went to Huntington, the Batys already had three children—Charlotte, Larilee, born in 1938, and Carl in 1941. After Charlotte, Helen recalls, "I had grown to love children," and when Don was born in 1945 he was cherished by both parents, at least for the first few years.

But by the time his younger brother, Doug, was born in 1947, the marriage was beginning to fall apart. "Three weeks before I had Dougie," Helen recalls, "Wilton accused me of having the child to keep a hold on him. I was shocked. I hadn't even known he was unhappy. He said I was a leech, a millstone around his neck. For him it broke up then. For me it took much longer."

Wilton remembers it differently. "Even in the early fifties I had a feeling we were doing all right. But as we moved along toward 1953 she began to feel that her life was 'zero, zero.' I was president of the New York Science Teachers Association and I needed lots of help typing materials. Helen worked at this very earnestly. But I guess in her supportive role she didn't feel very much satisfaction."

For whatever reason, in February 1954 Helen got a job of her own, as a "shopper" with William Storey, a Huntington lawyer who was counsel for Westinghouse on enforcement of fair-trade items. A lean New Englander with a stutter, Mr. Storey was divorced, and gradually he and Helen began to see each other outside business hours. Wilton feels Helen was attracted to Mr. Storey both because he was a lawyer and because he came from an old Brahmin family. "She always considered herself a Brahmin. And she'd say, 'I wasn't meant to be a school-teacher's wife. I was meant to be something more than that—a lawyer or a doctor's wife.' " Although Mr. Storey was by no means well off by then, he still lived in a rambling old white house with lots of fireplaces—very Brahmin indeed, compared with the Batys' small gray house with its sagging front porch and little green hedge.

Finally, after many shouted accusations, Helen left for Florida in December 1954 where she got a divorce the next year. In June 1955 she and Mr. Storey were married and moved into the big white house.

Meanwhile Mr. Baty had met Madeleine Arduino, the dark, intense daughter of Neapolitan immigrants who was then teaching at the Riverside Church Nursery School in Manhattan. In November 1955 they were married. So, suddenly there were two families living barely a mile and a half apart in Huntington—with the children caught in various stages between.

The support agreement gave Helen custody of the children until they were sufficiently mature to decide where they wanted to live. Charlotte, who had never been happy in the home, had already gone to live with Mr. Baty's brother in Ohio. Larilee, who was seventeen by then, decided to stay with her father. This left Carl, Don and Doug who, while Helen was in Florida, had also gone to live for a time in Ohio.

"We had a hell of a time getting them back," Mr.

Storey says. "I had to threaten to go out with a habeas corpus writ and get them on a kidnapping charge." This was the tone of relations between the two families for years to come. There were charges and countercharges, often ending in court, and sometimes more overt action. Once, Mr. Baty recalls, "I came home for lunch and found they'd backed a moving van up to the house and were cleaning the place out. Well, she had rights to some of those things, but there was nothing but a broken typewriter and a little flowered rug on the floor when I got home." Although the agreement provided that Mr. Baty could visit the boys once a week and have them with him during school vacations and ten weeks in the summer, the intense strain between the Batys and the Storeys made any precise schedule impractical.

Just what impact this fierce family conflict had on Don is difficult to gauge. "I really don't think it had a devastating effect on him," his father says. "Every divorce leaves some imprint on the children. But Don was not unloved by either parent; he had a place to go, two homes to go to, and he knew that all the time. I made it a point not to talk to the kids about the conflict except when I had to, and frankly I can't remember Don ever saying anything about the divorce in a positive or negative way."

Helen is sure there was no early effect. "His first two years were very nearly ideal. From my point of view he was entirely welcome. His father wasn't home much. There was no squabbling in the house. Don was a good baby. He never woke me in the hospital for extra feeding. Curiously enough, in light of his later history, I'd say he was even more willing to be led by other people— any authority figure—than other small children. And he was very fond, very protective of other children."

Larilee, who roomed with Don for his first six years, has similar memories: "Don was the most affectionate, sensitive and lovable of the three boys. I remember being in my bed either sick or upset, and little Donny, barely as tall as the bed, gently patting my shoulder and trying to comfort me."

But as Don reached grammar school—about the time the marriage was developing serious strains—the others began to worry about him. "Gradually he seemed to be a misfit in the family," Larilee recalls. "He was pudgy as a lad, the other boys were lean. He wasn't a quick learner and we often talked about Don having lower intellectual ability than the rest of us. Neither Carl nor Doug easily included Don in their activities and he was often left out. I always tried to protect Don from the teasing he got from other members of the family."

Doug, two years younger than Don, was regarded as the family's "bright" boy. Unusually deft with his hands, he was showered with acclaim for his accomplishments, such as making a nifty little racing car for a local soap-box derby. He and Carl were always working on mechanical projects together. "When I came into the family," Madeleine recalls, "Don clearly thought of himself as a dolt. He felt, I've got a bright little brother and I'm second-class."

And about this time a tough, stubborn streak began to develop. "He would resist with tenacity any effort to push him in a direction," Mr. Baty says. "Particularly if I had to punish him for any reason. Punishment of any kind with him resulted in a stubborn reaction which left you with the realization that you could beat that guy to death and he still wouldn't yield to you."

Don's tenacity showed up particularly in fights with his brother Carl. Four years younger and several inches smaller, Don was no match for Carl; but this disadvantage seemed only to whet his appetite for a scrap. (He almost never picked a fight with his younger brother, Doug.) Mr. Baty recalls: "Carl would invariably pin him down on the floor, but Don would never give up. He'd fight until his energy gave out in an almost frightening test of wills. His attitude seemed to be: I'm smaller than you but I won't let you push me under. You've got to recognize me as a human being and a person to be reckoned with." And though beaten time and again, he kept coming back for more with fierce determination. Once, Doug remembers, Don was so furious he tossed a kitchen knife at Carl. The knife shivered into a door inches from Carl's head.

The stubbornness increased and found a new target when Don and his brothers moved down the road to the Storeys'. For, at that time, Mr. Storey could be a difficult man to get along with. Larilee later described him as "a harsh, authoritarian disciplinarian, a supermasculine individual who demands submission from women and children." All the children, including three from Mr. Storey's first marriage who visited from time to time, were exposed to this side of him. But Don got the brunt because he rebelled the most. There were even some physical struggles. Mr. Storey recalls one: "I used to be the champion of my wrestling class at Harvard, and I put on holds which I knew could hurt. But even when I gave him quite a bit of pain he never for a moment gave in. The only way to have made him give in would have been to seriously hurt him."

In other ways, Bill Storey was a fascinating stepfather for an active boy. An outdoorsy man who loved to tramp the Long Island woods or sail the choppy waters of the Sound, he introduced the boys to the vigorous life. "I was raised in an atmosphere that made it seem important to me that boys be exposed to danger under supervision," he recalls. "So I started them off with a knife, then an ax, a rifle and finally a buzz saw. None of them were ever hurt." The Storeys still have the first chip Don ever took out of a tree with an ax.

Mr. Storey had been a scoutmaster and at this time he was teaching a group of Webelos ("We'll be loyal Scouts"), cub scouts in the last six months before they become boy scouts. The Webelos would gather every Saturday morning at the Storey house, where Bill would teach them how to build fires and tie knots. Carl and Don, who were already well versed in these skills, served as assistant instructors. Later, Don was a boy scout himself.

The family spent two summers on a New Hampshire farm where they did a lot of shooting (but not hunting; Mr. Storey never shot animals and neither did Don). Another summer they chartered a 32-foot sloop and sailed to Martha's Vineyard.

Mr. Storey also has an intellectual bent, with what Larilee describes as "an incredible fund of information" which he delighted in passing on to the boys. Much of it was on American history. For he came from a distinguished old American family which traced itself back to Lieutenant William Storey, an officer in the Battle of Breed's Hill (a musket from the battle hung over the fireplace in the Storey home for years), and later to Moorfield Storey, the eminent Massachusetts lawyer and private secretary to Charles Sumner.

The contrast between the Storey and Baty households could hardly have been greater. While the Storeys were proud of their colonial heritage, Wilton Baty joked about being the son of "an old Arkansas traveler and a woman who herded geese as a child in Czechoslovakia." The Storeys ran an orderly, almost austere house, while the Baty home at 24 Penataquit Place then, as now, was a jumble of children's toys, flowering plants, books, magazines, tools, electrical equipment and a bird's nest on the telephone table. While Wilton Baty was a vehement atheist, the Storeys turned after their marriage to the Methodist Church for a sustaining faith ("We are not religious people in the usual sense," Mrs. Storey says, "but everyone gets desperate enough to pray at times"). The Storey household was a strict one (in which, Larilee recalls, the boys were not supposed to talk at the dinner table unless spoken to), but the Batys let the children run wild through the house like the big friendly dogs and soft tabbies which could be found padding through the rooms.

For five years the boys were in and out of both households. They lived at the Storeys', but managed to drop by the Batys' after school or bicycle over on weekends. And not surprisingly, the sharp contrast between the two homes created some identity problems. All the boys were called Storey for a while, but Mr. Baty vigorously resisted this. Soon, Don in particular was wrestling with the question: Am I a Storey or a Baty? By the time he turned sixteen in the summer of 1960, he had largely resolved it. Exercising their prerogative under the separation agreement, he and Doug moved to the Batys' (carting their belongings over from the Storeys' in a two-wheeled trailer). Although Doug moved back with the Storeys a year later, Don's shift was permanent.

For the next few years Don's life in Huntington was uneventful—in fact, strikingly bland for a young man whose later days were so full of drama and confrontation.

He attended Huntington High School, where his father was still head of the science department, but never distinguished himself in any way. In fact, his lackluster record caused his father some concern. "He got zero out of high school, just sort of plodded through the days," Wilton recalls. "He never focused on anything, didn't really enjoy anything or anybody—classes, teachers or students. But he was never a discipline problem. He was just a blah.

"He didn't think of himself as much of a student, much of an athlete, much of a mechanic, much of anything. He even turned to Dougie if his bicycle needed work. One of the shocks of his life came from his I.Q. test late in that period when he found that he was as bright as any of the boys."

During these high school years there were only two things Don seemed to get any kick out of: reading and the sea. From the time he was twelve or thirteen, he read eagerly, but always on his own, books that were unrelated to formal classwork. J. D. Salinger was one of his early favorites. But more than anything, he liked to read of the sea. Starting with C. S. Forester's *Beat to Quarters,* he went on to plow through the entire Hornblower series and Hornblower became his first real hero. He also read and enjoyed Philip Wylie's *Crunch and Des,* a collection of short stories about charter-boat fishing. About this time he declared to the family that his ambition was to become a barge captain. Nobody was surprised because his reading reflected his fascination with the blue waters off Long Island. The summer he and Doug came to live with the Batys, Wilton bought them a little boat with an 18-h.p. outboard motor (the Storeys charged the boat was a "bribe" to get the boys to switch homes). Hour after hour after school and on weekends, Don and Doug would churn through Huntington harbor and the bay beyond "pounding waves." Or they would drop lines over the side and fish for porgies and blowfish.

Then one summer Don discovered water-skiing and this became his first true passion. It was a demanding sport for the short (five foot two), slight (110-pound) boy who had been too small for high school football or basketball. But he couldn't get enough of it, bracing his toothpick legs on the boards as they slapped across the waves and gripping the twisting tow rope with his bony little hands. And one soft summer evening, just for the hell of it, he skied nonstop all the way across the Sound to Connecticut and back—a total of twenty miles.

This sort of thing suggested that there was something powerful straining beneath Don's bland exterior. Just what it was nobody could be sure. Perhaps the remnants of that early bulldog tenacity. He no longer got into physical fights with his brothers, but there were other outcroppings of a stubborn will. Once, he got into a furious confrontation with Madeleine's mother, who had come to live with the family, and angrily proclaimed that everybody over fifty should be sent out on the ice like Eskimos to die. "He seemed to spend a lot of his time at loggerheads," Madeleine recalls. "He didn't back away from things. I'd say he was a cause waiting for a young man to espouse it."

But this latent cause never burst out as rebellion against the Batys. "It's pretty hard to rebel against Wil and me," Madeleine says, "We're fairly flexible. We believe that the home is here to serve the kids, and we don't get spastic about whether they're on time for meals. If they don't feel like chipping in and doing their share of the work around the house we do a little bit more. It's sort of hard to rebel against that."

And Don didn't. Years later, he wrote from prison that his father had been the single most important influence in his life. "Dad throws himself into whatever he does. His teaching, his hobbies, his infrequent urges to fix up the house are all infused with this tremendous drive and enthusiasm . . . I've brought the same enthusiasm into my antiwar effort that Dad brings to his teaching. I once described myself as having a head-on personality. I tend to tackle problems head-on. Grab the bull by the horns and go to work. Dad has often said that if I believed in war I'd make a helluva good soldier. I'm totally committed to ending this war and all other wars, just as Dad is totally committed to whatever he does. I think it is this kind of commitment, which I seem to have inherited from Dad, which accounts for the fact that I have acted on my antiwar beliefs."

Not everyone sees Mr. Baty that way. A big, jovial, unkempt man, who tinkers with second-hand cars and plays "Marrying Sam" at Huntington High's annual Sadie Hawkins Day, he strikes some as an amiable eccentric. Larilee, for example, remembers him as "a neutral factor" for most of Don's and her young lives. "Mother did the loving, the serving and the disciplining. Dad was in the background, calm by nature, but also calm because of a lack of involvement," although she adds that "after the divorce he became more forceful and dominant; the qualities of leadership and warmth he has always had professionally began to be present in his relationship with his children."

There was this passive side to Mr. Baty. Madeleine remembers a time when Don was in high school and the family went to Palisades Park in New Jersey. Don asked his father to ring the bell with the sledge hammer and his father reared back, clobbered the knob and sounded the bell loud and clear. "Donald was quite surprised that Wil was that strong, and about three days later he told me, 'You know, I've been thinking about Dad and that bell. Sometimes he is so quiet and steady that you forget how wonderful he really is.'"

But Don recalls chiefly his father's forceful side. He recalls when he was seventeen, Wilton and Madeleine decided to remodel the bathroom. They had a big old-fashioned bathtub resting up on blocks, but being bulky types, they liked the old tub and wanted to sink it in the new tile floor. This took a lot of scraping and grinding, which they did chiefly at night. Don recalls that his father "worked on it constantly for a number of days with a single-mindedness which was rather annoying, and which infuriated the neighbors, what with the continuous activity and banging and hammering at 3 A.M. in the morning. It kind of infuriated me too, 'cause I was trying to sleep in the next room. I wasn't interested in remodeling the bathroom, but I am interested in ending the war. And I have thrown myself into this effort just as Dad throws himself into his projects."

Don's relationship with his stepfather was more openly rebellious, but Mr. Storey clearly served as a model too. As a lawyer, he apparently inspired Don's early interest in the law. Moorfield Storey had known Oliver Wendell Holmes, and Mr. Storey met him as a young boy. Early in his teens Don read *Yankee from Olympus* and was fascinated by Holmes. But he was even more taken with *Inherit the Wind*, which he read over and over. Clarence Darrow became one of the major heroes of his youth, for it was less the majesty of the law itself than the stubborn defense of an underdog's rights which drew Don. And here Mr. Storey's own heritage and beliefs may have had some influence. Moorfield Storey was a Mugwump, and the Storey family, though scarcely radical, had the Yankee heritage of stubborn defense of individual liberties. Mr. Storey calls himself a "constitutionalist who puts a strong emphasis on the Bill of Rights." From 1937 to 1945 he was a farmer in Vermont, where, he says, "I got along well with those individualists up there because of my instinctive belief that every man has a right to be a damn fool." One of Mr. Storey's favorite aphorisms is "A man convinced against his will is of the same opinion still."

As for his mother, Don writes in a letter from prison: "Taking a walk in the woods with Mom is a great experience. She identifies many of the bird calls and much of the plant life. She'll quietly put a hand on your shoulder to catch your attention and point out a bird building its nest or a downy woodpecker climbing up an old dead tree. Her face will glow with pleasure if a flight of Canadian geese flies over."

And this he connects with his father's enthusiasm for life and nature. "Dad will take half an afternoon talking about the mating habits of blue-nosed baboons. He's filled with awe by the intricate workings of nature. He's glad to be alive. So am I. Life is great. Blue sky and pretty girls and oceans and mountains and interesting people to talk to. I love life. I respect life. I won't take life."

But this was a synthesis he made later. It was still unrealized in those teenage years which, except for the underlying tenacity and occasional outcroppings of passion, still seemed so outwardly bland.

In fact, Don's lassitude at high school was so pronounced during his senior year that Madeleine recalls, "We were not sure we could get him through; he just didn't see any point in it." By March that year he was ready to quit, but Mr. Baty arranged for Don to take his few required classes from 8 to 10:30 A.M. and have the rest of the day free. Somehow, in June 1964, he graduated.

Still fascinated by the sea, he had applied to the U.S. Merchant Marine Academy and passed most of the admissions tests. But he just couldn't get his weight up to the required 120 pounds (although he drank something like five banana milk shakes a day for weeks in a vain effort to put on weight). He was accepted by the New York State Maritime School, but by that time Don had decided he wasn't ready for higher education. He told his father he wanted to "see the world" first.

With money he earned at a Huntington boatyard and some added by his father, he bought a 250-cc Harley-Davidson motorcycle and set off for Louisiana—a natural destination because Carl was living there. On the way down, Don rode the bucking little cycle about seven hundred miles a day, ten or twelve hours through all kinds of weather. One day he had to stop to pour the rain water out of his boots. Like the water-skiing binge across the Sound, it seemed another of those periodic hints of Don's subterranean will.

And when he got to the Gulf he found a job which could hardly have been more demanding—on a barge searching for offshore oil. His crew played out a mile-long cable with sensors attached every fifteen feet. The sensors were planted in the mud with a long pole so that when explosive charges were set off they took seismographic readings of the Gulf bottom. Then Don's crew would go out again and pick up the cable, the worst part of the job. By then, the cable was a heavy, slippery snake covered with slime from the bottom. Leaning over the heaving barge side, sometimes Don could heave the cable out of the mud with a *zock*, but at times it was just too heavy and he had to call for help. Writing home that summer, he described it as "backbreaking, wet, soggy work."

The crew lived on a bunk barge for seven straight days. Then they had seven days ashore at Lafayette, Louisiana, where Don had a $7-a-week room. The other crew members were tough, swarthy Cajuns, much older, stronger men whom Don admired but never got close to. The food on the barge was hot Cajun stuff which Don never cared for.

There was the sea he loved—"the dolphins, and fish, and sun and all that," as he described it in one letter—but the work was tough, grinding and monotonous, and by fall he scrawled across the top of one letter: "I have built a prison for myself."

So nobody at home was surprised when he took off on his motorcycle again. He sped down the Florida coast and at Daytona turned his cycle onto the hard, smooth beach. "I went about ten miles on it, chasing bathers and fishermen and chasing the waves in and out," he wrote Doug. "Biggest kick of my life."

Finally he ended at Miami Beach, where he got a job

in a grocery store on Biscayne Boulevard. He was a "bag boy" making $1.05 an hour piling groceries into bags at the checkout counter, plus tips for carrying them out to people's cars (apparently his open, boyish face appealed to the old ladies who shopped at the store because he made $5.50 in tips alone his first day). He found Miami Beach "a beautiful, fantastic place," but also "macabre."

And he was getting homesick. So by winter he started cycling north again. He made it as far as Raleigh, North Carolina, where Larilee (now Mrs. William Suiter) was living. "He was frozen stiff," his father recalls. "He called us and I said, 'Look, leave the motorcycle there and take a bus.' He did, and at Christmas time he and I drove down to North Carolina in our little station wagon and picked up the cycle. It was a leisurely drive and we had lots of time to talk. Don told me, 'Dad, I'm really wasting my life. What can I do?'"

Mr. Baty suggested that Don start by coming home to live and enrolling at Suffolk Community College, a two-year school near Huntington. Don accepted the idea enthusiastically, and entered at midyear. He surprised himself and everyone else by making a B average that term. But Suffolk was a new school with meager facilities. It didn't have a library and Don had to study in the back seat of one of the family's old cars which he drove to school.

So the next fall he transferred to Harpur College in Binghamton, a four-year college which was part of the State University system. His B record at Suffolk made him automatically eligible for admission, but Harpur was a much more rigorous liberal arts institution which drew many city students who had their eyes on graduate school. Don found the atmosphere oppressively academic and didn't get along with the intense New Yorkers.

By the time he reached Harpur, Don was becoming growingly interested in psychology. Perhaps he was influenced by Madeleine, who had specialized in it during college and used it in her nursery-school work. But, as he later remarked in a letter, the desire to "help mankind" seemed to "run in the family." His father was a teacher, his mother and sister by that time were both in social work, his brother Carl was in sociology. The summer before, Don had worked as a counselor at Green Hills Country Day Camp near Huntington and was already beginning to talk about a career working with psychologically disturbed children.

In a general psychology course at Harpur he began running experiments on rats and started to get some strange results. The rats would run for the food pellets even before they received the signal. For weeks, while he battled a cold, Don re-ran the tests and puzzled over the animals' erratic behavior. Finally it dawned on him: he was sniffling his runny nose every few seconds and the rats had become conditioned by the sniffles rather than the light signals. Don was delighted and told the story to everyone he met.

He was also reading a lot of philosophy. "Nietzsche is my latest hero, kinda like Hornblower was," he wrote home late that winter. "I'd like to embark on his 'new mission.'" Don complained that most people he met dealt only with "shallow" ideas and that "the thoughts way down at the bases of all life are left untouched by almost everybody. It's too bad 'cause these are the important ones. Adults who have done a lot of thinking have trouble conveying their thoughts across the age barrier. They have trouble listening to my ideas in return because maybe they suppose I'm too young to have anything to say and we never really get anything going. People all over are hung up by religion and society and social status. Yeck! It makes me fear that Nietzsche's 'new mission' will never get off the ground."

Don also went out for the Harpur track team, and with his wiry body and endurance, might have made it. But he never could take competitive athletics seriously and skipped too many practices. He was fascinated that fall by another kind of water sport: a term-long competition to see who could stand under a running shower longest. Most of Don's friends were boys who preferred this kind of thing to long, dreary hours in the library. Soon they began dropping out of school. When Don was put on probation he realized Harpur's academic requirements were more than he wanted to take on. In the spring of 1966 he transferred again, to New Paltz State College in Kingston, New York, a less rigorous institution in the State University system.

By the time Don got to New Paltz he was preoccupied with the most intense emotional experience of his life.

In high school there had been one girl about whom he felt strongly. But Marilyn was something else again.

He had met Marilyn the summer before at the Green Hills Country Day Camp, where she counseled the four-year-olds and he had the eight-year-olds. "We both loved the pool and the kids," he recalls in a letter. "She radiated life. I took her water-skiing and found we both shared a love for the sea. She became an accomplished skier by the end of the season. She was feminine but hardly fragile. We went surfing, skiing and hiking together. I went into it with body and soul. The usual total commitment."

That fall, while Don was still at Harpur and Marilyn attended a Long Island community college, the relationship began to sour. Part of the problem stemmed from her parents. They thought Don was a bit kooky and they had another boy all picked out for her. When Don came home that Christmas they forbade Marilyn to see him.

Typically, Don took on the challenge with a seething intensity. "I responded poorly," he recalls today. "Rather than trying to understand her folks I started to kind of dump on them. Poor Marilyn was caught in the middle. It came down to a choice of me or them. Well, she wasn't prepared to give up me or her folks. I kinda barged through the mess selfishly. I wasn't sympathetic about Marilyn's trying situation. I don't think I even tried to understand. I simply exacerbated the problem by becoming possessive and jealous and an all-around crum."

But they continued to see each other. Defying her parents, Marilyn came up to spend a week with Don at the semester break in January. That summer, they both got counselor jobs at the camp again, and in the fall, Marilyn enrolled at New Paltz too. But starting in the spring, Don recalls, they began to fight a lot. "Became physically violent at times. Seems like we spent most of our time together hurting each other mentally and physically. Why didn't we break it off? I don't know. We couldn't. We tried a couple of times. We had some really bad fights. Some of the things I said and did were sick. During the fall of 1966 things got worse and worse. Finally she fell for another guy. By Christmas of '66 we both knew it was dead. Took me a long time to accept it."

It was a crisis period for Don, buffeted by powerful but often conflicting emotions. One of his consolations remained the outdoors. Far from the sea, he became active in the Outing Club and led several treks through the wilds of upstate New York. Once, after a canoe trip to Lake George which he described in a letter then as "the most fabulous weekend of my life," he expressed his ambivalent state of mind in some of the free verse he was beginning to write:

> Sometimes the whole goddam world
> and every goddam person in it
> and then this tree túrns to gold
> and a mountain turns to color.
> Sometimes the whole goddam world
> but not when trees turn to gold
> and mountains turn to color.

But, as the fall wore on, his mood turned ever blacker. By early winter he was writing:

> Keep your eyes open
> for suddenly the tide may turn.
> It often gives but small warning
> turning quickly and crashing in upon you.
> If only you had smelled it or heard the
> gathering roar,
> Perhaps you could have rallied a countercharge.
> Built a raft . . .
> But alas! You are caught. Trapped
> within the turmoil.
> A personal Hell gate.
> For though I am a strong swimmer
> —to fight a whole tide with no
> support is beyond me.
> And those who have your heart push
> you down for the third time.
> Half a man.

All through this period, Don was worried most by the uncontrollable violence of his feelings toward Marilyn. He had bruised her badly several times and was afraid he might really hurt her one day. When Marilyn left him he brooded even more deeply about the meaning of the violence within him. He recalled years later: "I've always had a temper. From what I hear, I threw some terrific tantrums when I was young. Not exactly a non-violent type. My intensity would often burst into violence. I had to learn to control my violent urges. Twenty-one-year-old men can't throw tantrums. My violence had destroyed and was continuing to destroy a beautiful relationship with Marilyn. I rejected violence."

And so, in the spring of 1967, Don's personal revulsion against the violence within him was merged and transformed into a more general rejection of violence in the world, specifically in Vietnam. It was as if his own personal concerns and the country's history had somehow fused.

Until that time he had little concern with current affairs and rarely even read a newspaper. "In 1965 or 1966 I thought little about the war, hoping it would be over before I graduated and lost my deferment. But the political situation was getting worse. By the spring of 1967 even an apolitical guy like I was couldn't really ignore the war. It was there. It was going to be there for a while. It was senseless."

Don dates his "antiwar feeling" from February 1967, a month or so after he broke up with Marilyn. He was taking a required course called General Education Forum. Each quarter the course dealt with a different topic of current interest, and that quarter it took up "The United States as Peacemaker." Much of it dealt with America's relations with the United Nations, but the Vietnam war kept creeping in, particularly with such guest speakers as Norman Thomas and Tom Cornell (one of the first draft-card burners who was later to serve a prison term for draft resistance).

"As the course progressed, it became obvious to me that the United States' involvement in Vietnam was clearly unjustified, and in the last half century, at least, the United States had been more of a warmaker than a peacemaker," Don writes. "This came as something of a shock. I had a great faith in this nation and it took quite a long time for me to realize that the United States was clearly in the wrong in Vietnam. Not only that, but the Johnson administration, and other administrations before his, were distorting the facts, indeed feeding outright lies to the public of this nation. These realizations were all part of a tremendous disillusionment. We didn't seem to be a peace-loving nation, after all."

But Don's agitated state of mind that winter seemed to demand a more personal confrontation with the war-makers. As he wrote later: "I was finding it hard to stay on the same campus with Marilyn and her new guy. I wasn't digging school. There wasn't anything I was ex-cited about. I was real down in the dumps. I wouldn't be missing much if I had to spend time in jail. There was nothing I wanted except Marilyn and she was gone . . . I was in a perfect position to make a dramatic protest against the draft and the war."

As if by some perverse providence, the vehicle for Don's protest presented itself when, on February 9 of that year, Don's draft board—Local Board No. 2 in Bay Shore, Long Island—abruptly reclassified him 1-A.

Until then, Don had had little notion of resisting the draft. He had registered promptly when he turned eigh-teen in 1963 and accepted a 2-S student deferment when he went to college. In a letter from prison, he re-members that during college the draft pressure "bugged him" because it kept him in a conventional channel when he yearned to explore outside it. "Because of the draft a guy couldn't be free. You either had to go to college, get married and have a bunch of kids, go into the Army or go to jail. There were numerous times when I wanted to drop out of college for a while and wander around find-ing out what life was all about. I wanted to be inde-pendent. Free. A man. But I had to stay in college or lose my deferment."

And when he was reclassified, without explanation, Don's first reaction was to get the deferment back as quickly as possible. He assumed that his board had made a mistake (most undergraduates with good records— and Don was on the dean's list then—were being deferred until they graduated). So he wrote them a note explain-ing that he was still only a junior and intended to con-tinue his studies for at least another year.

But soon this rankled him. In a letter home a few weeks later, he wrote, "Don't quite know what to do about this draft thing. It's really bugging me. I think if I was to fight for what I believe in I'd be fighting with the Viet Cong, not the U.S. I've been doing lots of reading on this subject. I firmly believe that we are the aggressors in this war. American foreign policy is really screwed up.

"I guess I could just send in my grades and an appeal and be done with it, but I refuse to do it. Next step is up to the draft board. If they call me I'm not going unless they let me fight on the Viet Cong side and I guess they won't let me do that. I don't want to kill anybody anyway. And I don't want to condone killing in any way, shape or manner . . . Even if they don't draft me this has got me thinking. How can I sit here and let people get killed because of our misguided foreign policy? How can all the intellectuals sit on their 2-S classifications and let this go on? I'm really getting upset over this whole thing now."

Late in February, Don decided he had to do something more concrete. He wrote a peace group in New York expressing his feelings about the war and the draft and asking what he could do. The group gave his name to a man organizing a mass draft-card burning as part of a peace march scheduled for April 15. The organizer wrote and suggested that Don might want to join them.

Don recalls weeks of "soul searching." Burning his card seemed like a drastic and irrevocable step. "It was a terribly difficult decision to make. There were a couple of nights there when I cried myself to sleep." But ultimately he decided he would. On April 11 he read a statement to a peace group at New Paltz telling them what he was going to do. On April 14 he sent a long, discursive letter to his draft board, which said in part: "Killing is not the way to solve anything. While we sit over here fat and happy and debate the issue, people are dying. If our homes were being bombed I am sure we would not be so ready to escalate.

"I decided to do everything in my power to end this senseless destruction of human life, and will not serve in this war or any war like it. I will no longer carry a draft card. I intend to devote all my time to the peace movement. I will not run to Canada. This is my country and I love it dearly. Because of this love I cannot stand by and watch people kill people in the name of freedom. I want to be part of this country, not ashamed of it.

"I hereby cease my relation with the Selective Service System, for the remainder of the Vietnam war. Yours in Peace. Donald C. Baty."

At 11 A.M. the next day, Don joined about seventy other young men clustered on an outcropping of rock in the Sheep Meadow of New York's Central Park. The meadow was aswarm with thousands of people gathering for a peace rally and march to the United Nations, and many of them drifted over to watch. The crush of milling, chanting demonstrators became so great that "marshals" had to form a human chain around the young men on the rock. There were a few speeches, a few songs. Then, here and there across the rock, flame leaped up from matches, cigarette lighters, an oil-filled coffee can. The young men gathered round, drawn to the flames like giant white moths. Dipping their draft cards in the yellow glow, they held the flaming white squares aloft while the crowd chanted, "Resist, resist."

"I was kinda scared and I burned my fingers," Don wrote later from prison. "But it certainly was a great feeling. It was an act of liberation. Not only was I making a dramatic protest against the war in Vietnam and the draft, but I was liberating myself. I was asserting my right to live in peace. I was asserting my right to be an individual. I've felt a lot stronger, a lot more confident since that moment.

"Everything else has followed from that action," he wrote, "all a logical extension of that first act."

Perhaps, but Don still had a way to go before he was willing to commit himself fully to pacifism. For, following his April 14 letter to his draft board, the board sent him a conscientious-objector-classification questionnaire. His letter had given no hint that he would seek such a way out. But the board always sends out this form in such cases, and Don did try to qualify, albeit in an unorthodox manner, for objector status.

He claimed exemption from both combatant and noncombatant training and service, but he made clear that this claim was not based on "religious training and belief" by striking these words from the form. He added, "Any convictions I have have arisen through a perusal of the facts concerning our involvement in Vietnam." Responding to a question about his beliefs on the uses of force, he wrote, "I am not a pacifist. If somebody hit me I'd hit back. I probably would have fought in World War II in a noncombatant capacity." And later in the form, explaining his unwillingness to serve, he said, "This conviction is not based on religious motives. Nothing in my religious training forbids me to serve in the Armed Forces. I simply feel that this is a senseless war."

This was Don's position when in April he became involved in the planning for a demonstration by the New Paltz Independent Committee to End the War in Vietnam against Navy and Marine recruiting on campus. This was the first major demonstration by the committee, which had been building strength at the college all year. One faculty member close to the committee recalls that Don was by no means a leader and seemed, in many ways, out of place: "He was different from so many of the other kids. He had no Marxist orientation. He wasn't even a radical. He just seemed like a rather excited young man. There was a burning quality in his eyes, an excitement, but also a confusion and an innocence. By the time I got to know him well he had already burned his draft card, and I remember he seemed terribly disappointed that they hadn't arrested him.

He didn't have long to wait. On the morning of April 24, Don joined several dozen demonstrators as they swarmed into the College Union building, where the Navy and Marine recruiters had set up their tables. Although warned by a faculty member that they were liable to arrest, they sat down around the tables. The college's acting president conferred with four of the demonstrators, among them Don, and offered them facilities for an outdoor rally, including a loudspeaker, if they would withdraw from the Union. They refused, although they finally left the building late in the afternoon.

The next morning they were back, and again sat down around the recruiting tables, this time blocking access. At 1 P.M., about a dozen Ulster County sheriff's deputies pushed through the crowd and formed a horseshoe around the demonstrators. For the next half hour the officers, their billy clubs held at waist level, glared at the still-seated students. About 1:30 P.M., Sheriff William B. Martin told them they were under arrest and ordered his men into action. "In what seemed like two seconds the sheriff's big goons came at us," Don later told the campus newspaper. Twenty-nine students were herded out the back door, loaded onto a chartered bus and taken to Town Hall, where they were arraigned on charges of disorderly conduct.

He was released late that night and promptly dropped out of college. For the next two months he shuttled back and forth along the East Coast between various events in the burgeoning peace movement and his own hearings at New Paltz.

His first move was to join the Boston-to-Pentagon Walk for Peace, sponsored by the New England Committee for Nonviolent Action. The walk had begun in Boston on March 25, reached New York by April 15 for the Spring Mobilization demonstration, and then continued on to Washington, where it arrived on May 9. Don joined it early in May, in time to walk through Laurel, Maryland, one Sunday morning as well-dressed suburbanites were just leaving Mass at a Catholic church. One woman leaned across the sidewalk and spit at Don as he went by.

This and other experiences on the walk helped transform Don rather quickly from an opponent of the Vietnam war to a full-blown pacifist. He was deeply impressed by many people he met on the walk and by "the love they generated in all directions." One of those who made the deepest impression on him was Erica Enzer, a heavyset middle-aged woman with a heavy Middle European accent, who was the CNVA staffer in charge of the walk. Miss Enzer remembers Don then as an "excessively pure" young man who had great doubts about the intense pacifism of those on the walk and about the methods they were prepared to use. "He was dubious about nonviolence, about the discipline it required, about the effectiveness of going to jail," she recalls. "He was constantly asking whether this or that tactic would really be effective." But Don stuck with the march into Washington and spent hours there talking with other convinced pacifists, among them Bradford Lyttle, one of the leaders of the movement who had been imprisoned for his refusal to serve in World War II.

Don also went home to Huntington for a while. His father recalls that Don seemed agitated and swept away by a rash of new ideas. "He was mouthing some of the things that were being mouthed by the most radical groups in America. He said there should be no recruitment on campuses. There should be no jails at all. Everything that was white was wrong; everything that was black was right. He said he wasn't going back to New

Paltz. It was just a dead little town with a dead little college. 'They are beginning to awaken a bit,' he said. 'We stirred 'em a little. Now we have to awaken the whole nation.' "

But almost as quickly as he picked it up, Don dropped much of the radical rhetoric. By summer, he was focusing on the issues which concerned him personally: the war and the draft. But now he was a militant pacifist. Abandoning all efforts to gain even a special conscientious-objector status, on June 23 Don walked into his draft-board office and handed in his 1-A classification card and with it a long mimeographed statement, which read, in part: "I am not going to wait for Johnson to declare peace. I have peace. I will not kill anyone. I am declaring my own peace. The Selective Service supplies the men to do the killing. Therefore I am not part of it. The Selective Service has sent me a classification card stating that I am 1-A. I am not 1-A. I am at peace. Therefore I am returning that card today."

And so from June on, Don threw himself fully into the peace movement. Later he was to see this as the time when he gained control over the forces surging within him. "I realized how my own violence had destroyed something beautiful," he wrote from prison. "I began to develop good control over myself. Emotions are fine but I had overdone it. As my emotions cooled I was better able to bring reason into play and reason tells me that violence never does anything but destroy and love never does anything but build. There is violence in every man but we can control it. Nonviolence is a discipline, a wonderful, fulfilling discipline. It doesn't come easy. It's something you strive toward. Inner peace. Inner love."

This is the way he saw it from his prison cell, but those who watched the process noted that Don's sudden conversion from violence to nonviolence did not drain any emotion from him. He transferred that emotion. He poured into the peace movement all the passion and tenacity which had been there all along in his early physical struggles, his marathon water-ski and motorcycle rides, and particularly his violent relationship with Marilyn. At last Don's "head-on personality" had found a cause to which it could commit itself totally.

"I am not a martyr," he wrote from one prison later.

"I am in the struggle because I find it fulfilling, indeed I would be half-dead without it."

As he recognized later, there was nothing of the soft, sentimental brand of pacifism in him. "I think it unfortunate," he wrote, "that the word 'pacifist' is sometimes confused with the word 'passive.' A pacifist, faced as he is now with hideous bombs, chemical warfare and countless wars, should be anything but passive. I like to think of myself as a militant pacifist. I have been aggressively pacifistic. Aggressively, but nonviolently, working for an end to the war and the draft. I have assaulted the American public with love and reason. Passive? Heck no! Pacifistic? Yes!!"

Don wasted no time launching his pacific assault. On June 29 his disorderly conduct case came to trial in New Paltz. Earlier in the spring, most of the twenty-nine demonstrators had pleaded not guilty and paid fifty-dollar fines. Don and seven others continued to plead not guilty, but on the 29th when Justice of the Peace Rexford Schneider found them guilty, six paid their fines and walked out of the court. Only Don and Diantha Perry, a twenty-year-old girl from Bard College, refused to pay and were sentenced to ten days in the Ulster County jail. Once in his cell, Don went on a hunger strike.

Mr. Baty drove up to see Don in jail. "It was a bear of an experience, I can tell you. The warden was blabbering, 'I have two kids in Vietnam and you've got to tell your kid . . .' and his guard went ahead of me and told Don, 'Your father doesn't like you.' Then they took me to Don. I looked at this kid. He was in this cage. See, it's open and there are all these cages, cages, cages with the light shining through them. Don had been a real problem to these people because he kept calling upstairs to the girl who was in another cage. He hadn't shaved and he was feeling pretty foggy, pretty low. He'd been fasting all that time. Ate nothing. He was protesting in his own way everything that was happening there, but the protest was falling on deaf ears. He was beginning to find out that once that iron gate clicks behind you you are just one of the guys in jail. They called him a noncooperative prisoner and treated him as one.

"Some of his colleagues went down to meet him when he got out. But he got out an hour before they got there. He went down to the local ham-and-egg place and had breakfast and then he walked out into a field and picked some flowers, and when his friends got there, he called, 'Hi, folks.' They called me up and said, 'We thought we were going to have to carry him out on a stretcher and here he comes out with flowers in his hands, saying 'Hi, folks.' "

Don came out of jail surer than ever that his life lay in the movement. This conviction was reinforced when he spent part of August attending the Peacemaker Conference at the Catholic Worker farm in Tivoli, New York, run by Wally Nelson, an active pacifist who was an articulate exponent of "noncooperation." Then, in September, Don moved over to the farm in Voluntown, Connecticut, which was the headquarters of the New England Committee for Nonviolent Action and was to be his home for the next nine months.

The New England CNVA, which Don first encountered during the Boston-to-Washington march, is a pacifist organization which grew out of the 1960 summer protests against Polaris submarines in New London and Groton. Founded by Marj and Bob Swann, two longtime civil rights activists and pacifists, the group moved to Voluntown in 1962. Life on the 40-acre farm, in the committee's own words, combined features of "a Gandhian ashram, an intentional community, a 'cause' organization office and a youth hostel." At any given time, twenty to thirty persons lived in the 235-year-old farmhouse, sharing meals, housekeeping chores, often personal savings and, of course, demonstrations, marches and vigils. Others drifted in and out for short stays.

From the start, Don was unusual. "Most people come up first just to look around and see if they like it," says Marj Swann. "But Don arrived with the intention of staying. He just jumped right in. I'd say his fundamental principles were pretty well set by then. He'd obviously been doing a lot of thinking over the summer. In fact, he was so sure about his feelings that he was sometimes accused of being self-righteous. He was extremely honest and outspoken and could be very blunt to the point of hurting other people's feelings. He could be very hard on his own contemporaries who weren't as dedicated as he was, particularly the hippie types who sat around smoking pot. But Don is extraordinary—his whole integrity and sense of responsibility. We've worked with hundreds of young people over the past years and I'd have to say that Don is the most impressive."

Don returned the admiration. "I think I learned more in the nine months I spent working with Marj than I did in fifteen years of school," he wrote.

He was more content at the farm than he could ever remember. Writing home in September, he noted that his car insurance was running out in October, so he would have no car from then on. "I just don't want one for the time being. I want to lead a simple, austere, rural life. Completely unfettered. I think we are often tied down by those things by which we middle-class Americans measure success . . . I feel the successful man is the man who has found out what he needs to do and then does it. I guess the hardest part is finding out what you need to do."

Part of Don's new austerity was a pledge of celibacy. He regarded this as a temporary step, designed to let him pour his full energy into the movement. "I only have room for one passion at a time," he told a friend. Marj Swann recalls "it was rather difficult for some of the young ladies at the farm because Don was a very attractive young man. I know one of them was determined to break down his barriers. I don't think she ever did."

The passion Don poured into the movement became clear on September 18, when he and seven others from the farm went to Hartford for a march organized by the Black Caucus to demand fair housing and protest "police brutality." The march was to wind through the Italian and Irish neighborhoods of the South End and there were fears about how the residents might respond. "We wanted to intercede in any violence that might develop," Marj Swann recalls.

"The march started off very peaceably," Don wrote a few days later, "but then about a hundred helmeted policemen came roaring up and blocked the street. Without any explanation the police then started to shove the demonstrators back . . . I asked why we couldn't keep going south on Main Street. The police only said, 'Go back or get in the paddy wagon.' Then suddenly I was grabbed by a policeman. I went limp. Two policemen carried me to a paddy wagon." Don refused to walk out of the wagon or cooperate in any other way and he therefore drew special attention from the police. "At one point two policemen grabbed me, forced my head down and shoved me head first into a young Negro, who had been arrested at the same time. They took him into an elevator, and just before the doors closed I saw a policeman sock him on the jaw. The policeman holding me said, 'Why did you push into that man?' I stammered that they had pushed me into him. The policeman said, 'Don't lie to me,' and hit me full strength on the cheek." Another policeman grabbed Don and fastened his arms behind his back with a metal ring. "He started to twist it and was calling me 'pig' over and over again. 'I'll make you walk, pig. Pig. Pig. Pig.' "

But Don only intensified his "noncooperation." He wouldn't walk. He refused a public defender. And he wouldn't eat. After fasting for nine days, he was brought to trial. While Don was waiting in the bullpen off the courtroom, his black co-defendant was sentenced to ninety days in jail for breach of the peace. Then the prosecutor dropped all the charges (including resisting arrest) against Don. This outraged him and later he picketed the courthouse carrying a sign: "Why was I released and not my black brothers?"

Even at times like this, Don did not lose his zest for other aspects of life. In the letter to his parents describing the days in jail, he recalled that the morning of the arrest he had driven a friend to Newport, Rhode Island. "We drove out Ocean Drive in time to see the 12-meter yachts heading out to blue water for the last day of the cup races. It was the most beautiful sight I've ever seen. The cup racers were being followed out to the starting line by an immense spectator fleet. All kinds of Navy ships and some of the finest yachts I've ever seen were pouring out of Newport harbor in an endless stream. I was completely overcome by the power and beauty of the scene."

But there was less and less time for such innocent pleasures. Only a few weeks after his release from jail, Don was off to Washington for the March on the Pentagon. This time, when he was arrested, he refused not only food but water. So they took him to the jail hospital and every morning awakened him at six for a vitamin shot in the arm. Five times a day they force-fed him through a tube in his nose.

On November 1 he wrote a letter to the Storeys in

which, for the first time in a long while, he harked back to some of the religious training he had gotten in their home. He said he'd been reading the New Testament. "There are certainly some beautiful thoughts in it. I just came across the quote about the lilies of the field— this sounds kinda vain but I feel like a lily of the field. I put my faith in men, and God if you wish, and strive to live in peace and I know I shall be clothed, fed and sheltered.

> I shall be clothed,
> for I am a lily of the fields.

. . . Christianity sure is confusing but I think with help I'll begin to understand a little what it's all about."

He also wrote a poem which he called "The Steps of the Pentagon Are Cold at 4 in the Morning":

> Why do some feel the faraway suffering
> and count the lonely hours
> protesting
> While others feel nothing
> and count the lonely hours
> nowhere
> Why do some men tremble
> at the sound of
> a plane
> While those who sent it
> worry about getting
> fat
> How can we make known
> our cause
> For those are our brothers whom
> we kill.

Eventually Don was brought to trial. Again he refused to stand in court, until the judge gravely lectured him. When Don finally did stand up, the judge gave him a suspended sentence. Back at Voluntown, he sat down and wrote the judge a long letter: "Hi. I'm back in Voluntown now. It certainly is nice to be out of jail. Now I can read the newspapers on the day they come, eat between-meal snacks, walk in the snow and, most important, love and be loved. Jail is a horribly impersonal place . . . Your courtroom can be a pretty impersonal place too . . . One of the things that bothers me about the courtroom procedure is that the purpose of the court is to find out whether a man committed a 'crime' or not, while his reasons for doing so are forgotten for the most part, dismissed as irrelevant. In my case, you and everyone else involved should have been asking themselves why I felt moved to protest the U.S. involvement in Vietnam—looking at my reasons, evaluating them —striving to find out if all these Americans and Vietnamese are dying needlessly. . . . It seems to me that you're being a little hypocritical when you deliver pious speeches to me about infringing on other people's rights by sitting down in the Pentagon parking lot, while at the very same moment the U.S. government, whose laws you seem bent on seeing upheld, be they reasonable or not, is dropping bombs on human beings, thereby taking their *God*-given right to live . . . With deep respect for you as a human being. Donald C. Baty."

In early December, Don was arrested again—the fourth time in less than six months—while demonstrating with a CNVA group outside an induction center in Manchester, New Hampshire. He refused to post bail and was held in the Hillsboro County jail for a week, during which he fasted. At the trial on January 12 he was fined $100 and appealed.

Two days later he was scheduled to report for a pre-induction physical on Long Island. When he got the notice, Don considered writing "the usual heartfelt letter with all the impassioned words condemning draft boards and wars and things." Instead, as he wrote his parents, "I decided to do something positive for a change. I baked some Christmas cookies with the help of one of the girls here and sent a box of them to the draft board. Kind of in the spirit of returning good for evil." With the cookies he sent a brief note saying he would not report for his physical and ending with "Merry Christmas. Enjoy the cookies." The board was not amused. It sent the cookies back unnibbled, along with another notice to appear for a physical on January 4.

A few days later, as snow fell on the fields around the farmhouse, Don wrote his parents, "Christmas finds me in a funny mood this year. I'm finding it hard to drum up any Christmas spirit. One of the peace groups is sending out a card with a sketch of a Vietnamese woman holding a dead child. The card reads, 'There is no peace this year.' I kinda feel that way."

A group from the farm did go out caroling one night —in front of a nearby jail and outside the Electric Boat Co. in New London which makes nuclear submarines. Don admitted that he ignored the words in most of the carols because he just didn't "really believe them."

But one song they sang was different. It was "I Heard the Bells on Christmas Day," with words by Longfellow, written after his son was seriously wounded in battle. Don wrote the next day that, standing outside the submarine plant in the snowy night, he "believed every word" as he sang:

> . . . in despair I bow'd my head;
> "There is no peace on earth," I said.
> "For hate is strong, and mocks the song
>   of peace on earth, good will to men."
>
> Then pealed the bells more loud and deep:
> "God is not dead, nor doth he sleep;
>   The wrong shall fail, the right prevail,
>   with peace on earth, good will to men."

There was time for Christmas festivities and some light-hearted horseplay at the farm that week. The others decided Don should have a "physical" after all. They gave him a real working over and declared him "1-AR— mentally and physically fit for resisting the draft." He even had to sign a loyalty oath—to his conscience. As a reward he was presented with a big gingerbread man.

Don's talents as a speaker and organizer were already recognized within the movement and he was in great demand up and down the East Coast. This concerned him. He wrote home that he still preferred "the personal witness type thing. I don't know if I have the patience and maturity yet to do the plodding, steady work involved in organizing." But he said he was "going to try and stay out of jail for a while. This last bout was pretty trying." So within the next few months he spoke to some young people in a church near Albany and at a high school on Long Island; conferred with representatives from the American Friends Service Committee about work on college campuses; helped organize demonstrations to back the upcoming Poor People's March; and worked to prepare for a vigil and demonstration in support of Dr. Benjamin Spock.

"Man, there's a lot going on," he scribbled in a quick note to his sister late in January. "We have to start making plans for the Democratic Convention in Chicago soon. I'm really afraid that one is going to go violent unless something happens. Chicago may be nothing but rubble by the end of August. Wake up middle class America! Your house is on fire and your children they will burn."

But then, in one of his introspective asides he wrote, "Boy, all I ever talk about is protesting. I took some time off yesterday though and went for a walk. Beautiful weather. I broke the ice and liberated the stream that runs through the woods behind the farm. Fell in like a clumsy oaf. Five times no less. Well, wet feet is a small price to pay for freedom."

But when he wrote that, Don knew his freedom was fast running out. The draft board was losing patience. When he was ordered to appear for his rescheduled pre-induction physical on January 4, Don sent the board a brief note: "Let me say I admire your persistence. Needless to say I won't take the physical." On January 18, the board declared him a delinquent and ordered him to appear for induction on March 4. The string was running out. Don knew that if he failed to appear he could be arrested.

So in the cold dawn of March 4, Don showed up in front of the board's office in a brick building in Bay Shore. With him were seventy supporters who picketed and handed out draft-resistance literature. Mr. Baty, Madeleine and Larilee were also there.

When the other inductees had clambered onto the bus bound for Fort Hamilton, Mrs. Carmella Dasch, the board's secretary, asked whether Don was going to get on the bus. He said he wasn't. The bus then drove off, and Don handed Mrs. Dasch his induction notice and a mimeographed statement entitled "I who have died am alive again today."

It read, in part: "On this day I am refusing induction into the armed forces. The repercussion of this act will follow me my whole life. Soon I will be put in jail. It means refusing to kill is a 'crime' in the United States of America . . . Refusing induction isn't a negative thing. On the contrary, it's a joyful affirmation of life and love. My mood as I contemplate this act of refusing induction can perhaps be summed up by a line in a poem by E. E. Cummings:

> I who have died am alive again today
> and this is the sun's birthday; this is the birth
> day of life and of love and wings: and of the gay
> great happening illimitably earth."

Don had one great happening left in him. On April 6 he joined a CNVA demonstration at the Philadelphia Naval Shipyard where the battleship *New Jersey* was being recommissioned for duty off Vietnam. It was a joint assault by land and sea. On land, more than a hundred demonstrators massed outside the base, where Secretary of the Navy Paul Ignatius was speaking to the guests. At sea, twelve protest boats tried vainly to maneuver past a cordon of Navy patrol ships toward the battleship. When most had turned back, Don and Bob Greene, in a tiny canoe, made a dash for the *New Jersey*. Later Don proudly recounted his exploit: "We didn't increase our paddling speed initially. We nonchalantly paddled right under the stern of the big police boat deep into the restricted area. Then someone noticed us, and half of the boats in the security fleet converged on us at full speed. We started to paddle like mad." Somehow they made it to within three feet of the bow of the great gray dreadnought before they were seized by Coast Guard and Navy men. They were held for a day in a Philadelphia jail and then released.

On May 18 a federal grand jury indicted Don for draft resistance, and he was ordered to appear for arraignment at 10 A.M. on June 13. Don decided that he wanted to seek sanctuary in a church. He was still by no means religious in any orthodox sense, but he had been reading the New Testament in jail and had had long talks with a Unitarian minister in Huntington. Sanctuary, he felt, was the best way to emphasize the "moral" issue in his stand.

Three or four Long Island churches offered Don sanctuary, but he settled on the Washington Square Methodist Church on West 4th Street in Greenwich Village because of its connections with the movement. He took his case directly to the church board, which voted seven to two, with two abstentions, to grant him sanctuary.

On the morning of June 13, when he was supposed to be appearing at court in Brooklyn, Don and about a hundred sympathizers showed up at the church. The pews had been moved back and to the sides, leaving a wide empty space in front of the altar where a press conference was held.

First, the church's minister, the Reverend Finley Schaef, explained the church's position. "The right of sanctuary in the Middle Ages was a right of impunity to crime," he said. "It was also a shield of innocence. The church, in granting sanctuary to Don Baty, is not granting impunity to crime, but rather declaring his innocence. He has committed no crime in refusing by conscience to kill."

Don read a short statement, in which he said, "I am not taking sanctuary to avoid arrest. I am taking sanctuary in order to continue the moral confrontation I began when I burned my draft card."

Then Don's mother spoke. She talked of Don's all-American upbringing: in a home with the Breed's Hill musket over the fireplace and an emphasis on freedom; in schools where he pledged allegiance to the flag and to American principles; in the Boy Scouts where he was taught the essentials of good citizenship; in church where he was taught "Thou shalt not kill"; and in college where he studied "what makes American democracy work." "It is not surprising that Don is here today when we consider the spoken ideals of his parents' generation. He must really have believed what we said we believed. The critical question and the surprising one is, Given that millions of men of Don's generation were raised in the same traditions, why isn't there one of them in sanctuary every morning in this country?"

Then Don, in a green corduroy jacket, his white shirt unbuttoned at the neck, clambered up on the altar. His sympathizers wedged in tightly around him. They shared bread and wine in symbolic communion. At 12:10 word came that a bench warrant had been issued for Don's arrest. They sang several choruses of "We Shall Overcome." Don suggested a few minutes of meditation.

The church fell silent. The noon sun streamed through the stained-glass windows.

Outside, a brown truck pulled up to the door. Six marshals in overcoats got down and walked into the church. Armed with a photograph, they quickly identified Don. Climbing over the other bodies around the altar, they seized him. Don went limp, except for two fingers held aloft in a V sign. The marshals lifted him and carried him spread-eagled out the door.

When Don had finished his summation, Assistant District Attorney Rosen stood to face the jury. In his hand he held a black-bound volume.

"Now, this looks like a book," he said. "It is a book, no different than the books that Mr. Baty probably has read throughout his life. There is a big difference what kind of book this is. Do you know who wrote this book? You wrote it, the judge wrote it, Mr. Baty wrote this— everybody out there wrote this. Why? Because Congress wrote it. This is our Congress, this is the law, the law of our land. Not Mr. Baty's law to do as he sees fit . . . This is a government of laws, not men. And that's where we get our strength . . . Mr. Baty received an induction order. You heard testimony that he knew there was a law which required his reporting. We ask you to pass upon the charge in the indictment and we ask that you return with a verdict in accordance with the evidence."

The jury took just twenty-seven minutes to find Don guilty.

Released in his father's custody, Don returned to Huntington that summer. He did some swimming and water-skiing, but he spent most of his time speaking to Long Island groups about why he was resisting the draft. On September 27, he returned to the Brooklyn federal court-house to hear Judge Mishler sentence him to four years in prison.

The next few weeks were difficult ones. "They shaved off all my hair this morning and gave me a set of pressed khakis to wear," he wrote on October 22 from the federal reformatory at Petersburg, Virginia. "There's a daily inspection and you get demerits if there's dust under your bed or if the bed isn't made right or something. I feel a little like I'm in the Army after all." A week later he wrote, "I'm amazed that the guards here, surrounded as they are with so many huge human problems, should be so concerned with such completely trivial details. They seem to be much more interested in the state of your extra blanket than they are in the state of your soul."

But gradually he got used to the routine and found ways of getting around it. He valued every moment he could get outdoors. "Every evening I sit on the chapel steps and watch the sunset," he wrote from Petersburg. A few weeks later he wrote, "Believe it or not it snowed Tuesday. Great, big, wet wind-driven flakes. It was great to walk in and feel the snow splat against your face. I got a runny nose."

Most of all, he read. Voraciously. James Hilton. Dostoyevsky. Vance Packard. Dietrich Bonhoeffer. John Gunther. Jean-Paul Sartre. Arthur Miller. And Thomas Wolfe. Reading *The Hills Beyond*, he wrote, "This'll be my first experience with Wolfe. From what I understand he's the J. D. Salinger of the middle-class people who are now running the Establishment . . . I just had a frightening thought. Will all the Salinger readers eventually become the middle-class people who are running the Establishment just as the Wolfe readers before them did? Will I eventually become a middle-class person helping to run the Establishment? Never! Never! Never! At least until I'm over 30. No! No! Never! Never! Never!"

And after reading Wolfe's "God's Lonely Man," Don wrote that it "really hit home." The essay, he said, "is basically an analysis of his own loneliness. I've been intensely lonely since Marilyn and I broke up and I began my confrontation with the U.S. government. I've learned to accept it. In a way I enjoy it. It certainly is maturing and as Wolfe points out, the fact is this: the lonely man, who is also the tragic man, is invariably the man who loves life dearly, which is to say, the joyful man. At one point Wolfe states that 'loneliness is the central and inevitable fact of human existence.' And he goes on to assert that 'Christ was as lonely as any man that ever lived.' How lonely it is to carry a cross, but oh how fulfilling."

In December, Don carried on his lonely struggle. He and four other draft resisters at Petersburg wrote to a federal judge in Richmond charging that the federal prison system was discriminating against them in a number of ways. The judge filed suit in their behalf. After a hearing, however, the suit was dismissed. Don and the four others, evidently regarded as troublemakers, were dispersed to different prisons.

On December 18, while awaiting the hearing, Don wrote to his sister: "Lots of people lately have been giving me this line about how I came to prison voluntarily. They say I made the decision to come here when I refused induction and I should therefore accept all aspects of my incarceration. I vehemently reject this position. I did not come here voluntarily. I was brought here against my will . . . I do not condone this imprisonment. I do not and will not any time in the future grant the United States government the right to put me in this cage . . . my fight for freedom did not end when I was arrested. Indeed, it was just beginning."

JERRY

In the sneaker-scuffed hallway of Walnut Hills High School, between matching Grecian statues of discus and javelin throwers, half a dozen F.B.I. agents and Cincinnati plain-clothesmen had thrown up a skirmish line. More policemen were clustered by the green lockers in front of the principal's office. It was Homecoming Day for Jerry Rubin, Class of 1956, and when Jerry comes home, Cincinnati doesn't take any chances.

Ray Brokamp, Walnut Hills' principal, was being particularly careful, for Jerry's return to his alma mater could hardly have come at a more embarrassing moment. Cincinnati was scheduled to vote a month later on a school levy. Three of the last four had been voted down, and school officials feared that if the Yippie leader was allowed to speak at Walnut Hills it could damage chances for the new levy. So, despite repeated requests by his student supporters, Jerry was warned that he would be arrested if he tried to speak on campus.

Ambling up the driveway toward the massive brick school that morning in April 1969, Jerry leered impishly as he savored the intriguing possibilities. Already facing three indictments, he didn't want another one, but he figured old Brokamp would try to avoid a messy arrest too. So, if he played it right he could stage a classic bit of Yippie theater which would enhance his reputation as the court jester of the Revolution. "Wow," he chortled with demonic glee, "it could be beautiful. 'Yippie Leader Goes Back to School. Students Defy Principal to Greet Alumnus.' Beautiful! Pure theater!" His stumpy (five foot six, 165-pound) frame was costumed for the part in buckskin half boots, brown corduroy pants, a red-and-yellow-striped polo shirt studded with buttons, and a red American Indian headband holding back his explosion of reddish-brown hair which tangled with his walrus mustache and wiry beard. As usual he was trailed by a platoon of reporters, photographers and television cameramen.

At first, the theater was subdued. When Jerry strolled through the school door, a husky man barred his way and directed him to the principal's office, where Mr. Brokamp said he would be permitted to stay only long enough for an interview with the *Chatterbox*, the school paper he once edited. By the time he finished his interview, hundreds of students were swarming in the driveway outside. Some were Jerry's enthusiastic supporters, a small group associated with the high school's underground magazine—among them Andy Schwartz, the Student Council president, who sported a large cardboard button on his chest which read: "The Forbidden Fruit. Rubin After School Today." Most of those outside were just waiting to board the yellow school buses, but when someone yelled "Here's Rubin!" they crowded round. And as Jerry swept down the driveway he carried many of the curiosity seekers with him. Soon, more than a hundred and fifty students were strung out behind him as he tramped across a lawn scattered with dandelions, through a shady park and along the sidewalk of Victory Parkway, where drivers speeding past peered out at the curious caravan. After about a mile, Jerry led them into the garden of the Friends Meeting House.

Surveying the students sprawled among the clover and violets, he said, "This isn't a class. I'm not going to talk like a teacher. Because to me schools are jails. Especially Walnut Hills. Walnut Hills is an elite school, which takes the children of the privileged from all over the city. It's a place where the rich teach the rich to replace them. Well, everything I'm doing now comes right out of Walnut Hills. Because when I was here I was so bottled up, just working for grades to get into college, respecting teachers who weren't worth respect. All these last years for me have been an effort to win back the innocence and enthusiasm that I had as a baby. That's what's happened in the last six years. We're creating a new culture. How many of you kids are going to college?"

Many students, who had been laughing appreciatively at Jerry's gibes, raised their hands. Taken aback, Jerry recovered quickly: "That's O.K. College is a good place to sit-in, get high, demonstrate, lock up the deans . . .

"But you've got problems right here," he mused, chewing on a blade of grass. "Did you see all those F.B.I. agents and police at the school? It was the closest thing I've seen to Chicago. And all because they were afraid I was going to show part of my body?" Rolling up his shirt sleeve, he stuck out a bony arm. "I've got an elbow." The kids rolled merrily on the grass.

"I might bring an elbow. But I wouldn't come into the school with napalm, guns, planes. They were afraid of obscenity. The only profane word I know is decency. It sounds like I'm spouting revolution—which I'm going to—but all I'm spouting now is the First Amendment."

The kids applauded. Then a slim boy with a dandelion chain draped over his shoulder-length hair rose and said, "We ought to do something about the school. Everybody knows about the study-hall doors being locked, so you can't even go out and get a drink of water. We ought to do something about that."

"What can we do?" a girl asked.

"One day we just get up and walk out," the boy answered, and many of the students clapped loudly.

Jerry smiled. "After today," he said, "maybe a little breathing space can be opened up at Walnut Hills. If you can get some I'll come back anytime."

"Graduation speaker!" someone shouted.

"Yeh, how about that!" Jerry cried delightedly. "Wow! Beautiful!"

After most of the audience had gone home, Jerry and his most ardent supporters gathered around a TV set to watch the news coverage of his day. When the announcer on Channel 5 declared, "Yippie leader makes like Pied Piper," everybody laughed and broke into wild applause. Jerry beamed. Then the announcer ran down other major headlines: "Harvard reoccupied, Cornell declared under emergency, Purdue students seize building."

"Another day in America," Jerry said with a little smile.

That evening, Jerry, his girl friend, Nancy, his younger

brother, Gil, and a few friends visited his family. Jerry's parents had died years before, but there were three uncles, Sid, Harry and Maurice Katz, and assorted cousins and in-laws around. The Katzes had never appreciated Jerry's style, particularly some of his irreverent gibes at the folks back home. Just a few months before, Jerry had told a Cincinnati *Enquirer* reporter in Washington, "I hated Cincinnati . . . I was bored. I had to get away from Cincinnati provincialism so I could be free and seek the truth." The Katzes had been hearing about that ever since —little remarks dropped at the barbershop or the country club such as "I saw they had a big writeup on your nephew, the Hippie-Yippie-Dippie" or "I don't know, Cincinnati always seemed pretty good to me, but I guess your nephew likes Moscow better."

But the Katzes were curious about their nephew. So some showed up for a small family reunion that night at Sid's house, a split-level ranch house in the Golf Manor section of town. When Jerry knocked on the door, it was opened by Sid. But what a Sid! He wore a brightly colored Mexican coat, a blue tie around his forehead, an electric guitar around his neck with a black skull-and-crossbones flag propped over it. Jerry guffawed and hugged Sid, always his favorite uncle.

Sid had once been a tap-dancer in vaudeville, strutting his stuff along the old Pantages and RKO circuits. Occasionally he had played M.C. too, polishing an endless supply of patter jokes. Slower on his feet now, a little pudgy, he sold movie advertising, the spots which show in small-town theaters or drive-ins extolling the wonders of oven cleaners or cross-your-heart bras. But he still twisted his bushy mustache into big stage winks and fenced at the world with the same Georgie Jessel thrusts.

"You know," he told Jerry after they were settled in his downstairs den, "I can't get away from you. Thelma and I were down in Florida this winter. We go into this store and there's incense so thick you couldn't see your hand before your face. Finally, we pushed through, and there on the wall is a big picture of you."

Jerry threw up his hands and hugged Nancy. "As far as I'm concerned," he shouted, "Sid Katz is the first Yippie. Absolutely. He's a Yippie."

Mildred, Harry's wife, turned to Jerry with annoyance

in her voice. "Are you laughing all the time, Jerry, or are you serious about all this stuff?"

"When you're laughing the most you're the most serious," Jerry said, draining his second Scotch and water.

"Well, if you're serious you shouldn't act like you do," Mildred said. "All that hair. The dirt. Everybody looks at you like you're a maniac—"

"Aunt Mil," Jerry interrupted. "Did you vote in the last elections?"

"No. Who could I vote for? There wasn't anybody to vote for."

"Then you voted right. You voted for Pigasus, the pig we nominated. We counted all the nonvoters as voting for Pigasus."

"You've told us everything you're against," said Marcia Bortz, one of Jerry's cousins. "But what are you for?"

"I'm for free—everything."

"Chaos," Mildred said. "That's what it would be. Chaos."

One of the brothers-in-law turned to Jerry. "Nobody has a right to eat free. These people on welfare want everything free. You should see what they do. I own real estate in town and a few weeks ago they went on a rent strike."

"Well, maybe you deserved it," Jerry said. "Are they slums?"

"Slums! They've got hardwood floors, air conditioning—"

The phone rang. Jerry, halfway through his third Scotch, picked it up and crooned, "Youth International Party."

Thelma, her arm suspended halfway toward the receiver, gasped, "How are we ever going to recover from this?"

"Did you hear that?" the brother-in-law said. "He called me a slumlord!"

"Don't you see," Jerry was saying, "capitalism itself has to be destroyed. Capitalism killed my father. He worked harder than anybody in this room . . ."

"If you ever had to go out and get a real job," snapped Marcia, "you'd feel different."

"A slumlord?" the brother-in-law said. "He's a maniac!"

"You know," somebody said, "they'll make a movie

out of this with Sinatra and they won't even call us in for side parts."

The Jerry Rubin Story, a zany Mike Nichols or Richard Lester production, would open with a long shot panning across the desolate Russian steppes and then slowly moving up a rutted road toward Kubsik, a small village near Kiev. It was from there that Hyman Katz set off for America in 1902.

He started as a peddler with a pack on his back, selling combs and cheap jewelry and patent medicines door to door through northern Ohio. When he built a little capital he opened a dry-goods store in Covington, Kentucky, across the river from Cincinnati. He had already sent for his wife and baby and established the Katz household in Cincinnati, then a largely German town.

As Russian Jews they suffered their share of social snobbery, but Hyman was a hard worker and by the time their children were grown the Katzes were fully established members of the Cincinnati Jewish community. The four sons, Harry, Maurice, Irv and Sid, all showed a knack for business, married and began adding to the Katz clan. But there was also a daughter, Esther, and when she was still unmarried at twenty-eight, the Katzes were worried. So they sent her off to Florida to find a lawyer or a doctor.

Esther didn't find a doctor or a lawyer; she found Bob Rubin instead. As Harry puts it, "Love kicked them in the teeth." Certainly their romance kicked the Katzes in the teeth. For Bob, a high school dropout who was working as a grocery-store clerk, was hardly their idea of a husband for Esther. Esther's choice was particularly hard on Hyman, who doted on his only daughter and didn't feel Bob was nearly good enough for her.

Esther brought Bob back to Cincinnati and married him, but a few weeks after Jerry was born—on Bastille Day, 1938—they moved to New York, where Bob opened a small candy store near Yankee Stadium. In 1942 he entered the merchant marine, and Esther took her four-year-old son back to Cincinnati, where she worked as a secretary in a doctor's office.

When the war was over, Bob went back to Cincinnati and found a job driving a truck for the Rubel Baking Co. Bernie, Harry's son, recalls that the Katz brothers considered Bob "a poor schlepper." The four Katz boys were particularly adept at the Jewish humor which began as a way of dealing with life in the ghettos of Kiev or Minsk but developed into a life style all its own. They got together frequently and their meetings were largely an exchange of wisecracks and quips, sometimes affectionate, at times almost savage. "It was a real act," Bernie's wife recalls. "But very ethnic. A bit like the Marx brothers."

The slower, more earnest bakery driver from New York just didn't fit into the tight little Katz clan. He couldn't keep up with the wisecracks. He wasn't "on the ball." Moreover, Jerry believes, his father may have seemed a little threatening. "The Katz side of the family always had this feeling of kind of being on the edge, that we hadn't really been accepted into America, that only when we had money and a big house and a big bank account and good ties would we be accepted. They were always afraid of scandals, of being embarrassed." The four brothers may have feared that Bob Rubin would embarrass them; they certainly feared he was going to be a burden. Finally, they found a solution: Esther and Bob would move in with the older Katzes, who now needed someone to look after them. The unwritten agreement provided that if the Rubins devoted themselves to the two old people for the rest of their lives they would get whatever money was left on their death.

Esther evidently welcomed the arrangement, for she seems to have returned her father's special affection. The family now concedes there was something a little too intense—"unhealthy," Jerry says—in the relationship between father and daughter. Not surprisingly, Bob resented the situation. Bernie Katz, now a psychiatrist, believes Bob felt somewhat "emasculated, not the master in his own house. His father-in-law was always there. Bob knew how the old man disapproved of him, and he knew how his wife doted on her father. Bob had to be an unhappy guy, at least at home."

Home, in those days, was 314 Northern Avenue in Avondale, a Jewish neighborhood a couple of blocks from the old Zoological Garden. The Katzes and the Rubins had separate floors in the two-story house, but they ate meals together. Yet, on Sunday afternoons when the rest of the Katz family would come over to visit the old folks, Bob Rubin would stay upstairs. He knew he wasn't wanted downstairs and he didn't feel comfortable there while the Katzes swapped what Jerry calls "their traveling sales-men's stories."

Other days, Bob worked a grueling shift. Six days a week, he got up at 3 A.M. so he could clamber into his bread truck about four o'clock for the morning route. He got home by noon, lazed around the house in the after-noon and had supper with the family, but went to bed early. It was a very different life from the one led by the Katz brothers and further set him apart from the family.

But if there was tension in the household, Jerry doesn't recall his first years as unpleasant. He believes he was truly loved. None of his grandfather's disapproval of Bob ever tainted his attitude toward Jerry. Quite the contrary. "He loved my mother so much that since I was her first son he just poured everything right out on me. I could do no wrong."

Likewise with his parents. "They wanted a child so bad-ly that they would do anything for me. They had just total dedication to me. And that's kind of a key as to why I could become so rebellious. See, my father would put his foot down. He'd punish me—turn me over his knee or even slug me. But he didn't really mean it. I knew they loved me so much that if I cried I'd get my way, if I screamed I'd get my way, if I insisted I'd get my way. It was really total toleration, total permissiveness. Many of the tactics I now use I learned at home. I learned just how far to push before you got totally wiped out. I learned how to play one parent off against another, be-cause my mother didn't really approve of some of my father's methods. A kid is brilliant that way, you know, he can really pick up all sorts of nonverbal things. He knows just what will happen if he cries. Living in that home was like an education in psychological warfare. I'm really convinced that the whole of my recent activity in the movement has been a playing out on a massive politi-cal scale of the things I learned in the family."

The first target of his rebellion was Orthodox Judaism. Hyman Katz had brought an Orthodox faith with him from Kubsik. He didn't answer the phone on the Sabbath, wore his hat on Fridays, kept a kosher table, and warned Jerry not to marry a *shiksa*. On Saturdays he would take Jerry's little hand in one of his wrinkled old palms and lead him off to temple. But Jerry was repulsed, almost sickened, by what he found there.

"All those old men shaking their gray heads under their yarmulkes," he recalls. "I hated it. All those old men shaking their heads! I became a Communist right then."

A little while later, Jerry told his horrified grandfather that the way to solve the Jewish problem was to stop being a Jew. "I asked myself, What does that mean—Jew? I'm not taking the responsibility for two thousand years. I have no psychological heritage in the Maccabees and the Judabees and the Jujubees and all the Egyptian slaves and so forth. I have got no cross to bear. If the Jews disappear tomorrow it won't bother me at all." This sort of thing was not uncommon in Jerry's circle. One of his closest friends a few years later was Yigael Goldfarb, who changed his name first to Leon Goldfarb and then to Leon Kenman (there was an apocryphal story that he changed it again to Sean Kenman).

Hyman insisted that Jerry have an Orthodox bar mitzvah at thirteen. But otherwise, Jerry gave little quarter in his battle with the faith of his fathers. He went to Hebrew School for a few years but recalls that he was consistently the worst student there and never learned Hebrew. He stopped going to temple altogether. Jerry would never have gotten away with this had he not received at least covert support from his parents, who did not share his grandfather's orthodoxy. "My parents weren't really religious at all. They respected my grandfather, but they just didn't believe in all that stuff. I took that from them and carried it a step further. Their position gave me kind of a stage from which to rebel against my grandfather on the religious issue. Sort of intermediaries."

Mildred recalls other forms of rebellion. "I remember once when Jerry was little he lay down in the street and kicked his heels, saying he wouldn't go any farther. Maybe the first sit-in," she says with a hint of auntly pride. "He gave Esther all kinds of trouble. She couldn't handle him."

Esther, a gentle, quiet woman, was the only one of the Katz children to graduate from college (the University of Cincinnati). She liked to read, and she played the piano. Jerry recalls that he had "deep conversations" with his mother and believes he inherited something from her—"the gentle side of me, the intellectual side." But he resented her weakness, her vulnerability and family loyalty which made them live with her parents.

Unlike some others in the family, Jerry recalls his father as "a very strong personality," and he sees this as one reason for his rebellious nature. "The only way I could survive in the house was to become very strong too. That just produced a very strong personality in me. I wanted a reason for everything I was supposed to do. My father said, 'Because I said so,' and I'd say, 'That's no reason.' I became a bratty, rebellious, screaming kid."

One of the things Jerry recalls rebelling against first was the "total racist environment" of the neighborhood. Avondale was Jewish, but blacks were moving in rapidly. "It was a very unhealthy social situation. The Jews were scared of getting knifed in the back. They didn't want to live next to blacks and started moving out en masse. I was intensely aware of all this, and from the start I tied it up with all the Jewish provincialism I rejected. I particularly identified that kind of thing with the Katzes. Being upper-middle-class while we were lower-middle-class, they always managed to live one concentric circle further away from the black ghetto than we did."

When Jerry was eight, though, the Rubins did move— to 835 Hutchins Avenue, about half a mile from the old house where his grandparents remained. The new house was in a neighborhood with fewer Negroes, but the move was apparently inspired less by racial than by family conflict. Bob Rubin had finally persuaded his wife they should have their own home, probably using Gil's impending birth as the excuse. Jerry recalls the five years they spent on Hutchins Avenue as more relaxed and happy ones, chiefly because his father felt master in his own house.

In those years—from age nine to fourteen—Jerry lived largely for sports. And this brought him closer to his father, for Bob Rubin was a sports fanatic. He helped found a Boosters Club for Cincinnati's hockey team and Jerry remembers watching with awe as 200-lb. Bob pounded on the seats and roared his encouragement to the roughnecks on the ice below.

But it was baseball that really engaged Jerry's emotions. The Reds were in sad shape then, regularly finishing toward the bottom of the National League. But Jerry didn't care. Sometimes his father would take him out to

Crosley Field and together they'd cheer on Ted Kluzewski and his hapless mates. The rest of the time he followed the games on radio, traded baseball cards, read sports pages and baseball magazines.

When he was ten he decided he was going to be a major-league player. For a while he played second base on a team at the Jewish Center. But he was always the last kid chosen in pick-up games, so he soon shifted to managing the team. His father (who had become a cub master when Jerry joined the cub scouts) now became the "supermanager" of Jerry's team, coached third base and helped them win the league championship.

When Jerry was fourteen, his grandmother had a stroke, and since there was nobody else to take care of her, the Rubins moved back with the old people—this time at 1816 Catalina Avenue in Bond Hill, a solidly Jewish middle-class area about two miles further out. The new house, which was to be Jerry's home until he left Cincinnati, was a two-story brick box with green shutters and a little white portico supporting a porch, on which his grandfather and grandmother would sit in folding chairs on sunny afternoons. Again the Rubins lived upstairs and the Katzes downstairs, but this time the Katzes were feebler and needed more attention. Jerry recalls that the smell of approaching death pervaded the house.

That fall, Jerry entered Walnut Hills High School, two years after he should have. Walnut Hills, which drew the best students from all over the city, started in the seventh grade. But Jerry, whose elementary-school record had been mediocre, failed the entrance exam. This was a devastating blow. He remembers breaking into tears when he heard the exam results. Most of his friends were going on to Walnut Hills, and for the next two years he had to attend Samuel Ach Junior High School, a rougher, racially mixed and academically lackluster school further downtown.

This hit Jerry particularly hard because it seemed to reinforce the class distinctions which he began to see between the Rubin and the Katz sides of the family. "They had better cars; they had better furniture; they went to better restaurants; and then this." Lower-middle-class Jews generally went to Samuel Ach while the upper-middle class often went to Walnut Hills. And Johnny Katz, Maurice's son who was Jerry's age, had made Walnut

Hills in the seventh grade. Nobody let Jerry forget that.

The family encouraged competition among the various cousins, but particularly between Johnny and Jerry because they were so close in age. Jerry recalls his parents' painful reminders that "Johnny's doing so well." Johnny, in turn, resented his grandfather's showing favoritism toward Esther's children, which became clear one Hanukkah when he gave Jerry a bicycle and Johnny a silver dollar. Yet the boys managed somehow to become friends. They went to the neighborhood Forest Theater (a movie house which Johnny recalls as "the Midwest distributor of ringworm"), and on Saturday afternoons they'd ride the Reading Avenue bus downtown to a matinée at one of the big movie palaces, then browse through the library or look for weird items in the pawnshops along Vine Street.

Yet the competition was still keen, and Jerry was determined to follow Johnny to the big school on the hill. For two years he worked with only this in mind. He remembers "snowing" his teachers by writing extra papers and doing extra homework. "When I wanted something I'd really go after it. I'd overkill." After eighth grade, he coasted into Walnut Hills.

Then as now, Walnut Hills ranked as one of America's best high schools. Harold Howe II, later the federal Commissioner of Education, was the principal, and the school had a superb record for placing its graduates in the country's best colleges. For Jerry it was an achievement just to get in. But he brought to school a gnawing sense that he didn't belong there.

"I didn't arrive with any inherited prestige. I didn't know most of the people there. Most of them came from better parts of town. They'd all been friends together. I came from the lesser part of town. They were just richer and there was like an inferiority relationship there. I had to prove myself."

His proving ground was the *Chatterbox*, the weekly student newspaper. Jerry's attraction to newspapers grew directly out of baseball. Once he had abandoned his ambition to play professional ball, he decided to be what the sports pages called a "scribe." Jerry covered a few games for the mimeographed paper at Samuel Ach, and at Walnut Hills quickly became the school's ace sportswriter. Every afternoon he was out covering one team or another. By his junior year he was elected sports editor, a position usually held by a senior. Johnny Katz recalls that Jerry tried to turn him into a sportswriter: "I wrote 'coach' once, and he said I should never say that, always say 'mentor.' He had the lingo down pat."

But already his interests were broadening to include the rest of newspapering. "I wanted to be where the action was. At first that meant sports. Then it meant other kinds of action." His senior year, Jerry became co-editor of the *Chatterbox* along with a quiet girl named Sheila Karam.

"Jerry ran the paper," recalls Alexander Gleason, the *Chatterbox*'s faculty adviser. "He was so cocky, so sure of himself, that he made Sheila play second fiddle. She deeply resented that and often broke into tears when Jerry ignored her. Jerry could be very abrupt and even arrogant. Mind you, he was good. He'd been elected on the basis of his drive, his devotion to the paper, and his sheer professionalism. He bought the *New York Times* style book and made people conform to that. He was a perfectionist, a taskmaster, a bug on accuracy and details. But he could be terribly intolerant of somebody who wasn't as good as he was. If somebody goofed he'd ride roughshod over them, and his sharp cutting voice and exasperated gestures made it worse. He'd blow his top, yell, pound the table. I'd say 'Jerry, take it easy.' But he'd say 'They shouldn't be here if they're no good.' He particularly had it in for Dick Levy, the sports editor, who he thought was doing a lousy job. Jerry really lacerated him. It was brutal, vicious."

Jerry drove his colleagues hard in his determination to win an all-American rating from the National Scholastic Press Association. He was crushed when the paper fell 90 points shy of the 1700 required for that honor (it was judged "a neat, appealing paper which might be able to use a bit more zip in its makeup").

During his year as editor, the *Chatterbox*'s editorial page was hardly incendiary. On Memorial Day it urged students to show "worship and reverence" for the fifty school graduates killed in World War II. A front-page editorial urged support for the Student Council's Clean-Up Week. Another chided students for discourtesy in assemblies. But there was a streak of iconoclasm. Although Jerry had joined Sigma Delta Chi (the best Jewish fraternity), by his senior year he was a strong opponent of fraternities (called "social clubs" at Walnut Hills). On November 15, 1955, he mobilized a majority of the paper's staff behind an editorial urging sophomores not to rush the clubs. The editorial noted that "most of the clubs segregate and discriminate by race and religion. They teach their members to live only with the same general type of person . . . Through this type of discrimination the social club becomes the breeding ground for prejudice and discrimination on a larger scale." The clubs' supporters replied that the clubs were traditional at Walnut Hills. So Jerry struck back in another editorial: "It would seem unquestionable that traditions are not valuable but detrimental when they prohibit clear thinking and obstruct the establishment of new, constructive customs."

Except for this anti-fraternity campaign, Jerry was by no means a rebel at Walnut Hills. He wore clip-on bow ties and flannel shirts when most others at the school were wearing reps and oxford button-downs (but Johnny Katz is sure this was not a sign of rebellion but because Jerry "just didn't know any better"). He didn't get along well with most upper-middle-class Jews at school, but this was because he still didn't feel comfortable with them, not because he consciously rejected their values.

Yet Jerry believes today that in one sense he was a rebel "because I had something I believed in with incredible passion and inflexibility and totalness. That added up to rebellion at a place where popularity was everything. Nobody was supposed to take anything he did all that seriously. But I was a total reporter fanatic, asking all kinds of questions, writing them down. I was a character. I wasn't overtly snubbed, but I was always on the fringes of the real 'in' group because I was just too intense."

Jerry went at journalism every moment he could find. One summer he attended a five-week course at the National High School Institute of Journalism at Northwestern and ranked first in the class of sixty student editors. His junior year, he and another student began providing sports statistics on local high school teams to the Cincinnati newspapers. All weekend, they would work on the complex summaries, hunched over their adding machine and charts. Then Jerry would rush to get copy ready for the *Chatterbox*'s Thursday deadline.

Sometime in between he sandwiched some school-work. His work was erratic—A's and B's in subjects like English and history which interested him, often D's in math, the sciences and languages which bored him. Because of the low marks, Jerry failed to get elected in the winter of his senior year to the Quill and Scroll Society, an honor awarded for journalistic achievement (and a minimum academic record). He was bitterly disappointed and raised his grades enough to be elected the following spring.

In his senior-class poll, Jerry didn't win any of the traditional categories—"most likely to succeed," "most popular," or "best all-around"—but he was voted the "busiest" boy in the class.

Jerry believes his enthusiasm for newspaper work then was related to something happening at home. For during the same period, Bob Rubin, the candy-store owner turned bread-truck driver, the man the Katzes considered a "poor schlepper," was going through a metamorphosis. In 1954, when Jerry was a junior, the Secretary-Treasurer of Teamsters Local 114, the Cincinnati bakery drivers union, resigned in midterm. Bob Rubin decided to run for the vacant office. Jerry recalls his father on the telephone every night saying, "Hello, I'm Bob Rubin. You don't know me, but I'd like you to vote for me." His slogan was "5 in '55," meaning that within the next year he would get the drivers' workweek reduced from six to five days.

To everybody's surprise, he won. The victory meant more money and a new car to replace the four-year-old one. But more important, it meant a whole new life style. Instead of getting up at 3 A.M. he now rose at nine. Instead of a bakery driver's uniform, he wore a suit and tie. Instead of doing physical labor, he was now a "union leader." Jerry might be expected today to sneer at this conversion to middle-class mores. Instead, he emphasizes that his father became simultaneously "a real crusader, out there battling for the working man."

He carried out his crusade, Jerry recalls, with the assistance of Jimmy Hoffa, then the chairman of the thirteen-state Central Conference of Teamsters. Until then Cincinnati and southern Ohio were relatively free of Hoffa's influence. But in late 1954 Bob Rubin allowed Hoffa's men to take over negotiations with Cincinnati's bakeries on the understanding that they would get him the five-day week.

The negotiations failed, and in February 1955 the bakery drivers went on strike. Until mid-April they stayed off the job, preventing bread from reaching retail stores. The strike was marked by minor violence: a warehouse was broken into and thirteen hundred sliced loaves strewn across the floor. One wholesale grocer reported that rocks had been heaved through his window.

Rubin denied his union had been involved in these incidents. But he said he had received several telephone threats that his house would be "blown up." Another caller warned, "Don't let your kids out of the house." Jerry doesn't recall the specific threats, but he remembers the strike as a period of great drama and confrontation.

There was less confrontation than met the eye. When the strike was five weeks old, Hoffa came to Cincinnati and urged the drivers to go back to work. He told them the strike couldn't be won on such a narrow front, and that he would soon call an area-wide strike. For weeks the drivers resisted Hoffa's advice. But on April 18 they gave in, accepting an $8-a-week raise in lieu of the reduced workweek.

Most drivers felt Hoffa had sold them out as part of a deal for more favorable terms in the Dayton region. But Jerry doesn't see it that way. "Hoffa's approach was the only one that would work. That was his goal, to stop the wheels of the country on any given day for any union. That's approaching the old I.W.W. vision. That's real working man's power. I really dig that and I really dig Hoffa. That's why he's in jail, not because of corruption, but because he had the vision of crippling the country to get what he wanted instead of asking 'May I have it, please?'"

And Jerry identifies his father with Hoffa. Shortly after the strike, Hoffa put the local under his own "trusteeship," apparently as punishment for disregarding his back-to-work advice. Two of its top officials were forced out, but Bob Rubin was retained and worked quite contentedly for nineteen months as Hoffa's "employee." Jerry recalls: "He had a picture of Hoffa in his office; he kind of modeled himself after Hoffa; and he had Hoffa's feeling that we can use any tool, any weapon to get what we need."

By this time Hoffa's troubles with the McClellan Committee and the courts had begun, but Jerry recalls that his father heatedly defended him. "Dad was totally behind Hoffa in that whole attack and against the Kennedy types who wanted to 'clean up the unions.' Once, my father spoke to a group of my friends who were against Hoffa because that was the intellectual thing to be, and he convinced them that they were all pro-business snobs. He showed them they were trying to put unions under restraints that business had never followed."

Local 114 regained the right to govern itself in June 1957, and simultaneously fought a bitter internal battle. An insurgent, overtly anti-Hoffa group fought Rubin, using posters showing him and Hoffa with their arms around each other. In his campaign, Rubin favored ending the trusteeship and made no open show of support for Hoffa. But after he won, he announced that he was backing Hoffa for Teamsters' president because Hoffa had pledged he would get the local its five-day week. "My people want five days at any cost," Rubin said. "If I had to align myself with Al Capone I'd do it to get the five days."

But a few days later, Jim Luken, president of the Teamsters Joint Council for southern Ohio and a determined enemy of Hoffa's, showed up at the meeting called to instruct the local's convention delegate (Bob Rubin). "I told them that after fighting so hard to get back their own self-government they couldn't back Hoffa now," Luken says. "I got them to endorse Tom Haggerty. Rubin didn't even have the guts to stand up and fight me, and he went down to Miami and cast his vote for Haggerty."

Luken believes that was typical of Rubin. "Jerry is really dramatizing his father. Bob Rubin was more intelligent than the average Teamsters official. He was an excellent politician—the old fence-mending type. He was very efficient, ran a good office and a good credit union. But Bob Rubin had absolutely no guts. He was with Hoffa when it was healthy to be with Hoffa; he was with me when he thought it wise to be with me. He blew with the wind."

Jerry can't accept that version of his father any more than he can the Katzes' condescension toward him. "My father was a fighter. He said, 'The bread driver's the boss.' Now you can see that isn't a Katz quality. To the Katzes the bread driver delivers bread, period, and keeps his mouth shut. For my father the Katzes' suburban, middle-class thing was just totally foreign. He wasn't into their verbal games. He wasn't a cynic like they were. My father was very naïve. I've got a lot of my father's naïve enthusiasm.

"In that sense, my whole life has been a battle of the Rubins against the Katzes. I see my life as just a straight line. The Katzes are the Johnsons, are the Nixons, are the professors. They have that same quality of lack of faith in life. You know, the kind of people that have totally given up on themselves or on society and therefore everything is a joke, everything is cynical. My father wasn't like that. He enjoyed his work. Sometimes I'd go along on his bread route with him and, you know, he'd always take time, carry the bread in and say 'How are you?'— very gregarious, very humorful. He was never a snob at all. The Katzes were snobs. From their suit-and-tie, middle-class, salesman point of view my father was always a schlepper. But he didn't look at things that way. Even when he was a union official he was always very egalitarian. I got some of that from him. I'm a lot like my father."

With some of his father's enthusiasm, Jerry went to work for the Cincinnati *Post* three weeks after he graduated from Walnut Hills. Joe Quinn, a veteran sportswriter who handled high school events, had been impressed by his statistics work and recommended that the paper hire him. That first summer, Jerry spent much of his time as a "runner" to the race track, bringing back the racing results and compiling the charts.

That fall, he went off to Oberlin (after being turned down by his first choice, Northwestern). A few days before he left, he posed for a fashion layout under the caption "You've Got to Look Collegiate, Collegiate Man." The blurb under the first picture read: "Jerry Rubin polishes up for his freshman year at Oberlin College in a blue-gray flannel suit with a three-button coat. The $49.95 ticket admits a college man to four years at fraternity rush parties, campus chapel, dances, plays and faculty teas."

Although he now regards places like Oberlin as "a lot

of academic bullshit," he was by no means unhappy there. He was suspended briefly for a complex college prank involving fake letters to public figures. But he did well enough academically and socially. In a letter to a friend that first winter, he wrote: "I'm pretty satisfied with Oberlin. First, the college has the myriad advantages offered by an out-of-town school. The dependence upon yourself and the meeting of new people, I consider to be terrific rungs along the ladder of growing up . . . Oberlin's dormitory life is great but the work load is great, too. The girls here are both good and bad. I've had about seven dates with two make-outs." If Jerry had any complaint it was about the college's attitude toward sports. "Sports at Oberlin," he wrote in the same letter, "is geared to build character. We play foes like Wittenberg, Hiram, Otterbein. Wooster beat us in football 59-0." And he added, "You can see what Oberlin is doing to me. I'm covering a wedding."

But the wedding—of New Jersey's governor, Robert Meyner, and Helen Stevenson—provided one of the biggest stories and most exciting experiences of Jerry's young life. Helen Stevenson was a distant cousin of Adlai Stevenson, whom Jerry idolized. This hero worship dated from Stevenson's first race, in 1952. "I can remember one day that summer I was about to go swimming at the Jewish Center and I just happened to turn on the TV and there was Adlai giving the introductory address to the Chicago convention. I don't think I even knew who he was then. He was a real dark horse and I was just fourteen years old. But, wow, I fell in love with him. He was so funny!

"I was two hours late to the Jewish Center. I just stayed and watched Stevenson. And for the rest of that year I was hooked. I kept a scrapbook on him and argued for him at school, at home, everywhere." Jerry didn't have to convince his family. His grandfather was a passionate liberal Democrat, voting the straight Roosevelt-Truman-Stevenson line. Jerry calls the rest of the family "mechanical Democrats." They were going to vote for Stevenson, but they didn't want to be bothered with Jerry's constant chatter about him. Uncle Harry remembers one day that summer he and Sid were watching a ball game when "Jerry just marched up and switched the channel to a Stevenson speech. We said, 'What the hell are you doing, Jerry, turn it back,' and he said, 'This is more important.' This from the baseball nut! It started a hell of an argument."

Jerry believes that Stevenson attracted him partly because what he stood for was in such sharp contrast to the Katz way of life. "My uncles were commercial, business-oriented people. Stevenson was the first thing in American public life that I saw as an alternative to that. He was idealistic, especially in that first campaign, and his speeches were like poetry. That was my first exposure to politics, but in a way it wasn't even politics. An election is a sports event, and I think I really saw it as a ball game then. I was a Stevenson fan like I was a Reds fan. When I root for something I'm always very dogmatic and very total about it."

When Stevenson lost the first time, Jerry took it very hard. "I cried and cried. Then I developed a very elitist point of view. I decided that the American people were just too stupid to know a good man. It was so obvious that Stevenson was better than that dumb general, but the people went out and voted for a father figure. I think that implanted in me at a very early age a disbelief in elections. I was still strongly for Stevenson in '56, although a little less enthusiastic because he seemed to be more of a politician that time."

But when Stevenson showed up for the Oberlin wedding in January 1957, two months after his second defeat, Jerry's enthusiasm poured back. He was determined to meet the great man, and as campus stringer for the *Cleveland Press,* set out to get an interview. When Stevenson arrived at his hotel, Jerry boldly buttonholed him in the lobby and the governor invited him to breakfast the next morning.

The interview yielded little news. Jerry asked him whether he planned to run for President again. Stevenson at first said flatly, "I have no intention of running for office again," but when Jerry pressed him he said, "No, I can't see myself running for governor or President again." Jerry wrote what he recalls as a "nice little character portrait" of the governor and phoned it in. A few hours later he turned on the radio and heard: "Adlai E. Stevenson, discussing politics at Oberlin today, left the door slightly ajar for another try at the Democratic presidential nomination." The United Press had picked up the story and rewritten it to stress the slight ambiguity in Stevenson's two responses. Aghast, Jerry called a Stevenson aide and apologized, but the aide said calmly: "The governor is used to such distortions; if it gets too bad we'll just have to deny it." Jerry remembers thinking, My God! My first big story and the guy I admire most in the world is going to deny it.

He never did. And this taste of big-time journalism convinced Jerry that he didn't want to stay at Oberlin. The Cincinnati *Post* had offered him a full-time job, and the vision of finally being a reporter far outweighed the attractions of college life. He took the job, moved in with his family again, and registered on the side at the University of Cincinnati.

He'd been on the job only a few weeks when he scored the sports scoop of the summer. Claude Osteen, a sensational Cincinnati high school pitcher, was being pursued by half a dozen major-league teams, including the Reds. Scouts were swarming all over him. Pat Harmon, the *Post*'s sports editor, decided that since Jerry was about Osteen's age he might gain his confidence: "I told him to go out, camp at Osteen's house and see what he could get." What he got was every cub reporter's dream: an eight-column banner across page one on his story that Osteen would probably sign with the Reds. He did the next week and Jerry sighed with relief. "It was a gamble," he confesses now. "He might have gone to three or four clubs; I gambled on the Reds and won."

The *Post* was impressed and gave him more baseball assignments. When James Farrell, the author of *Studs Lonigan* and a rabid baseball fan, came to town, Jerry went to the ball park with him and did a lively feature story about his impressions of the game. "I had very high hopes for Jerry," Harmon recalls. "He could have been a first-rate sportswriter."

But Jerry had also made an impression on Leo Hirtl, the *Post*'s city editor, and in the fall Hirtl asked him to move across the room and become the *Post*'s youth editor. Jerry accepted immediately. "I was no longer quite the sports nut I'd been. Partly it was getting to know the players; whenever you get up close the myth disappears. And because I was also friendly with Gabe Paul, Jr., the son of the Reds' general manager, I found out something about the management side too and I'd begun to see the game less as a field for heroics than a business like everything else."

Most of all, though, there was the chance to be an editor at the age of nineteen. His job meant editing and partly writing a two-page youth section on Wednesdays and writing his own column, *Campus Capers,* every Friday. If Jerry disdained Cincinnati student life at this time, there was scarcely a hint of it on his youth pages. Except for a brief feud with the city's parochial schools, the pages took the trivia of teenage life with an almost painfully straight face. A typical column reported: "Mary Dirr, XU Homecoming Queen, is winner of her bout with the flu. After a week of groaning, she is rarin' to reign Saturday at the Armory-Fieldhouse dance." The page regularly carried record requests to disk jockeys ("Bob Braun: Will you play 'Tammy' for Walt? I think he's mad at me. Nancy"); a *Teen of the Week* column ("Miss Rosemarie Klick, 18, fresh from high school, finds her first full-time job 'really fascinating'"); and a letter column called *Sound Off* ("Dear Jerry—I am against teenagers going steady. They are too young to settle down to one person. They have plenty of time for that later on. They should play the field during high school"). The front pages that fall were carrying streamer headlines on the school-integration crises in Little Rock and Nashville.

Jerry's job made him almost an instant celebrity. His parents were proud, particularly his father, who was always saying, "Do you know what my son is? He's a reporter."

On November 5 the youth page reprinted a story about Jerry from the University of Cincinnati paper. "The dynamic, crew-cut, jabberin' Rubin, insisting he is only a sophomore at UC, is well on his way to newspaper brilliance." Noting that Jerry worked forty hours a week on the *Post* in addition to a full schedule at the university, it concluded: "This young editor's motto is 'working hard, keeping busy, meeting people, watching his mistakes and keeping on top of all news angles.'" With the story ran a big picture of the young editor at his desk; alert dark eyes staring out at the camera; close-cropped hair; a phone under his smooth chin; checked sport shirt tucked neatly into dark slacks; his feet, clad in white bucks and argyle socks, propped professionally on the desk's right-hand drawer. Other pictures from the same period show the same bright-eyed, bushy-tailed young reporter on the make. Something about those pictures—perhaps the jaunty little bow tie he almost always wore—suggests Jimmy Olsen, the eager, young copy boy who trailed Clark Kent and Lois Lane through the Superman strip.

Some who knew Jerry then suggest a less flattering comparison—Sammy Glick, the ambitious, often ruthless young Hollywood mogul in Budd Schulberg's *What Makes Sammy Run?* Jerry resents this comparison: "Remember there was only one other Jew on the *Post* at that time. So what does a Protestant do when a driving young Jewish reporter comes on the paper? He immediately associates him with an archetypal character—he's not a human being, not Jerry Rubin, he's Sammy."

Archetypes aside, most people who knew Jerry then remember him as being unusually ambitious. "He was dedicated to success," Alex Gleason recalls. "It was almost an obsession. And he had to be a success that could not be matched with other dedicated persons. It had to be unique." Stan Dahlman, Jerry's immediate superior while he was youth editor, recalls: "Once he asked me, 'Who do you think is the best man in here?' I said, 'It's difficult to judge; there are different criteria,' but Jerry snapped, 'There's only one job here I want. That's the editor. All the rest are copy boys.' "

At the University of Cincinnati the verdict was similar. Dick Gabriel, a friend there, recalls: "He was really driven. He seemed to have an appetite that he couldn't satisfy. For position, power, social recognition. Jerry was always an outsider here and I think he had a deep yearning to belong, to do something big, to be famous." Dan Beaver, a history professor who was the only faculty member Jerry knew well at U.C., says, "He struck me as an upwardly mobile type, very much on the make, always on the lookout for the main chance. He wanted to be recognized as somebody whose words counted."

As a child he told Mildred, "Aunt Mil, you're going to hear from me." And Jerry concedes: "From an early age, I knew I was going to affect history in some way. I knew I was going to be famous."

But Jerry was willing to work hard for what he wanted. Leo Hirtl recalls that one day he kept Jerry going ten straight hours and forgot to send him to lunch. "Finally I told him I was sorry he'd been held so late. But

Jerry thanked me for the wonderful experience. And he wasn't kidding."

And there was an appealing kind of naïveté about him. "He didn't have the smart-alec, quasi-sophistication of most of those Walnut Hills kids," a friend recalls. "He was really kind of innocent."

But it was difficult to retain enthusiasm and naïveté for long around the Cincinnati *Post*. The *Post* was a dreary operation. It regarded the opening of a new shopping center as page-one news. It enthusiastically supported "anti-smut" campaigns in Cincinnati and when civil libertarians denounced newsstand raids the *Post* refused to record their protest. The building on Eighth Street had a grand marble lobby, but the fourth-floor city room was drab, musty and filled largely with veteran reporters who had long since lost whatever imagination they started with.

There were a few young reporters who bridled at the paper's stodginess and met over lunch for what one of them describes as "group-therapy" sessions. "We would moan and groan," he recalls, "about the narrowness of the management, the Neanderthal editorializing of the chain, the general cheapness and intellectual suffocation. Jerry usually came along and joined in our teeth-gnashing with a will, which was a little bit remarkable for someone who hadn't seen much of the world."

But Jerry had seen enough by then to blight his vision of journalism. "I learned that the guy who writes a story makes the story. The guy being interviewed is just a helpless subject. I'd take guys and with a few fancy paragraphs I'd romanticize them out of all recognition. The high school kids used to call it 'the Rubin treatment.' In my political activism since, I've used these same tools to manipulate the media. I know what the media want. I know the little things they need to blow something up out of all proportion."

Most disillusioning, though, was the deadwood around him in the city room. "See, I go on the paper and I just love it. I mean everybody should work fifteen hours a day, man, we're covering the world; we're telling people where it's at—what a responsibility! I was like bright-eyed all the time, asking 'Who's there?' 'What's there?' 'Let's do this,' 'Let's do that,' and what do I find?—'Eight to five,' 'Where's my salary?' 'This is a drag.' It was like a department store. I was the only person who enjoyed what I was doing. Everyone's attitude when I suggested something was 'Ah, why bother? I'll get my paycheck on Tuesday just the same.' At four o'clock, no matter what story they were working on—they could have been on the most important story in the world—*vroom*, down the elevator."

In reaction, Jerry often let his paycheck sit at the window for weeks on end. Living at home, he didn't need the money right away. "Then one day I'd come in and pick up three or four checks. All those sixty-year-old men were kind of angry at me, this punk kid who's not doing it for money.

"It really bothered me, though, that nobody enjoyed their job, because I wanted to enjoy it. So I said, Well, maybe it's the people's fault; maybe they aren't very talented. But I'd go to lunch with them and I'd find them funny and interesting, really good people, very alive at lunch. Then we'd go back to work and they'd just sit there. Finally it came to me. They don't feel part of it. They're hired help. I didn't have to be Karl Marx to figure that out. If people feel part of something, if their ego's involved, then they'll enjoy it. This really radicalized me. I can remember telling people it would be better if we all owned the paper, all shared in the money, and then elected a city editor. Or switched around. 'You be city editor this week; I'll be sports editor.' They would say 'That's communism,' and I'd say 'I don't care what you call it. Okay. If that's what it is, then I'm a communist.' I'm not saying I became an ideological communist then. Because I then would go right back and write about fraternities. But a person grows in fits and flashes, and the frustration on the paper was one of those big fits."

One of the flashes came on May 13, 1960, when Jerry driving to work, heard on the radio about police turning fire hoses on Berkeley student protesters outside the House Un-American Activities Committee hearing in San Francisco. "I remember saying to myself, Wow, that's me being washed down the steps. I knew then that someday I would go to Berkeley myself and be a trouble-maker." Jerry may be exaggerating his certainty, but the San Francisco protests did give Jerry his first glimpse of a radically different life style. He was still a few years away from adopting it himself, but the image of students being washed down the steps stayed with him.

Two weeks later, Jerry quit the paper. The editors were dismayed. They'd been talking about Jerry's becoming "the next Harry Taylor," a flamboyant journalist who started in Cincinnati and became Scripps-Howard's ace roving reporter until he was killed in the Congo in 1961. But Jerry had another model in view. When he quit he told Dick Thornburg, the *Post*'s editor, "I'm going to be back on your pages one day as the next Walter Lippmann."

Jerry had been reading Lippmann—particularly his early works, such as *Drift and Mastery* and *A Preface to Politics,* which struck him with their radicalism. "Lippmann was a flaming socialist in those books, talking about the evils of big business, corporations, nationalism. And I began to get interested in combining journalism and history the way he did. I began to see myself as a Lippmann, as the country's leading pundit."

He went to the University of Cincinnati summer school and then plunged into a full academic program that September. Majoring in history, he wrote his senior paper on Lippmann. And he began talking to Dan Beaver about graduate school. "I was puzzled," Beaver says, "because I'd never seen any deep intellectual interest there. He'd always been running so hard toward a newspaper career. Now suddenly there was this shakiness with regard to objectives."

It was a time of flux for Jerry. Within two years his grandmother and grandfather died. On August 31, 1960, his mother died too, although it was no great shock because she had been ill for months with cancer. That summer, Jerry moved out of the house and into the YMCA near the university campus. But he took little part in campus life ("It's a streetcar college. You rape it. You come for what you need and you leave").

Jerry's mind was still very much on his own future. After flirting with American graduate schools that fall, he decided against the straight academic life and applied for a scholarship to India. Why India? He recalls being "turned on" by several Indians he met at the YMCA. He believes Nehru's India also appealed to him as the "opposite extreme" from an America he growingly rejected. "I liked the idea of bringing the passionate voice of the

suffering peoples back to the doorstep of white middle-
class society," he says now.

If these were his reasons, he soft-pedaled them in his
letter asking Dan Beaver for a recommendation. India,
he told Beaver, offered "ripe opportunities for a student
of political science" and "material for my writing ambi-
tions."

Later, after he was granted a scholarship to the University of Lucknow, he gave several other reasons in interviews with Cincinnati newspapers. "I want to go where I
won't get the East versus West philosophy—it's not the
thing of the future," he told a *Post* reporter. "In Russia
there is too much propaganda. Africa is too primitive. I
am not allowed to go to China. The important thing of
the future is objectivity. If the two sides don't kill each
other first, someone—a third party—should be around
to bring the best of the two systems together. India is
where the old and the new, the East and the West, meet."
To the University of Cincinnati paper, Jerry stressed the
dangers and adventure in going to a city "only five hundred miles from Communist Tibet." He told the *Chatterbox* he knew he would have to act as a representative of
the United States and therefore not give hasty opinions
or be careless in his dress. "As for religion," the apostate
Jew said, "they have Hinduism, Buddhism and Islam. I
think I'll try all three, and if my soul gets saved in the
process, so much the better."

Jerry left for India that June—via Britain, France and
Germany. On July 2 he was in a West Berlin youth
hostel when he heard his name announced on a loudspeaker. There was a message to call the American con-
sulate, where a consul told him his father was dead. Jerry didn't hesitate. He got on a plane and flew right back
to Cincinnati.

This seemed a bit out of character for an ambitious
young man so eager to break free of Cincinnati. His
uncles could have handled the funeral arrangements. But
Jerry probably felt a touch of guilt. His father had been
ill with a heart condition for some time and hadn't wanted
Jerry to leave. ("He didn't understand my fanatic desire
to make something of myself," Jerry recalls. "I figured
I wasn't going to wait around until he died. I had to lead
my own life.")

Death revived what was left of his family loyalty, and it focused on Gil. "I didn't want to see the Katzes have Gil. I knew they hated my father. I knew they would raise my brother subtly against my father. They would bring him up to be a Katz and I just didn't want to see that happen."

The devotion which Jerry proceeded to shower on Gil was unprecedented. He had always rebelled against the close-knit Jewish family and at school he showed little capacity for friendship. "He couldn't relate to people well on a human level," Dick Gabriel says.

Now somewhere he found reserves of warmth and affection for his new role as legal guardian and virtual father to the fourteen-year-old boy. "I was almost evangelical about it," Jerry says now. "I thought, Here I can create a perfect human being." Gil, a warm, gentle boy who takes after his mother, remembers: "Until then Jerry had been a distant figure. I didn't know what to expect when he got back. But he was just incredibly protective."

Money was no problem; their parents had left a substantial estate in trust for the boys. They set up a bachelor household on the second floor of the family home, renting out the downstairs, and sharing the cooking, cleaning and washing chores. That summer was devoted to getting Gil into Walnut Hills. Like his brother, he had failed the test for seventh-grade entrance. Through July and August, Jerry tutored Gil in reading and math and kept him at his books. When Gil passed the test and entered Walnut Hills that fall, Jerry shared his triumph.

In September, Jerry went back to school too, as a graduate student in political science at U.C. He quit after six weeks. He did not feel he was rejecting learning—just the university's version of learning. "I decided I could learn more by myself. I'd sit at my desk at home and pile fifty books in front of me—philosophy, the Greeks, Plato, Christianity, history, World War II, George Kennan. I made my own schedule—nine to ten, read this book; ten to eleven, read that book. It was nutty. I read almost nothing. It would get to be ten o'clock, I'd have a little coffee and start thinking about how much I hated Cincinnati."

In those months, sitting at his desk in the little upstairs room on Catalina Avenue, Jerry's bitterness toward Cincinnati reached its peak. Perhaps it was the all too brief taste of foreign lands; perhaps it was the delayed shock of four deaths in the family within two years; more likely, it was the accumulated frustrations of twenty-three years pouring forth now on what had become the symbol of his antagonisms: the Katzes and the way of life he associated with them.

The word he used then was "provincialism." Gil recalls: "That's all he'd talk about, how 'provincial' Cincinnati was. He wouldn't even go to regular movie theaters any more; he'd only go to art movies."

Art movies led Jerry into his first demonstration. One of the few places in town which showed foreign films was the Unitarian Church. One night there, he met some people who were forming a peace group, Citizens for Nuclear Disarmament, and the next Saturday he joined the little band on downtown street corners handing out leaflets against fall-out shelters. "It was kind of pitiful," he says now.

If there had been a full-fledged peace movement then, it might have served to channel his growing anger. As it was, he recalls, "I just stagnated. I was bitter about everything—family, school, the whole city. The Katzes and Cincinnati were sort of synonymous to me. I thought there was nothing of value there at all. It ought to be destroyed, or we ought to get out."

At first, Jerry set his mind on getting to India and taking Gil with him. But he ran into a major obstacle: the trustee of his parents' estate, a Cincinnati lawyer named Al Katz. Although he was no relation to the family Katzes, Jerry almost gleefully found what he now called the "Katz quality" there too. "Only he was worse. He said India was out. It was a backward country. There were lions in the streets. Lifelong sickness. Gil's a young boy. He should grow up with other boys." It was a real problem because Al Katz controlled the money.

So Jerry began playing games with Katz, just as he had with his parents years before. His first move was to persuade Katz that Gil wanted to go to India. "Jerry sent me to see Katz," Gil recalls, "but he coached me carefully beforehand. I said I was coming without Jerry's knowledge. I said I wanted to go to India more than anything. But Katz saw right through it." Then Jerry came up with a shrewder scheme. They would propose the one place Katz, as an Orthodox Jew and Zionist, couldn't object to:

Israel. This worked. In June 1962, after a round of rather uncomfortable dinners with their uncles, Jerry and Gil left for Israel.

Israel was not merely a stratagem. From Cincinnati, Jerry saw it as a healthy antidote to middle-class Jewish life in America. "I'd always known there was a lot of talent in the Jewish people. The people are good, I thought, but it's the situation they're in. If you're a Katz and you're in that situation there's nothing you can do. But maybe in Israel it'll be different. I wanted to see people dancing in the streets, sharing things, creating new institutions. I wanted to see the new man."

Within months he was as disillusioned with Israel as he had been earlier with sports, newspapers and universities. Studying Hebrew in Jerusalem that summer, Jerry found that the indispensable words were *"Kama ze oleh"* ("How much does it cost?"). Most Israelis, he decided, were not very different from Cincinnati Jews; they were just at an earlier stage. "It was a society in an early consuming stage," he says now, "people just getting into nice apartments, having a refrigerator, a car. An ascendant middle class, very proud of its privileges, very competitive, very little idealism. So here I came for idealism, and I got—America."

In a letter to a friend that year, he wrote: "The Jewish emphasis on everything makes all so provincial, and youthful capitalism is something ugly to see. The emphasis on the private over the public can drive one batty. For the tourists they have just built a beautiful hotel on top of the beautiful Haifa mountain. For the tourists looking down on the sea it is enchanting; for those looking up on the mountain, that giant big building commands attention and ruins everything. Everything for the dollar . . ."

Jerry enrolled that fall at Hebrew University. He couldn't understand lectures in Hebrew, so he spent most of his time in the library reading—chiefly American sociologists. He recalls it today as "a lot of bourgeois bullshit—why people are friends and silly things like that." The one author who excited him was C. Wright Mills "because he was the only one asking who's got power and what values do they use their power for? Everyone else was kind of assuming the world as given, and then like asking how do starving children relate to their first piece of bread?"

A letter the next spring to a friend in Cincinnati suggests that the university wasn't quite as arid as Jerry remembers. The letter recounts a series of long conversations with Walter Kaufmann, the German-American philosopher and authority on Nietzsche who was a visiting professor there that year. The dialogue indicates that Jerry was already a utopian socialist. He wrote: "Kaufmann told me he thinks I am the most optimistic person he's ever met. When I said, 'Justice will come when each man in society has the opportunity to ask, How can I best spend my life? and then does it,' Kaufmann remarked, 'Most people would find they have no answer to that question . . .' And then he argued: 'Total equality is impossible and undesirable . . .' I answered: 'Equality is not complete likeness but equal opportunities for each individual to develop himself to his fullest. A society without economic motivations could find another way to get undesirable work done, maybe a rotation system, maybe making the work desirable. The great sickness of an acquisitive society is that society makes a man who works for money and is therefore alienated from himself, nature and others . . .' "

With this state of mind, it is not surprising that Jerry's best Israeli friend, Avishai Ehrlich, was a Communist. They met at a demonstration against Eugen Gerstenmeier, president of the West German Bundestag, who was visiting the university. The Communist Party cell there organized a militant protest, sneaking demonstrators into the hall who shouted and showered leaflets every time Gerstenmeier tried to speak. Watching the action, Jerry fell into conversation with Avishai, and soon they became close friends.

At twenty-two—three years younger than Jerry—Avishai was already an important functionary in the cell and well read in Marx, Lenin and other socialist writers. He was the first Communist Jerry had ever met—in fact, the first coherent radical. "I was really curious. I wanted to meet some of these far-out Reds. I bombarded Avishai with questions about Communists and Marxism."

But skeptical and probing in his old reportorial manner, Jerry was no pushover for indoctrination. Avishai recalls that during one of their first conversations Jerry asked him, "Have you read everything Marx wrote?" Avishai said he hadn't. "How can you call yourself a Marxist then?" Jerry asked.

Avishai had met the type before. "We had a lot of Americans in Israel who came during the early fifties. They were good democrats. They were against McCarthyism, they fought discrimination, chauvinism and things like that. But they weren't socialists yet. Jerry was like that, particularly at the start. He said he wasn't satisfied with how things were going in the States, but he wasn't specific. And I think he was a little afraid of us. He wasn't sure what Communists were. We were little devils in the beginning."

Jerry began going to meetings and parties sponsored by the cell and soon he relaxed and even joked about his Communist friends. Avishai recalls how they used to put on other American students. "We'd sit down at a table with some Americans and Jerry would introduce me as 'my friend, the card-carrying Communist.' I had no card. But every American boy believes in the card-carrying Communist and, of course, the card has to be red. Well, it happens that the Israeli Health Service card was red, so I'd pull that out and everybody would just stare . . ."

When Gil moved to a kibbutz, Jerry shared an apartment with a Southern Rhodesian named Goldon, the first black person he'd ever known well. Jerry was one of the first whites Goldon had ever known well and he was often suspicious and sensitive. Once, they were riding in a Tel Aviv cab together. When the driver learned where Goldon was from he said, "Roy Welensky's the premier there, isn't he?" Goldon took out his pen and wrote on his palm, "Jews always at the top." Jerry has never forgotten that scrawl on a black man's hand.

By that fall, Jerry and Gil were ready to leave Israel. Avishai recalls that Jerry was "not yet really a Marxist—he accepted some but not all." Jerry still saw himself more as an academic than an activist and wanted next to study sociology at Berkeley (he wrote then that he needed time "to build a career"—a concept which is anathema to him now). When he left Jerusalem he gave Avishai a copy of George Homans' *The Human Group* (a decidedly non-Marxist work) and a note which outlined his

plans for the next ten years. These included a trip to
Cuba, a Ph.D. in sociology (by 1967), then trips to
Russia and China for "comparative analysis."

On the trip home the brothers stopped off at a friend's
villa in Florence (where Jerry denounced their hostess
for the way she treated her servants); in Würzburg, Germany (where Jerry had a long argument about American foreign policy with a friend serving in the Army
there); in London (where they came out of a movie to
see a headline announcing John Kennedy's assassination
and Jerry remembers thinking, If you want to be king,
some of the people don't want to be subjects); and in
Cincinnati (where they had nothing much to say to the
Katzes and left for Berkeley after less than a week).

When they reached the Coast, they got an apartment,
Gil started at Berkeley High School and Jerry enrolled
as a "special student" at the university. He went to a
few lectures by Seymour Martin Lipset and read some
more Mills, but his heart wasn't in it. Within six weeks he
dropped out.

It was a strangely abrupt end to his quest for a Ph.D.,
which less than two months before he had solemnly
inscribed on his ten-year program. It wasn't his first
change of heart, of course. He'd left Oberlin, left the
Post, left the University of Cincinnati graduate school
and Jerry concedes, "I'm a quitter; if there's something I
don't like I just quit it and go somewhere else."

Yet there was something more definitive about this
move. Perhaps Jerry had been fooling himself when he
thought he was attracted to Berkeley by its sociology department. For four years he had carried the image of
Berkeley students being washed down the City Hall steps.
And in the years since 1960, Berkeley had emerged even
more sharply as the pacesetter in youthful protest. Perhaps, all the way from Jerusalem, Jerry had been drawn
to the one place in America where he might act out the
protest which had been building within him.

He did not wait long. Even before he quit the university, there was a "shop-in" at a Telegraph Avenue grocery store which didn't hire Negroes. At first Jerry was
put off by the tactic—militant for the time—of filling up
shopping carts, then arriving at the checkout counter
with no money. But then, he began to enjoy the scenes of
helpless chaos. Soon he was showing up every afternoon

and filling his cart more quickly than anybody else. "I loved it," he recalls.

Jerry joined CORE and took part in several major anti-discrimination campaigns, which he found "beautiful emotional experiences." But civil rights were not really his bag. That was the year of Mississippi Summer. But at the same time the Progressive Labor Party was organizing a trip to Cuba—which was part of Jerry's ten-year scenario. So while other students streamed south to work on voter registration, Jerry and eighty-three others left for Castro's forbidden island.

Since they were defying a State Department ban on travel to Cuba, they had to travel fourteen thousand miles by way of Czechoslovakia to get to an island ninety miles off the Florida coast. But it was worth it. Jerry came to Cuba with much the same expectations he had brought to Israel. He had been deeply impressed by Mills' *Listen, Yankee,* an early defense of Castro's revolution; he had been outraged by the Bay of Pigs; he looked to Cuba as an island of idealism in a sea of Katzian cynicism. And this time he was not disappointed.

"Cuba just took me totally. I remember saying to myself this is the first place, outside of Berkeley maybe, where the atmosphere is healthy. The first place where people care about one another, where people really feel bad when someone else gets hurt. You could feel mass enthusiasm on the streets, energy everywhere. In factories, guys would say 'Look, this is my factory.' It was like fantastic. I just never slept."

But there was the other side of Jerry too, always alert to his opportunities. On June 17, shortly after they arrived, he wrote Raul Roa, the minister of foreign affairs, asking permission to stay in Cuba to write for American magazines and to work on a book "about the people of revolutionary Cuba." He never heard from Roa. He did meet Castro and Che Guevara ("Che told us that he'd like to go to North America and fight there, in 'the stomach of the beast,' and this really blew the minds of those of us who imagined ourselves Latin American revolutionaries"). So in August, feeling like a dangerous parasite "injected into the small intestine of the enemy," he returned with the group to New York, where their passports were promptly confiscated.

That fall Jerry wrote a long magazine article on

Cuba. It was not a one-sided picture. Jerry noted the suppression of political opponents, the controlled press, the proliferation of bureaucracy. But these were outweighed by his description of a government "schooling its people, wiping out racial discrimination, developing an underdeveloped country, enlisting the energies and enthusiasm of its people and giving the poorest man a chance to advance." And touching the themes which had become the leitmotifs of his own consciousness, he called Cuba "a land of idealism" where there was "no trace of cynicism or a 'what's in it for me?' attitude," and contrasted this with the small middle-class Jewish community in Cuba which was holding desperately on to "the million-dollar Jewish Community Center [which] has not been taken over, although the present size of the community hardly warrants such a building."

Back in Berkeley that fall, Jerry had no difficulty maintaining his revolutionary élan. For on September 16 the university banned advocates of "off-campus political issues" from their traditional stand on a strip of university property along Telegraph Avenue. The Free Speech Movement was born. And to Jerry it was "a projection of Cuba, you know—mass rallies, Mario Savio, the whole community fighting against the university, the brotherhood that results when people get involved in fighting for their rights and try to create a whole new world. Like I'd gone to Cuba and here it was right here."

Jerry was "just one of the troops" in the movement, present at all the rallies and demonstrations, but not a leader. He joined a thousand others who occupied Sproul Hall on December 2, but he left before the police stormed the building.

When the exhilarating three months of confrontation ended in January 1965, Jerry was at loose ends. He was one of the few political radicals to support the Filthy Speech Movement ("It was a natural extension—Free Speech meant the right to say 'fuck' if we wanted to"). But dirty words did not offer much of a cause for the future.

For a while he hesitated, still unsure whether he wanted to commit himself entirely to radical activity or whether he could combine it with a more traditional career. Sometime that winter, he wrote out another list of objectives in order of priority. In the "A" category he listed "Mississippi" and "Book-Rebels in America," a study he planned to write. Under "B" were "Anti-Imperialist Activity," "Venezuela–Latin America" and "Return to Cuba"; the only "C" was an entirely new option, "Law," and "D" was his discredited, but not quite discarded, old love, "Journalism." At the bottom of the list as "E" he placed "Education by Study Marxism."

Within weeks, Anti-Imperialist Activity had shouldered its way to the top. Jerry remembers asking himself, How do we take all the energy, the beauty, the excitement of the Free Speech Movement and channel it into something even bigger? With a keen sense of the possibilities for the future, he decided to zero in on the Vietnam war. "I figured we had the university on the run now. Why not go after Johnson and the war?" His first technique was the teach-in, then popular on campuses across the country. "We decided to have the biggest, wildest teach-in of all."

By early April 1965 he was driving single-mindedly ahead. A note to a friend that month reveals the hardheaded organizer trying to build a movement out of the squabbling factions of the Berkeley Left. "I as a person right now am interested less in theoretical exactness than in making a difference in the struggle." He identified three main factions—"the left sectarians" (Young Socialist Alliance and the Progressive Labor Party), "the social democrats" (Students for a Democratic Society and the W.E.B. Du Bois Clubs) and "the activists" (Mario Savio, Congress of Racial Equality and Student Nonviolent Coordinating Committee). He felt the sectarians offered the least promise; the social democrats more "with care," and the activists "most, but need to be politicized." But he would "work with anyone of the three who can go in the streets and make a difference. My goal is not a demonstration of 300-500 hards but the largest number of softs."

Jerry got his softs—ten thousand to fifteen thousand at any one time sprawled on a softball field for thirty-six hours that May to hear, among others, Bertrand Russell ("The world is confronted with a great danger; the danger of subjection to the United States") and Norman Mailer ("Listen, Lyndon Johnson, you've gone too far this time. You're a bully with an Air Force and since you will not call off your Air Force there are young peo-

ple who will persecute you back . . . They will go on
marches and they will make demonstrations and they will
begin a war of public protest against you which will never cease.")

Mailer was right. Jerry and the other teach-in organizers decided they could not stop there. So the Vietnam
Day Committee was born. Its founding statement articulated almost for the first time—certainly the first time in
Jerry's life—a coherent if oversimplified radical position
for America in the sixties: "Vietnam, like Mississippi, is
not an aberration—it is a mirror of America . . . We
must make connections. The Los Angeles riots in the
summer of 1965 are analogous to the peasant struggle in
Vietnam. The Free Speech Movement at Berkeley is
analogous to both Los Angeles and Vietnam. Peasants
throughout the world, ghettoized Negroes and other poor
people in America, and middle-class American youth are
all part of the same movement. Liberalism cannot solve
our problems; only direct collective political action by
the oppressed themselves. We must build a movement
which makes these connections . . ."

The committee set up headquarters on the ground
floor of a pink rooming house near the university. For
the next few months it was the most frenetic spot in
America's emerging radical movement. "It was fantastic
just walking into that place," Jerry remembers. "We all
had this incredible energy then. We believed we could
stop the war if we just made enough noise. The floor was
bursting with energy. We were telephoning across the
country—two thousand dollars a month in phone bills.
We had fifteen different committees—committees to talk
to soldiers, committees to plan civil disobedience. Fantastic!"

But this burst of enthusiasm was all too brief. The
committee successfully blocked several troop trains bound
for the Oakland Army Terminal, making front-page news
around the country. But its major project, an October 15
march on the terminal, turned into a fiasco. Fifteen thousand demonstrators gathered at the university in the early
evening and marched down Telegraph Avenue, singing
freedom songs. But at the Berkeley-Oakland line they
were confronted by a phalanx of police with clubs and
gas masks. Many of the marchers wanted to go on and
dare the police to stop them. But the steering committee

huddled and voted five to four to turn around. In the minority, Jerry resigned in protest the next week. He later rejoined and helped organize several more marches that fall, but the spirit had gone out of the VDC. The following spring its office was blown up.

The next step almost had to be jail. Most of the activists in Berkeley had been behind bars at least once, but Jerry was becoming known as a slick manipulator who worked behind the scenes. It was hard to hold your head up in the movement without some kind of prison record. So Jerry was by no means unhappy when, on December 14, 1965, he and three others were sentenced to thirty days for their roles in a San Francisco demonstration against General Maxwell Taylor. As he was led from the courtroom, Jerry shouted, "Our act was a political protest. Our punishment is political. We are today political prisoners."

But even as a political prisoner Jerry found jail unbearable. "The boredom, the waiting for the hours to tick away, destroys part of your soul. But I had to admit that jail is an effective tool for a ruling class because it did take something out of me. It slowed down my step. I took a couple of months to get my confidence back, to get careless again, because you have to be careless, daredevilish and adventurish in these things."

Perhaps it was this temporary caution which led Jerry that spring into the most conventional—and frustrating—segment of his Berkeley career: managing Robert Scheer's campaign for the Democratic congressional nomination in the Seventh District. The Scheer boom came chiefly "out of the hills," from professors and other liberals who lived in redwood, plate-glass splendor on the green slopes behind the university. But Jerry admired the articulate young *Ramparts* editor and saw the campaign as a chance to reach thousands of new constituents with an antiwar message.

Jerry managed to bring many of his friends from the VDC into the campaign. But the clash between the "liberal" and "radical" wings of the campaign eventually got out of hand, and he was dismissed as campaign manager. To clinch Jerry's disillusionment with conventional politics, Scheer lost narrowly that June.

The morning after Scheer's defeat found Jerry sitting in SDS national headquarters in Chicago writing a long letter to Nancy Kurshan, a pretty, dark-haired, twenty-one-year-old graduate student he'd met in Berkeley the fall before and fallen in love with. Nancy was still deeply involved with another man and was spending the summer with him at Cornell. Hunched over a desk in the deserted office in the heart of the Chicago ghetto, Jerry poured out his love for her, his loneliness, his intense depression and doubts about the future. He had been talking with Paul Booth, then the SDS national secretary, about a job in the organization. But this was by no means certain and Jerry was also thinking about writing a book or leaving the country again. "Problem is, Nancy, I just don't know what I want to do," he wrote.

Perhaps for the first time he was beginning to grapple seriously with what he called "my achievement drive, which is too damn high for my own sense of balance." That year, Jerry had begun to smoke pot a little and now he wrote, "In a sense, I think, LSD and pot signifies the total end of the Protestant Ethic: fuck work, we want to know ourselves. But, of course, the goal is to free one's self from American society's sick notions of work, success, reward and status and to find and establish oneself through one's own discipline, hard work and introspection. Can you do this while encapsulated within the institutions of America (the university, the newspaper)? Can you do that while trying to change the society? . . . I guess the task is to make clear, to make available the image or the opportunity for honest, expressive, self-fulfilling work and relate that to mind-expression. If such could be done, maybe an alliance after all could be built between the political and the bohemian tendencies. Frankly, honey, I see this—not electoral politics—as the real job of the New Left."

This idea of merging a self-expressive life style with radical politics was percolating in Jerry's mind when, in August, he received a subpoena to appear before the House Un-American Activities Committee. He remembers considering "the old Communist Party approach—you know, the committee's illegitimate, so don't go, or if you go, take a total civil-liberties approach, cite the Fifth Amendment and all that." But after talking with many friends—particularly with Ronnie Davis of the San Francisco Mime Troupe, the country's pioneer in guerrilla theater—Jerry decided: "Hell, I don't want to fight

HUAC. I want to use this to project an image across the country. But I can't do that with words because you just have to answer their questions, and if you don't they'll hammer you down and say, 'Are you a Communist?' Suddenly I saw it had to be a costume, a total costume which would do two things—first, get its own message across, and second, ridicule the whole thing because even they can't take themselves seriously if you're sitting there in some outlandish costume."

So Jerry went down to a theatrical costume store and plunked down twenty-five dollars for a Revolutionary War uniform. The uniform, a rather dashing affair with lots of gold braid, may have fulfilled another need too. For Jerry has always had a thing about heroism. "Young kids want to be heroes," he says. "They have an incredible energy and they want to live creative, exciting lives. That's what America tells you to do, you know. The history you learn is hero-oriented: Columbus, George Washington, Paul Revere, the pioneers, the cowboys. America's promise has been 'Live a heroic life.' But then, when it comes time to make good on its promise, it can't. It turns around and says, 'Oh, you can get good grades, and then get a degree, then get a job in a corporation, and buy a ranch house and be a good consumer.' But kids aren't satisfied with that. They want to be heroes. And if America denies them an opportunity for heroism they're going to create their own."

On August 16 Jerry wore his uniform into the caucus room of the House office building. As he anticipated, he was the immediate hit of the chaotic four-day proceedings. Yet, Jerry could not maintain his mocking style. The long statement he handed out the opening day had a few nice touches—"I wear this uniform to symbolize the fact that America was born in revolution, but today America does violence to her own past by denying the right of others to revolution"—but most of it was as turgid and outraged as any Old Left tract: "I take these hearings deadly seriously. They are dangerous . . . We shall never be silent . . . You can silence us only by killing us . . . History will condemn you." On the last day of the hearings, Jerry was so outraged at not being allowed to testify that he was arrested for disturbing the peace. The merger of style and protest was still incomplete.

It began to take form in Berkeley that fall. Nancy

finally succumbed to Jerry's insistent courtship and settled
down with him in a small apartment off Telegraph Avenue in the heart of Berkeley's student quarter. Together
they began smoking pot regularly. "Drugs became a big
part of his life," Nancy recalls, "and it began to change
him."

"From the moment I started taking drugs regularly,"
Jerry says, "I just loved it. I loved sex under drugs. I
loved movies under drugs. And my whole sense of politics
changed. Like under drugs the experience is an end in itself. I began to see that we had to create a movement
that was an end in itself—not an external goal or revolution, but living revolution every day."

Even then there was an unresolved tension in Jerry
between the loose life style associated with drugs and his
older, harder political style. After his costumed appearance before HUAC he was widely regarded as a producer of radical spectacles, the Cecil B. DeMille or P. T.
Barnum of the Left. But he was annoyed by this. "I was
embarrassed by that reputation. I tried all the time to
convince people that I was political, that I had a goal."

For there was still more than the bay between Berkeley and Haight-Ashbury. The freaky, zonked-out style being developed on the misty slopes of the Haight had still
made few inroads into intense, political Berkeley. Berkeley radicals rarely went to the Haight and Jerry was
still a Berkeley radical. On October 7, 1966, two groups
converged on the San Francisco City Hall—one a "Love
Delegation" in golden robes bearing magic mushrooms
to "turn on the mayor"; the other, an SDS group, with
Jerry as its spokesman, come to hold a press conference.
The two outfits stared at each other with ill-disguised
antagonism.

And in a letter later that fall, Jerry recorded his dismay after hearing Richard Alpert, an advocate of mind-
expanding drugs and a hippie hero, speak at Berkeley—
"He was a sad sack in my view. Told all that the truth
lies within, that change externally was impossible . . .
I'm getting increasingly bitter as I see the cop-out of
youth . . ."

Only two months later, Jerry was actively seeking a
synthesis of the two strands of disaffection. Announcing
he would speak at the hippie-sponsored "human be-in"
at the Polo Grounds, he said he and other radicals "share

a common identity with the community of Haight-Ashbury. Our struggle to create meaningful communities is the same—in Berkeley and in Haight-Ashbury . . . The 'political radicals' and the 'hippies' are 'turned off' by the same things in this country . . . We will 'tune in' to a new community, based on love and sharing . . ."

But when Jerry spoke in a similar vein at the be-in, it was a fiasco. The vast gathering of flower children, wandering barefoot in the grass, many of them stoned out of their minds, were in no mood for even a relatively hip rap by a politico from across the bay. Stew Albert, one of Jerry's closest friends then and now, believes his experience that afternoon helped complete the shift his personal experience with drugs had begun. "Jerry asked himself, 'Why didn't I go over?' and then, 'What's wrong with me?' Some people say Jerry got into the whole cultural thing because the political thing had run out of steam. Sure, it was politically expedient, but it also was a way of coming to terms with himself. Jerry had always been incredibly ambitious, and the cultural revolution made him come to terms with that hard drive."

But there were a few more testing grounds for the "new Rubin." One was his race that spring for mayor of Berkeley. The Scheer campaign had disillusioned him about conventional politics, but even then he had played around with ideas for a truly unconventional campaign. Once, he scrawled several proposed "stratagems" for Scheer, including "Burn down Slum House," "Marx-Jefferson Day $100-a-plate dinner," and "Operation Subversion on campus." None of these ideas were accepted, but Jerry had always wondered what would happen if they were.

So when someone suggested that he take on Republican Mayor Wallace Johnson in the April 1967 election, Jerry decided to run a campaign based on the tactics of the *Provos*, the zany Dutchmen who were the spiritual fathers of the Yippies. Stew Albert became his campaign manager and together they gleefully planned "the zaniest campaign the country would ever see" (among other things, Jerry planned to resign if he won and let a panel of citizens take turns as mayor). But two things happened—the liberals and the "straight Left" threw up their hands in horror at his ideas, and Jerry suddenly got the even freakier idea that he might win if he played it just half straight. Even then, his platform was probably the most daring ever offered by an American candidate: legalization of pot, free heroin for addicts, legalization of abortions, gradual disarmament of the police force, and abolition of the draft. Only in Berkeley could a candidate running on that platform have gained 22 percent of the vote (Mayor Wallace got 69 percent in the four-way race).

His defeat left Jerry mired in depression again. The campaign had absorbed all his money, including five thousand dollars left him on his twenty-fifth birthday under his father's will. That summer, Jerry helped organize a cross-country "peace-torch marathon," which deteriorated into a typical Berkeley factional squabble. On July 6 the *Barb*, Berkeley's underground paper, announced that Jerry was going overseas as its "foreign correspondent." It said he would travel for two or three years in Europe, the Mideast and Africa with his "bride-to-be," Nancy. And it quoted Jerry as saying, "When I came to Berkeley four years ago I believed the intellectual would be a major force for social change . . . I can't say I'm leaving Berkeley with any feeling of enthusiasm or optimism."

But a month later, Jerry found himself deeply involved in another New Left project. David Dellinger, chairman of the National Mobilization Committee to End the War in Vietnam, asked him to be project director of the October march on Washington. Jerry had known Dellinger since the Vietnam Day teach-in and he admired him. So he postponed his trip abroad and brought Nancy to New York.

His second day there, he met the man who would complete his transformation—a wild-haired, beak-nosed, freak-out acidhead named Abbie Hoffman. As Stew Albert sees it: "The hippie thing in California had already made Jerry realize he was in the movement as much for personal liberation as for political liberation. In Abbie Hoffman he found a man who had developed a style of action which would liberate the person involved as well as changing society. If it was Hippie which gave Jerry a sense of his own liberation, it was Abbie and Yippie which gave him a way of carrying it out."

"Abbie had this incredible effect on me," Jerry concedes. "Just revolutionized me." He grew his hair long (until then Jerry had been a short-hair, although in Berkeley he sported a handlebar mustache as his "revolutionary symbol"); shucked his white shirt and slacks for the more freaky garb of the East Village; and started dropping acid regularly ("just the grooviest sexual and emotional experience, and so ecstatic that if everyone did it it would just be like heaven on earth").

When Timothy Leary, the high priest of the drug cult, came to New York that winter, he pronounced Jerry "changed"—no longer the "driving radical shouting activist slogans" he remembered from the San Francisco be-in only a year before, but a "relaxed, jolly," almost elflike creature. "The dogmatic leftist activist chapter had been written, and here was Merry Jerry the Lycergic Lenin, the grass Guevara, the mescaline Marx."

Abbie showed him new tactics too. For he and his friends in the East Village were then pioneering a "protest as theater"—most spectacularly demonstrated by the showering of dollar bills onto the floor of the New York Stock Exchange. Already disposed to the theatrical style —perhaps an inheritance from Sid's vaudeville routines —Jerry was entranced. As he rollicked around New York with Abbie and his zonked-out colleagues—Ed Sanders, Keith Lampe, Paul Krassner, Jim Fouratt—he found Dave Dellinger's straight radical line increasingly difficult to take ("Dave was all the time worried about how to get the Women for Peace to accept civil disobedience—I just couldn't worry about things like that; relations started getting very tense").

The split broke into the open with the publication of an issue of the *Mobilizer* (the organ of the Mobilization Committee) containing an article by Keith Lampe predicting that during the March on the Pentagon "a thousand children will stage a Loot-in at department stores to strike at the property fetish that underlies genocidal war . . . seven tailored fraternity boys will wrestle LBJ to the ground and take his pants off." The Mobilization "straights" suppressed the issue. From then on, although Jerry continued as project director for the march, he spent most of his time working with Abbie on his scheme to "levitate" the Pentagon.

The march itself (during which he was arrested again) left Jerry ecstatic. "It made me see that we could build a movement by knocking off American symbols. We had symbolically destroyed the Pentagon, the symbol of the war machine, by throwing blood on it, pissing on it, dancing on it, painting 'Che lives' on it. It was a total cultural attack on the Pentagon. The media had communicated this all over the country and lots of people identified with us, the besiegers."

But Jerry saw something else at the Pentagon: "I saw a new person. A young kid whose hair was long, who was sticking his nose out at America, saying I want a whole different life. He was getting high all the time, having more sex, having more fun than middle-class America. He was a revolutionary; his brothers were the Panthers and the Vietnamese. But he saw that it wasn't enough to fight for the Vietnamese because you're fighting for your own fucking freedom too. He wasn't at the Pentagon the way the radicals were in the Berkeley days—to present demands, express an ideology, be consistent with page three hundred of Marx. He was there out of fun, because it was the thing to do, excitement, action, and being young. What was he? I didn't know. But I knew no organization—not Mobilization, not SDS—spoke for him. Somebody had to."

So Yippie was born. New Year's Day in Abbie's apartment, Abbie and his wife, Anita, Paul Krassner and Jerry were rapping out their ideas for a massive youth festival during the Democratic convention in Chicago. "But we realized that we couldn't build things around just a youth festival. That's just an event. We had to build it around a new person. Let's create a new figure, we said, a longhaired, crazy revolutionary. I said it had to have youth in it because we definitely believed it was a generational thing. And it had to be international because we envisioned youth festivals in Russia, in Latin America. And I think it was Krassner who put it together, who said, 'Uh huh, Yippie—Youth International Party.' Right away I dug it."

Lots of others didn't dig it at all:
• the Old Left (Fred Halstead, presidential candidate for the Socialist Workers Party, in a debate with Rubin— "Jerry defines ideology as a disease of the brain . . . I have to plead guilty. I read books and I try to learn from the past . . . And in order to get the masses you have to achieve unity of diverse forces, and that takes

some careful detailed work, some boring, yes, some boring things");

• the Berkeley radicals (Michael Rossman, a leader of the Free Speech Movement, in an open letter to Jerry in the *Berkeley Barb*—"Living in New York you have forgotten San Francisco. I see you surrounded by death, wanting to reach out in a gigantic gesture of life. But you can't do it save by leaving the old behind: a redefinition of Leader in the new wilderness of the Media won't do it, you can't reach out larger than yourself");

• the rock musicians (*Rolling Stone*, the voice of the rock world, warned that Jerry was trying to lure people to Chicago with "media gamesmanship" and "the potent charm of music of the young," but really was inviting people to "serious injury and possible death");

• the cultural rebels ("You radicals are all alike, lashing out at the approaching armed tractor with Yo-Yos," Phil Ochs told him);

• the nonviolent movement ("When he tells us he supports 'everything which puts people into motion, which creates disruption and controversy, which creates chaos and rebirth, he might easily be one of the Fascist intellectuals explaining the merits of German National Socialism," said David McReynolds of the War Resistance League);

• eventually even Abbie Hoffman (who fell out with Jerry in Chicago and later wrote, "Jerry's a tough son of a bitch. He's got a hell of a fuckin' ego . . . Jerry wants to show the clenched fist. I want to show the clenched fist and the smile");

• Mayor Richard Daley of Chicago (who said the leaders of the demonstration in Chicago were "nationally known agitators who had arrived fresh from triumphs at Berkeley and Columbia . . . [and] came into the city of Chicago for the avowed purpose of a hostile confrontation with law enforcement");

• and undercover policemen ("Rubin became extremely agitated and began shouting 'Kill the pigs! Kill the pigs!' according to Robert Pierson, a cop who infiltrated the Yippies to serve as Jerry's "bodyguard" during the Chicago convention).

On this and other "evidence," Jerry was indicted by a Cook County grand jury for solicitation to commit mob action and later, with seven other "leaders" of the Chicago demonstrations, by a federal grand jury for crossing state lines with intent to incite a riot.

Although far more worried than he let on, Jerry welcomed the indictments in bravura style. "This is the greatest honor of my life," he told a press conference after the federal action. "I hope that I am worthy of this great indictment, the Academy Award of Protest . . . It is the fulfillment of childhood dreams."

And, in a sense, it was.

JOHNIE

Before Gospel, or Song,
always
most sweetly sung by those most suffering
and therefore the near-exclusive property
of this Earth's most fucked-over creature . . .

Blues sung, forgotten
    flowers growing where blood flowed
And strong men baptised
    in the memory of fathers whose genitals
Had been shorn off, left to sway in the wind.

"It was always funny to me that before the Emancipation Proclamation black people sang work songs and that after the Emancipation Proclamation black people sang the blues. Nobody would willingly sing blues, you know. Blues have to come from the heart. And blues are more than a song. They're my writing, too. I try and write what's there, what I feel at the moment. I don't edit because then I'd be picking words with somebody in mind. No, it's like, 'Johnie Scott, say exactly what you feel.' I know what I feel."

Sick baby sick black baby sick trapped black baby
sick trapped motherless black baby that can
never be because of mother unwed mother unwed welfare
mother unwed underfed welfare mother starving self
to feed the infant lest momma cool her love and drown the
child.

Johnie Scott first felt the texture of his strange world on May 8, 1946, in Cheyenne, Wyoming. Strange place indeed for a black baby to gulp his first American air.

The Scotts were from Grambling, Louisiana, a town slow and soft as the bayou's green water, where their folks had been farmers for generations, and before that, slaves. John Scott and his wife-to-be, Mattie, had grown up within a few miles of each other on all-too-similar dirt farms. John's father died when he was in the fifth grade, so he quit school and picked cotton to help support the family. When war broke out, John was drafted and the Army shipped him here and there around the country until finally they parked him for the duration at Fort Francis E. Warren in Cheyenne. Home on furlough in 1944, in his crisp khakis with the single gold Pfc.'s chevron shining on his sleeve, he looked pretty good to Mattie. So she married him and, at seventeen, went off to live in that dusty city hunkered down on the Great Plains just before they meet the Rockies.

There were only fifteen Negro families in Cheyenne then, not counting the handful from Fort Warren. The Scotts lived in the tiny black section and never felt part of the rambunctious cow-and-railroad town. They met little outright prejudice, if only because they rarely strayed from the Army post or darky town. Once, when they did go downtown to the movies, the cashier told them they'd have to sit upstairs. John asked why and was told, "There's a whole party downstairs." Somehow that seemed more unfair than down South where there just would have been a sign, COLORED UPSTAIRS.

Cheyenne County Memorial Hospital wasn't used to black people either. Mattie recalls that she got no personal nursing and no anesthetic. She passed out from pain, cursing the hospital. Amid the curses, Johnie was born.

And so they had no regrets when, a few months later, Pfc. Scott got his discharge. John and Mattie had seen enough of the world to know they didn't want to go back to Grambling. They'd heard about the California boom towns and decided to get themselves a piece of that boom. So off they went to Los Angeles, leaving little Johnie with a grandmother in Rouston, Louisiana, until they got settled.

His first memories come from those months on the farm—surprising ones for such a bucolic setting: "falling into the muddy pigpen, with pigs running all over and squealing and me more scared than the pigs 'cause I couldn't get no grip in standing up . . . sprinkling bread on the floor so one of the chickens would come in and as he reached for the crumbs Grandma would bring her ax down and chop his head off . . . the BB gun that nearly broke my hand off . . . my dog, Duke, that got run over by a truck . . . riding on a bike with my Uncle C.L. when a bunch of dogs got after us and I fell off and nearly got bit until C.L. drove them off with a stick."

In 1947 Mr. Scott found a job in a lumberyard, and with all his savings, bought a small frame house on a street grandiloquently called Imperial Highway. He sent for Johnie, and the family was together again. But one night, when Johnie was four, their old kerosene stove exploded. Johnie remembers rushing into the night in his underclothes and watching with his two sisters while the house and everything they owned burned up.

For a while they lived with friends and neighbors. Then they moved into the heart of Watts, to the Jordan Downs Housing Project, a huge tract of stucco-and-brick public housing that was to be Johnie's home for the rest of his youth. There the family continued to grow. "Seems like every time he looked at me I was pregnant," Mattie recalls. "All the different methods they have now I didn't know about, so I was having babies fast." Every two years there was a new child, until there were six: Johnie, Lana, Rhonda, Rosalind, Agnes and Irvin.

Meanwhile Mr. Scott discovered the California boom wasn't much of a boom to a man who'd dropped out of the fifth grade and had nothing to offer except the strength in his big hands. He moved from one job to another—the lumberyard, the railroad, the transit company, North American Aircraft, the docks—sometimes holding two jobs at once, hustling any way he could to get the long green. Johnie remembers him as "a short, heavy-muscled man, quick to laugh in a high, cackling voice, yet very sensitive to the stigmas that latched onto the back of an illiterate immigrant from the South."

Slowly his pride was nibbled away by all the layoffs, the hours on hard benches in personnel offices, the white men shaking their heads and saying "Nothing for you today," and most of all, by Mattie's constant pleading for grocery money when there was nothing in his pocket.

> Raw, outside in the wind
> where it hurts to breathe
> where my father died
> JUST LIKE I AM DYING.

The pleas changed to demands and then to accusations. Soon Johnie's parents seemed to be shouting at each other all the time. "When my mother was mad she was mad; she didn't care what came out. My father was always kind of a religious man, you know, who would rather fight than cuss." So they fought. When he was seven or eight, Johnie remembers standing at the bottom of the stairs watching his parents arguing up above. "Mother grabbed a chair, a little child's chair. My father took the chair and told me to come up and get it. My mother told me I better not move and I remember looking up there and seeing them both and wanting to do both and at the same time I didn't want to see anything happen. So I just turned around and went out the door, the tears coming down my face."

Soon Mr. Scott began staying away nights and weeks and then whole months. "He stayed gone more than he stayed home," Mattie says. "He just walked away whenever he felt like it." Usually he didn't go far and she would hear about him from people on the street, how they'd seen him here or seen him there the other night, but he didn't come near the house. Finally, to pay the bills, Mattie got a job as a nurse's attendant at Los Angeles County Hospital—a dirty job emptying bedpans and making beds soiled with the sputum of dying old men. In 1956 she and her husband worked out a legal separation, and Mattie reluctantly went on welfare— "county aid," as they call it in Los Angeles.

Mattie doesn't like to talk about the days on county aid ("It brings back things I've tried to forget"). But Johnie concedes he resented it. "The social worker was always coming, knocking on the door, wanting to look around and see if there was a man there. She tried to be kind, I guess, but she was white and she was nosy, extraordinarily nosy, and I made it a point to leave when she came in. I never dug the whole aid thing. But I see now that it was the only chance my mother had unless she was going to go on the streets."

A lot of mothers did, mothers of guys Johnie knew. They'd walk the streets at night over around 103rd and Beach, waiting for white men in big convertibles to come cruising by and pick them up. "I never liked to go down in that area because it was really rough," Johnie says. "But once in a while I would and I'd see the mother of some cat I knew. I'd see her from a distance and I'd cross the street so she wouldn't see me. Of course, you never mentioned that you saw 'em."

Mattie had too much pride for that. Like countless other ghetto women, she somehow got by on the welfare check—and her dreams.

> The Living Statistic—at 35 years of age, a single woman with six kids and a $65-a-month apartment where the water pipes have leaked forever and the roaches share the community life-style . . . a black woman who has seen man after man walk through her doorway between her crying children and her empty refrigerator—a man who promised love, a way out of the projects, affection that would obliterate the memory of that man who walked out so many years ago—only to leave her shattered, a useless relic of adoration that no longer glistens when a caring hand moves to smooth its troubled brow.

The welfare check would buy only the cheapest food: for breakfast, oatmeal; for dinner, pinto beans seasoned with a couple of ham hocks; and for lunch—talk. "Yeh, you'd talk some guy at school into giving you something from his lunch bag. You knew who had the biggest lunches and you'd talk, you know, you'd beg."

School was the 102nd Street School, just a few blocks across the Projects, and one of the first things he learned there was that he was "colored." After the first day, his mother asked how he liked the teacher. He said he liked her. Then Mattie bent down almost conspiratorially and asked, "Is she white or colored?" Johnie, only five, had never thought about his color before. On the streets he saw only black people, but school complicated things because there was a white principal, some white teachers and some white students—although most of them were

Mexican-Americans, considered white by Negroes but colored by whites.

At the start, school was mostly fights or the threat of fights. "Guys were always saying, 'I'm gonna see you after school,' 'I'm gonna beat you up,' 'So-and-so is looking for you.'"

Often these were empty boasts. But when Johnie was seven he got into a fight with a boy who attacked his oldest sister, Lana. The boy broke a bottle over his head, opening a gash it took sixteen stitches to close. The next year, another boy hit him with a flaming strand of clothes-hanger wire snatched from an incinerator.

That was school—until one day in the first grade, the teacher took Johnie's class over to the old Watts public library behind the railroad tracks. The librarian read to them awhile, and then everybody filled out forms and got a library card. Most of the kids didn't come back, but Johnie did. "I just dug the library. Mainly because it was the first place I knew that was really quiet. It was a change of pace from all that hassling and bickering at home. It was peace."

Then, like an addict who goes from cocaine to heroin, Johnie discovered the real thing—books. And he was hooked. "I started reading fairy tales because they were visions, you know. They could take your mind places. You weren't in Watts any more. And I dug the visions. Oh, they were wild! You had everything in there, everything you would ever want to see. You had old orders toppled and new orders moved in. You had whole new codes of good and evil. And all the stories involved men who would fight to establish right. And that's very important. Richard Wright once wrote: 'Don't necessarily fear me, but the young ones who can interpret the fairy tales.'"

Johnie didn't interpret them then; he was drawn by the lilting words alone. In the rustling gloom he read through all the fairy tales the old library had, and then moved on to adventure stories and travel books and novels. He always had out five books, the library's limit, to read at home.

But books were no asset at school, where most of the kids thought they were sissy stuff. In public, Johnie went along, even joining his friends in jeering the grinds who carried books to school. He learned an even more

striking lesson when he was advanced from the fourth to
the fifth grade for a paper he did on his ·own: a detailed, illustrated discussion of the human reproductive
system. When he showed it to his mother, she scolded
him and told his father to beat him for looking into
things he had no business with. The next day, Johnie told
his teacher he didn't like the fifth-grade kids and wanted
to go back with his friends. He went back and he was
more careful in the future. But in the library or in a corner at home he continued to read hungrily.

> . . . you entered into the coldest contract.
> Accepted the legacy of the Word.

Johnie doesn't believe that stuff about In the beginning was the Word. "No, in the beginning was the experience, then came the Word." And even fairy tales couldn't
wipe out Watts. Once, in the library, he opened a book
and found a silverfish nibbling the page. "You can never
get away from insects. There's more of them than there
is of us."

Silverfish and spiders and flies. Roaches that "carpeted the floor from wall to wall as soon as the lights
were turned out." Then there were the rats—grinning
little monsters that could bite a child's nose off in the
dark. But most of all, Watts was dogs: strays and wander-
ers, wild scruffy hounds with yellow fangs and frothy lips,
loping in packs through the streets, yelping at cars, over-
turning trashcans, chasing little black boys all the way
home. Johnie was terrified of dogs.

But there were other more dangerous denizens, most
of them in the Parking Lot. The Parking Lot wasn't for
cars. It was for people. People who drifted in off 103rd
Street, which Watts just calls the Street because that's
where the action is, like 12th Street in Detroit, Lenox Avenue in Harlem, Pennsylvania Avenue in Baltimore.

The Parking Lot was a big vacant space between the
Jordan Downs Housing Project and 103rd Street. There,
as the fading California sun was replaced by the flashing
red neon sign over Bob's Fine Liquors, men and boys
drifted together into hard little knots of urgent consulta-
tion or wider spatterings of loud, joshing banter. There some
of the neighborhood gangs would gather: the Orientals,
the Majestics, the Huns, the Barbarians, the Italians—the

last named not because they were from Naples or Sorrento but because of the pointed shoes they wore.

You could find anything you wanted in the Parking Lot: a dice game, with the ivories skittering crazily on the uneven ground; a pull of cheap red wine from somebody's brown sack; a packet of "horse" (heroin) or capsules of "red devils" (Seconal); or word on a new hustle.

Like most Jordan Downs boys, Johnie was a hustler. The Parking Lot was his stamping ground. By the time he was twelve he was drinking White Ripple, the only carbonated wine on the market. It was easy enough to get. You just stood in front of Bob's Liquors until a wino came by and gave him forty-five cents—thirty for the Ripple and fifteen to buy himself a drink. Johnie smoked, too—first cigarettes, and soon pot. The harder stuff was all around him, too. Once, in the Parking Lot, he asked an older man for a cigarette. "Man," the hustler said, "I ain't got nothing for you but a habit."

Sooner or later, Johnie tried almost everything the Parking Lot had to offer—for a while even some petty crime. Picking things off store counters; jimmying vending machines; stealing hubcaps and batteries off cars. Once Johnie got caught shoplifting; the manager took him in the back room and whipped him, then let him go. Another time, a policeman shot at him and two other guys as they were stealing a battery. And once, in the middle of the night, the police came to his house saying somebody stole a loaf of bread and people said it was Johnie Scott. "I hadn't been out of the house all day, except for school. But they rode me all through the Projects, prodding me, you know, 'Did you steal it? If you didn't, who did?' And obviously I wasn't going to rat on anybody, even if I'd known. Because I got to live there. But they put the fear of God, or at least the fear of white men, in my heart.

"Right away I started to hate the police. And I still do. They're the occupation force, the Gestapo. They could really scare you, roaring along with their sirens blaring. But much more when they came swooping down silently, jumped out of their cars, and did you in—*blam, blam, blam* and you're dead. Once, right across from where I live, I saw these cats in a stolen car and the police came up behind them and blew out the back window with their shotguns. One of the cats was killed right off.

The other one got out and sat down on the curb holding his head. He had a big white rag around it and it was spouting blood. See, the top of his head had been blown off and he was dying, right there. The police just stood around with their shotguns and stuff, you know, to keep the people back. Then this girl threw a bottle at the police. One of them pointed his shotgun and said, 'Do that again and we're going to shoot.' So the people backed off and watched him die.

"Another time, this friend of mine, Ronnie, and two other cats stuck up the Jack-in-the-Box drive-in restaurant. They were running away when Ronnie dropped this bag of silver. His partners were already in the car and they yelled, 'Come on,' but he ran back to grab this bag of nickels and dimes when the police swung up and gunned him down. They never yelled 'Halt' or whatever. Ronnie didn't even have a gun. He was just trying to run. But they blew him away."

> It was a time of steel flashing and hands
> grasping and eyes bulging from skulls
> and blood leaking to the sidewalk
> running in the gutter coming up to
> help float a little child's paper ship.

Somewhere out there was America's second largest state and third largest city. But until Johnie was in his early teens he saw little of California or Los Angeles beyond Watts. His life was bounded by 92nd Street, Imperial Highway, Central Avenue and Alameda. But even much of Watts was foreign to him: the pastel-colored stucco bungalows where the "middle-class" porters and janitors and waiters lived.

Johnie's world was the Projects, cramped brick rectangles occupied largely by first-generation families from Louisiana, Mississippi and Texas who were still strangers in the city. "You could always tell a brother from the Projects," Johnie says. "They were just different. If you got old quickly in the city, it happened even quicker in the Projects. They were a reservation in the middle of a ghetto. Talk about separatism! I was about as separate as I could get right there."

His first expeditions into the wide white world were grammar school "culture trips" downtown: to museums,

the planetarium, the opera or the theater. The produc
tions rarely meant much to him—"Cinderella, Snow
White and that sort of thing"—but his brushes with
whites did.

Once, going into a theater, they passed a busload of
white kids from another school; one boy leaned out a
window and shouted, "Look at them niggers" and the
others laughed. "I'm going to get him," Johnie growled to
his friend Bernard. Inside, they followed the white kid
into the men's room and beat him up. The boy told his
teacher, who came after them. Johnie remembers "sitting
up front with my hands folded, trying to look comfy. But
the teacher shined this light in my face, and the white
kid said, 'That's him.' So they dragged me out and I had
to say I was sorry. But I wasn't sorry, not really." Back
at school, a Negro teacher gave Johnie his "swats,"—a
beating with a big wooden paddle. But that didn't stop
him. On other culture trips Johnie and his friends beat up
more white boys, sometimes in the washrooms, sometimes just in the darkness of the aisles where they
couldn't be seen.

Johnie's parents never would have expressed open anger at whites. They were soft-spoken Southern Negroes
who, from all appearances, knew their place. But Johnie
believes the roots of his anger go deep into his family—
and beyond.

"My father never told me to hate white people. But
my father hated being broke. And I guess the Communists got the answer for that, you know, for people that
hate being broke. You can direct your anger against the
ruling classes. My father wasn't no Communist. But his
experiences radicalized him. Revolution begins at home."

His mother never had much contact with whites—
pleasant or unpleasant. In Grambling she'd lived in a totally segregated community; she'd left as a young girl,
and had lived in the ghetto ever since. At home, she had
other things to worry about: the next meal, shoes for six
kids, the rats that got into the flour. But Johnie can remember her talking about "white crackers." He believes
the agony of her ancestors was in her bones. "You just
don't forget those steel manacles. Being chained head and
foot. You don't forget being sold, like cattle. You don't
forget them babies dying. You don't forget none of that."

How many more years, Lord?
   Before our, my troubles, personal, soon be over?
How many years, Lord
   Before that happens here?

Not all ghetto life is grim. There was the day Johnie
found a paper bag full of money in the Parking Lot, apparently thrown away by a fleeing thief. He took most of
it home to his mother, but stowed the rest away for
popsicles and soda. "For a while I ate well," Johnie recalls. "I owed it to myself."

Every Sunday afternoon there were the flicks down at
the old Largo, Watts' only movie house. Kids could get in
for fifteen cents. Johnie would take his sisters, protecting
them from tough guys who might grab their money
while they stood in line. He liked the old Flash Gordon
and Tarzan films. Now Tarzan annoys him—"all that
chest-thumping, the white God who kept the natives in
fear"—but then it was just a good flick. "I dug things that
had action and emotion, and I always got totally involved
in movies like that, so I didn't even know what was going
on outside."

And, of course, there were girls. By the time he was
fourteen or fifteen, Johnie was already "messin' with
chicks." Tall, lithe and full of jive, Johnie did well. "One
year I had eight or nine girl friends at the same time. I
used to be scared to go out at lunchtime. I'd eat my
lunch up in the hall, because if one girl saw you with
another one there would be trouble. Couple of my girls
even got in a fight one day. I never did like monastic girls,
you see. I liked them wild and fast."

   A poor pimp on the corner
      dressed in his finest rags
   with a white soft-top '62 Cadillac
      shining next to him 21 years old
   loaded off them narcotics looking
      you in the face, Me, his woman dis-
   concerted actually shamed not looking at
      you but away, smiling and talking quietly
   she ain't but 17 herself, what he got to say
      that ain't been written down yet?—"Man,
   I can get pussy when I can't get bubblegum."

As Johnie plunged deeper into the street life, he found himself increasingly in trouble at school. Mattie didn't understand what was happening because Johnie had always been such a good boy at home. "I had less trouble out of him than any of the children," she says. At Edwin Markham Junior High School, he was a good student and was placed in a special, experimental program stressing English and social studies.

But he rankled under classroom routine and discipline. Mrs. Mills, who taught one of his experimental classes, had particular trouble with him. "I just didn't dig her," Johnie explains. "She came on like a Marine sergeant, always trying to drill us right on line because we were supposed to be the 'hopes' and all that stuff. She was black, but she was worse than the white teachers because she was trying so hard to push the white dogma, the white way: 'Don't talk back,' 'Cough up the right answer quick,' 'Just accept all this.' And I wasn't going to be trained as nobody's Pavlov dog."

There was constant friction in the classroom. Johnie recalls teachers saying, "Johnie Scott, why don't you shut your mouth?" "Johnie Scott, why don't you sit down?" "Johnie Scott, why don't you stop fooling around?"

Johnie struck back by putting tacks on the teacher's chair, writing gibes on the blackboard or doing other calculated mischief. He became adept at calculating just how far he could go with a teacher before it brought him serious punishment. "I'd sit in class the first couple of days and figure the teacher out and then adapt my methods accordingly."

This psychological warfare, which made the teachers wary of him, made Johnie a hero to other students. In his last year at Markham he was elected student-body president. Mischievous, perhaps a bit cocky, but he was still no rebel. At his graduation ceremonies that February, he delivered a decidedly upbeat peroration (with apologies to Longfellow):

> "Lives of great men all remind us
>   We can make our lives sublime;
> And departing, leave behind us
>   Footprints on the sands of Time.

"All those big voluptuous blondes who were used as sex symbols to get you to buy everything. All that 'Blondes have more fun' stuff. Hell, we were taught in school that this country went to war with Germany because we were fighting that kind of racist ideology, and here was the tube propagating all the blond, blue-eyed thing all over again."

Gradually he was fitting the jagged pieces of his life into a pattern—and he didn't like what he made of it. He'd seen his father slogging from one ill-paid job to another, always the last hired and the first fired. Sometime during high school he decided that wasn't for him. Carried to an extreme, it was the old Mantan Morlin, Stepin Fetchit stereotype—the lazybones nigger shuffling off to work. Johnie found the stereotype curiously apt. "In a way old Mantan should have shuffled because he had no reason in the world to get to that job. The Man tells you, 'Be industrious, get to the job quick, even if it ain't but fifty dollars a week.' But Mantan says, 'Naw, I ain't gwan to get to no job quick that is payin' fifty dollars a week.' He should have shuffled and stammered and everything else because that's all that job was doing to him. It was killing him.

"Oh yeh, there were all kinds of killing. Take the twelve-year-old kids in the Projects who dealt heroin; not the ones who shot it, but the kids who dealt. That's killing, too. That's insidious death. The Man supplies the stuff, but he has twelve-year-old kids deal it for him. That's the mark of a good killer because you don't have to be present at all, you don't have to run the risk of being called a pig or a racist. Do you wonder why people get to the point where they call white people devils?"

> Uniformed cop standing shotgun beneath arm
> over the body of a dead Negro.
> Child down the block,
> he, too, the child, also shot!

The worst kind of killing went on in the schools. The killing of young minds. Dead before they were ten. And Johnie saw it all: the neighbor who didn't learn his ABC's until the seventh grade; the Mexican-Americans, from homes where only Spanish was spoken, branded as "non-learners" because they were slow with English; the eleven-year-olds, bored with school, who got their kicks stealing cars and ended up in Youth Authority Camps where they fell even further behind their classmates.

No wonder they were bored. Their teachers were bored, too. Johnie recalls his teachers as "old, old beyond their years." Most had long since given up trying to make school a learning experience. For most of them, too, it was a minimum-security house of detention where they had to keep the inmates in some kind of order for six and a half hours a day. They "taught" their classes by ancient outlines, emphasized memory and rote recitation, and handed out meaningless homework assignments ("What did you do over the summer?" and "Write a one-paragraph autobiography"). In one class of sixteen, only three bothered to hand in their homework.

Most of all, Johnie remembers the waste, the waste of human potential which didn't fit into Jordan's rigid categories. There was Ramon, a Negro of vast natural talents blessed with an almost photographic memory. At nineteen, Ramon was expelled from Jordan. He'd been sitting in a science class puffing on a cigar. The teacher, actually a gym instructor, asked him what he was doing, and Ramon replied, "I'm showing where I got more sense than you, fool, trying to teach a class you obviously can't handle." So a "potential prodigy" was put out on the streets and was soon in trouble with the law.

Above all, Johnie was overcome with "a sense of powerlessness"—the powerlessness of his people before the cop with a nightstick, the welfare caseworker with her check, the newspaperman with his printing presses, the Man with his white skin.

> Take me away from this
> make me beautiful in this filth,
> turn my shoes to glass, give
> me carriages and horses and
> fine-tailored footmen, make
> me an object of love!!!

And yet, Johnie saw a way out—education. He had continued to read, and though his grades slipped somewhat when he began chasing girls, he was still near the top of his class.

In Watts schools, sheer survival was an achievement.

Some 750 students entered Markham Junior High with Johnie in 1959; 550 graduated in 1961; 250 of these entered Jordan; by their senior year, there were only 107 left; 97 graduated.

The attrition rate was particularly high among girls. Dozens of girls Johnie knew dropped out because they became pregnant—among them, one president of the student body. Several girls withdrew after they were raped—one in a classroom during the lunch hour. Others left to support their family. Often, this meant walking the streets around 103rd and Beach.

Students who stayed enrolled attended only sporadically. Jordan's official enrollment was 1,400; but its average daily attendance ran closer to 800; on rainy days, about 400.

The average grade point of a Jordan graduate the year Johnie graduated was 1.8 (D—), and the average reading level was 6.0 (sixth grade).

Yet those who survived were encouraged to see better things ahead. Johnie's class called themselves Les Améliorants (The Improvers). And his yearbook was dedicated to two renowned Jordan graduates: Glenn T. Seaborg, the nuclear scientist and Nobel Prize winner, who graduated from Jordan in 1931, when it was still a predominantly white school; and Stan Sanders, a recent Negro graduate who became the school's first Rhodes Scholar.

"The pathway of life traveled by these two alumni is open to other Jordanites," the yearbook said. "They are inspiration for those who sat in the same classrooms, walked the same halls and departed through the same doors leading to the future."

The future? As graduation approached, most of his classmates were exhorted to "get a job," "go into the civil service," "join the Army." But Johnie was among the few the teachers thought might make it. With their encouragement he applied to seven colleges: Harvard, Yale, Stanford, U.C.L.A., Carleton, Whittier and Pomona.

Meanwhile, Johnie had caught the eye of Stanley Meyer, a former theater-chain executive and TV producer, who helps underprivileged young people get into college. "You could say my avocation is helping people regardless of race, creed or color," he says. "I'm like the song 'People who like people are the luckiest people in the world'—I just like people. And I happen to think that if there's going to be any future to the world it's going to be through education, not violence."

In more than twenty years, Meyer has developed close ties with admissions directors at many colleges, particularly in the Ivy League. Each year, Los Angeles high schools suggest "deserving young men" to him, and if he approves he recommends them to Yale, Dartmouth or Stanford. Stan Sanders, Jordan's first and only Rhodes Scholar, was one of his finds—and ever since he has paid particular attention to Jordan.

Meyer met Johnie first at lunch with several top Jordan "prospects" that winter. He liked him immediately, and this impression was strengthened by a follow-up letter from Isaac H. McClelland, Jordan's principal. McClelland wrote enclosing Johnie's College Board scores (618 on the verbal, 478 on the mathematics portion of the Scholastic Aptitude Test; 94th percentile in the Iowa Test of Educational Development):

"In evaluating the scores of our students on various achievement tests, it is necessary to remember that our students, due often to cultural deprivation, do not score at the extreme top level of the 98th or 99th percentile," McClelland said. "In the talent search, therefore, it has been our experience that those students who score from the 90th to the 96th or 97th percentile represent our most capable performers." He emphasized Johnie's unusually high score, by Jordan standards, on the verbal section, and his 3.01 grade average—nearly double the Jordan average. "Based upon the above considerations," he said, "I think we can pick Johnie Scott as an exceptional candidate coming from the environment he does."

Selecting Johnie as his "number one choice of the year," Stan Meyer pushed hard for him at Harvard. Seeking to increase its Negro enrollment, Harvard was receptive. One day in June a letter on fine-grained stationery told Johnie he had been accepted as a member of that venerable college's 328th freshman class.

> Dreams of pretty Eldorados
> and huge houses at the crest
> of Sugared Hill—Black People
> who have *promised* Themselves

red-vest shiny-faced butlers
thereby continuing the Slavery.

"It was almost with an attitude of revenge that I walked into the school office and showed everyone my letter of acceptance," Johnie recalls. He was one of only fourteen Jordan graduates that year to get into college, and the first Negro to go directly from Watts to the Ivy League.

Mattie was "filled with rejoice, overwhelmed, proud—I cried a little." His classmates threw him some parties. And the girls were impressed. "They started diggin' me, because I became a success to them." Palmy days.

"But the ghetto has a habit of reaching into your life just when you think you've climbed the top of the mountain, and in one fell swoop, bringing you crashing to the bottom to be buried beneath the following rocks." Barely a week later, Johnie learned that one of his sisters was pregnant—the work of Johnie's best friend.

Furious and despondent, Johnie did something he'd never done before. He sought out his father. Borrowing a friend's old Chevy, he drove down the strip of Central Avenue some called Black Broadway to the place where his father boarded.

He found him in his room, and for three hours they talked: about their family, not the Ozzie-and-Harriet-and-David-and-Ricky family Johnie saw on television, but a shattered black one; about the divorce, not the glamour-queen-drops-third-husband-to-pick-up-fourth kind he read about in the papers, but the kind that ends in a boarding-house room; about how lonely his father's life was, but how eventually you got used to it; about his father's years in the Army; about school; and finally, about his pregnant sister. His father told him to go off to college and study hard. There were certain things in life that couldn't be avoided, he said with a shrug.

So, after boning up on Greek literature at Metropolitan Junior College, Johnie was off to Harvard. His family all came to the airport: his mother with tears in her eyes; his brothers and sisters, still kidding him about being a "Haaavad maan"; Mr. Anderson and Mrs. Trotter, two high school teachers; even his father, tall and grave in an ill-fitting suit. They took lots of pictures—among them, one of Johnie standing solemnly between two Amer-

ican Airlines clerks. Then the loudspeaker called Flight
362 and it was time to board the big jet for the first
flight of his life.

He'd taken along some Greek plays to read, but he
spent most of the trip with his face to the window. "I'd
never seen that much green countryside in my life, particularly at the end when we started coming in low over
Massachusetts. It was like on TV or in the movies and it
really tripped me because I thought I might like to live
that way someday."

He hauled his suitcases up to his room on the third
floor of Weld Hall, a Victorian brick pile in the center of
the Yard. Then he wandered out across the Square to the
broad green sweep of the Cambridge Common and sat
there awhile on a bench "checking out" all the trees,
and the plaque marking the spot where George Washington rallied the colonial armies, and the Radcliffe girls
jouncing by in their cashmere sweaters and soft, sham-
pooed hair.

That night, he took the subway down to Boston and
ate dinner at the Union Oyster House. "I still had a little
change people at home gave me, so I decided to have
my first lobster. I figured I owed it to myself." The lobster, the milky clam chowder, and the glass of beer that
washed it down were all nice, but they only reinforced
the feeling that he didn't belong in this amber world of
tradition and wealth. "It was as though Cain had slipped
unawares into the Garden of Eden again," he wrote later;
"but this was a Cain that didn't know what his crime
was, nor where he was, but only that he did not belong
there."

And this sense of Harvard's strangeness was only underlined the next night when he went to a party in Roxbury, Boston's black ghetto. In the Common he'd met a
"brother" who gave him an address and told him to come
on by. "Wherever you go, from city to city, the first people you look out for are black people in hopes of finding
the life. It was refreshing to hear the music, to know
there was life in Boston."

But a few hours later, walking through the Yard with
the funky blues still in his ears, he heard the first winds
of the New England winter rustling the elm trees overhead, and he shivered.

Cold shaft of wind on the neck's back the tunnel ahead
dark still the magic lantern moves on, a speck of light
at the cave's end.

His premonitions were still more than balanced by the
excitement of his new world. On October 13 he wrote
Stanley Meyer on his new Harvard stationery with the red
Veritas seal at the top. "Harvard is the most liberal and
responsive school in America," his adviser had told him,
and now Johnie reported, "I have found full acceptance
here . . . Harvard has an awful lot to offer outside of the
lecture halls and libraries, I am finding out. This is quite
an experience, something that I can never forget."

He wrote of Peter Scott Ivers, a classmate from a
wealthy Boston family, who, he said, "has shown me that
even among the wealthy . . . sincerity of purpose plus a
genuine enthusiasm for life and people exist. This Sunday we, that is, Peter and I, are to go to one museum
with which he is familiar, and afterwards ride through
the country. We shall see those 'leaves turn.' Maybe, if we
have time, we'll buy some apple cider from one of the
farms that dot the countryside and sample New England
at its best."

Peter was the first close white friend Johnie ever had.
And the fact that he was wealthy, socially well connected
and bright only made Johnie more aware of the specialness of their relationship. "Any time we needed a car,
Peter could go home and get the Cadillac, you know, the
black Fleetwood. His father bought two every year, just
took them in and picked up two new ones. But Peter
didn't let money faze him. He went on and became what
he was. In prep school, he'd scored in the top thirteen in
the country in Greek and he could have been a Greek
scholar. But he got involved in the theater and in women.
He joined a rock band and played the hippest harmonica
you'd ever want to hear. That's giving praises to a white
boy, but Peter was heavy."

He couldn't say the same for most of the white boys
he met at Harvard—starting with his roommates. Neither
of them had known many Negroes before. One came from
a small town in Oregon where no Negroes lived. The
other was from Los Angeles, only a few miles from Jordan
Downs, but his neighborhood was overwhelmingly white
and he rarely went near the ghetto.

Music was their biggest friction point. Johnie remembers coming back to their suite late at night after a drinking spree and finding one roommate lying on his back in the middle of the living-room floor listening to Mozart. "I'd walk over, take the record off and say, 'What's this Mozart shit? Take it into your room and play it because I want to go to bed and I don't want to hear that silly shit coming through my doorway.' And that would start it. They'd say I didn't appreciate culture, and I'd say, 'That's right; I'm culturally deprived just like you people are.' They didn't dig it either when I'd play Miles Davis on my little record player. They were squares."

If he could take umbrage at Mozart, he reacted even more angrily to the well-meant but clumsy queries of his classmates. One night, at a B'nai B'rith party, a bespectacled young man in a tweed jacket groped his way out of the darkness and said, "I don't want to sound prejudiced, but don't you feel uncomfortable here?" Johnie stared him down and then said, "It's not so much a question as to whether I feel uncomfortable as it is whether you feel uncomfortable."

Or, over dinner at one of the long wooden tables in the Freshman Union, someone would ask, "What does your father do for a living?" Johnie would feel a twinge of shame and somehow avoid answering, but later he would burn with resentment over the question. He still does. "It's a thing about white boys, you know, they got to ask you where you come from, and where your daddy works, and how much your daddy makes, and where your momma and them go to school. That's what Harvard and schools like that are all about. You see, they're establishing the social totem pole of the future, you know, who's going to be where, and they're trying to figure out where you're at so they can make an allowance for you. They're not ever going to dig niggers, but they can make an allowance for one. After all, why not say one of your best friends is a black from Watts, and he was poor, and he made it, and I sympathize with you people completely, but look at Johnie. I was to become their new whip for beating black people.

"I stopped that right there. I said, 'Bullshit' and 'Fuck you! Don't use me for a front.' "

Cool boogie cooking mommas shaking that thang
brothers getting down party-popping drinking
Cutty Sark and milk over the rocks bourgeois
pretenders but too black to bother about the
extras like two cars, your own pad, kids to
raise who are doing well in school.

From the start, Johnie was uncomfortable in class. At
first, his problems seemed largely technical. As the October winds blew through the Yard's drafty old classrooms,
Johnie shivered in his Southern California clothes. Stan
Meyer had told him to call if he needed anything ("I'm
like the United States Marines"). So Johnie asked for some
warm clothing, and back came word: "Buy what you
need and send me the bill." At J. August he selected a
coat, suit, sports jacket, two pairs of slacks, two shirts,
shoes and rubbers. The Canadian winds could blow as
they might. Johnie was outfitted for an Ivy League winter.

But even in tweeds and button-downs, Johnie felt ill at
ease shoulder to shoulder with all those attentive young
men in the stately gloom of Sever and Emerson halls.

Chinese philosophy was his best course. "I dug that Oriental stuff. I remember one phrase—'Wealth stands by
wealth; influence is greater than effort. To he that hath
is given while poverty clamors in vain.' You see, I had
all the reason in the world to take Chinese philosophy.

"The only problem is that in those courses you're not
supposed to dig them, you're just supposed to study them.
Yeah, that was the problem with me. I'd take the classes
not just seriously but enthusiastically. But the Man always tried to make it cut and dried and that's when I'd
start getting revolted."

Johnie admired his teachers' obvious learning and analytical powers. "There was this fellow Fenton I had in
my writing course. Very Brooks Brothers, you know.
That was the way he carried himself, the way he attired
himself. He was a beautiful thinker, too, but he never
could dig my papers because he was always too busy being analytical. I could never get involved in class discussions because everybody would be talking in those cold
terms. I was into 'stream of consciousness.' It was funny,
because I dug writing and the rest, but that class was

boring, it wasn't interesting, there wasn't nothing in there challenging."

Likewise, in Humanities I, Johnie read T.S. Eliot and Ezra Pound for fun. "I just read them and dug them." He didn't bother with the papers and flunked Humanities that term.

In Natural Sciences 6 (cultural anthropology), Johnie got interested in Africa. On his own, he read Robert Ardrey's *African Genesis*. But he hardly ever went to class and flunked Natural Sciences, too. French was simply more than he could handle, or cared to handle. He dropped out after eleven weeks.

In late fall he wrote Stan Meyer to report that he was being put on probation. "I hate to hear it," Johnie wrote. "I know I am not that dumb . . . Mr. Meyer, you must be terribly disappointed in me. I beg you, though, don't give up on me. I am determined not to be the 'first' after 17 years to cast a blight on your record . . . College, not just Harvard, means a great deal to me. It stands for a chance to be something I had always dreamed of . . . When I said that I have always wanted to be a great man, I meant it."

Johnie had become a "problem" for the advisers and "baby deans" in University Hall: men with marvelously Puritan names like Dana Cotton and Christopher Wadsworth called him in and asked what the trouble was ("How are things here at Harvard for you?" "Oh. They're all right, I guess." "Like the way they've been treating you here?" "Yes. Everything's all right." "Guess it's kind of different from Watts, eh?" "Yes. It is a little different from Watts.")

Well-meaning men. Kind men. But they never seemed to connect with Johnie's life. "Every time I talked to them they were symbols of the very life I was having trouble with. The tweed coats and everything. They never had to worry. They knew they'd drive home at the end of the day to a fireplace, hot apple cider, and gin if it was snowing outside, turkey, you know, London-broil dinners, the whole New England thing. They had homes, not like the Projects back in Watts, but homes like homes should have been. Christmas like *The Christmas Carol* by Charles Dickens—Scrooge, Tiny Tim, especially the Spirit of Christmas Past."

Even Archie Epps, Harvard's only black dean, was difficult to talk to. "Archie was O.K., I guess. The first black dean in the Ivy League, pushing to get more blacks admitted. That was cool. But he was always Archie C. Epps, Jr., in his double-breasted Saks Fifth Avenue jacket. That tells the story."

At times Johnie could overcome his sense of distance from the Harvard scene. Once, with a classmate, he took a canoe trip down the Concord River, watching the fish glinting beneath the surface, the brilliant fall colors along the banks.

Then his sister's swollen body swam into view and he remembered where he belonged.

thoughts that I carried with me into the river
where the fish indeed were silver where the water
in truth was sky-blue where the sense of moving
in good circles was certainly the sensation of
growing out of one world into another, into
the hot-cinnamon hot apple cider hot gin cold snow
white snow Christmas Time not wanting to go home,
not home not away from what it is that you left Home for.
Then to realize that to stay is to deny oneself
the privilege of suffering,
the highest human privilege. A birthright for your kind,
What did they always say,
            "Everyday
            Everyday I sing the Blues.
            I said that everyday,
            Everyday I sing the blues."

So gradually Johnie turned to his own—to the handful of Negroes at Harvard. There were thirty-two in the class of 1967—twice as many as the year before—but still barely three percent of the class. They were scattered all over the Yard, most of them rooming with white boys, meeting only in classes or in the Union. But before many months had passed, they had sought each other out and formed little blood knots to which they could turn for warmth after chilling excursions into the white world of the university.

In Johnie's knot there was Elvin Montgomery, a New Orleans brother who hated the white man but loved the white woman; Conway Augustus Downing, Jr., of Newport News, Virginia, and Andover, known to one and all as Sugar; Thaddas Alston, a laborer's son who grew up on the levees in Cairo, Illinois, and got his education in the streets of Chicago; John Potts, a wealthy dentist's son who went to Kent and shot pool all the way through; U. C. Clark III, whom they called Baby Huey because he was only five foot three; Tony Williams, a hulking football player they all liked because he had a stack of soul records.

At first they didn't do much but party. "Yeh," Johnie remembers, "wherever we went was a party. We were a party. Like we'd go to parties and people thought they were partying but we'd become the party." They'd sit out on the big front porch of Weld Hall on football weekends, the whole group sharing a fifth of white port which they mixed with a lemon and called a "shake-em-up." White boys would come by with their dates, imitation minks draped over their shoulders, and look up wondering what "those Roxbury kids" were doing in the Yard. They got so many stares, they started spending more time in Roxbury, hitting the bars and the pool halls where all the faces were black.

Johnie was closest of all to Thad Alston, perhaps because they were both from the Projects. Whether in Watts or on Chicago's west side, the Projects are much the same; and from that common experience grew a natural affinity. "I was tired of trying to relate to middle-class people, black or white," Thad recalls. "There just weren't that many black people at Harvard who even knew what poverty was. Johnie and I knew. We reacted to lots of things in the same way because we'd led the same kind of life."

Ironically, they met while trying to grab a new rung on the ladder out of that life—by pledging Alpha Phi Alpha, the largest, most prestigious Negro fraternity in the country.

Founded in 1906 by seven Negroes who couldn't get into Cornell's white fraternities, it has since attracted an astonishing roster: W.E.B. Du Bois, Thurgood Marshall, Adam Clayton Powell, Dick Gregory, "Cannonball" Adderly, Edward Brooke, Whitney Young, Martin Luther King, and at one time, twenty-nine of the thirty-three presidents of predominantly Negro colleges.

The Alphas have all the paraphernalia of other fraternities: symbols ("the Sphinx"); riddles ("S-Scholarship;

P-Perseverance; H-Honesty; I-Initiative; N-Nobility; X-
is for the role we shall play as Alpha Men"); creeds ("As
a Sphinxman, I will uphold high scholastic standards,
high moral character, brotherhood, personal progress,
loyalty and the chastity of womanhood"); and hymns:

> The mystic Sphinx to us an aim doth signify
> We cherish all thy precepts and ideals
> The path is hard; the vigil long and dutiful
> Our hearts forever mindful of thy task.

Harvard doesn't recognize national fraternities, but Alpha Phi Alpha had a metropolitan chapter which drew
students from Harvard, Boston University and M.I.T. In
November, Johnie, Thad and six other Boston area students began pledging the chapter.

It was a long, hard, rigorous pledge. "The technique
was to find your breaking point," said Stan Goldsboro, a
Boston University sophomore who was in Johnie's group.
"They paddled you and that sort of thing, but most of
the breaking was psychological, not physical. They kept
you working all the time—memorizing things, doing
tests and tasks, and somehow you were supposed to maintain a B average."

After a few weeks, five of the eight starters dropped
out, leaving just Thad, Stan and Johnie. "It was tough,"
Stan says. "But we stuck it out. And it brought the three
of us awful close together. I'd spend almost every day at
Harvard in either Johnie's or Thad's room, studying together, talking together. I cried. I saw Johnie cry. I saw
him cry for me."

And there were good times, too. Parties. Cheap wine.
Girls. With Johnie, always girls.

> and after all the chanting
> then gurus with perfumed candles
> performing the dance of the lights
> while women garbed in flowers
> hang above one's head, my head, their
> bodies begging for,
>> no, their pale bodies mocking
>> my own need to be loved by offering
> flesh as tho liver to the panther.

"Johnie was very desperate for a female companion who would listen and try to understand him," Stan recalls.

First he tried Radcliffe girls. "There was this white girl over there, Susan. She was a Jew, which made her more attractive to me than the blondes. I had a thing against blondes. Susan was pretty and all that. But she was too busy trying to be heavy and profound. She had one of those I.Q.'s of 180 plus, but was stupid. A lot of Cliffies were like that. They'd want to meet you and all. But I couldn't relate to them. They were just smart. Cliffies didn't have no soul."

After Susan and a few others, white girls began to bug him. "I know cats in the streets who would eat those bitches alive," he wrote. "Would grab them by the neck. Hurt them, in the dark, with fouled breath."

So he turned to black girls. He went out with some "Deltas"—sisters from a Negro sorority—and was even voted "Delta sweetheart" once. The girls were impressed by a black man from Harvard. "I was a success. I was somebody to be looked at, and emulated and to get a little pride off."

Soon he was taking out two girls regularly. One was Eve, a bright, light-skinned West Indian, born in England, living with her middle-class parents in suburban Randolph, and going to Boston University. The other was Liz, a Roxbury girl, deep into the life of the ghetto, particularly dope. Thad and Stan liked Eve and thought she was just the girl for Johnie. They pointedly disapproved of Liz. But although Johnie could see all their arguments for Eve, he felt strangely drawn to Liz. She was part of his world, a world he felt increasingly guilty for seeking to escape.

> what words, that made me ashamed
> for ever having spoken aloud of beggars,
> of winos, of prostitutes and pimps,
> of hustlers and sharpies and chippies
> and chumps, of dice-shooters, murphy men
> sweet daddies yes, and sugar mammas,
> made me ashamed for speaking of them
> as Them or They or He or She maybe It
> perhaps What but never Me never We
> not once Us avoiding fuss
> afraid inside of scaring people

afraid inside of lots of things,
myself, myself, my place of what place meant.

Johnie found it increasingly difficult to study. "When
the three of us went to Lamont Library," Stan recalls,
"Johnie would run off a verse of poetry about Thad and
me. I'd get really pissed off and say we ought to study.
But Johnie was feeling the futility, the irrelevancy of it
all." Once he complained to Stan about the literature
courses: "You go to class and read Jane Austen who
wrote about those English ladies. Why can't we read
Baldwin and Wright? At least they're writing about us."
This was 1964, several years before the clamor for Black
Studies began.

"Johnie saw that the university was asking him to
'achieve so you can be something you aren't—and maybe you don't want to be,' " Thad says. "So working toward
academic excellence, in a way, was alienation of self.
Johnie was asking himself not only 'Where do I fit in at
Harvard?' but perhaps more important, 'If I get through
here where will I fit into the things I'm used to—my
family, the people on the street, the ghetto world?' "

"Johnie saw that we'd made a mistake," says Stan.
"We tried so hard to assimilate at an Eastern white university we almost forgot what it was like to be on the
block. But we'd gone so far we felt we could never go
back. We had terrible guilt feelings. We felt trapped."

At times, particularly when he'd been drinking, Johnie
could find his way back to the ghetto style. Conway
Downing recalls: "In our little group, everybody had a
nickname and Johnie's was Super Nigger, or Sup for
short. I guess we called him that because he seemed to
be very worldly at times, very hip in the street sense. He
used to dance this weird Johnie Scott dance—hands and
arms out, eyes flashing. That was one of the main reasons
he and I became friendly. I'd just gone through four
years of prep school, four years of discipline and per-
severance. All of a sudden I was trying to find my identity again and Johnie helped me."

Conway found his identity partly by becoming treasurer of the Civil Rights Coordinating Committee, a Harvard group which supported the Southern integration
struggle. Thad Alston was vice-president, but the overwhelmingly white group had difficulty enlisting Negroes.

Although two of his close friends were officers, Johnie never joined. "He helped me out a couple of times selling magazines and stuff in the Union," Conway recalls. "But he was no activist." Thad remembers how deeply Johnie resented the attitudes of white liberals who criticized Negroes for not getting into civil rights work. "He said white folks who never had to work or sacrifice for anything couldn't understand why black folks didn't go south." Conway concluded: "Johnie just wasn't that concerned with the civil rights thing."

On the edges of the civil rights thing there were already outcroppings of what later became known as the Black Revolution. Johnie believes he was drawn to this half-formed movement even then, but he gave few signs of open identification. He did go to hear Malcolm X at Eliot House that winter and remembers "digging it." But Conway recalls that Johnie's poetry that year "dealt a lot more with love than it did with black subjects," and Stan says, "Johnie saw the absurdity of going to a meeting of blacks and seeing who was going to talk the baddest about the white man. He also felt it was a lot of bullshit to have Afro-American History Week because, as he'd say, 'Nobody needs to tell me I'm black.' "

We as black people
We as American marginals—a movement from
   Aboriginals
—we who could point with shame and mocking laughter
at the bearded grizzled face the exposed breast the
high-rumped women the skinny naked little children and
speak of civilization in grand wordly ways
while somehow or another, I know not how,
it was hard to forget, it is too hard to forget,
but more than that,
the Past is Not to be Forgotten.

Spring, the gentle, pale-green Cambridge spring, brought feelings too strong for Johnie to handle.

First, there was joy. Although his average was far below the required B, the Alphas felt Johnie had so much else going for him that they got a waiver of the grade requirement from the National Office, and he, Stan and Thad became Alphas. "It was the only thing the whole year that made Johnie happy," Stan recalls. "It was something he never thought he could do. The fraternity was overwhelmingly middle-class, but there he was, a boy from the Projects. We went out and got drunk."

Then there was grief. On Easter Sunday, his mother called to tell him his close friend, Marvin Mack, had been killed the night before. "She said some fellows had been jumping on a little dude. Marvin broke it up and said, 'If you jump on him you got to jump on me.' So the brothers went home, got their shotgun and blew Marvin away. My mother said she hated to tell me but she figured I'd hear anyway and it would be easier this way."

It wasn't. "For a while I cried. Then, for two weeks I walked around that campus in a daze. I didn't show up at classes. I didn't care about school any more. I'd known for a long time I was out of place at Harvard. But Marvin's death really opened my eyes. I realized my morality wasn't based on a white system of calculated goods and evils, traceable down to Plato and Hesiod, but rather on the social and cultural orientation of the slums—in which evil has been taken for granted."

Then there was panic. Because of all the time he spent on the Alphas, girls and poetry, Johnie was in deep academic trouble. "I am terribly frightened at times at the intense competition here for marks," he wrote Stan Meyer. "It is very akin to war. Sometimes, like today, I wonder if I am the type of person who can survive this fiercely competitive atmosphere."

With finals approaching, he went into an orgy of cramming. "From May first on, Johnie and I both lived on Dexedrine," Thad recalls. "He really busted his ass. But it was too late. I flunked one course. He flunked a lot."

His friends suspect that, consciously or not, Johnie wanted to flunk out. "There are all sorts of ways to give up if you really didn't want to stay at Harvard and had no business coming in the first place," Thad says.

"I think Johnie left Harvard out of guilt," Stan Goldsboro says. "I think he felt guilty about not wanting to tell us about his parents who never went to college, who were poor and lower-class. He sort of tried to come here and take on a different role. But he felt guilty about it. He was too sensitive to really get away with it. So he went home."

Johnie flew to Los Angeles on June 7, knowing he would never be back. "I hadn't got my marks yet, but I knew how badly I'd done. I remember looking down from the plane and seeing those same little houses and trees and rolling hills I'd seen on that first flight the September before. Only this time I was going the other way. My mother met me at the airport. I was back in my world."

Three weeks later, Christopher Wadsworth, a senior freshman adviser, advised Johnie that the Administrative Board had voted to "informally discourage" him from returning to Harvard. His mother took it very badly. Johnie, too, was sunk in depression.

He got a job that summer working the graveyard shift at Disneyland. A $72-a-week janitor. ("It seemed like they lifted all of Disneyland eight feet off the ground every night and told us to sweep, mop and wax it.") It was a weird life: midnight to 8 A.M. dragging a mop through that neon-lit, pastel-tinted Fantasia, then home to the gray-brown Projects dusky under the low-lying smog.

Weirdest of all on August 11.

> If you ain't got no bread
>   then you can't eat
> It's as simple as that.
>   Rome wasn't burnt in a day
> America won't burn that quickly,
>   *either.*

He had worked his usual shift the night before, then dozed a few hours before the traffic outside woke him, his head still throbbing from lack of sleep. He was eating supper at 7 P.M., when Marquette Frye and his brother were stopped by policemen for drunken driving at Avalon Boulevard and 117th Street. Two hours later the radio reported that trouble had broken out in Watts.

"That wasn't Watts over there on Avalon. But people around my place began saying, 'Well, if we're going to get blamed or dumped on, let's give them something to do it for.' Because our reputation was at stake, you know. If we were going to do it, we were going to do it right."

Watts did it right. Up and down 103rd Street ran the graduates and dropouts of David Starr Jordan High School, breaking store windows, pulling out pastel slacks and color TVs and cases of canned soup—anything they could reach through the shards of shattered glass.

The prime target was Martin's Department Store at 103rd and the tracks—the biggest furniture store in southern L.A. Anybody could get credit at Martin's ("Easy terms," "No Finance Co. to Deal With," said the signs across its aluminum front), but by the time the store added on interest and other carrying charges, you ended up paying half again what the item would have cost outright.

"Oh, yeah, we all knew Martin's," Johnie says. "Everybody had credit there. Our houses were full of their stuff. That is, until you missed a payment. If you missed one you didn't get to miss another. You'd always see that big truck from Martin's out in front of somebody's house in the Projects, the furniture being carried out, while the momma stood out on the porch with her hand on her head, cussing them out. She'd be trying to meet their notes on a county welfare check and all. But that didn't matter. Out the door it went.

"So, naturally, when people had their chance at Martin's they took it. I remember Freddy riding down 103rd Street sitting in the back of his father's pickup with a sofa on top of his head, shouting, 'Get it all now; do your Christmas shopping now.' People just stripped that store bare. And then, because we all knew they had everybody's records on file in a little box, somebody threw some cocktails in there and burned it all down, records and all."

Down the street, Mr. Kay tried a stratagem to save his store. He had all the furniture dragged into the street, where Johnie saw him, hands outstretched, pleading with his old customers: "Please don't burn my store down. Take the furniture. There it is. But please don't burn the store."

"Kay, a Jew man from Beverly Hills, was another of those kind that loved credit," Johnie says. "He loved to give you five years and you wind up paying twice the original price. So people took his furniture and then some brother, laughing, threw a Molotov cocktail into the store anyway. While it burned, Kay sat on the curb in front of the store, with his head in his hands, crying."

At another store down the block, the crowd ripped

iron bars off the windows to get at rows of glittering patent-leather shoes. "Then, when they thought everybody was out, a fellow threw a fire bomb in. But a baby was still in the store. The mother started screaming, 'My little baby,' but they couldn't get it out. The baby just burned up."

All along 103rd, stores were burning—so many that the next day someone dubbed it Charcoal Alley. Later, Los Angeles officials blamed The Magnificent Montague, a disk jockey on KGFJ, for fueling the spree with his chant "Let's all get together and burn," which was picked up and transformed to "Burn, baby, burn." But Johnie recalls that the line was popular long before the riot. "At parties, when some cat was out on the floor dancing, really doing it, we'd all yell, 'Burn, baby, burn,' especially at girls. So when things started on the street, it just seemed appropriate."

Johnie got a few of the goodies. "I got my mother a case of Scotch," he recalls. "But I didn't make no money like I should have. That's what I'm mad about in retrospect. Everybody else made money selling stuff they took."

But the riot snapped Johnie out of his depression. One night, while gunfire crackled outside, he called Thad in great excitement. "The shit hit the fan," he said, "and I'm here."

> The screaming children
> wandering the streets,
> their hands no longer flesh
> but fiery gases,
> the heat of stores burning
> erasing memories,
> my careless fingers
> playing unmindful Havoc
> with a mutilated brain.

The riots changed more than Johnie's mood. Within weeks Watts became the focus of a dozen investigations —governmental, academic, journalistic—and everybody was looking for bright, articulate blacks. "They found out there was a cat there who'd gone to Harvard and, whoosh, suddenly everybody wanted to talk to me."

Within a month, he went to work for Occidental Col-

lege's Research Laboratory in Urban Culture on a study
funded by the Labor Department—assigned to interview
Watts youngsters, sixteen to twenty-two years old, who
had left school but were unemployed. "My purpose," he
wrote Stan Meyer, "[is] to log and write up the reason
why these people cannot get ahead, why they are so
frustrated, why tensions boil and well up within the
breasts of these, my people, and suddenly explode in one
chaotic blast."

He said he hoped the study would help bring urban
renewal, upgrading of schools and more jobs to Watts.
"But for me the most enjoyable, yet frustrating, aspect of
the work is that I am privileged to delve deep beneath
the eye of the black metropolis and peer into the souls of
black and yellow peoples, their cries and damning calls
ringing in my ears. I feel as though my own being at
times must break in the face of the discontent and im-
patience, at the frustration and, most deplorable of all,
hopelessness of ghetto peoples."

About the same time, Budd Schulberg began his Watts
Writers' Workshop. Visiting Watts just after the riots,
the Los Angeles author had asked, "What can I do?"
Someone suggested he teach writing; so he posted a notice on the bulletin board of the Westminister Neighborhood Association: "Creative Writing Class—all interested
sign below." The response was slow and suspicious, but
gradually would-be writers started showing up at his
cubbyhole in the association's green stucco building just
off Charcoal Alley.

One of Johnie's friends had gone to the workshop and
tried to take him along. Johnie refused, perhaps because
the memory of Harvard's tweedy English teachers was still
fresh in his mind. But, eager for a professional reaction
to the poetry he'd been churning out, Johnie let his friend
take Schulberg two of his poems. Before he knew it,
they had won the workshop's poetry award. Schulberg
told him his poetry was "great stuff."

Overwhelmed by acclaim from a famous white writer,
Johnie decided, "Wow, maybe this is the cat who could
help me with my writing." So he plunged into the workshop that spring of 1966, coming down every Wednesday night to read his poetry and listen to other Watts
writers like Leumas Sirrah (Samuel Harris spelled backward), a high school dropout who lived alone with a

black cat named Thought; Birdwell Chew, a fifty-three-year-old self-educated woman from Texas; and Harry Dolan, a former city-hall janitor who showed up one day with a briefcase full of unfinished manuscripts.

The workshop thrived. It outgrew the old cubbyhole and moved to the Watts Happening Coffee House down the street. Later that spring, with money donated by Schulberg's friends, they moved again to their own building, a nine-room house which they named the Frederick Douglass Writers' House. Here there was room for some members to live, and the workshop became more of a genuine writers' community.

Soon it was attracting national attention. *Los Angeles Magazine* printed some of its products, including eight of Johnie's poems. Reporters came to interview them. That summer, NBC-TV did an hour-long special called *The Angry Voices of Watts,* on which Johnie and others read their poetry. In December, Johnie, Harry Dolan and Schulberg went to Washington to testify before the Senate Committee on Government Operations then looking into ghetto life. After Johnie told something of life in Watts, Senator Abraham Ribicoff called his testimony "as moving and memorable as anything that has come before the United States Senate."

In between, Johnie continued to work in Watts. He helped produce the Watts Summer Festival on the first anniversary of the riots and he organized a group called Young Men for Total Democracy to keep pressure on the federal government for more and better-placed funds. As he wrote Stan Meyer, he had come back to his "point of starting: that being none other than the ghetto, Watts."

> In these forbidden jungles of
>   My Own People, as We exist in a
> Nightmare so ashamed have We grown
>   of Our own bodies, so ashamed to
> Speak of ourselves, Our peoples,
>   as beautiful but even deeper in the
> Slumworld's womb, O Lord, we have
>   somehow begun to call ourselves more
> Fit than other peoples to survive.

But Johnie was concerned with personal as well as collective survival. His mother had once warned him, "You can either follow the others and die here, or else pull yourself up out of this ditch." He had had his chance at Harvard and muffed it. Now, even while he helped his neighbors on their long road up, he burned impatiently to get out of the ditch again.

"There is shame," he wrote Harvard's Dana Cotton. "Yet there is still within me a spark which will not cease to burn, and that spark is saying to me to show you and others that I am not a failure." To Stan Meyer he wrote, "I do not intend to quit. I refuse to die."

As a start, Johnie enrolled in September 1965 at East Los Angeles Junior College. He got into an advanced writing course and did some debating (taking third place in a statewide oratorical tournament). But such small successes only emphasized how far he had fallen. For East Los Angeles was about as far from Harvard as you could get. Most of its students were Mexican-Americans or lower-middle-class whites. Johnie and his friends didn't even consider it a college; they called it JUCO. And Johnie yearned to get back to a real college. It became his "consuming desire," he wrote Stan Meyer. "I want to get into school so bad until at times I feel as if I must cry."

In February 1966 he wrote Chris Wadsworth, asking readmission to Harvard. Junior College, he said, had been "a hell for me—a place where I had to learn to resolve my shame." At times, he confessed, a return to Harvard seemed almost the completion of a dream. "I would be the poor black boy, climbing out of the ghetto to face the glaring lights and wistful angels of Harvard, celestial palace . . . only to be crushed, to fall down, down, down unholy streets to land amidst the mocking voices and leering faces of neighbor and old-time friend, of sister and mother smirking under breath . . . and then to set out, to admit the defeat; and then lift myself by the bootstraps on back to Cambridge and there, doing what few others have ever done, feel that I have done all I lived for . . ."

Harvard said it would take him back, but only if he started all over again as a freshman. Johnie wouldn't do that, and again Stan Meyer interceded. He called the dean of admissions at Stanford and said, "I want you to do me a personal favor. I have a young man who can be the new James Baldwin." Stanford agreed to take him as a sophomore.

So, one day that September, Johnie was off to college again. Almost immediately, he was more at home at Stanford than he'd ever been at Harvard. Its Moorish campus was distinctly Californian, and its climate was warm enough for Johnie to dress as he liked without worrying about the tweedy types who intimidated him in Cambridge.

Moreover, his growing recognition as a poet gave him a degree of self-confidence. Stanford's English department recognized that it had a student of pronounced though unorthodox talent. Johnie was invited to attend graduate seminars and evening meetings where authors like John Barth and Jack Hawkes spoke.

Perhaps most important, he found a girl who seemed to meet all his needs—Joyce Hurdle, a Stanford sophomore from a middle-class black family. They met his first week there and soon were keeping regular company.

At times that fall, Johnie felt he could really "make it" at Stanford, and making it big was still very important to him. He went to the Stanford-California game that fall and loved it. "I've made the two big traditionals in this country: Harvard-Yale and Stanford-Cal. The only one I've missed is the Little Brown Jug—Michigan and Michigan State. The way I understand it, those are the big things in this country as far as college life goes. I've even got the tickets saved. I save little things like that because they're kind of important in a way."

But as the fall wore on, Johnie felt growingly uncomfortable. The administration had arranged for him to live in the Alpha Delta Phi fraternity house to save rent. One of the wealthiest fraternities on campus, Alpha Delta Phi was almost entirely white, with only three blacks among its sixty-five members. His fraternity brothers weren't overtly hostile. But they treated him much as they would a live-in maid, as if he were there to get a job done and otherwise keep quiet. Johnie moved out, renting a place across the Freeway—the dividing line between predominantly white Palo Alto and predominantly black East Palo Alto. He was back in the ghetto.

For his fourteen months at home had taught him an important lesson. No matter where he went, he could never really escape the ghetto. "You can take a man out of the ghetto," Johnie concluded, "but you can't take the ghetto out of the man." And you shouldn't even try, because that's where a black man gets his strength. "It's like the story about Hercules and the giant. The only way Hercules could beat the giant was to lift him off the ground. All his strength came from his mother, Earth.

"I realized that the slum world gave birth to me. Out of her womb I came. And I came to love her. Maybe she was a bit of a whore, but I didn't like white boys snickering at her. The more I thought about her, the more I preferred her that way. There's a lot of wisdom in the ghetto. Up on the walls recently the cats have been writing, 'God is the Sun.' I dig that, because I see black people as Sun people. After all, that's where our lives have always been—out under the sun. And I think of white people as coming from the ice climes, the ice caves."

Already in Watts that year, Johnie had met the new breed of black nationalist. For a while he dabbled in "the Muslim thing," going to mosque, eating at Shebazz's Restaurant, dating the Muslim sisters. "I dug all that because that's where the black people of the day were." And although raised a Baptist and still profoundly influenced by the old-time religion, Johnie almost took out his X. Johnie X.

> What has happened?
> That I am told by those so near me
> That Belief in You,
> O LORD,
> Makes fast and binding the shackles
> Of a slave!

Black nationalism was blooming in the San Francisco area, too, and Johnie was soon caught up in it. St. Clair Drake, the black historian, lived in Palo Alto and ran a workshop which, Johnie wrote then, "vitalized the thought process of myself and others in illuminating the African and American Negro role in the world community." Syrtillah Cabot, a former SNCC worker, and Bob Hoover, a black educator, also influenced him.

But the prime influence on Johnie that year was LeRoi Jones, then teaching at San Francisco State. He had read LeRoi's poetry and regarded him as the quintessential black poet. "LeRoi's head was where mine was. He wasn't one of those black writers who tried to negate their color and talk about being universal. He openly proclaimed himself a black poet. I dug him because he could have made the New York café society set, but instead he packed his bags and went back to Newark. No black man had done that before, except Richard Wright who was an expatriate all those years. LeRoi stayed in America, but still he split. I identified with him because I thought his break with New York was a lot like my break with Harvard."

Johnie's emerging radicalism remained intensely black. He felt scant sympathy with white radicals like David Harris, the Stanford senior who was among the first in the country to burn his draft card. "Dave read a lot of Camus, but he wasn't militant really. He was like a lot of white boys who don't become activists until they're faced with the draft."

When his own draft notice came that summer, Johnie saw the issue not as American militarism but as a black man's survival. And he accomplished that not with a symbolic act like burning his draft card but with a street man's hustle.

"When I got down to the induction center I said I wanted to see the psych. They sent me up to this booth where there was a little white man in a little white coat. I told him, 'Looky here, I got some things I want to tell you.' Then I recited my poem about 'I think I'm going outside and be a sniper' and I talked about dropping atom bombs and about Saladin the Moor. The little white man wrote 'hostile, antisocial' on my slip and told me to go get my clothes and get out."

Back at Stanford that fall, Johnie became increasingly concerned about the black man's survival there—not his physical survival but his survival as a black man.

There were about a hundred and thirty blacks at the university by then, but they were nearly invisible, lost among thousands of whites. And their invisibility was more than just a matter of numbers, Johnie thought; it was a matter of identity.

"Black people had no identity here at all. They were white, or I should say they were preparing, training, to be white. They didn't even come together much. They were scattered all over the campus in different dormitories. Alone. Isolated. Afraid to play their music loud and the rest."

Johnie and his friends had heard about black student groups then being formed on other campuses and they decided that was what they needed at Stanford. So one evening in October 1967 the Black Student Union was born.

"We didn't have no heavy ideology then," Johnie recalls. "It was mainly just the idea of getting to know one another, getting to feel one another." They brought leaders of other black organizations to campus to advise them on "how to get yourselves together," and sponsored dances and parties at which Stanford's blacks met and talked about their common problems.

Art Harris, a popular basketball player, was elected chairman ("He was a model the bourgeoisie could identify with"), but Johnie emerged as one of the Union's most effective spokesmen. As a member of the liberal arts students' association, he demanded and helped elect more black representatives to student government. *The Stanford Daily* opened its columns to him and he wrote a long article calling the Union the spearhead of "Black Consciousness."

Yet, his very prominence on campus only sharpened the conflict which was growing within him. As a black man, Johnie often became so angry at the racism he saw around him that he talked of revolution. As a slum child who had scrambled into two of America's best universities, he yearned to make it big in the white man's world. As an artist, he often dreamed of rising above all such categories. In his last years at Stanford these three conflicting impulses nearly tore Johnie apart.

> Trying to act civilized and completely failing
> My own upbringing My own world having consigned
> Me to those poems others could not write.

Early in January, barely three months after he helped form the Black Student Union, Johnie and six of his friends resigned. The schism was rooted partly in personality conflicts, but there was more to it than that.

In part, it was a class split. Like Johnie, most of those who quit came from the ghetto. In a letter explaining their position, Johnie quoted a passage from LeRoi

Jones: "The middle-class black bourgeois intelligentsia was very probably the worst thing that ever happened to the street brother."

And most of them were also artists—writers, painters, musicians—who felt uneasy with the straight political-racial formulations of the BSU leaders. "We are Black students," Johnie wrote. "Yes. But, even more, we are artists . . . striving with our own ghetto-made images and slum-indentured cultures to add . . . all of this to a much grander race than Our Own or that of The White Man . . . the Human Race."

There may have been an element of opportunism in this. As artists interested in getting their works published, shown and produced, Johnie and his friends wanted to make use of white funds, public or private. The BSU, on principle, was opposed.

Lest they be seen as assimilationists, their letter denounced the BSU leaders as "Compromisers, unwittingly yet unerringly diluting the blood of righteous anger." Yet anger was never really the issue. Both groups were angry; their styles were different. BSU expressed itself in toughly worded but hard-headed and pragmatic programs demanding specific administration steps. Johnie and his friends were aesthetic rebels—often more revolutionary-sounding, but actually less sure of what they wanted.

Constituting themselves as "Afro-West," they devoted themselves to what they called the "black cultural revolution."

They wanted to "end the prostitution of black art" by cutting the ties which made black artists dependent on white producers, patrons and critics. "We should have black cultural institutions, where a black man can go and sell his work and not suffer for lack of exposure," Johnie says. "We need black publishing companies, black newspapers, a black literary magazine as heavy as the *Atlantic*."

But they saw cultural revolution as much more—as a way of changing a whole people's consciousness, an essential prelude to political revolution. "That's where the Communists and the rest fell down," Johnie says. "They dealt with people as though they were strictly political beings. But people work, people play, people laugh, they fornicate, they go through all the changes that make life what it is.

"Jean Genet has a phrase in *The Blacks*—'Let Negroes negrify themselves: pump black blood through those veins.' That's what we're trying to do, pump black blood through our veins, our people's veins. Stop trying to write like white people, stop trying to write like Castro or Mao. Write like black people. Blackness is feeling, emotion. In our poetry, our music, we were trying to bring out this feeling."

But there were few black cultural institutions around. If Johnie wanted to express himself, he had to do it through whites.

In the spring of 1968, Ram's Head, a Stanford theatrical society, commissioned him to write the *Gaieties* revue for that fall's Stanford–Cal-game weekend. The equivalent of Harvard's Hasty Pudding or Princeton's Triangle show, it was a distinction for a rising young writer. Johnie worked all summer on a script he called *David*— a bluntly autobiographical story about a Stanford student from Watts.

But after reading it, Ram's Head decided not to produce *Gaieties* that fall. Johnie was furious, and vented his anger in his *Daily* column: "Don't ever ask a black man for the truth as though you can handle it—no, don't do that and then have that black slapped in the face . . . the truth, Dear Sirs, is that right here, not in Viet Nam, but right here at Stanford and a million other strongholds of white power is where genocide is being waged against the colored people of the world . . . 'genocide' is being waged here in the form of a one-way fronting-off of the black psyche with white quasi-Victorian postures of moral indignation . . . when black art, which is black life, cannot enter the system normally, then it is left with precious few alternatives."

Sometimes his rage was so strong it frightened him and he pulled back, seeking alternatives. Often that was dope: speed, pot, LSD, heroin, cocaine, morphine, just about anything to dull his anger.

> . . . Instead of anger, or fear,
> or polemic against the White Man,
> raging until my skull burnt out on speed
> that white shit crystal loving methedrine
> and anything else to fit the mold of he who

lived fast fast fast fast wanted to die but couldn't
say so because that wouldn't have been cool . . .

Work was piling up: term papers, reading assignments,
exams. Johnie was getting better marks than he got at
Harvard, but they still weren't good enough, He knew
he couldn't afford to flunk out again.

The Pressures:
Building up and about to make you cop out
for keeps. This time
your friends won't forgive you, but should that matter
after all weren't you brought up to be a two-time loser?

The pressures, the anger, the drugs, the late nights,
the poetry were destroying his home, too. He had married
Joyce the year before and they had a son. But Joyce, used
to a more stable world, couldn't keep up with Johnie's
sharply fluctuating moods. When she learned he'd had a
child by another woman, she left—returning only when he
said he couldn't live without her.

. . . trying to do the impossible
which is a poet trying to live the narrow life
of domestic trying to live the quiet life when
his blood boils to be free when his nature calls to
be free when he feels that the times call to be free
when he screams that his people cry to be free . . .

At times, he had to scream out loud.

By early 1969 Johnie had brought Afro-West back into
the Black Student Union, becoming artistic director of
the merged organization. And BSU was on the move. On
February 4 it presented twelve demands to President
Kenneth Pitzer: among them, demands for an Afro-
American Studies Department, an Afro-American Cultural Research Institute and at least one black faculty member in every department. At a rally that day Johnie said,
"The black intellect is stripped here." Lashing his audience
as "damned apathetic," he said Stanford's black movement had just begun. "We're still asking for reforms, but
when it gets to moving don't complain about blacks not
working through channels."

Three weeks later, four hundred students gathered for another rally outside the president's office. Told he was out to lunch, they marched on the Faculty Club, where they refused to leave until President Pitzer came to the door, promised more negotiations, but warned, "We've got to consider this in an orderly fashion." Chanting "Now! Now! Now!" the crowd marched to the cafeteria, where they seized food from the counters and refused to pay. Johnie clambered onto a table and told the demonstrators that blacks had to control their own cultural life at Stanford. "We want all this," he said, "because it's right." A few minutes later, two dozen blacks raced into the Stanford Bookstore, smashed display cases, turned over shelves and swept thousands of books onto the floor. "It was like a hurricane," one dazed employee said.

> I am that Voice
> moving slowly within
> the hurricane's eye
> crying out in whispers.

But Johnie wasn't swept away by the hurricane of black militancy any more than he was by the other winds which gusted through his life. Slowly he realized he could never give himself wholly to anything. He was a marginal man.

"All black people are marginal. The very color of your skin puts you outside the mainstream of American life. And all real writers are marginal—James Joyce was marginal, so was Faulkner, so was Steinbeck—in the sense that they feel an alienation from society. But my alienation is of a different order because I'm both black and a writer. I can't go all the way with the militants because I have to function as a writer. I got to make it in this white man's system. But the system all the time moves you toward marginality. It drives a black man toward extremes. So I don't really belong anywhere."

> Yes, it is time that I, as Outsider,
> came in for a while from the rim's edge
> and shared with you that which I have found . . .

> Outsider, outsider singing a song
> running along once here now gone
>   Outsider Outsider.

After

These, then, are ten young Americans. I present them as nothing more: not as symbols, not as models, not as spokesmen for their generation. Certainly they are not typical of their peers, not even of the disaffected minority. For I realize now that I was drawn to them as subjects for these portraits by a certain intensity, a way of driving experience to extremes, which distinguishes them from others who may share many of the same basic impulses.

This individuality did not diminish my interest in them; it only strengthened it. For we have had all too much talk of "youth," "students" and "radicals"—as if there were some prototype in flowing hair, granny glasses and denim jacket offering a ready-made laboratory for analysis. If my work on this book has taught me anything, it is that today's young people are as richly variegated, as stubbornly idiosyncratic, as their elders and can only be understood in highly personal terms.

This raised a problem which bothered me as I wrote: how to deal with those personal experiences which obviously had deep psychological implications for the development of the personality. These portraits are rife with them—Sue's persistent weight problem, the traumatic death of Jim's older brother, Groovy's emotional disturbances which disrupted his schooling and required treatment. I could not ignore such matters. Yet, as a journalist who had read only a smattering of psychological literature, I could not adequately interpret them. To properly evaluate the importance of these factors, even an analyst would need to rely on material from dreams, fantasies and free association which I did not have. Ultimately I decided to proceed with great restraint in these areas: to report what I knew, offer at most a few cautious suggestions, but to steer clear of amateur psychiatry.

Yet one psychologically important aspect of these lives consistently fascinated me: the complex relationship between generations. That relationship—or the seeming lack of it—was what struck most readers of the Linda Fitzpatrick story. The "two worlds" of Linda—Greenwich, Connecticut, and Greenwich Village—seemed light-years apart. The readers' letters I received remarked on how little the parents seemed to know of Linda's other world. They talked of "the incredible generation gap" and "the yawning chasm between parents and child."

Linda's story was accepted as a paradigm of the generation gap, a concept which had gained a firm hold on the public mind. The "gap" was already conventional wisdom, accepted as given in any discussion of the "youth problem." But somehow it struck me as too pat an explanation for what happened to Linda and, by extension, what was happening to many other young Americans.

In the winter of 1968 the *Times* asked me to follow up Linda's story with a nationwide survey of the "drug problem." And one of my first interviews was with Erik Erikson, the eminent professor of human development at Harvard. When I asked Erikson what he thought of the generation-gap concept, he answered somewhat as follows: "The values of any new generation do not spring full blown from their heads; they are already there, inherent if not clearly articulated, in the older generation. The generation gap is just another way of saying that the younger generation makes overt what is covert in the older generation; the child expresses openly what the parent represses."

I jotted down that answer in my spiral notebook and went on with the survey. But in the spring and summer of 1968 as I interviewed for the book, I kept coming back to Erikson's formulation. Of all the explanations of the generational relationship I had heard, it was the only one which seemed to clarify the young lives I was encountering.

In the fall of 1968 I went to Harvard as a Nieman Fellow and enrolled in Erikson's graduate seminar. By then

I was well into this book, but I was undoubtedly influenced by Erikson's perspective. At times this worried me. For I was fully aware of my limitations in this area. Moreover, I was concerned not with elaborating a theory but with the specifics of ten lives. Yet, in those very specifics I kept finding further applications and variations of Erikson's original insight. These complex echoes and interconnections between parental behavior and children's values continued to fascinate me.

What follow are merely some of the hints, speculations and subjective reactions which came to me as I approached these ten lives from Erikson's perspective. I have tried to retain an essentially journalistic voice—drawing largely on material I have already reported, eschewing psychological jargon or overly theoretical formulations. I have made no effort to work out a fully coherent explanation equally applicable to all ten lives. In some places the perspective seems useful; in others it doesn't. Finally, there are many important aspects of these immensely complex lives that I have not even tried to deal with in this section. By focusing on the generational relationship I do not mean to suggest that it explains everything. It is merely the aspect that interests me most.

To many in the mid-sixties, hippies like Linda, Groovy and Jim seemed strange apparitions on the American scene. Their weird dress, bizarre hair styles, communal living arrangements and, above all, their drug habits seemed a radical departure from the bland, understated, moderate, hard-working, get-ahead fifties. Seen from this perspective, the hippies, almost overnight, had baldly rejected everything the previous generation lived by.

But, applying Erikson's insight, things looked somewhat different. To be sure, the adult generation does proclaim its adherence to the traditional values of the Protestant Ethic: hard work, frugality, self-control, postponement of pleasure. On public occasions (and many private ones) Americans still pay lip service to the Pioneer Spirit, in which we strive to dominate our environment much as our forefathers did when they carved clearings in the wilderness.

But, increasingly, those values have been outrun by events. The work habits appropriate to life on the American frontier or even to early industrialism no longer make much sense in the sybaritic suburbs of the sixties. And Americans have adapted their lives, if not their rhetoric and their self-image, to changed conditions. The father may still go off to "work" every morning, but his job these days is likely to involve more shifting of paper and bank drafts than it does actual production. He may complain that there is less and less to "do." More important, the children grow up at home in their mother's world, symbolized by the supermarket, the shopping center and goods to buy, to consume, to enjoy. In fact, American values are rapidly becoming spending rather than work, consumption rather than production, taking from life rather than shaping it.

The hippie drug culture is a dramatic sign of that shift —the covert theme in the older generation becoming overt in the younger. Drugs, at least marijuana and the hallucinogens, are associated not with action, production, achievement and work, but with passivity, consumption, introspection, hedonism. They are literally consumed— swallowed, smoked, sniffed or injected. And they work their effect on the consumer—the reverse of the pioneer's shaping of his environment.

Today's adults, too, depend heavily on drugs—alcohol, tobacco, the amphetamines and barbiturates. But the values these drugs symbolize are still covert. When the father downs three martinis coming home on the club car he rarely admits to himself he is seeking pleasure; he says he needs the drinks to relax after a hard day's work and to recharge his batteries for the next day. When his son smokes marijuana he openly proclaims that he turns on for "kicks," or pleasure. One generation's forbidden fruit becomes the daily bread of the next.

In turn, this may influence the parents' and the older generation's view of youthful behavior. If the germ of that behavior is there—but suppressed—in the older generation, its uninhibited appearance in the young may stir up no little guilt in the parents. And guilt is rarely an aid to understanding or compassion. There is an old saying: "The most effective way to punish your parents is to imitate them"; if so, many parents today are being subtly tortured by their own children.

Seen in this light, the "two worlds" of Linda Fitzpatrick may not have been quite so disparate as they first appeared. Few American communities have mastered the fine art of consuming better than Greenwich, Connecticut. The giant fieldstone or white frame houses, set on rolling lawns with swimming pools and tennis courts behind them, are stocked with an ample selection of appliances, accessories, fine foods and liquors from the American cornucopia. And everything else the suburban heart could desire is available in the smart shops downtown.

Linda never broke completely with that world. Until near the end, she shuttled back and forth, unable to let go of the comforts and advantages her home life provided. Her first open aberration was the shoplifting at Oldfields, a revealing crime indeed for a girl who could afford to buy anything she wanted. Even in the Village, her friends recall, she never lost her "rich-girl aura." David recalls she had "a thing about money." She talked constantly about it, about how she was going to earn forty thousand dollars a year and rent "a big apartment on the Upper East Side." Susan recalls that Linda first expressed open affection for her Village friends by buying them a huge bag of groceries, full of particularly expensive items. Later, she'd come into town with thirty dollars or forty dollars to buy acid or pot for everybody. "She bought us all kinds of things," says Mark.

And then there was the intriguing question of Linda's mother. A lively woman with strong artistic impulses, she evidently found suburban life dull and made frequent trips into New York seeking more excitement and stimulation. Ultimately she ran off altogether. It is not clear how much Linda knew about her real mother, but Mr. Fitzpatrick is said to have told her, "You're just like her." Was Linda, in some respects, recapitulating her mother's behavior—or at least her father's image of her mother? For, despite their clash of temperaments, Mr. Fitzpatrick was clearly attracted to Patricia. Later he suppressed this attraction, changing Linda's name to remove the "Binger," shutting Patricia out of his life so completely he did not even like to mention her name. Was Linda making overt certain themes implicit but covert in her parents' lives?

Jim may be an even better example of the same process. San Leandro is not nearly so affluent as Greenwich. But it is a prime example of the new consumer-oriented suburbs which sprang up all over the country, notably in California, after World War II. The Chamber of Commerce calls it "a shopper's paradise," well symbolized by the huge Bay Fair Shopping Center ("The Center with Everything in the Center of Everything").

Young veterans like Jim's father, back from the war and determined to make up for lost time, bought and consumed, often beyond their means. Jim recalls "the materialism, the things . . . all the stereos and the cars and the houses and the money . . . I never wanted any of that stuff. And it was kind of *shoved down my throat* all my life. You know, it was 'Here, buy this. Here, buy that. Do you want this? Do you want that? You can have whatever you want.' "

But increasingly his father turned to his own form of consumption—alcohol—going from a genial Irish drunk to an alcoholic. He became incapable of "doing" anything, the true consumer, acted upon rather than acting. After their parents' separation, Jim's older brother partly filled the father's role. But after his death the dominant influence in Jim's life became his mother. Unable to serve as a model for male activism, she could only feed him, comfort him, make him feel good—even to the point of doping him with tranquilizers for two straight weeks after his brother's death.

I do not find it surprising that, given his upbringing, Jim should have become the passive, pleasure-seeking, perpetually drugged young man I met. Wasn't he acting out attitudes inherent in the community, personified by his father and nurtured by his mother?

There are a few skimpy parallels here with Groovy. Like Jim, he grew up virtually without a father (although he clung tenaciously to his father's photograph, tried to grow a mustache like his and, in a sense, imitated his father's peripatetic life). Again, the dominant influence was his mother, not perhaps quite so indulgent as Mrs. Murphy, but scarcely a strict disciplinarian.

Yet the pattern doesn't really fit Groovy very well. Nothing fits Groovy very well. He was an original, a tortured tumbleweed among the flower children. Most of the hippies were middle-class and suburban children, who dropped deliberately into the East Village or Haight-Ashbury. Groovy was a natural dropout, who quite by chance found the hippie scene there to drop into. Two decades ago he would have dropped out too and ended as a leather-jacketed motorcycle tough or a gentle, aimless wanderer through America's shantytowns.

I have tried to deal with the ten as individuals, avoiding wherever possible the labels which have so often hampered our understanding of today's youth. Rigid categories have lost much of their meaning as the lines between "hippies," "yippies," "radicals," "draft resisters" and the like have increasingly blurred and shifted. Yet at times it is necessary to employ rough groupings. Linda, Groovy and Jim, whose disaffection is largely in the area of style and culture, may fairly be called "hippies." John, Don, Sue and Dave, more concerned with the redistribution of power in American society and in the world, can properly be called "radicals." Jerry falls somewhere in between, consciously seeking an amalgam of life style and political revolt. Roy and Johnie, whose disaffection grows largely out of their blackness, must be put in their own category.

The most popular view of today's young radicals is that they are flaming rebels against their parents, particularly against their fathers. One prominent sociologist has written a massive work tracing the source of their radicalism (and that of other young radicals throughout history) to the oedipal urge. Undoubtedly there are such urges in all of us. But among the radicals in this book I saw little evidence of outright rebellion or hatred of their fathers. I found far more evidence of continuity with their parents, especially their fathers.

Yet, if the continuity in the hippies' families was subtle and ironic, with buried themes erupting in surprising fashion, in the radicals' families it was more direct. As Kenneth Keniston has pointed out, most of today's young radicals are children of old radicals, liberals or, at least, humanists. The values in the parents' lives are echoed rather clearly in their children.

Yet, here too, there is a subtle kind of inversion. For, as Keniston has noted, many of these parents have failed to implement their stated values and beliefs. Cowed by McCarthyism, made cautious by age or professional responsibilities, they may nominally hold to their earlier positions, but in fact let them atrophy for lack of exercise. They become less vital for the parents, giving way to the more pragmatic concerns of daily life. Accordingly the radicals' most common critique of their parents (and their parents' generation) is hypocrisy: that they profess all the right values but fail to act on them. The radicals want to act.

In a sense, then, they too take what have become covert themes in their parents' lives and make them overt.

There is an element of this even in Jim. His mother is a striking example of a parent who proclaims the "right" values but declines to act on them: "I didn't like the society we live in any better than they [the hippies] do. I just knew I couldn't change it. I always taught my children to conform outwardly, not inwardly. I told them questioning, doubting inwardly, was fine. But everybody has to conform outwardly . . ." Yet she is disgusted with the "hypocrisy" of life in Halcyon, conceding "it was all a front and our kids saw through it." Jim too talks of hypocrisy: "What began to get me over there was how it was all a farce, a bunch of lies . . . What America says it stands for and what it really stands for are two different things." He makes a few half-hearted stabs at doing something by attending a few peace demonstrations. But ultimately the other theme wins out: "I think it would be nice to change society . . . but there's nothing I personally can do to change it. Except be what I am."

Dave is a better example. The continuity with his parents is striking. Apparently it ran in the family. Oliver, who writes of his "deep respect for the life work of my father," says, "What I wanted for David was to have the same relationship with me that I had with my father." By that he didn't mean indoctrination but the natural transmitting of "a heritage." In this respect, I find Dave's upbringing almost ideal—a loving, flowing interplay with his parents in which values and ethics were certainly transmitted but which left Dave ample freedom to carry them where he would.

Those values, as Dave describes them, were "humanistic, libertarian, democratic, universalist." They were also, in the best meaning of the word, radical. The Goldrings joined the Communist Party not as arid dogmatists but as sensitive persons seeking a way to halt the slide toward economic disaster at home and fascism abroad; they left the party because they could no longer stomach its dogmatism. Oliver's continuing radical-humanist concern was then channeled into the Progressive Party.

But the advent of McCarthyism—dead rats on the doorstep, glass in the driveway, threatening phone calls and the brush with the Un-American Activities Committee—took its toll. In the fifties, Oliver pulled back, burying his radicalism under more mundane concerns. He calls this "the period of disjuncture which has given the New Left such a vivid sense of independent discovery." An apt description. For it was just this interim, when such commitments were put away on the shelf like fine old first editions, cherished but now a bit irrelevant, which allowed Dave to pluck them out again with such excitement.

In the sixties, his parents resumed some activity—in the civil rights and antiwar movements. But by then Oliver's radicalism was tinged irrevocably with academic professionalism. Opposing efforts to put the college on record against the war, he argued that "the only proper institutional stands for the college are on issues scrupulously identified as educational." He stressed "the theoretical struggle."

Once Dave, too, had been absorbed in theory and pointing toward a professorial career. But in his last year at Harvard he increasingly rejected the traditions and trappings of academic life in favor of activism outside, and even against, the university. In some respects he also rejected his father as a model, at least that aspect of him symbolized by that professorial figure he glimpsed trudging through the snow on Massachusetts Avenue, "going to work." But in place of that professorial image he put a radical image which had also been a prime theme in his father's life. Dave now made it the dominant theme in his. Don is much less a radical than Dave. Ideas, systems, power relationships concern him less than moral witness, ethical values and personal relationships. Yet in this area he, too, seems to be acting out certain themes in his family. Here I am tempted to go back one generation further, to Grandfather Baty who "just wouldn't bow to the necessity of limiting himself in any way." Is there perhaps something there that echoes in his grandson?

There is certainly continuity with the next generation. Don writes that the desire to "help mankind" seemed to "run in the family," citing Madeleine's interest in psychology and her nursery school work, his mother's and sister's social work, his brother's study of sociology. And he says the greatest single influence on him has been his father. "Dad throws himself into whatever he does. His teaching, his hobbies, his infrequent urges to fix up the house are all infused with this tremendous drive and enthusiasm . . . I've brought the same enthusiasm into my antiwar effort that Dad brings to his teaching. I'm totally committed to ending this war and all other wars just as Dad is totally committed to whatever he does."

There was little outright rebellion against Wilton, in part because he was so easygoing. "It's pretty hard to rebel against Wil and me," says Madeleine. "We're fairly flexible." But certainly Don, driven by urgent passions which I don't claim to completely understand, went to extremes which at times astonished, even distressed, his father. For Wilton is hardly an activist. He may bring great enthusiasm to bear on his teaching or the bathroom tub, but his ethical humanism and political liberalism have never been channeled into social causes.

Don's mother recognized this gap between values and action in her speech at the altar of the Washington Square Church. Citing all the fine ideals implanted in Don during his upbringing, she says "it is not surprising that Don is here today when we consider the spoken ideals of his parents' generation. He must really have believed what we said we believed."

Sue believes her stand on the race issue can be traced back to her parents' attitude, which she sees as an unusual one for the South. "They were paternalistic, yes, but their paternalism was really a kind of basic human decency towards other people. They approached Negroes as human beings who were less fortunate than they were but nevertheless human beings."

And she feels she owes her parents still more than that. "I got many of my basic values from them. They were both decent, kind people. I never saw them hurt anyone. I'm sure I wouldn't be what I am today if they hadn't instilled those values in me."

Yet, clearly, Sue carried the implications of those basic values beyond her parents' wildest dreams. The civil rights movement was one thing, but the peace movement and Sue's other radical activities were quite another. At times, as I talked to her mother in her Savannah parlor, she seemed to be saying, "Certainly we told Sue all men were equal in the sight of God, but we never thought she'd go this far." They never sought to restrain her, but Sue put reins on her own activity for fear of embarrassing them or, worse yet, rupturing the family ties which meant so much to her. Finally, her parents' warm and understanding letter after the auto accident convinced her that they would love her no matter what she did.

But Sue's radicalism was nurtured by a community wider than just her home. Or to put it differently, her home was far larger than her parents' house. It included the Methodist Church, which taught her the fatherhood of God and the brotherhood of man. "I took those doctrines seriously. After all, I said them every Sunday. I took them literally too. I thought you were supposed to. I was very upset when I found out that other people didn't; that, for example, they didn't apply to black people, not even to all white people." When the Belmont Methodist Church turned Abel Musorewa away from its doors, she put a label on it: "hypocrisy." The church's values were fine; it just failed to act on them.

But ultimately her radicalism grew from something still bigger—the South itself, or at least that part of it with which she could identify. As Ed Hamlett aptly put it, Sue is "rooted in time and place." Her political views are not abstract dogma; they are "soul, heart and gut stuff." So she is constantly searching for continuity with the South that is in her gut. When SSOC was formed, it sought "a new South, a place which embodies our ideals for all the world to emulate." It sought to "come to terms with our own backgrounds" by emphasizing what was good in the Southern white's heritage. "We had to find ourselves rooted in history," Sue says. "We had to show that we weren't that different; that the ideas we represented had some kind of tradition in the South and that there had been other people who had gone through the same things we were going through." This was not always easy for Sue because many Southern whites—"the out-and-out racists, the Klansmen, the women who shouted dirty names at Negro children"—were clearly her enemies. "But I could never reject the average white Southerner because that would have meant turning against my family. I always believed that there were deep reservoirs of very decent, good, even radical feelings in many rural Southerners which could be tapped if only we worked hard enough."

This ambivalence is partly resolved in the week after her father died. Resenting most of the provincial racist whites in Savannah, but stirred by their warmth and support during that terrible week, she is finally "thrown back against my roots in a way I hadn't been for years" and comes to understand that "that was my father's life, a part of it and a part of mine."

In John, the continuity is far more with his childhood community than with his parents. Rather bland, generally permissive and unpolitical, the McAuliffs established few strong themes which their son could either accept or reject, the major exception being his mother's Catholicism which provided the target for John's first rebellion. It is tempting to point to his father's streak of independence— placing a Kennedy sticker on his front door because he was getting "sick of all these people voting and thinking the same way just because everybody else was doing it."

But John's ornery individualism owes more to Indianapolis' brand of militant eighteenth-century liberalism (we now call it conservatism). The major intellectual influences in his youth were Stan Evans' *Indianapolis News;* the Intercollegiate Society of Individualists and John Stuart Mill's *On Liberty*, with its central doctrine that "every man should have unlimited freedom as long as his freedom didn't interfere with anybody else's freedom." This doctrine was still a fertile source of American political thought, capable of nourishing both the stubborn conservatism of Young Americans for Freedom and John's libertarian radicalism. As John notes, his radicalism is hardly typical of the New Left, stressing "the anarchistic 'every-man-should-be-free' thing" more than the "communal drive" so strong in today's movement. In fact, he sees a clear line of development from the libertarian ethos of his Indianapolis days: "I don't think I've really changed so much. What change there has been came as a result of learning more about the world rather than shifting my basic values. Even my attitude toward the federal government. Indianapolis was always an anti-establishment town, very paranoid about the Eastern liberal establishment they thought controlled the country. Well, I haven't made such a big switch emotionally. I still don't trust Washington bureaucrats—I just don't trust them for different reasons now." Indianapolis might not recognize John as its ideological heir, but to me the lineage is clear.

Cincinnati and the Katz brothers would recoil in horror at the suggestion that Jerry was any heir of theirs. And yet, what about the Katzes' wisecracking humor, the ethnic act which Bernie's wife likened to the Marx Brothers? Sometimes it was gentle, sometimes savage, but always it had that mocking tone which has become a feature of Jerry's put-on style. And what about Sid the Vaudevillian, the old tap-dancer and MC on the Pantages Circuit, whom Jerry now calls "the first Yippie"? As Robert Jay Lifton has pointed out, mockery is one of the central techniques of today's young, and it is an interesting one. For it gains its power precisely from acting out the most lurid—yet often the most secretly appealing—fantasies of the old. Jerry, with all his hair, his war paint, his drugs, his sexuality, is one of its most skilled practitioners.

But if Jerry borrowed the style of the Katz brothers, he rejected their substance. Their antithesis he found in his father. And in "the battle of the Rubins against the Katzes" he sees the meaning of his whole life. "The Katzes are the Johnsons, are the Nixons, are the professors. It's that same quality of lack of faith in life. My father wasn't like that . . . Even when he was a union official he was always very egalitarian. I got some of that from him. I'm a lot like my father."

I wonder whether Bob Rubin was quite the strong, dedicated man Jerry now pictures. Certainly, the Katzes still regard him as a "poor schlepper," a weak man dominated by his wife and his father-in-law. Jim Luken cannot accept Jerry's description of him as a fervent Hoffa man determined to use any methods to advance the interests of the working man; he says Bob had "no guts" and "blew with the wind." Perhaps he was a bit of all these things. But what strikes me as most interesting is that Jerry should have picked out his father's most forceful side to model himself after. Both Don and Sue seem to have done a little of the same thing. This suggests that children may embellish their parents' traits to establish the continuity they yearn for.

Roy and Johnie do not need to seek out continuity. It is there all too clearly in the one attribute they and their parents can never shed: their blackness. The very experience of being black in America is enough to nurture a deep and abiding resentment. Yet, until recently, most Negroes had to keep those resentments bottled up or, worse, channeled into self-destructive activity. Only within the past decade has a young black man been able to give full vent to the anger and pride latent but largely unexpressed in his people.

Roy's parents were soft-spoken Southern Negroes, deferential and unassertive. Yet there were subtle cues which Roy picked up quickly: talk of "white trash" and "crackers," his father's pleasure when Joe Louis beat Max Schmeling, and their quiet satisfaction when Eisenhower sent troops into Little Rock. More, even bolder cues, came from Henry Boyd, the teacher who taught black history in order to give his students pride in themselves and awareness of their own possibilities. But, dependent on white men for his own position, he never spoke openly against them. When Roy took these cues and ran with them, his parents not surprisingly urged caution; but they never tried to hold him back. Ultimately, as if Roy had uncovered the strength which lay within them all the time, they marched beside him through the streets of Holly Springs.

I was struck by the title of the play which first involved Roy emotionally in the movement: "Seeds of Freedom." Just as Sue was compelled to search for "roots," so Roy sought "seeds" from which something bigger could grow. Medgar Evers, the most readily accessible black model in Mississippi, was the most obvious seed, but I would suggest that Roy's whole upbringing scattered seeds which later bore fruit. He eagerly seized the opportunity for education, to rise in the world, but at Brandeis he recognized that he could not rise at the price of self-denial. "To survive psychologically," he said, "a black living in a predominantly white society needs something to relate to, to go back to. You need a base and you find that in the black community."

Johnie's parents were Southerners too and just as cautious as Roy's. Mr. Scott, his pride nibbled away by the endless search for work, drifted off to a boarding house, where he later told Johnie there were certain things in life that couldn't be avoided. Yet Johnie sensed there was anger burning deep within his father. "My father never told me to hate white people. But my father hated being broke. And I guess the Communists got the answer for that, you know, for people that hate being broke. You can direct your anger against the ruling classes. My father wasn't no Communist. But his experiences radicalized him. Revolution begins at home." His mother, preoccupied with the daily need to feed and clothe her children, didn't seem to worry much about social injustice. But Johnie believes there was an ancestral agony in her bones. "You just don't forget those steel manacles. Being chained head and foot. You don't forget being sold, like cattle. You don't forget them babies dying. You don't forget none of that."

And Johnie couldn't forget. He craved the excellence and grace of Harvard. But, as Thad put it, "Johnie saw that the university was asking him to 'achieve so you can be something you aren't—and maybe you don't want to be.' Working toward academic excellence, in a way, was alienation of self." So Johnie reached back to the ghetto, to Watts. "I realized that the slum world gave birth to me. Out of her womb I came. And I came to love her." And with a poet's gift, he found a striking image for the unbreakable ties he felt with the ghetto: the old tale of Hercules and the giant, "all of whose strength came from his mother, Earth."

These then are ten of your children, America. Their strengths, yes, and their weaknesses too, come from you. Not always in clear, linear fashion, often with surprising twists and convolutions, but ultimately the material seems to be there in the lives of the preceding generation. Like clay, the past may be pulled and molded into new shapes, but it is always the past becoming the future.

Yet, you may ask, isn't this begging the question? If Erikson is right, if each generation tends to make overt what is covert in the preceding generation, then what is so special about the generational relationship today? Why is the seeming disjuncture between generations so much larger today than it was two or three or four decades ago? One answer may be the sheer speed of the technological and social change we have experienced in recent years. Disjuncture, it seems, comes from the gap between what we say we are and what we really are. It is this gap which children seem so uncannily adept at finding and exploiting. But this gap is understandably widest at times of rapid change. In the nineteenth century it might have taken twenty or thirty years for the values and assumptions of a generation to seem ill-fitted to the times. Today that can happen apparently overnight. Perhaps that is why we have the impression now that a new generation is born every three or five years.

Perhaps, then, we have been paying too much attention to the wrong "gap." Perhaps, instead of endless examination of "the generation gap" we should be more concerned with the gap between what we say and what we do, the gap between the American dream and the American reality. Perhaps we should spend more time asking ourselves whether the unspoken values and assumptions we all carry around with us still adequately reflect the kind of world we live in.

I am not suggesting that today's youth have stumbled on some immutable new values and eternally valid assumptions. Far from it. If Erikson is right, then this process will continue; today's young people will inevitably begin talking one way and acting another, and their children will smell out that hypocrisy and turn it against them.

My work of the past two years has not persuaded me to accept wholesale the values and assumptions of any of the ten young people in this book. But the experience of examining closely their assumptions has taught me one valuable lesson: the compelling need to constantly re-examine my own.

On October 15, 1969 (Moratorium Day), two nice 17-year-old kids killed themselves so that people would think about peace and love. . . .

Craig & Joan
Two Lives for Peace

by Eliot Asinof

Their town hushed it up. The 24 last notes they left were never delivered and never made public, except for one poem which slipped through the authorities. Their parents were ashamed of them; their friends didn't understand; the reason for their deaths was turned into nothingness by the very people whom they loved enough to die for.

This is the true story of Craig Badiali and Joan Fox of Blackwood, New Jersey, who couldn't live in the world the way it is and hoped by their deaths to change it.

Soon to be a major motion picture.

A DELL BOOK $1.25

If you cannot obtain copies of this title from your local bookseller, just send the price (plus 15c per copy for handling and postage) to Dell Books, Post Office Box 1000, Pinebrook, N. J. 07058. No postage or handling charge is required on any order of five or more books.

*Biggest dictionary value
ever offered in paperback!*

The Dell paperback edition of

THE AMERICAN HERITAGE DICTIONARY
OF THE ENGLISH LANGUAGE

- Largest number of entries—55,000
- 832 pages—nearly 300 illustrations
- The only paperback dictionary with photographs

These special features make this new, modern dictionary clearly superior to any comparable paperback dictionary:

- More entries and more illustrations than any other paperback dictionary
- The first paperback dictionary with photographs
- Words defined in modern-day language that is clear and precise
- Over one hundred notes on usage with more factual information than any comparable paperback dictionary
- Unique appendix of Indo-European roots
- Authoritative definitions of new words from science and technology
- More than one hundred illustrative quotations from Shakespeare to Salinger, Spenser to Sontag
- Hundreds of geographic and biographical entries
- Pictures of all the Presidents of the United States
- Locator maps for all the countries of the world

A DELL BOOK 75c

If you cannot obtain copies of this title from your local bookseller, just send the price (plus 15c per copy for handling and postage) to Dell Books, Post Office Box 1000, Pinebrook, N. J. 07058. No postage or handling charge is required on any order of five or more books.

75¢

DELL
75¢
REF

Dell
0207

Based on the new best-selling—
AMERICAN HERITAGE DICTIONARY—
the freshest, most innovative, most useful dictionary
to be published in this century

THE
AMERICAN HERITAGE
DICTIONARY
OF THE ENGLISH LANGUAGE

- Largest number of entries—55,000

- 832 pages—nearly 300 illustrations

- The only paperback dictionary with photographs

AMERICAN HERITAGE DICTIONARY

440-00207-075

DELL

How many of these Dell bestsellers have you read?

DELL Bestseller List

1. **MILE HIGH** by Richard Condon $1.25

2. **THE AMERICAN HERITAGE DICTIONARY** 75c

3. **THE ANDROMEDA STRAIN** by Michael Crichton $1.25

4. **CATCH-22** by Joseph Heller 95c

5. **SOUL ON ICE** by Eldridge Cleaver 95c

6. **THE DOCTOR'S QUICK WEIGHT LOSS DIET** by Irwin M. Stillman, M.D., and Samm Sinclair Baker 95c

7. **THE DOCTOR'S QUICK INCHES-OFF DIET** by Irwin M. Stillman, M.D., and Samm Sinclair Baker 95c

8. **THE MIDAS COMPULSION** by Ivan Shaffer $1.25

9. **THE RICHEST MAN IN THE WORLD** by JP $1.25

10. **NEVER CRY WOLF** by Farley Mowat 50c

If you cannot obtain copies of these titles from your local bookseller, just send the price (plus 15c per copy for handling and postage) to Dell Books, Post Office Box 1000, Pinebrook, N.J. 07058. No postage or handling charge is required on any order of five or more books.